OPTIMAL LINKING GRAMMAR

Supported by data from linguistic fieldwork conducted in the Faroe Islands and Iceland, this book presents a pioneering approach to syntactic analysis, Optimal Linking Grammar (OLG), which brings together two existing models, Linking Theory and Optimality Theory (OT). The latter, which assumes spoken language to be based on the highest-ranking outcome from a number of competing underlying constraints, has been central mainly to phonology; however, its application to syntax has also gained ground in recent years. Combining the models into OLG not only provides a robust account of case-marking phenomena in Faroese and Icelandic; it also explains a wide range of sentence types, including passives, ditransitives, object shift and word order variation. The book demonstrates how OLG can resolve numerous issues in competing theories of formal syntax and how it might be successfully applied to other languages in future research. It is essential reading for researchers and students in syntax, morphology, sociolinguistics and European languages.

DANIEL GALBRAITH completed his PhD in Linguistics at Stanford University. His research interests are in syntax, morphology, case and metrical phonology. For the last four years, he has worked on voice assistance and other linguistic projects in the technology industry, currently at Google.

In this series

141. MISHA BECKER: *The Acquisition of Syntactic Structure: Animacy and Thematic Alignment*
142. MARTINA WILTSCHKO: *The Universal Structure of Categories: Towards a Formal Typology*
143. FAHAD RASHED AL-MUTAIRI: *The Minimalist Program: The Nature and Plausibility of Chomsky's Biolinguistics*
144. CEDRIC BOECKX: *Elementary Syntactic Structures: Prospects of a Feature-Free Syntax*
145. PHOEVOS PANAGIOTIDIS: *Categorial Features: A Generative Theory of Word Class Categories*
146. MARK BAKER: *Case: Its Principles and Its Parameters*
147. WM. G. BENNETT: *The Phonology of Consonants: Dissimilation, Harmony and Correspondence*
148. ANDREA SIMS: *Inflectional Defectiveness*
149. GREGORY STUMP: *Inflectional Paradigms: Content and Form at the Syntax–Morphology Interface*
150. ROCHELLE LIEBER: *English Nouns: The Ecology of Nominalization*
151. JOHN BOWERS: *Deriving Syntactic Relations*
152. ANA TERESA PÉREZ-LEROUX, MIHAELA PIRVULESCU AND YVES ROBERGE: *Direct Objects and Language Acquisition*
153. MATTHEW BAERMAN, DUNSTAN BROWN AND GREVILLE G. CORBETT: *Morphological Complexity*
154. MARCEL DEN DIKKEN: *Dependency and Directionality*
155. LAURIE BAUER: *Compounds and Compounding*
156. KLAUS J. KOHLER: *Communicative Functions and Linguistic Forms in Speech Interaction*
157. KURT GOBLIRSCH: *Gemination, Lenition, and Vowel Lengthening: On the History of Quantity in Germanic*
158. ANDREW RADFORD: *Colloquial English: Structure and Variation*
159. MARIA POLINSKY: *Heritage Languages and Their Speakers*
160. EGBERT FORTUIN AND GETTY GEERDINK-VERKOREN: *Universal Semantic Syntax: A Semiotactic Approach*
161. ANDREW RADFORD: *Relative Clauses: Structure and Variation in Everyday English*
162. JOHN H. ESLING, SCOTT R. MOISIK, ALISON BENNER AND LISE CREVIER-BUCHMAN: *Voice Quality: The Laryngeal Articulator Model*
163. JASON ROTHMAN, JORGE GONZÁLEZ ALONSO AND ELOI PUIG-MAYENCO: *Third Language Acquisition and Linguistic Transfer*
164. IRINA NIKOLAEVA AND ANDREW SPENCER: *Mixed Categories: The Morphosyntax of Noun Modification*
165. ABRAHAM WERNER: *Modality in Syntax, Semantics and Pragmatics*
166. GUGLIELMO CINQUE: *The Syntax of Relative Clauses: A Unified Analysis*
167. HENK J. VERKUYL: *The Compositional Nature of Tense, Mood and Aspect*
168. SANDRO SESSAREGO: *Interfaces and Domains of Contact-Driven Restructuring: Aspects of Afro-Hispanic Linguistics*
169. GREGORY STUMP: *Morphotactics: A Rule-Combining Approach*
170. DANIEL GALBRAITH: *Optimal Linking Grammar: A Theory of Morphosyntax*

Earlier issues not listed are also available

CAMBRIDGE STUDIES IN LINGUISTICS

General Editors: U. ANSALDO, P. AUSTIN, B. COMRIE,
T. KUTEVA, R. LASS, D. LIGHTFOOT, K. RICE, I. ROBERTS,
S. ROMAINE, M. SHEEHAN, I. TSIMPLI

Optimal Linking Grammar

OPTIMAL LINKING GRAMMAR

A THEORY OF MORPHOSYNTAX

DANIEL GALBRAITH

Stanford University, California

CAMBRIDGE
UNIVERSITY PRESS

Shaftesbury Road, Cambridge CB2 8EA, United Kingdom

One Liberty Plaza, 20th Floor, New York, NY 10006, USA

477 Williamstown Road, Port Melbourne, VIC 3207, Australia

314–321, 3rd Floor, Plot 3, Splendor Forum, Jasola District Centre, New Delhi – 110025, India

103 Penang Road, #05–06/07, Visioncrest Commercial, Singapore 238467

Cambridge University Press is part of Cambridge University Press & Assessment, a department of the University of Cambridge.

We share the University's mission to contribute to society through the pursuit of education, learning and research at the highest international levels of excellence.

www.cambridge.org
Information on this title: www.cambridge.org/9781009015875

DOI: 10.1017/9781009030663

© Daniel Galbraith 2023

This publication is in copyright. Subject to statutory exception and to the provisions of relevant collective licensing agreements, no reproduction of any part may take place without the written permission of Cambridge University Press & Assessment.

First published 2023
First paperback edition 2025

A catalogue record for this publication is available from the British Library

ISBN   978-1-316-51659-1   Hardback
ISBN   978-1-009-01587-5   Paperback

Additional resources for this publication at www.cambridge.org/9781009015875

Cambridge University Press & Assessment has no responsibility for the persistence or accuracy of URLs for external or third-party internet websites referred to in this publication and does not guarantee that any content on such websites is, or will remain, accurate or appropriate.

For Caroline, Samuel, my parents
and friends
Soli Deo Gloria

Contents

List of Figures   xiii
List of Tables   xv
List of Abbreviations   xvi

1 **Introduction**   1
    1.1 The Puzzle of 'Quirky' Case   5
    1.2 Theoretical Overview   8
       1.2.1 Linking Theory   9
       1.2.2 Optimality Theory   18
       1.2.3 Competing Grammars   23
    1.3 Empirical Findings   27
    1.4 Structure of Book   31

2 **Case Study: Non-Nominative Subjects**   33
    2.1 Icelandic Oblique Subjects   34
    2.2 German Pre-Verbal Dative Experiencers   39
    2.3 Faroese Clause Structure   43
    2.4 Faroese Dative Experiencers   53
       2.4.1 Subjecthood Tests   53
    2.5 Summary of Chapter   60

3 **Overview of OLG**   62
    3.1 Linking Theory   62
       3.1.1 From Conceptual Structure to Semantic Form   63
       3.1.2 From Semantic Form to Syntax   66
    3.2 Optimality-Theoretic Syntax   71
    3.3 Summary of Chapter   75

4 Faroese Dative Subjects — 76
- 4.1 Introduction — 76
- 4.2 Overview of Data — 77
- 4.3 Surveys on Quirky Case — 82
  - 4.3.1 Faroese Quirky Case Survey 1 — 82
  - 4.3.2 Faroese Quirky Case Survey 2 — 88
  - 4.3.3 Icelandic Quirky Case Survey — 92
- 4.4 OLG Analysis — 95
  - 4.4.1 Case and Agreement Constraints — 96
  - 4.4.2 OLG Analysis — 98
  - 4.4.3 Factorial Typology — 102
- 4.5 Summary of Chapter — 103

5 Competing Grammars — 105
- 5.1 Two Kinds of Dative Case — 107
  - 5.1.1 Accounting for 'Weak' and 'Strong' Dative Case — 108
- 5.2 Competing Grammars Model of Nominative Substitution — 110
- 5.3 Competing Grammars and Social Meaning — 117
- 5.4 Bimodally Distributed Judgements: Dialects or Noisy Data? — 121
  - 5.4.1 Bimodal Clustering: Investigating Disagreement in Judgements — 122
- 5.5 Neural Approaches — 131
- 5.6 Summary of Chapter — 136

6 Faroese Passive — 138
- 6.1 Introduction — 138
- 6.2 Survey Data — 138
  - 6.2.1 Faroese Passive Survey 1: No Agent Phrase — 139
  - 6.2.2 Faroese Survey 2: Passives with Agent Phrase; Sentences with *tróta* — 143
  - 6.2.3 Summary of Faroese Passive Survey Results — 146
- 6.3 OLG Analysis — 146
- 6.4 Case Preservation and 'Dative Sickness' — 149
  - 6.4.1 A Word on Icelandic 'Dative Sickness' — 154
- 6.5 Summary of Chapter — 155

7	**Ditransitives**		**157**
	7.1	Ditransitive Verbs in Faroese	157
	7.2	Survey Data: Faroese 'Give' Passive	160
		7.2.1 Faroese 'Give' Passives Survey 1: Colloquial Context	161
		7.2.2 Faroese 'Give' Passives Survey 2: Formal Context	162
	7.3	OLG Analysis	165
		7.3.1 Position of the Goal and Theme Arguments	168
	7.4	Survey Data: Icelandic 'Give' Passive; Other Faroese Ditransitive Passives	170
		7.4.1 Icelandic Survey on 'Give' Passive	170
		7.4.2 Faroese Survey 3: Other Ditransitive Passives	173
	7.5	Summary of Chapter	178
8	**Alternative Hypotheses**		**179**
	8.1	Woolford (2007): An OT Account	179
	8.2	Jónsson (2009): 'Covert Nominative'	185
	8.3	Asarina (2011)	188
	8.4	Summary of Chapter	192
9	**Syntax in OLG**		**193**
	9.1	Introduction	193
	9.2	Phrase Structure	194
		9.2.1 G<small>EN</small>: A Tree Adjoining Grammar	195
		9.2.2 Phrase Structure Constraints	201
		9.2.3 Deriving Word-Order Typology	203
	9.3	Movement, or Fillers and Gaps	206
		9.3.1 Base Order	206
		9.3.2 Scrambling, or Word-Order Optionality	209
		9.3.3 Traces, or Co-Indexed Gaps	211
		9.3.4 A Note on Locality	215
		9.3.5 Section Summary	216
	9.4	Syntactic Features	217
		9.4.1 Feature Identity	219
		9.4.2 Feature Realisation	220
		9.4.3 Subcategorisation	221
		9.4.4 Section Summary	222
	9.5	OLG Syntax in Practice	222

xii   *Contents*

	9.5.1 Input to Syntax	223
	9.5.2 Deriving an English *Wh*-Question with Do-Support	225
9.6	Faroese Clause Structure Revisited: OLG Account	228
	9.6.1 Ranking Arguments	229
	9.6.2 Factorial Typology: Faroese Clause Structure	238
9.7	Information Structure	240
	9.7.1 Case Study: Scandinavian Object Shift	241
	9.7.2 Factorial Typology: Information Structure	251
9.8	Summary of Chapter	253

10 Conclusion — 255
   10.1 Overview of Findings — 255
   10.2 Avenues for Future Research — 256
      10.2.1 Dative-Accusative Case Frames — 256
      10.2.2 Diachronic Changes in Case Systems — 259
      10.2.3 Adverbial Adjunction and Information Structure — 262
      10.2.4 Other Topics — 263
   10.3 Final Summary — 265

References — 267
Index — 291

An online appendix can be found at www.cambridge.org/9781316516591.

Figures

3.1	OLG grammar model	65
3.2	Architecture of grammar in Optimality Theory	72
4.1	Faroese quirky case survey 1: Mean acceptability by word order	85
4.2	Faroese quirky case survey 1: Mean acceptability by object case and subject number	86
4.3	Icelandic quirky case survey: Mean acceptability by agreement and dative intervener	93
5.1	Architecture of competing grammars model	109
5.2	Faroese competing grammars: Subject case by register	113
5.3	Faroese competing grammars: Subject case by lexeme	114
5.4	Faroese competing grammars: Subject case by speaker age	115
5.5	Example of a bimodal distribution of judgements	123
5.6	Faroese quirky case sentences with SVO word order: Scatter plot of judgements	124
5.7	Faroese quirky case sentences with medial adverbs: Scatter plot of judgements	125
5.8	Bimodal clustering: Density plot of beta for Faroese sample	127
5.9	Bimodal clustering: Density plot of beta for Icelandic sample	130
5.10	Competing grammars: Deep neural network for binary classification	133
6.1	Faroese passive survey 1: Mean acceptability by verb and passive type	141

6.2	Faroese passive survey 2: Mean acceptability by verb and passive type	145
7.1	Faroese 'give' passive surveys: Mean acceptability by word order and theme case	164
7.2	Icelandic 'give' passive survey results	172
7.3	Faroese ditransitive passive survey results: Active versus passive	176
7.4	Faroese ditransitive passive survey results: Word order	177
8.1	Faroese survey results on *tróta*	190
9.1	Tree Adjoining Grammar: Substitution	196
9.2	Tree Adjoining Grammar: Adjunction	196
9.3	Tree Adjoining Grammar: Example of adjunction	199
9.4	Tree Adjoining Grammar: Example of substitution	200

Tables

1.1	List of fieldwork surveys	28
2.1	Faroese clause structure	51
3.1	Case constraints	74
4.1	Frequencies of subject case by verb token in blog corpus	81
4.2	Faroese quirky case verbs: Sentences in survey 1	83
4.3	Faroese quirky case verbs: Sentences in survey 2	89
5.1	Faroese quirky case verbs: Sentences in survey 1	122
5.2	Faroese quirky case survey 1: Bimodal clustering results	126
5.3	Icelandic quirky case survey: Bimodal clustering results	129
6.1	Faroese passive sentences	140
7.1	Faroese ditransitive verbs	175
9.1	Constraints governing positions of syntactic elements	208
9.2	Faroese sentence types: Hypothesised winning candidates	229

Abbreviations

Language abbreviations

Dan.	Danish
Dut.	Dutch
Far.	Faroese
Fin.	Finnish
Ger.	German
Guj.	Gujarati
Hix.	Hixkaryana
Ice.	Icelandic
Kaq.	Kaqchikel
Kor.	Korean
Lav.	Lavukaleve
Lit.	Lithuanian
Nah.	Nahuatl
Nep.	Nepali
Swe.	Swedish
Yup.	Central Siberian Yup'ik

Glossing abbreviations

ABS	absolutive
ACC	accusative
ACT	active
ADESS	adessive
ART	article
COLL	collective number
COMPL	completive aspect

CONT	continuative aspect
DAT	dative
DEF	definite
DISTPST	distant past tense
EMPH	emphatic particle
ERG	ergative
EXPL	expletive
F	feminine
GEN	genitive
IMP	imperative
IND	indicative
INF	infinitive
INS	instrumental
INTERROG	interrogative mood
INTRANS	intransitive
LOC	locative
M	masculine
N	neuter
NOM	nominative
O, OBJ	object
PART	partitive
PASS	passive
PERF, PFV	perfective
PL	plural
PRES	present tense
PRT	particle
PST	past tense
RECPST	recent past tense
REFL	reflexive
S, SUBJ	subject
SG	singular
SUP	supine

1

Introduction

Since the earliest work in generative grammar, theories of natural language syntax have proliferated and developed along disparate and often contradictory paths. Nevertheless, the content of the human language faculty, or at least the part of it pertaining to sentence-building, has continued to be the principal locus of investigation. Issues such as defining grammaticality, the 'poverty of the stimulus' problem, how to delimit the typology of possible languages, and the relation between so-called competence and performance remain central to the discussion, albeit with ostensibly little consensus across camps. One need look no further than the contrasting traditions of transformational approaches, which typically posit derived structures and movement as a fundamental syntactic mechanism (Chomsky 1965 and subsequent studies), and those which reject transformations in favour of enriched theories of the lexicon and feature-structural representations, such as Lexical-Functional Grammar (Bresnan 1982 and subsequent studies) and Head-Driven Phrase Structure Grammar (Pollard and Sag 1994). Yet a third dimension underlying the syntax debate is that of the connectionist versus computational or algebraic cognitive models, that is, whether the human language faculty is best viewed as a formal system of manipulating symbols, as a neural network which encodes weights learned from external stimuli, or as some fusion of the two (see Pater 2019 for a recent summary). Perhaps the most well-known example of an explicitly hybrid approach, adopting both formal representations and connectionist assumptions, is Optimality Theory (OT; Prince and Smolensky 1993), in which formal constraints are ranked and violable, and the task of the learner is to acquire the language-specific ranking. Finally, a fundamental concern of syntactic theory has been the restrictiveness of Universal Grammar (UG), a topic which in the 'Principles and Parameters' tradition has centered on the problem of parameter-setting: how to account for the full typological range of attested languages and the acquisition thereof while minimising the formal machinery attributed to UG (see, e.g., Huang and Roberts 2016 and references therein).

This book is written in order to contribute to the above discussions from a unique perspective: one that combines both computationalist and connectionist assumptions, posits a rich feature-matching apparatus as opposed to transformations, integrates insights from the Minimalist literature (Chomsky 1995 and subsequent studies), and proposes a holistic framework for syntactic investigation. In particular, three strands of preceding literature are built upon here: an Optimality Theoretic approach to constraint interaction applied to syntax (see Grimshaw 2001, Legendre et al. 2001, among others), an approach to feature-mapping between grammatical levels based on Linking Theory (LT) (Kiparsky 1997, 2001), and a model of morphosyntactic variation and change (Kroch 1989a,b, 1994, Pintzuk 1999, among others). Although OT-based analyses are commonplace in phonology, there remains a relative dearth of in-depth studies in the syntax literature from an OT perspective. The second key aim of this volume is to provide substantial empirical support for the proposed theory via a detailed case study of morphosyntactic phenomena in two closely related languages, Icelandic and Faroese (see Þráinsson 2007, Þráinsson et al. 2004/2012 for recent treatments). A considerable amount of new data from the author's fieldwork conducted on the Faroe Islands and Iceland is presented with respect to the theoretical questions of focus. An additional purpose of this book is to provide a sufficiently explicit description of the core aspects of the theory to enable future researchers to test the framework against new data, including detailed discussion of methodological concerns. Significant efforts have been made to support the presentation of data with statistical rigour, including plots and figures where appropriate. The section on competing grammars also touches on machine learning approaches to modelling grammatical variation, attempting to bridge the perceived divide between neural network and algebraic formalisms while acknowledging the importance of sociolinguistic factors in the selection of variants.

While, in principle, any generative theory of syntax must speak to the full range of possible syntactic phenomena, special attention is given here to one particular subdomain, namely grammatical case. Since case touches on both the semantics–syntax and syntax–morphology interfaces, it represents a good testing ground for grammatical hypotheses. Zooming in yet further, the central problem explored in this book can be summarised by the following high-level question: how can we approach a unified account of case-marking, particularly in those instances where morphological case does not transparently map to grammatical function? The theory of case has been a topic of considerable debate and little consensus in the syntactic literature. The phenomenon of non-nominative subjects has been the focus of much discussion, particularly since the classic works on Icelandic (Andrews 1976, Levin and Simpson 1981, Zaenen et al. 1985 and subsequent studies). Indeed, the majority of theories of 'quirky' case have, to a greater or lesser extent, built upon a framework that assumes Icelandic as the archetype. However, a closely related language, Faroese, has been largely neglected despite it exhibiting case-marking patterns that differ from Icelandic in challenging ways. In the chapters which follow, it is argued that even apparently idiosyncratic Faroese and Icelandic case-marking patterns are in fact predictable from general principles, which in turn have implications for the kinds of case systems we expect to encounter cross-linguistically.

As noted above, a version of Kiparsky's LT is adopted here (Kiparsky 1997, 2001), which acknowledges both syntactic positions and case morphology as means of licensing arguments and does not collapse argument structure into syntax. Instead, information relevant to case assignment is encoded via features that link the levels of abstract, morphosyntactic and morphological case. Abstract case is defined by a hierarchy of theta-roles, which itself is derived from the Semantic Form of the verb (Bierwisch 1986, Wunderlich 1997). By assuming a separate abstract case representation distinct from syntactic positions, we allow for phenomena where a single grammatical function may be instantiated by several different morphological cases (e.g. subjects in Finnish) or indeed multiple positions (e.g. subjects in Icelandic). However, this additional generative capacity is not unconstrained: as highlighted in Section 2.1, syntactic configurations which license structural cases may share certain properties, such as being specifiers of a head in the extended verbal domain. These generalisations are captured via interaction of constraints on phrase structure and feature identity, as laid out more fully in Chapter 9. By acknowledging the availability of positional licensing in some languages, we also capture the fact that mismatches between positional and inflectional case may be tolerated, as in Faroese and Icelandic. Moreover, by giving syntax access to inflection, that is, distinguishing morphological exponence from case within syntax, we cover instances where a syntactic operation appears to track morphology, such as the dependence of agreement on case. In the chapters which follow, I will show that the range of observed variation in argument realisation is both readily explained and appropriately constrained by the proposed model.

Also following Kiparsky (2001), matching between levels of case is implemented in OT (Prince and Smolensky 1993, McCarthy and Prince 1995), which provides a way of formalising the generalisation that many linguistic phenomena involve markedness hierarchies, that is, a default or 'elsewhere' form with potentially increasingly specific forms depending on the relevant grammatical conditions. Case is a prime example of this, where in accusative languages nominative is the unmarked subject case and non-nominative subjects the more marked form. Under OT, grammar is an optimisation of conflicting pressures, the set of which is universal, but the ranking of which is language-specific. This book explores the hypothesis that a set of appropriately ranked, violable constraints is able to account for a range of case-marking, agreement and word-order facts in Faroese and Icelandic and correctly generates case-marking patterns in other typologically disparate languages.

Moreover, this proposal integrates a competing grammars model of synchronic intra-linguistic variation that goes beyond mere descriptive adequacy, providing a framework for approaching morphosyntactic variables that incorporates both internal and external factors.[1] Morphosyntactic variation is attributed to a probabilistic calculus, in which grammars are selected from a set of rankings available to the speaker according to differently weighted factors that depend on the variable in question. It is possible to test the competing grammars hypothesis empirically by training a model on corpus data, learning the weights assigned to relevant factors and predicting when a speaker

---

[1] See Kroch (1989a,b, 1994), Santorini (1992, 1993), Pintzuk (1999), Wallenberg (2016), among others, for the origin of this idea in the context of language change and Fritzenschaft et al. (1990), Yang (2000, 2002), among others, for similar ideas in the acquisition literature.

is likely to select a given grammar. The accuracy of the model can be verified through logistic regression and basic machine learning techniques, an exciting avenue for future research. Therefore, this approach also presents an opportunity for developing computational methods to explore central questions in syntactic theory.

All of the above theoretical claims are buttressed by empirical evidence from extensive surveys conducted in the Faroe Islands and Iceland, as well as from corpora and native speaker consultations; the significance of the findings is demonstrated by repeatable statistical models of the patterns observed in the data. Thus, this volume aims to account not only for discrete variants, such as case selection or available argument positions in syntax, but also the kinds of grammatical, information-structural, sociolinguistic and contextual factors that contribute to case-marking in actual usage. The adoption of these three components – i.e. LT, OT and the Competing Grammars Model, hereafter abbreviated to *Optimal Linking Grammar (OLG)* – provides a cross-linguistically tractable framework for approaching case-marking phenomena that is not only descriptively adequate but is ultimately more explanatory than most contemporary approaches to case in the generative syntax literature.

1.1 The Puzzle of 'Quirky' Case

This section introduces a phenomenon which necessitates a detailed account of how grammatical relations, syntactic structure and morphology interact. Case-marking in Insular Scandinavian languages is an oft discussed topic, but there remain interesting questions to be answered, one of which is revealed by comparison of experiencer-stimulus predicates in the two languages. In both Faroese and Icelandic the standard transitive case-marking pattern is nominative–accusative, but some verbs occur with non-nominative higher arguments (1–2).

(1) a. Far. *Eg sá gentan*
I.NOM saw girl-the.ACC.SG
'I saw the girl'

b. Far. *Henni manglar mat*
her.DAT lacks.3SG food.ACC.SG
'She lacks food'

(2) a. Ice. *Ég sá stelpan*
I.NOM saw girl-the.ACC.SG
'I saw the girl'

b. Ice. *Mér   ógna   þau   vindaský*
me.DAT terrify.3PL those.NOM.PL winds.NOM.PL
'I am terrified of those winds'

c. Ice. *Hana   vantar   peninga*
her.ACC lacks.3SG money.ACC.SG
'She lacks money'

The sets of verbs which mark subjects with non-nominative case overlap across the two languages, but the Icelandic set is much larger than the Faroese and with a greater variety of case frames (see Þráinsson 2007:156–172). Moreover, in Faroese verbs with accusative subjects are no longer commonly used, unlike in Icelandic (2c). The central empirical question addressed here is: why are Faroese and Icelandic sentences with dative subjects different with respect to their object case and agreement? The distinction is illustrated in (3).

(3) a. Ice. *Mér   líka   hundar*
me.DAT like.3PL dogs.NOM.PL
'I like dogs'

b. Far. *Mær   dámar   hundar*
me.DAT likes.3SG dogs.ACC.PL
'I like dogs'

As can be seen in (3), in Icelandic the object argument in such sentences bears nominative case and triggers number agreement on the finite verb, whereas in Faroese the object bears accusative and occurs with default third person singular verb agreement.[2] On the surface, it is surprising that this phenomenon, a highly marked structure cross-linguistically, should exhibit such differences between two closely related languages, where the sentence type in question has the same origin in Old Norse sentences with preverbal datives (van der Gaaf 1904, Jespersen 1927, Allen 1995, Rögnvaldsson 1995, Barðdal and Eyþórsson 2003). Moreover, since it has long been known that Icelandic marks objects with nominative case in the presence of dative or genitive subject case, it is unexpected that Faroese marks the object with accusative in such predicates. Additionally, it remains to be explained why Icelandic sentences with non-nominative subjects

---

[2] It has also been observed that full person agreement is not possible with nominative objects in Icelandic (Sigurðsson 1991, 1996, Taraldsen 1995 and subsequent studies), but this fact is tangential to the case-marking difference, since the patterns can be explained solely in reference to number agreement; that object agreement is 'impoverished' relative to subject agreement is unsurprising given the markedness of object agreement more generally.

exhibit object agreement in number while the same apparent structure in Faroese exhibits non-agreement in number, or perhaps agreement with a null expletive (Barnes 1986, Þráinsson et al. 2004, 2012).

If the dative argument in (3) in both languages is a true subject by standard criteria, which does seem to be the case (Zaenen et al. 1985, Barnes 1986), and if it is corroborated by results from fieldwork presented in this volume, the difference in object case cannot rest upon a difference in subjecthood of the dative. It is interesting, however, that the difference in object case co-varies with a difference in number agreement. Therefore, the main hypothesis to investigate is that these facts are connected. The OLG account presented here posits that **the difference between Icelandic and Faroese dative-subject predicates results from a conflict between two pressures: (i) to mark the object with regular structural case, and (ii) to agree with an overt nominative argument.**[3] If these pressures are weighted differently in the two languages, with Icelandic preferring object agreement and Faroese preferring accusative structural case, the sentences in (3) have an explanation. Furthermore, such an account appeals to general principles rather than *ad hoc* idiosyncrasies and makes testable predictions about the typology of languages with case-marking.

In order to test this claim, two other reasonable hypotheses must first be ruled out:

(i) **Different structural object position**: if Icelandic and Faroese can be shown to have a distinct object position in these languages, *and* said position is shown to be associated with nominative case-marking in Icelandic, the difference could be attributed to the configuration of the object with respect to other clausal elements.

(ii) **Lexical case-marking**: if the Faroese accusative object case can be shown to be lexically assigned (i.e. associated with the subset of verb lexemes marking dative case on the subject), previous analyses of Icelandic could be retained, in which accusative case is unavailable due to some kind of 'nominative first' preference (e.g. Yip et al. 1987).

---

[3] By 'object' is meant the syntactic instantiation of [–HR] abstract case, which in these languages is standardly an argument which occupies object position (V,Comp). For the purposes of the constraints, an object is defined by the abstract case features, which different languages realise differently in morphosyntax.

In order to rule out these hypotheses, we must test whether the object in each language (a) behaves like a regular object with respect to its structural position and (b) bears structural or lexical case. One means of investigating (a) in Scandinavian languages is the phenomenon known as *object shift*: if the object in both languages behaves no differently with respect to object shift, this constitutes evidence for it being structurally the same as a standard transitive object. Regarding (b), it is possible to determine whether the case is structural or lexical by testing *case preservation* behaviour: in Icelandic, when an object marked with lexical case, such as dative, is passivised, the corresponding subject of the passive 'preserves' case and is not replaced by nominative. In contrast, structural object case (accusative in both languages) is replaced by nominative on the passive subject. If the Faroese verbs which mark accusative object case passivise and the subject of the passive is nominative, this is consistent with the case being structural and not lexical.

These phenomena were investigated in extensive fieldwork on the Faroe Islands and Iceland via surveys and consultations with native speakers of each language, the results of which suggest that (i) and (ii) are not viable explanations for the observed patterns. Moreover, the data collected *are* consistent with the OLG proposal, namely that the key difference is a preference in Icelandic for agreement with a nominative argument conflicting with a pressure to express structural object case, whose relative importance is reversed in Faroese. These results have implications beyond Scandinavian languages, since they indicate that similar conflicting pressures are responsible for case-marking and agreement patterns in multiple disparate language families. Indeed, it has already been shown that a very similar interaction of constraints can account for Indo-Aryan case-marking and changes in case and agreement systems within that family (Deo and Sharma 2006, Kiparsky 2017).

1.2 Theoretical Overview

The OLG proposal involves three central theoretical assumptions which are shown to be necessary to account for the range of data observed in Icelandic and Faroese alone and also provides a flexible enough framework to generate realistic typologies of case systems beyond Scandinavian. These three pillars build upon previous work in the morphosyntax literature but also innovate in terms of the specifics of case theory and how grammar competition is modelled to capture intralanguage variation.

1. **Linking Theory (LT)** (Kiparsky 1997, 2001): case is determined by semantics, syntax and morphology, and the *linking* between these levels determines the output.

2. **Optimality Theory (OT)** (Prince and Smolensky 1993): grammar is a *harmonic optimisation*, that is, a universal set of violable constraints with language-specific rankings.

3. **Competing grammars model (CGM)** (Kroch 1989a,b, 1994, Pintzuk 1999): native speakers have synchronic access to multiple competing grammars, where a grammar is defined by a constraint ranking; grammar selection is probabilistic.

This book posits that such a theoretical apparatus is in fact necessary for empirical reasons and makes better sense of the data than a theory which collapses all of case and agreement into the syntactic component. Moreover, it does not attribute the difference between Icelandic and Faroese to mere language-specific exceptions or idiosyncrasies but to general principles of language. Each component of the theory also makes testable predictions that are demonstrably borne out crosslinguistically.

1.2.1 Linking Theory

Originally proposed by Kiparsky (1997, 2001), the basic premise of LT is three distinct levels of case: abstract, morphosyntactic and morphological. Abstract case is generated from a Semantic Form representation of the predicate and its argument structure. Morphosyntactic case is so called because languages may make use of *syntactic position*, *case inflection* or both to instantiate case within syntax. Finally, morphological case is a representation of mapping morphosyntactic case to morphology, that is, the morphemic representation of case that feeds the pronounced surface form. All three of these levels are represented by the binary features [±H(ighest)R(ole)] and [±L(owest)R(ole)], which refer to a hierarchy of thematic roles. These features 'mean' something distinct at each level, since semantics, syntax and morphology manipulate distinct types of elements: for example, [+HR] may be paraphrased as 'most prominent argument' at abstract case, 'subject position' or 'nominative inflectional case' in morphosyntax, and 'nominative morpheme' at morphology. The theory also presupposes Lexicalism, in which word-formation is subject to pre-syntactic lexical constraints as opposed to syntactic transformations, and therefore words enter syntax fully inflected (Chomsky 1970, Halle 1973, Siegel 1974 and subsequent studies). Importantly, this does not rule out syntactic constraints targeting sub-parts of words, such as case or agreement morphemes; it simply rules out the *construction* of words by syntactic rules or constraints (e.g. some aspects of Distributed Morphology [DM], see Halle and Marantz 1993, 1994 and subsequent studies). In that sense, the theory adopted here joins a family of theories that combine lexicalism with a constraint-based architecture, such as Lexical–Functional Grammar (Bresnan 1982) or Head-Driven Phrase Structure Grammar (Pollard and Sag 1987, 1994). However, it should be noted that LT is not necessarily incompatible with many of the ideas espoused in DM-based approaches: for instance, since spellout is post-syntactic in DM, mismatches are also possible between morphological case and the features syntax operates on. In DM, such mismatches may also differ across languages according to differing inventories of pronounceable morphemes; thus, there is an optimised mapping between two domains (which in OLG is expressed in Optimality Theoretic terms). Hence, the LT component of OLG can be seen as a complementary proposal which builds upon ideas present in the literature rather than opposing all developments of DM. It is, however, opposed to some of the more derivation-based proposals and explicitly constrains the range of possible mismatches between levels.

Kiparsky (2001) provides evidence from Finnish for the necessity of three levels of case. The table in (4) shows the paradigms of structural cases for nouns and pronouns as typically presented in pedagogical grammars:

(4)

Finnish structural cases 1

	Nouns: 'bear'		Pronouns: 'you'	
	SG	PL	SG	PL
NOM	*karhu*	*karhu-t*	*sinä*	*te*
ACC	*karhu, karhu-n*	*karhu-t*	*sinu-t*	*te-i-dä-t*
GEN	*karhu-n*	*karhu-j-en*	*sinu-n*	*te-i-dä-n*
PART	*karhu-a*	*karhu-j-a*	*sinu-a*	*te-i-tä*

The distribution of the accusative singular in *–n* in the noun paradigm is formalised as Jahnsson's Rule, which can be paraphrased as 'verbs with no overt subjects govern the endingless accusative, verbs with overt subjects govern the *–n* accusative' (Kiparsky 2001:3). What counts as an overt subject is a complex question, but the key issue is how to account for the apparent three-way allomorphy of accusative case, viz. the suffixes {*–t, –n, –Ø*}.

According to Kiparsky, the best analysis of allomorphy of the structural case suffixes is to treat these three as syntactically conditioned realisations of abstract accusative case; the paradigm shown in (5) better represents the alternatives:

(5)

	Finnish structural cases 2			
	'bear'		'he/she, they'	
	SG	PL	SG	PL
NOM	karhu	karhu-t	hän	he
ACC	—	—	häne-t	he-i-dä-t
GEN	karhu-n	karhu-j-en	häne-n	he-i-dä-n
PART	karhu-a	karhu-j-a	hän-tä	he-i-tä

In other words, the accusative case paradigm is not an instance of suppletive allomorphy but of three distinct ways of mapping *abstract* accusative to syntax, that is, the *morphological* genitive or nominative in nouns, with the additional possibility of morphological accusative in pronouns. One piece of evidence for this is that in co-ordinate structures, a shared argument must be assigned the same case in each conjunct, which means that a nominative subject is paralleled by a nominative object but not an accusative object (6).

(6) a. Fin. *Mikko   pyörty-i   ja   (Mikko)   kanne-ttiin   ulos*
Mikko.NOM faint-PST.3SG and (Mikko.NOM) carry-PASS.3SG out
'Mikko fainted and (Mikko) was carried out.'
b. Fin. *Hän   pyörty-i   ja   *(häne-t)   kanne-ttiin   ulos*
he.NOM faint-PST.3SG and (him.ACC) carry-PASS.3SG out
'He fainted and (he) was carried out.'

Verbs in the active, like *pyörtyi* 'fainted', assign nominative to their sole argument, whereas passives such as *kannettiin* 'was carried' assign either (i) 'endingless' nominative case to their sole overt argument if it is nominal (here *Mikko*) or (ii) morphological accusative if it is pronominal (here *hänet*). Ellipsis is possible in (6a) because the shared argument *Mikko* is assigned morphological nominative case by both verbs, whereas in (6b) ellipsis is prohibited because the shared argument gets a different morphological case from each verb. If the generalisation is formulated using abstract case alone, ellipsis in (6a) should not be allowed since *Mikko* would bear abstract accusative;

likewise, morphological case alone does not capture the fact that these allomorphs share the grammatical function of object and adds needless complexity by having to re-state the distribution of the nominative, genitive and accusative in every analysis of abstract accusative.[4]

Returning to dative subjects in Icelandic and Faroese, it is clear that the grammatical function of subject (i.e. abstract nominative case), maps to non-nominative morphological case. In these languages, both of which have a marked nominative, both structural position and case inflection are available for marking grammatical relations; OLG treats case on *positions* and on *items* occupying those positions as language-dependent varieties of morphosyntactic case. Abstract case maps directly to structural position in languages with positional licensing: that is, subject position bears [+HR] positional case and object position [−HR]. The important case-matching constraints target the mapping from positions to items (e.g. ensuring that an argument bearing [+HR] occupies a position matching that feature), whereas MAX constraints ensure that abstract case features are instantiated at the level of morphosyntactic case (e.g. penalising an output without a [−HR] feature when one is present in the input).

Although this apparatus may initially appear redundant, it is empirically necessary to maintain the distinction between Semantic Form, structural position, case inflection in syntax and morphological spellout. This volume adds to Kiparsky's evidence for the necessity of a three-level case approach, one illustrative example being passives of ditransitives. Ditransitive actives have three arguments, and the application of passivisation demotes the subject, resulting in a two-argument predicate with a passive verb. In Icelandic, Goal-Verb-Theme order in the passive, or promotion of the structurally higher object, is most frequent (Þráinsson 2007:135–136):[5]

(7) a. Ice. *Einhverjum útlendingum   var   seldur*
 some.DAT.PL foreigners.DAT.PL was.3SG sold.NOM.M.SG
 harðfiskurinn
 dried.fish-the.NOM.M.SG
 'Some foreigners were sold the dried fish.'

---

[4] See Kiparsky (2001:5–7) for further Finnish evidence of the necessity for both abstract and morphological case, including examples showing that objects in *-n* are morphologically genitive, not accusative.

[5] The nominative masculine singular morphology on the participle *seldur* 'sold' in (7a) shows that there is object agreement with *harðfiskurinn* 'dried fish', whereas in (7b) the neuter singular participle *skilað* 'returned' is default agreement morphology (i.e. non-agreement with either dative argument).

b. Ice. *Foreldrunum   var   skilað   börnunum*
parents-the.DAT.PL was.3SG returned.N.SG children-the.DAT.PL
'The kids were returned to the parents.'

The argument occurring to the left of the finite auxiliary in these examples, being neither the highest nor lowest theta-role at the level of Semantic Form, bears the abstract case feature [−HR−LR]. However, Spec,TP in Icelandic bears [+HR] positional case at the level of morphosyntax, since it licenses subjects. Moreover, the *item* in Spec,TP in both examples (7a–b) (the goal argument) bears dative morphosyntactic case, which here matches abstract but not positional case. In (7b), both arguments exhibit case mismatches, since the theme argument also bears dative lexical case assigned by the verb *skila* 'to return, hand back', resulting in an item, *börnunum* 'the children', bearing [−HR−LR] case in a position associated with [−HR] (V,Comp). Finally, the morphological spellout of the case realises the case inflection, not the structural position: the nominative theme in (7a) bears the morphology that corresponds not to its abstract case nor to its syntactic position but to its morphosyntactic case inflection. The pattern in (7a) can be schematised as follows:

(8)

Semantic role	Goal	Theme
Abstract case	[−HR−LR]	[−HR]
Morphosyntactic case: position	[+HR]	[−HR]
Morphosyntactic case: item	[−HR−LR]	[+HR]
Morphological case	[−HR−LR]	[+HR]
Morphology	[DAT] → *-um*	[NOM] → *-urinn*
Phonology	*útlendingum*	*harðfiskurinn*

As is evident, abstract case and syntactic position cannot be collapsed, since the thematic role of goal or recipient in (7a–b) does not correspond to the abstract case of subject position. Likewise, at the level of morphosyntax the case inflection cannot be collapsed into syntactic position, since there are mismatches (e.g. the dative goal argument bearing [−HR−LR] in the position bearing [+HR]). However, this example does not prove that what I am calling morphosyntactic case inflection and morphological case should remain separate. My reasons for maintaining the distinction are that syntactic operations must make reference to case inflection (e.g. whether an argument is a viable target of agreement), and said operations do not depend on the allomorph of the case (i.e. morphology 'proper').

In Icelandic, nominative objects trigger number agreement with the finite verb, but objects bearing other cases do not:

(9) a. Ice. *Mér   líka   hestar*
        me.DAT.SG like.3PL horses.NOM.PL
        'I like horses'
    b. Ice. * *Ég   lásu   bækurnar*
        I.NOM.SG read.3PL books-the.ACC.PL
    c. Ice. * *Hann   sakna   þeirra*
        he.NOM.SG miss.3PL them.GEN.PL
    d. Ice. * *Hún   köstuðu   boltunum*
        she.NOM.SG threw.3PL balls-the.DAT.PL

Even when subject agreement is unexpected, such as when the subject is accusative, number agreement is not possible with a non-nominative object, showing that the rule is not simply 'agree with the object if subject agreement fails':

(10) a. Ice. *Hana   vantar   vinnu*
         her.ACC.SG lacks.3SG work.ACC.SG
         'She lacks work'
     b. Ice. * *Hana   vanta   vini*
         her.ACC.SG lack.3PL friends.ACC.PL

The relevant property of a potential agreement target in Icelandic therefore seems to be nominative case-marking, not grammatical function. In other words, agreement is sensitive to case inflection, and if agreement also depends on syntactic configuration, there must be some syntactic representation of case inflection (Preminger 2011, in contrast to Bobaljik 2008). It turns out to be quite difficult to prove that the level of case being targeted by agreement is morphological, or in OT syntax terms, whether the losing candidates are ruled out at the semantics–syntax evaluation (the position argued for here), or the syntax–morphology evaluation. Under lexicalist assumptions, the relevant case information is present in the set of input candidates at both levels. However, some pieces of evidence point in the direction of agreement targeting both case-marking and syntactic position, and hence for distinguishing morphosyntactic and morphological levels of case.

Preminger (2011:25–40) presents data relevant to this question from three Kichean languages (a branch of Mayan) spoken in Guatemala: Kaqchikel, K'ichee' and Tz'utujil. Each of these languages has no case morphology on full noun phrases, that is, it makes use of positional licensing, but exhibits an ergative agreement pattern which also indexes case as shown in (11–12):

(11) TRANSITIVES:
    a. Kaq. *rat   x-Ø-aw-axa-j   ri achin*
           you.SG PFV-3SG.ABS-2SG.ERG-hear-ACT the man
           'You (sg.) heard the man'
    b. Kaq. *ri achin x-a-r-axa-j   rat*
           the man PFV-2SG.ABS-3SG.ERG-hear-ACT you.SG
           'The man heard you (sg.)'

(12) INTRANSITIVES:
    a. Kaq. *ri achin x-Ø-uk'lun*
           the man PFV-3SG.ABS-arrive
           'The man arrived'
    b. Kaq. *rat   x-at-uk'lun*
           you.SG PFV-2SG.ABS-arrive
           'You (sg.) arrived'

There are, therefore, distinct agreement morphemes for ergative agents of transitive verbs on the one hand, {-*aw*- 2SG, -*r*- 3SG} in (11), and for patients of transitives and subjects of intransitives on the other, {-*a(t)*- 2SG, -Ø- 3SG} in (11) and (12). Thus, we can see that the verb morphology must have access to the case of the argument(s), which is determined by syntactic position in these languages. Indeed, the kind of indexing of arguments in (11–12) is far from rare cross-linguistically: of the 378 languages listed in the World Atlas of Language Structures for the feature of verbal person marking, 193 mark both agent and patient arguments on the transitive verb, 47 of which also do not have morphological case marking (Iggesen 2013, Siewierska 2013).[6] Some examples from Hixkaryana, Lavukaleve and Nahuatl illustrate this:

(13) **Hixkaryana** (Derbyshire 1977, examples from Kalin 2011:9, 11, 24):
    a. Hix. *kuraha y-   onyhorye- no   biryekomo*
           bow   3S.3O- make-   IMPPST boy
           'The boy made a bow'
    b. Hix. *biryekomo komo y-   on- yetxkoni   kamara txetxa wawo*
           child   COLL 3S.3O- eat- COLL.DISTPST.CONT jaguar forest in
        amnyehra
        long.ago
           'The jaguar used to eat children in the forest long ago'

---

[6]Further information is available online at http://wals.info/, accessed on 6/19/18. Languages under the heading 'verbal marking of both A and P arguments' include both those in which marking of both arguments is obligatory, and those in which marking of either or both arguments is conditioned on discourse, syntactic or other contextual factors (e.g. topic marking in Tswana or definiteness in Swahili, see Creissels 2006).

16 *Introduction*

    c. Hix. *yawaka ryhe   w-   ɨm-   yako,   Waraka wya*
           axe   EMPH 1S.3O- give- IND.RECPST.COMPL Waraka to
        'It was the axe I gave to Waraka'

(14) **Lavukaleve** (Terrill 2003:227):

    a. Lav. *ali   na   mola   ga   e-   o-   le*
           man ART.M.SG canoe.N ART.N.SG 3SG.N.O- 3SG.S- see
        'The man saw the canoe'

    b. Lav. *aira   la   ali   na   a-   o-   le*
           woman ART.F.SG man ART.M.SG 3SG.M.O- 3SG.S- see
        'The woman saw the man'

(15) **Nahuatl** (Launey 1981:38, cited in Baker 2008:201):

    a. Nah. *Ø-   quim- itta cōōhua in pilli*
           3SG.S- 3PL.O- see snakes the child
        'The child saw (some) snakes'

    b. Nah. *Ø-   qu-   itta in cihuātl in calli*
           3SG.S- 3SG.O- see the woman the house
        'The woman saw the house'

Not all languages without case marking exhibit positional licensing; for example, verbal agreement may license arguments via noun class concord (such as in Zulu, see, e.g., Henderson 2011, Marten and van der Wal 2014), or the language may make use of extensive noun incorporation (such as Oneida, see e.g. Koenig and Michelson 2015). Nevertheless, the phenomenon of verbal agreement targeting argument positions is consistent with the hypothesis that agreement is dependent on syntax-internal case. By contrast, it is difficult to capture the ergative agreement pattern in Kichean if agreement constraints come into play at post-syntactic EVAL, since arguments in such languages do not bear morphological case and hence are only distinguishable to verbal person marking by their syntactic position.[7]

Another relevant data point is 'dative intervention' in Icelandic: in transitive expletive constructions with a dative argument intervening between the finite verb and the nominative, number agreement is not possible with either the dative intervener or the nominative (16):

---

[7] Preminger (2011:99–133) provides further argumentation in favour of agreement being a syntactic operation but presupposes the VP-Internal Subject Hypothesis and movement to canonical subject position in French and English, assumptions not shared by the account proposed in this book.

(16) **Icelandic** (Holmberg and Hróarsdóttir 2003:1000):

a. Ice. *Það finnst/*finnast [mörgum stúdentum] [tölvan*
   EXPL finds.3SG/*PL many.DAT.PL students.DAT.PL computer-the.NOM.SG
   ljótan]
   ugly.NOM.SG
   'Many students find the computer ugly'

b. Ice. *Það finnst/*finnast [einhverjum stúdent] [tölvurnar*
   EXPL finds.3SG/*PL some.DAT.SG student.DAT.SG computers-the.NOM.PL
   ljótar]
   ugly.NOM.PL
   'Some student finds the computers ugly'

c. Ice. *Einhverjum stúdent finnast [tölvurnar ljótar]*
   some.DAT.SG student.DAT.SG find.3PL computers-the.NOM.PL ugly.NOM.PL
   'Some student finds the computers ugly'

If number agreement in Icelandic were evaluated at the syntax–morphology interface, it would be difficult to formulate the generalisation for (16) without referring to syntactic structure. One could state the generalisation informally as 'match the number feature of the finite verb to that of the most prominent nominative argument unless another oblique argument intervenes'. Minimally, the clausal domain of agreement must be specified, which on an OT framework requires the winning output candidate to include a representation of constituent structure. If the evaluation at which (16b) is the winner did not include argument *positions* in the set of output candidates, it is not clear how to capture the fact that the dative argument is structurally higher than the nominative. Hence, the hypothesis that candidates which fail on agreement constraints are evaluated at phonology involves an additional stipulation, that phonology accesses syntactic positions, not simply linearised items. A simpler solution is to assume that agreement is evaluated at syntax, since there is much stronger empirical support for the necessity for output candidates to contain positional licensing information (in contrast to Bobaljik 2008).[8]

Finally, a word on the mapping between these levels of case. OLG does not assume a feature unification approach but rather an identity-based matching of feature values; in other words, [+HR] matches [+HR] only and fails to match [−HR] or [+HR+LR]. This is possible in a theory of hierarchically ranked, *violable* constraints, in which mismatches are tolerated given the right ranking. Such an account preserves both the

---

[8]For further discussion and an OT account of dative intervention in Icelandic, see Hrafnbjargarson (2001).

apparent universality of constraints such as 'a sentence must have a subject' while allowing for exceptions within a language (such as ellipsis or subjectless sentences in English) as well as cross-linguistic variation (e.g. radical pro-drop in Japanese and Korean). Descriptive generalisations of the form 'do X unless Y unless Z ...' are prime candidates for such an analysis, which recognises the existence of 'elsewhere' cases and a hierarchy of markedness. In the case of Icelandic and Faroese, the bare-bones generalisation is 'subjects are nominative (elsewhere case) unless the verb marks lexical case (marked case)'. This idea is at least as old as the Sanskrit grammarian Pāṇini, who captured the observation that there is a logical ordering to the application of rules. Optimality Theory (Prince and Smolensky 1993) offers a robust framework for implementing these generalisations, as well as a means of testing hypotheses through the generation of factorial typologies of possible output grammars; the basics of this approach are discussed in the following section.

1.2.2 Optimality Theory

The *locus classicus* for OT is Prince and Smolensky (1993). The fundamental concepts behind OT are that 'Universal Grammar consists largely of a set of constraints on representational well-formedness, out of which individual grammars are constructed' and that constraints are 'highly conflicting and make sharply contrary claims about the well-formedness of most representations'; thus, OT presupposes 'a means for precisely determining which analysis of an input *best satisfies* (or least violates) a set of conflicting conditions' (Prince and Smolensky 1993:2). These elements, namely a set of universal, conflicting, violable well-formedness constraints and a mechanism for evaluating output candidates, form the backbone of OT-based approaches to grammar. In Chapter 9 the specifics of the proposed OT model of grammar are laid out in detail; here, a brief summary is given of why OT is both necessary and sufficient to answer the central case-marking question in Faroese and Icelandic, as well as an overview of the OT mechanisms most relevant to the proposed analysis.

One important indicator of the need for a violable constraints model of case-marking is the possibility of mismatches between abstract case, structural position and case inflection discussed in Section 1.2.1. In most sentence types in both Faroese and Icelandic, case inflection does track structural position, that is, subjects occupying Spec,TP are marked nominative and objects occupying V,Comp marked accusative. However, a number of 'unless' statements must be formulated in order to account for instances where the case-marking does not match grammatical function. Furthermore, these statements must be hierarchical, since there are elsewhere cases within subsets of sentence types (i.e. 'unless' statements embedded under other 'unless' statements). For instance, to return to the examples in (2), in Icelandic most monotransitive predicates have a nominative–accusative case frame (17a). In quirky case predicates, the subject is marked with a non-nominative case, and in most instances the object is marked nominative and triggers number agreement on the finite verb (17b). However, a smaller number of quirky case verbs mark *both* the subject and object with accusative case (17c).

(17) a. Ice. *Ég   sá   stelpan*
             I.NOM saw girl-the.ACC.SG
             'I saw the girl'
     b. Ice. *Mér ógna   þau   vindaský*
             me.DAT terrify.3PL those.NOM.PL winds.NOM.PL
             'I am terrified of those winds'
     c. Ice. *Hana vantar   peninga*
             her.ACC lacks.3SG money.ACC.SG
             'She lacks money'

The descriptive generalisation here regarding the object case is: the object is accusative, *unless* the subject is non-nominative, *unless* the non-nominative subject is accusative. One reason we should treat the accusative–accusative frame as a sub-type of quirky case predicate rather than a separate generalisation is that the object is also nominative-marked when the subject is genitive (18):[9]

(18) Ice. *Hans er bráðum von*
          his.GEN is soon   hope.NOM
          'He is expected soon'

Therefore, if we formulate a rule for accusative subjects that does not interact with other rules, we are losing the observation that non-nominative subjects in Icelandic always trigger nominative object case

---

[9] As Þráinsson (2007:170) explains, these genitives are quite restricted, and so it may necessitate a different analysis from other quirky case predicates; however, the genitive argument does behave like a subject with respect to the standard tests, and the key point here is that the object is nominative-marked rather than accusative or dative.

and number agreement *unless* the subject is accusative. This interaction can easily be captured via OT constraints. The standard object case inflection in monotransitives is accusative, which matches abstract accusative case and the accusative position V,Comp. The constraint responsible for this could be a MAX faithfulness constraint, which ensures that elements present in the input (here [−HR] abstract case) are realised in the output (here [−HR] morphosyntactic case). Hence, we can formulate the constraint MAX[−HR] as in (19):

(19) MAX[−HR]: Assign a violation for each [−HR] abstract case feature on an input argument that is not realised by a [−HR] morphosyntactic case feature on an output argument.

Evidently, there is a constraint conflict behind examples like (17b), since MAX[−HR] is violated by the nominative case inflection on the object. Moreover, there is a mismatch between subject position [+HR] and the dative case inflection [−HR−LR]. This suggests a *higher-ranked* constraint ensuring that lexical case-marking is realised (20):

(20) MAX[LEXCASE] (MAX[LC]): Assign a violation for each lexical case feature on an argument at the level of abstract case that does not correspond to the same lexical feature value on an argument at the level of morphosyntactic case.

Hence, if MAX[LC] is ranked above a constraint enforcing a match between structural position and case inflection, such as MATCHCASE (21), MATCHCASE will be violated while MAX[LC] is not; thus the subject case in (17b) is derived.

(21) MATCHCASE (MC): Assign a violation for each positional case feature matrix $F[vals_{pos}]$ that is not identical to its corresponding item case feature matrix $F[vals_{item}]$.

However, this does not explain the nominative object case. Some other constraint must be responsible for ensuring that there is some nominative in the clause, which would not be the case if the object was marked accusative. In addition, number agreement is only possible in quirky case predicates when the object is nominative. Let us hypothesise a constraint AGR[+HR] which is violated when no local nominative is agreed with in number:

(22) AGR[+HR]: Assign a violation for each finite verb whose number agreement value is not identical to that of an argument bearing [+HR] morphosyntactic case in the same clause.

If the Icelandic ranking of these four constraints is Max[LC] » Agr[+HR] » Max[–HR] » MC, we derive *all* of the observed behaviour for free: since Agr[+HR] outranks Max[–HR], nominative object case will be a preferred candidate over accusative object case when there is no other nominative present. Since Max[LC] is ranked above MC, it is possible to derive non-nominative subject case and non-accusative object case. Finally, provided one assumption is made regarding the accusative–accusative case frame, the constraints we already have also generate the most embedded 'unless' statement: if the accusative object case in the ACC-ACC frame is lexically assigned, it falls under the purview of Max[LC], and given that Max[LC] is ranked above Agr[+HR] on this hypothesis, the pattern falls out from the ranking. It is not possible to use the passive diagnostic to test whether the object bears lexical case in (17c), since such verbs do not passivise in Icelandic, perhaps due to a thematic restriction (Þráinsson 2007:258); nevertheless, given the constrained distribution of accusative co-occurring with non-nominative subjects, lexical accusative object case is a reasonable hypothesis. The three tableaux for (17) are shown below, with simplified notation for the purpose of exposition:

Icelandic NOM-ACC **monotransitive**

/[+HR], [–HR]/	Max[LC]	Agr[+HR]	Max[–HR]	MC
☞ a. NOM-ACC				
b. NOM-DAT				*!
c. NOM-NOM			*!	*

Icelandic DAT-NOM **monotransitive**

/[LC:[–HR–LR],+HR], [–HR]/	Max[LC]	Agr[+HR]	Max[–HR]	MC
a. NOM-ACC	*!		*	
☞ b. DAT-NOM			*	**
c. DAT-ACC		*!		*

Icelandic ACC-ACC **monotransitive**

/[LC:[–HR],+HR], [LC:[–HR],–HR]/	Max[LC]	Agr[+HR]	Max[–HR]	MC
a. NOM-ACC	*!		*	
b. ACC-NOM	*!		*	**
☞ c. ACC-ACC		*		*

The inputs to these tableaux contain a representation of abstract case, and the constraints here hold of the mapping from abstract to morphosyntactic case; the output candidates contain lexemes already occupying positions in a syntactic tree structure with case-inflectional features present. Our main focus here is the mapping from abstract to morphosyntactic case (i.e. from semantics to syntax), which involves input–output faithfulness constraints (e.g. Max[−hr]), markedness constraints (e.g. Agr[+hr]) and output well-formedness constraints such as MC, which penalises output candidates containing a mismatch from position to item case. Clarification of the precise theoretical claims made with respect to the architecture of grammar is provided in Chapter 9. Further information on these tableaux, the constraints and empirical support for the analysis of Icelandic and Faroese quirky case predicates can be found in Chapter 4.

Above, we have seen an example where a hierarchy of violable constraints is both necessary to avoid losing generalisations and sufficient to generate the correct output forms. Now we will see that the central issue of why Faroese marks objects accusative in quirky case predicates also receives a straightforward, principled explanation if the OLG model is adopted. It was hypothesised that the range of Icelandic case frames in monotransitives is explicable by the interaction of four constraints, with the ranking Max[LC] » Agr[+hr] » Max[−hr] » MC. When we approach the Faroese data, there are only two possible case frames in the contemporary language: nom-acc and dat-acc.[10] A reasonable hypothesis to explore would be to use the same constraints already proposed for Icelandic, but with the ranking Max[−hr] » Agr[+hr]:

Faroese nom-acc monotransitive

/[+hr], [−hr]/	Max[LC]	Max[−hr]	Agr[+hr]	MC
☞ a. nom-acc				
b. nom-dat				*!
c. nom-nom		*!		*

Faroese dat-acc monotransitive

/[LC:[−hr−lr],+hr], [−hr]/	Max[LC]	Max[−hr]	Agr[+hr]	MC
a. nom-acc	*!	*		
b. dat-nom		*!		**
☞ c. dat-acc			*	*

This is an empirical claim, since it entails that the Faroese accusative case in quirky predicates is structural, not lexical: these objects should therefore **behave like regular structural objects**, for example, with respect to object shift or case non-preservation in the passive, which does turn out to be true, as discussed in Chapters 4–6. Moreover,

---

[10] Genitive case has essentially fallen out of use as a structural case in contemporary Faroese. Although acc-acc occurs in some fossilised expressions, these are rare and are generally assumed not to be representative of the modern Faroese system (Þráinsson et al. 2004:253).

it entails that **non-agreement in the Icelandic** DAT-NOM **predicates should not be possible**, since if AGR[+HR] is the right constraint, third person singular agreement with a plural nominative object should not satisfy the constraint and therefore be judged unacceptable, another fact corroborated by fieldwork data presented in Section 4.3.3 of Chapter 4. If the ranking MAX[–HR] » AGR[+HR] is correct for Faroese and the formulation of each constraint is on the right track, the prediction is that **nominative objects should be impossible across the language, not merely in quirky case predicates.** It turns out that this holds true for the contemporary language, despite some claims that have been made and repeated in the literature (Asarina 2011:136, Þráinsson et al. 2012:272–273). All of these empirical predictions are explored with respect to Faroese and Icelandic data, provided in Chapters 4–7; a brief overview of the findings from fieldwork is given in Section 1.3. An additional way of testing the hypothesis – another advantage of OT – is to generate a factorial typology of the possible grammars with these constraints and violations. In Section 4.4.3 we will see that the four constraints described in this section generate case frames attested in other languages in addition to the Faroese and Icelandic types under discussion.

While similar versions of OT have been proposed to account for case-marking phenomena with or without the LT framework (see, e.g., Kiparsky 2001, Donohue 2004, Deo and Sharma 2006, Woolford 2007), the primary contributions brought to discussion by this book include (i) an explicit account of a wider range of Faroese data than heretofore examined, (ii) a specific mapping computation between abstract and morphosyntactic case that generates realistic factorial typologies, and (iii) a competing grammars model which accounts both for lexically/grammatically determined variation *and* the capacity for case selection to convey social meaning. Moreover, in Chapter 9 an OLG analysis of object shift is presented which captures Holmberg's Generalisation through adverbial scope and information-structural constraints without presupposing verb movement. In the next section, an overview of the competing grammars model of morphosyntactic variation is given.

1.2.3 Competing Grammars

As stated in the previous section, in OT a grammar is effectively a snapshot of a specific constraint ranking. Constraint rankings make predictions that are borne out empirically; it is possible to test whether a hypothesised ranking matches observed data within a language, e.g. the prediction that nominative objects should not be possible in Faroese. However, some phenomena exist which are difficult to capture by a single constraint ranking. One such phenomenon is 'nominative substitution' (Jónsson and Eyþórsson 2005) in Faroese quirky case predicates: it is possible to replace the dative case on the subject with nominative case, yielding a standard monotransitive NOM-ACC case frame. This is effectively an 'overwriting' of lexical case, since the standard variant of the same verbs (e.g. *dáma* 'like'), is to mark the subject dative. It is not a question of by-speaker variation, for example, if one speaker always produced nominative and another always dative; rather, two possibilities coexist within a speaker's competence: one the more cross-linguistically marked but standard and more frequent in corpora (dative subject), the other the less cross-linguistically marked but non-standard and stigmatised (nominative subject). Moreover, use of the nominative variant carries social meaning, being associated with childishness, anti-purism and commonly attributed to Danish influence (Petersen 2010). Indeed, the same speaker can be found using the same verb with a different subject case even within the same text.

This presents a conundrum for the theorist, since there is a discrete binary variable, namely dative and nominative subject case, which requires a different morphosyntactic analysis. It is, of course, possible to stipulate two lexemes for the verb in question, one of which marks nominative and the other dative; however, this seems to miss important facts about the diachronic trajectory of the system and about sociolinguistic meaning. As can be observed more broadly in Faroese, quirky case is gradually being lost over time: accusative subjects have fallen out of usage, and the range of verbs with dative-marked arguments is drastically reduced in comparison to Icelandic. Another interesting observation is that the verbs which allow nominative substitution, such as *dáma* 'like', do have a passive form with a nominative subject, whereas verbs more resistant to nominative substitution in the active, such as *tørva* 'need', do not passivise. This mirrors case-preservation behaviour in dative-object verbs, where some verbs, such as *hjálpa* 'help', do not preserve case in the passive (i.e. the subject surfaces as nominative), while others, such as *takka* 'thank', do preserve case (i.e. the subject retains dative case). Therefore, it seems that these facts are *systematic*: an *ad hoc* stipulation of a different lexeme for each variant would involve an excessive amount of redundancy and misses the generalisation that lexical case-marking is being lost in various different constructions. The relevant constraint conflict is between preserving lexical case and marking regular nominative subject case, that is, MAX[LC] and S[+HR], which enforces nominative subject case. This requires two rankings: MAX[LC] » S[+HR], which yields lexical subject case, and S[+HR] » MAX[LC], resulting in nominative subject case.

It is argued here that the most flexible and empirically sound way to model these types of variation is to propose that a given speaker has simultaneous access to multiple competing grammars, where a grammar is activated probabilistically. The probability that a given grammar is accessible depends on factors that bear different weights depending on lexical semantics, grammatical context and socio-pragmatic context. This proposal expands upon the competing grammars idea discussed in previous work such as Kroch (1989a,b, 1994), Pintzuk (1999), among others. Kroch (1994), in particular, suggests that this concept is helpful for understanding synchronic variation within a speaker, including for apparently unvarying morphological paradigms; an idea also explored by Wallenberg (2016) regarding extraposition. A very similar concept to competing grammars was posited in the acquisition literature by Fritzenschaft et al. (1990); the notion is also present in Yang (2000, 2002) as part of his model of acquisition and implicitly as a theory of intraspeaker variation. In this work I focus more on the synchronic dimension rather than diachronic or acquisitional concerns, but the model is readily compatible with the idea that language change occurs when one grammar wins out over another through both internal and external pressures. The following aspects of the CGM put forth in this book are particularly important:

i. The number of grammars/rankings accessible to a speaker is not unconstrained: only those rankings that yield actual attested variants are accessible in production.[11]

ii. The selection of a grammar can be modelled statistically, with fixed effects that differ in their significance to the speaker's calculation.

---

[11] I do not make further claims here about listener hypothesised rankings or the probability of selecting a specific ranking among several that result in the same output; such questions are well beyond the scope of this book.

26 *Introduction*

iii. The relative weight of grammatical and social/contextual factors depends on whether the variant conveys indexical meaning in addition to semantic content: when the variable is above the level of consciousness (see Labov 1966, 2001, 2007, among others), social factors take on greater significance, whereas when the variation is primarily lexical–semantic, lexeme choice, including surrounding syntactic context, will be the strongest factor.[12]

iv. The model is falsifiable by examining actual data: if the factors claimed to be significant in one sample of the sentence type do not emerge as significant in another sample of the same sentence type, e.g. two comparable subsets of a Faroese corpus with tokens of *dáma*, the hypothesis is rejected.

An advantage of CGM is its compatibility with game-theoretic approaches to pragmatic and social meaning: in Section 5.3 a version of the Rational Speech Act model proposed by Goodman and Frank (2016), Burnett (2017) *i.a.* is discussed and applied to the nominative substitution phenomenon in Faroese. Moreover, CGM is easily applicable to *systematic* changes in grammar. One pertinent example in Faroese is that nominative substitution in the active of dative-subject verbs and case non-preservation in the passive of dative-object verbs is explicable by the same constraint interaction; thus, there is a 'preserving' and 'non-preserving' *grammar*, not merely (non-)preserving constructions or lexemes, even if lexeme is the strongest predictor. The loss of lexical case represents increasingly frequent activation of the non-preserving grammar, resulting in an increasing probability over time that learners acquiring the language will hypothesise the non-preserving grammar.

It may be argued that CGM is too unconstrained with respect to the large number of rankings yielding the same output, but if the grammar selection itself is also probabilistic, the search space of reasonable ranking hypotheses is drastically reduced. A speaker is assumed to have knowledge of the whole grammar of the language beyond the specific construction, and therefore is extremely unlikely to hypothesise rankings which would yield unattested forms in other

---

[12] We include syntactic context in this because most of the cases of syntactic change previously analysed as competing grammars, which show contextual effects on frequency of variants, also show effects of syntactic context which cannot be attributed solely to specific lexemes. For example, in phenomena such as the rise of *do*-support or change from OV to VO word order, syntactic factors such as whether the sentence is declarative or interrogative, or the relevant clause is matrix or subordinate, also play a role.

constructions. For instance, both Faroese and Icelandic are languages which exhibit lexical case-marking. When a Faroese speaker selects the ranking S[+HR] » Max[LC] yielding nominative subject case, it is highly improbable that this ranking also includes a markedness constraint *CaseInfl ranked above Max[LC], since this would result in a language without inflectional case-marking (such a ranking would, however, be reasonable for a language like English or Danish). One can easily imagine a probabilistic approach to CGM that builds on prior work, such as Maximum Entropy or Stochastic OT; for further discussion of such approaches, see Boersma (1998), Boersma and Hayes (2001), Goldwater and Johnson (2003), Jäger (2007), Pater (2009) *i.a.* There is not enough space in this book to explore the manifold implications of CGM for morphosyntactic change; the primary aim is to posit the model as a way of understanding intra-linguistic and intra-speaker variation, phenomena which have too often been neglected in the theoretical syntax literature, particularly in the frequent attribution of variation to lexical or language-specific idiosyncrasies. In this way it is hoped that OLG bridges a gap between robustly quantitative and abstract representational approaches to morphosyntax, both of which are data-driven, but which have much to benefit from each other in arriving at a deeper understanding of morphosyntactic variation.

1.3 Empirical Findings

This section summarises the empirical findings from the author's fieldwork conducted on the Faroe Islands and Iceland, in addition to corpus data. The survey data is available online at the permanent URL purl.stanford.edu/nd533ns7207 (Galbraith 2017). As the focus of this book is to explain case-marking patterns in Faroese and Icelandic, multiple surveys were distributed to native speakers of each language, which elicited acceptability judgements on the sentence types most relevant to the phenomena under discussion. Table 1.1 shows details of the surveys; the numbers in parentheses indicate the number of fully complete responses, the remainder providing partial responses. The Stimuli column does not include filler sentences interspersed with the target sentences for judgement, which were included in all surveys except number 1. It is important to note the following: surveys 2 and 6 were conducted as two separate surveys, one with the sentences embedded in a colloquial context and one placing them in a formal context; the groups of speakers for the colloquial and formal surveys did not overlap, and the analysis is based on the combination of the two (i.e. the figure of 158 total participants represents a combination of both groups of speakers). Moreover, the two Icelandic surveys 3 and 7 were tested as one single survey with the same group of speakers, and stimuli of each sentence type were interspersed; the results were split for ease of exposition. Finally, the same goes for Faroese surveys 5 and 9, that is, both passives without agent phrase and *tróta* were tested in the same survey with the same group of speakers. For clarification it is indicated which sets of speakers are the same in the column 'Group'.

Table 1.1 List of fieldwork surveys

№	LANGUAGE	SENTENCE TYPES	GROUP	SPEAKERS	STIMULI	SECTION
1	Faroese	quirky case predicates	A	23 (14)	15	4.3.1
2	Faroese	quirky case predicates	B	158 (46)	28	4.3.2
3	Icelandic	quirky case predicates	C	28 (14)	54	4.3.3
4	Faroese	monotransitive passives, no agent phrase	D	42 (22)	25	6.2.1
5	Faroese	monotransitive passives, with agent phrase	E	37 (15)	45	6.2.2
6	Faroese	passive of 'give'	B	158 (46)	28	7.2.1–7.2.2
7	Icelandic	passive of 'give'	C	28 (14)	54	7.4.1
8	Faroese	ditransitive passives	F	18 (13)	31	7.4.2
9	Faroese	verb *tróta*	E	37 (15)	16	6.2.2

Statistical models were run on the results of these surveys to establish the significance of grammatical factors affecting the mean acceptability judgements. The sentence stimuli are laid out in full either in the section discussing the data or in Appendices B1–B5. Histograms of the distribution of responses for each sentence in the surveys are given in Appendices C1–C9.

The following points summarise the key findings from the fieldwork and survey results:

Quirky case predicates

a. In both Icelandic and Faroese, the object of a quirky case verb behaves like a regular object with respect to object shift and negative scrambling:

i. In Faroese sentences without auxiliaries and with the main verb in T, full DP objects are only accepted when the object occurs in V,Comp, while pronominal objects are accepted with shift (though there is disagreement on whether they may remain in situ); in Icelandic, shift was accepted with pronominal objects and less consistently with full DP objects.

    ii. In Faroese sentences with the finite auxiliary in T and the main verb in V, shift is impossible across the board, but negative scrambling is accepted when the object is negative-quantified; the same results held of Icelandic.

b. In Icelandic, sentences with nominative objects and no number agreement (i.e. third person singular morphology on the verb) were rejected across the board; moreover, sentences with an intervening dative argument were judged significantly worse than those without an intervener. No evidence was found for a dialect or speaker group which consistently accepted agreement across the intervener in this sample (in contrast to Sigurðsson and Holmberg 2008).

Hence, the data are consistent with the OLG hypothesis that these accusative arguments in Faroese are structurally regular objects, and that number agreement with the nominative is a pressure in Icelandic that rules out the possibility of accusative object case. These results also speak against the hypothesis that the difference in object case between the two languages is due to a different object position. This was explored further by investigating passives of both mono- and ditransitive predicates in Faroese in order to verify whether nominative 'objects' ever occur in Faroese.

Passives

a. In Faroese, impersonal passives were judged across the board less acceptable than personal passives; the choice of verb interacts with type of passive, so that the personal improves acceptability over impersonal to differing degrees depending on the verb. Passives were universally judged less acceptable with an overt agent phrase than without.

b. Mean acceptability of the passive of *geva* 'give' was so low in Faroese as to rule out the construction as ungrammatical; the only word order of a Faroese 'give' passive that approached a mean of

      3 acceptability was the Theme-Verb-Goal order, that is, not the order where the argument in object position is nominative.

  c. In Icelandic, survey results confirmed the two acceptable orders of the passive of *gefa* 'give' reported in the literature (Þráinsson 2007:134–136): Goal-Verb-Theme and Theme-Verb-Goal.

  d. In Faroese, the acceptability of ditransitive passive is strongly dependent on the verb lexeme, with certain verbs not permitting the construction; additionally, the Theme-Goal and Theme-only word orders were judged significantly better than Goal-Theme, which was rejected across the board.

The important conclusions from the passive surveys are that (i) by far the most significant factor in the availability of passive in Faroese is the verb lexeme, and (ii) the purported 'nominative objects' in passives with Goal-Verb-Theme order were not accepted by any Faroese speakers in the sample, contrary to what has been reported (Þráinsson et al. 2012:272–273). Of course it could be the case that a different sample of speakers would accept this word order, but it would need to be shown that this sample is not representative with respect to this variable.

    To conclude this section, the data gathered in extensive fieldwork on the Faroe Islands and Iceland are largely consistent with the OLG hypothesis that the object in both Faroese and Icelandic dative-subject predicates behaves just like a regular object with respect to its structural position, and that therefore accusative case-marking in Faroese is expected; in that sense, it is *Icelandic* that needs explanation. Furthermore, the fact that Icelandic speakers rejected non-agreement with the object in these sentences shows that number agreement is a considerable pressure, which is formalised as the constraint AGR[+HR]. Finally, results also show that the supposed nominative objects in Faroese ditransitive passives are not accepted and that the only possible word orders in Faroese when a three-argument verb can be passivised are those in which the nominative theme occurs in subject position. In each section describing the outcome of the given survey, an analysis of the facts is presented using the OLG framework, with the aim of demonstrating that the constraints and implementation proposed not only achieve descriptive adequacy but also offer a deeper explanation for the patterns observed.

1.4 Structure of Book

In this section, an overview of the structure of the book is given.

In Chapter 2 a review of the literature concerning so-called 'quirky' case is presented, starting from the initial work on Icelandic and the subjecthood of the dative arguments, in contrast with preverbal datives in languages such as German. An overview of Faroese clause structure is given, presenting fundamental starting assumptions regarding the non-quirky case data. Finally, it is established that the Faroese dative experiencers in such predicates are true subjects by the standard tests, confirming the conclusions of Barnes (1986).

Chapter 3 provides an overview of the two main components of the OLG approach, namely LT and OT. The basic starting assumptions of each of these formalisms are presented, thus laying the foundations for the analysis of the data discussed in Chapters 4–7.

In Chapter 4 a summary of Faroese non-nominative subjects is presented, followed by survey results from the Faroe Islands and Iceland. Discussion follows of the Semantic Form of the relevant verbs and the OLG analysis of the difference in object case-marking between the two languages.

In Chapter 5, the CGM of variation in Faroese dative subject case is described, supported empirically via logistic regression with data from the Faroese blog corpus. Finally, a Rational Speech Act model of the social meaning conveyed by the case variable is presented.

Chapter 6 discusses the passive of monotransitive verbs in Faroese, with survey data that establish the dependence of passive acceptability on choice of verb lexeme. Case preservation is then discussed and further support given for the competing grammars model by showing the inter-relatedness of the availability of passive and loss of lexical case-marking.

In Chapter 7 the topic of ditransitive verbs in Faroese is broached and further data from fieldwork laid out. Passives of 'give' in both Faroese and Icelandic are discussed, in addition to other triadic verbs in Faroese. These facts are analysed through the same OLG framework, with the conclusion that nominative objects are in fact not accepted in Faroese; thus, ditransitive passives do not threaten the OLG hypothesis.

Having reviewed the crucial data, in Chapter 8 some alternative accounts of case-marking in the literature are discussed. This chapter deals with one OT-based account as well as broadly Minimalist approaches. It is concluded that while these analyses do provide some insight into the case-marking phenomena in question, ultimately the OLG approach shows that Faroese and Icelandic are predictable from general principles of case systems rather than idiosyncrasies of language-specific syntactic configurations; moreover, OT-based approaches have readily demonstrable cross-linguistic traction due to the ease of generating factorial typologies.

In Chapter 9 a detailed exposition is given of the mechanics of the OLG approach, working through an English example within OT syntax. Extensive argumentation is provided for the ranking assumed for Faroese in order to account for the non-quirky case sentence types presented in Chapter 2; an illustrative example is also given of how OLG can explain Holmberg's Generalisation if the right assumptions are made regarding adverb adjunction. It is argued that this theory is able to account for a far broader range of data than those phenomena examined in the preceding chapters.

Chapter 10 concludes the book.

2

Case Study: Non-Nominative Subjects

One of the most illustrative domains of grammar for testing theories of syntax is that of case. What has traditionally been called 'case' requires multiple levels of linguistic analysis, since it is inherently an interface phenomenon, between semantics and syntax and between syntax and (morpho-)phonology. The relations between thematic roles, argument structure, grammatical function, syntactic configuration and morphological exponence can all figure in the case equation. Moreover, the appellation 'case' has been applied not only to traditional grammatical relations (i.e. subject, object, etc.) but also to functions as disparate as locative or prepositional meanings (e.g. Estonian, Tsez), a combination of information structure and grammatical function (e.g. Japanese, Korean) or even more specific meaning, such as the formal ('similar to') and identical ('same as') cases of Manchu.[1] Case, therefore, offers a uniquely challenging arena for syntactic hypotheses and for delineating the division of labour between semantics, syntax and morphology. This becomes particularly apparent when we examine those case-marking patterns where there is no neat alignment between grammatical levels. One such phenomenon is that of non-nominative

---

[1] More confusingly, in the Principles & Parameters/Minimalist literature, the capitalised term 'Case' has been used with a very specific technical meaning that pertains to licensing of NPs within syntax (Chomsky 1981, Vergnaud 2008 and subsequent studies). I do not use this meaning of 'case' unless indicated in the text.

subjects, that is, when the argument mapping to the grammatical function of subject does not map to the typical case borne by subjects. In this chapter, a brief introductory overview of the topic is presented, in addition to a summary of prior work on Faroese clause structure. Once these preliminaries have been established, we turn to the central research question, namely how best to account for the observed differences between Icelandic and Faroese theoretically, and hence what we can learn from these languages about case systems more broadly. This chapter assumes familiarity with syntactic theory and notation within the Government and Binding (GB)/Minimalism tradition.

2.1 Icelandic Oblique Subjects

It has long been established that Icelandic features arguments that pass tests for subjecthood but are marked with some morphological case other than nominative, the unmarked subject case in the language. Zaenen et al. (1985:446) presented the problem as follows: in Icelandic passive sentences with an initial dative argument (23), the structure could either be (24) that of an impersonal passive with a topicalised object or (25) a true dative subject.

(23) Ice. Þeim   var   hjálpað
         them.DAT was.3SG helped
         'They were helped'

(24)

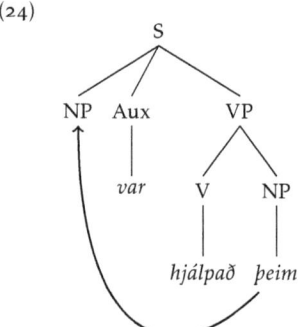

(25)

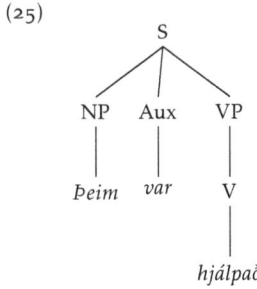

Zaenen et al. (1985) found that hypothesis (25) was consistent with results of diagnostics that pick out a collection of subjecthood properties, both in terms of thematic prominence (e.g. ability to control PRO, being antecedents of reflexives) and structural position (e.g. subject–verb inversion, extraction and subject ellipsis). It has been argued that in Icelandic, transitive subjects are base-generated in Spec,vP and may remain there or move to Spec,TP[2] or Spec,CP,[3] depending on the construction (Þráinsson 2007:46–64). The structural diagnostics employed to test for subjecthood demonstrate that these dative arguments pattern like subjects, not like topicalised objects, and thus appear in Spec,TP and arguably Spec,CP when sentence-initial. In (26) the subject–verb inversion test is illustrated with a topicalised XP preceding the finite verb and subject following the verb in Spec,TP.[4]

---

[2] In much of the literature the relevant head is called I or Infl, and it has been proposed that separate heads may be necessary for I(nflection), T(ense) and Agr(eement) (Pollock 1989 and subsequent studies); in order to build up a case without presuming such a 'Split-IP' analysis, this will be notated as T without assuming the distinction to be required.

[3] Vikner (1995:138) proposes that the finite verb in Icelandic main clauses moves to C and the subject to Spec,CP in subject-initial sentences, since V2 appears to be a general property of the language.

[4] In this overview, for passives the longstanding analysis where subjects are derived from the active is presented (Chomsky 1957, 1975 and subsequent studies), and hence prior to passivisation the object DP originates in the complement of V; this is not the OLG analysis of passive, as discussed in Chapter 9.

(26)

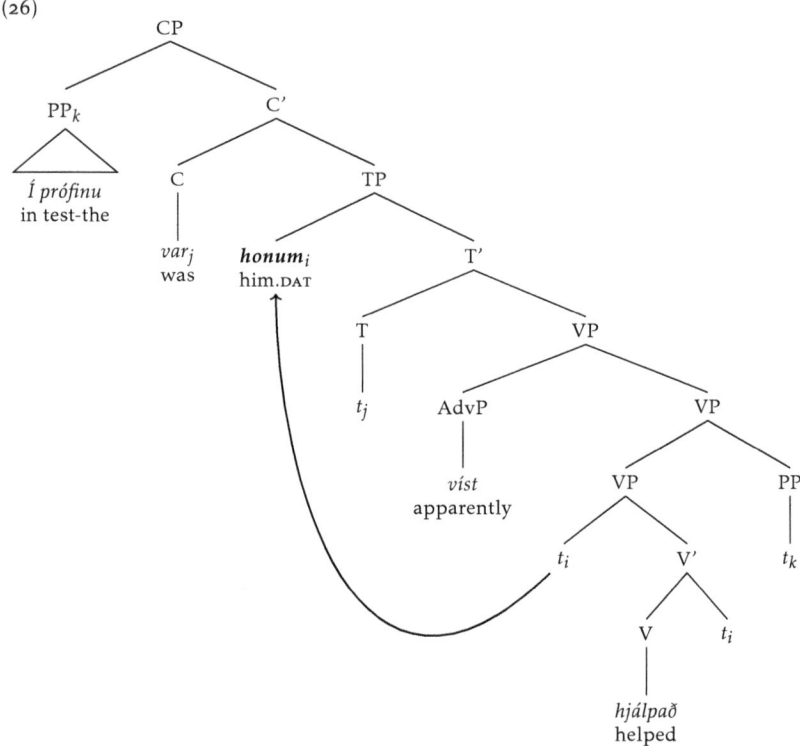

In non-subject-initial sentences with V2, it seems that nominative subjects occur in the same position as the dative argument in (26):

(27) Ice. *Hana hefur **hún** ekki lesið*
it.ACC has she.NOM not read
'That (one), she hasn't read'

(28) Ice. *Ekki hafa **þeir** lokið verkinu í dag*
not have they.NOM finished work-the.DAT today
'They have not finished the work today'

(29) Ice. *Það hafa **nokkrir kettir** verið í eldhúsinu í dag*
EXPL have some.NOM cats.NOM been in kitchen-the.DAT today
'Today some cats have been in the kitchen'

Here it is assumed, following Þráinsson (2007:28, 46), that the subjects in (27–29) occupy the specifier of T, since there is independent evidence that finite main verbs and finite auxiliaries occupy either the T or C head (depending on whether the subject immediately precedes or follows the verb). Icelandic data show that non-finite verbs must occur after negation or sentence-medial adverbs, and finite verbs must precede these elements, both in matrix and subordinate clauses (30–31):[5]

(30) a. Ice. *Jón* **hefur aldrei** *(*hefur) lesið bókina*
John.NOM has never has read book-the.ACC
'John has never read the book'
b. Ice. *Jón* **las aldrei** *(*las) bókina*
John.NOM read never read book-the.ACC
'John never read the book'

(31) a. Ice. *Ég spurði hvort Jón* **hefði aldrei** *(*?hefði) lesið bókina*
I.NOM asked whether John.NOM had never had read book-the.ACC
'I asked whether John had never read the book'
b. Ice. *Ég spurði hvort Jón* **læsi aldrei** *(*?læsi) bókina*
I.NOM asked whether John.NOM read never read book-the.ACC
'I asked whether John never read the book'

There is also evidence that a specifier position lower than Spec,TP can also license subjects, which for now is notated Spec,vP. Evidence for this comes from sentences in which the subject follows the sentence-medial adverb (Þráinsson 2007:17, 47):

(32) Ice. *Það höfðu* **aldrei margir** *lokið verkefninu*
EXPL had never many.NOM finished assignment-the.DAT
'There were never many people who had finished the assignment'

However, since the adverb *aldrei* could be adjoined higher (say, to T), in which case the finite verb would be in C, the subject in (32) could also be in Spec,TP; this is the analysis adopted in Section 2.3 regarding Faroese subject positions. Nevertheless, expletive constructions in which the subject occurs below the non-finite main verb occur in Icelandic, a position assumed to be V,Comp, as in (33):

(33) Ice. *Það hafa verið* **nokkrir kettir** *í eldhúsinu í dag*
EXPL have been some.NOM cats.NOM in kitchen-the.DAT today
'Today some cats have been in the kitchen'

For now, given the possible word orders in (27–33), we assume that minimally Spec,TP and Spec,CP are subject-licensing positions in Ice-

---

[5] See Angantýsson (2007:238), Þráinsson (2007:58, fn.28). This is somewhat of an oversimplification, since the judgements for Icelandic V3 vary depending on the type of embedded clause, matrix verb, pronominal versus full DP subject, and so forth. See Angantýsson (2007) for a detailed treatment of V3 in Icelandic.

landic and that V,Comp also may be occupied by a subject if the right information-structural conditions hold.[6] Let us assume a working definition of subjecthood consisting of both (a) displaying the binding properties picked out by raising, control, reflexivisation and other tests, and (b) obligatorily occupying subject-licensing positions. Much work subsequent to Zaenen et al. (1985) has proposed that the non-nominative arguments in active sentences with nominative lower arguments (e.g. dative-experiencer verbs) exhibit the same properties as these subjects of passives, in spite of the observed object-agreement pattern (Yip et al. 1987, Sigurðsson 1989, 2004, Jónsson 1997–1998, among others). Barðdal (2001) argues that a construction-based account of dative-nominative predicates is necessary, since either argument can behave as a subject with respect to the subjecthood tests; however, this behaviour is restricted to a subset of experiencer verbs with identifiable common lexical–semantic properties,[7] a set that excludes *leiðast* 'find boring' in (36–40).[8]

---

[6]OLG assumptions regarding positional licensing are laid out in detail in Section 3.1.

[7]Barðdal (2001:57) analyses these as several varieties of psych-verb, although her proposal is that the dual-subject behaviour is a property of the construction rather than idiosyncratic verb semantics. The most frequently presented example of the DAT-NOM/NOM-DAT alternation is *henta* 'please', contrasting with *líka* 'like', which always has a dative subject:

(34) a. Ice. **Mér** hefur alltaf hentað **þetta**
me.DAT has.3SG always pleased this.NOM
'I have always been pleased with this'

b. Ice. **Þetta** hefur alltaf hentað **mér**
this.NOM has.3SG always pleased me.DAT
'This has always pleased me'

(35) a. Ice. **Mér** hefur alltaf líkað **Guðmundur**
me.DAT has.3SG always liked Guðmundur.NOM
'I have always liked Guðmundur'

b. Ice. * **Guðmundur** hefur alltaf líkað **mér**
Guðmundur.NOM has.3SG always liked me.DAT

[8]Examples adapted from Sigurðsson (2004:141–143). Some speakers may reject (37) due to dative intervention effects, but judgements vary on this (cf. Sigurðsson and Holmberg 2008); the same sentence with singular 'book' as the object is accepted by all, since third singular agreement may either be an instance of number agreement (with a singular) or default/failed agreement.

REFLEXIVISATION

(36) Ice. **Henni**$_i$ *leiðast*   *bækurnar*   *sínar*$_i$/**hennar$_i$
        her.DAT bore.3PL books-the.NOM.PL self's.NOM.PL/her
        'She finds her (own) books boring'

SUBJECT–VERB INVERSION

(37) Ice. *Þá* *hafa*   **henni** *líklega*   *leiðst bækurnar*
        then have.3PL her.DAT probably bored books-the.NOM.PL
        'Then, she has probably found the books boring'

RAISING

(38) Ice. **Henni** *virðast* [*hafa*   *leiðst bækurnar*]
        her.DAT seem.3PL have.INF bored books-the.NOM.PL
        'She seems to have found the books boring'

CONTROL

(39) Ice. *Hún*   *vonast til* [*að* **PRO**   *leiðast ekki bækurnar*]
        she.NOM hopes for to   PRO.DAT bore.INF not books-the.NOM.PL
        'She hopes not to find the books boring'

EXCEPTIONAL CASE MARKING

(40) Ice. *Ég*   *mundi telja* [**henni** *hafa*   *leiðst bækurnar*]
        I.NOM would believe her.DAT have.INF bored books-the.NOM.PL
        'I would believe her to have found the books boring'

Many other tests have been employed which verify the subjecthood of these arguments according to our working definition (see e.g. Sigurðsson 1989:204–205, 1997:302). Hence, most theoretical analyses of the Icelandic facts have been built on the assumption that non-nominative subjects occupy subject positions and co-occur with nominative objects (see Þráinsson 2007:156–172). One corollary of this: if we approach other languages with pre-verbal dative experiencers, e.g. German, and if the diagnostics for Icelandic turn out to be portable to said language, we would expect either: (i) the same results hold and the dative experiencers are subjects by our definition, or (ii) we see different results and the datives are non-subjects.

2.2 German Pre-Verbal Dative Experiencers

What we find in German is that the same diagnostics can be applied and that the results are consistent with the relevant datives being *non*-subjects. This was noticed as early as Cole et al. (1978), cited by

Zaenen et al. (1985). For instance, in German, subjects of infinitives can be controlled (41a), including nominative-marked subjects of passives (41b), but in the passives of dative-object verbs (41c), the corresponding argument in the active cannot be an understood subject of an infinitival (i.e. arbitrary PRO):

(41) a. Ger. *Im Sommer zu reisen ist angenehm*
in summer to travel is agreeable
'To travel in the summer is nice'
b. Ger. *Aufgenommen zu werden ist angenehm*
admitted to be is agreeable
'To be admitted is nice'
c. Ger. * *Geholfen zu werden ist angenehm*
helped to be is agreeable
'To be helped is nice'

Likewise, EQUI-control is possible in German in both actives and passives (42a–b), but not when the PRO subject would be non-nominative (42c):

(42) a. Ger. *Er hofft weg zu gehen*
he.NOM hopes away to go
'He hopes to go away'
b. Ger. *Er hofft aufgenommen zu werden*
he.NOM hopes admitted to be
'He hopes to be admitted'
c. Ger. **Ihm/*Er hofft geholfen zu werden*
him.DAT/he.NOM hopes helped to be
'He hopes to be helped'

Thus, German can be shown to behave differently to Icelandic with respect to subjecthood of these oblique arguments. We draw the same conclusion in German for the pre-verbal oblique arguments of actives (i.e. constructions not derived from passives):

(43) a. Ger. *Mir ist übel*
me.DAT is nasty
'I am nauseated'
b. Ger. * *Mir hofft übel zu sein*
me.DAT hopes nasty to be
c. Ger. * *Ich hoffe übel zu sein*
I.NOM hope nasty to be
'I hope to be nauseated'
d. Ger. * *Übel zu sein ist unangenehm*
nasty to be is disagreeable
'To be nauseated is unpleasant'

Therefore, it seems that we can conduct similar tests in German to those for Icelandic, which pick out the same control properties. Hence, one reasonable hypothesis would be to posit that these arguments also are *not* situated in the German syntactic positions available to subjects, by contrast with Icelandic. This is in fact what one proposal by Haider (2010) suggests: he argues that case in German is not 'positional' in the sense that the base order of arguments is determined by lexical argument structure (i.e. along the lines of a theta-role hierarchy) rather than assuming unique licensing structural positions (Haider 2010:259, 267). One piece of evidence for this is the fact that nominatives are licensed in contexts which would require object-to-subject raising in English (44):

(44) a. Ger. *dass man   ja Kindern   Märchen   erzählen muss*
         that one.NOM PRT children-DAT fairy.tales-ACC tell   must
         'that one must tell children fairy tales'

   b. Ger. *dass ja Kindern   **Märchen**   erzählt werden müssen*
         that PRT children-DAT fairy.tales-NOM told   be   must
         'that children must be told fairy tales'

   c. Ger. [VP *Märchen   erzählt werden*] *muss Kindern   heute nicht*
         fairy.tales-NOM told   be   must children-DAT today not
         'Children must not be told fairy tales today'

   d. Ger. [VP *Märchen   erzählen*] *muss man   Kindern   ja heute nicht*
         fairy.tales-ACC tell   must one.NOM children-DAT PRT today not
         'One must not tell children fairy tales today'

The nominative in (44b) probably occurs in a VP-internal position, in the same place as the accusative in the active. However, to verify this we must consider that the dative could have been scrambled in front of the nominative. One fact that speaks against that hypothesis is that the main verb plus the direct object can be fronted regardless of grammatical function (44c–d). Haider (2010:260) notes that this property of allowing VP-internal nominatives is shared by Icelandic:

(45) a. Ice. *að **henni/stelpunum**   líkuðu hestarnir*
         that her.DAT/girls-the.DAT liked horses-the.NOM
         'that she/the girls liked the horses'

   b. Ger. *dass **ihr/den Mädchen**   die Pferde   gefielen*
         that her.DAT/the girls-DAT the horses.NOM pleased
         'that the horses pleased her/the girls'

The claim is that although in both languages the arguments are merged according to some lexical argument structure ranking, that is, the dative precedes the nominative in sentences like (45), in Icelandic the dative argument raises to the higher Spec,TP subject position – and precisely because German does not have this positional licensing requirement, the dative argument in fact remains in the highest argument position of the verbal projection. However, it should be noted that since in Icelandic the subject may also remain VP-internal in certain constructions, occupancy of Spec,TP should not be construed as the only subject-defining property in Icelandic; let us merely state that Spec,TP is the standard subject position, provided other factors do not hold (such as the subject remaining in V,Comp in presentational constructions). See Haider (2010:259–271) for additional discussion, the conclusion being that 'it is reasonable to continue assuming that a German dative object stays in its object base position just like any other object' (Haider 2010:270).[9]

To summarise thus far, we have seen that Icelandic oblique arguments behave like subjects with respect to binding properties as well as structural position, here assumed to be Spec,TP (and Spec,*v*P when following a sentential adverb or Spec,CP in subject-initial sentences). German, on the other hand, displays the inverse properties, namely, that oblique arguments are not able to control PRO and (if we accept Haider's point regarding German argument structure) are not occupying standard subject position. With this background in place, that is, having some predictions for what a non-nominative subject language should look like (Icelandic) versus a language without oblique subjects (German), we can approach the Faroese data.

---

[9]It should nevertheless be noted that some have argued against this conclusion: Barðdal (2002) and Barðdal and Eyþórsson (2003), for instance, hold that the at-issue dative arguments do in fact behave as syntactic subjects with reference to reflexives, conjunction reduction and control of infinitival PRO. On the other hand, these behaviours are more restricted than they are in Icelandic; for example, the subject of a second conjunct can be unexpressed if and only if the first conjunct subject bears the same morphological case (Barðdal and Eyþórsson 2003:757). Barðdal and Eyþórsson suggest that the difference between Icelandic and German ought to be viewed as on a gradient rather than categorical. However, they do not discuss or give an explicit account of the syntactic position occupied by the dative argument in these instances. Thus, it remains a strong possibility that although the German obliques may display more of the cluster of subjecthood properties than previously claimed, the position they occupy may not be a licensing position in German like Spec,TP is proposed to be in Icelandic.

2.3 Faroese Clause Structure

Relatively little prior work exists on the architecture of the Faroese clause. The main primary source is the grammar by Þráinsson et al. (2012).[10] Most of the basic questions about Faroese clause structure receive preliminary treatment in Þráinsson et al. (2012:236–248); some relevant sentence types are given in (46a–k).

(46) a. Far. *Tey hava aldri lisið bókina*
     they.NOM have never read book-the.ACC
     'They have never read the book'

   b. Far. *Tá hava tey lisið bókina*
     then have they.NOM read book-the.ACC
     'Then they have read the book'

   c. Far. *Eg haldi, at Jógvan (aldri) hevur (aldri) lisið bókina*
     I.NOM think that John.NOM never has never read book-the.ACC
     'I think that John has never read the book'

   d. Far. *Hon spurdi, hvør (aldri) hevði (?aldri) lisið bókina*
     she.NOM asked who.NOM never had never read book-the.ACC
     'She asked who had never read the book'

   e. Far. *Eg ivist í, um hon (altíð) sigur (?altíð) satt*
     I.NOM doubt in whether she.NOM always says always true
     'I doubt if she always tells the truth'

   f. Far. *Tey lósu aldri bókina (*aldri)*
     they.NOM read never book-the.ACC never
     'They never read the book'

   g. Far. *Tann gamla bilin vil eg ikki hava*
     the.ACC old.ACC car.ACC will I.NOM not have
     'The old car, I don't want'

   h. Far. *Eg las ikki bókina (*ikki)*
     I.NOM read not book-the.ACC not
     'I didn't read the book'

   i. Far. *Eg las (*ikki) hana ikki*
     I.NOM read not it.ACC.F not
     'I didn't read it'

   j. Far. *Eg havi ongan sæð (*ongan)*
     I.NOM have nobody.ACC seen nobody
     'I haven't seen anyone'

   k. Far. *Eg havi ongan næming tosað við (*ongan næming)*
     I.NOM have no.ACC student.ACC spoken to no student
     'I haven't spoken to any student'

It will be immediately observable that, like Germanic languages other than English, Faroese has finite V2 as indicated by the relative position

---

[10] First edition 2004, but citations here are from the updated 2012 edition.

of the auxiliary/finite verb and sentence-medial adverb or negation (46b–g). Moreover, like in Mainland Scandinavian but unlike Icelandic, full-NP objects may not precede negation even though pronominal objects do (46h–i), i.e. Faroese does not exhibit full-NP object shift (Holmberg 1986 and subsequent studies); nevertheless, there is a kind of 'negative shift' in that negative objects do precede the non-finite verb, whether direct objects or complements of prepositions (46j–k).

Another important point to note is that unlike in Icelandic, in Faroese non-bridge-verb clausal complements (46d–e), the adverb–finite verb and finite verb–adverb orders are not equally acceptable; there is significant inter- and intra-speaker variation here, as many find the finite verb–adverb order questionable or unacceptable. This is one of the few areas of detailed prior work: Vikner (1991) and Barnes (1992) made the first proposals that Faroese is not as free as Icelandic with respect to word order in embedded clauses. Rohrbacher (1994) provides the analysis that the verb in Faroese stays low and does not raise to T apart from in 'residual' examples (Rohrbacher 1994:130–135). Likewise, Heycock et al. (2010, 2012) show that while Faroese speakers' acceptability judgements do not show a completed change to a Mainland Scandinavian-type system with no V-to-T in embedded clauses (after carefully controlling for embedded V2), they do appear to show that V-to-T is significantly less available than it is in Icelandic. Hence, some account of both orders must be made, since although one type of grammar may be significantly preferred over the other, the type in which V-to-T is more available nevertheless represents a stage in the history of Faroese that is documented.[11]

---

[11] Lockwood (1977) and Barnes (1986) provide a couple of examples of embedded clause orders with modals and auxiliaries (47–48), cited by Rohrbacher (1994:49):

(47) Far. Eg segði tað, at hann (skuldi) ikki (skuldi) havt nakað
I.NOM said it.ACC that he.NOM should not should have anything.ACC
'I said that he shouldn't have anything'

(48) Far. Tey nýttu fleiri orð, sum hon (hevði) ikki (hevði) hoyrt
they.NOM used several words.ACC that she.NOM had heard not heard
fyrr
before
'They used several words that she hadn't heard before'

This contrasts with Mainland Scandinavian, such as Danish, which prohibits the V-Adv order in the embedded clause (Rohrbacher 1994:49 *mutatis mutandis*, citing Vikner 1991):

Finally, in order to account for three-argument predicates such as double-object constructions, an additional object position must exist below sentence-medial adverbs, and the main verb cannot occur to the left of the adverb (50a–b). Additionally, the order of indirect and direct object cannot be swapped (50c).

(50) a. Far. *Ivaleyst skulu tey ongantíð selja dreingjunum teldurnar*
doubtless shall they.NOM never sell boys-the.DAT computers-the.ACC
'No doubt they will never sell the boys the computers'

b. Far. * *Ivaleyst skulu tey selja (ongantíð) dreingjunum (ongantíð)*
doubtless shall they.NOM sell never boys-the.DAT never
teldurnar
computers-the.ACC

c. Far. * *Ivaleyst skulu tey ongantíð selja teldurnar dreingjunum*
doubtless shall they.NOM never sell computers-the.ACC boys-the.DAT

Since a finite main verb occurs to the left of all three arguments (51), it is reasonable to posit that in the absence of an auxiliary the finite verb occurs at least as high as T, and possibly as high as C given the post-verbal subject.

(51) a. Far. *Ivaleyst góvu tey ongantíð dreingjunum teldurnar*
doubtless gave they.NOM never boys-the.DAT computers-the.ACC
'No doubt they never gave the boys the computers'

b. Far. * *Ivaleyst góvu (ongantíð) tey dreingjunum (ongantíð)*
doubtless gave never they.NOM boys-the.DAT never
teldurnar
computers-the.ACC

Binding facts also support the analysis that the indirect object is structurally higher than the direct object. Since Barss and Lasnik (1986), it has been standardly assumed that the indirect object position precedes the main verb, perhaps by means of a VP-shell (Larson 1988); in examples like (50a) the main verb would therefore move to the left of the indirect object but not across the adverb. However, since OLG is OT-based, we do not stipulate movement, merely that the verb occurs in a position structurally higher than the two objects in the winning candidate, and that the recipient asymmetrically c-commands the theme argument (see Section 7.3.1).

---

(49) Dan. *Jeg ved ikke hvorfor koen (*står) altid står inde i huset*
I know not why cow-the stands always stands inside in house-the
'I don't know why the cow always stands inside the house'

Given these facts, let us test the hypothesis that the following basic clause structure holds of Faroese (cf. Þráinsson 2007:17–19 for the Icelandic facts). This is the maximal structure necessary to account for the sentence types discussed in Section 2.3; usually the optimal output candidate will have all and only the structure necessary for the input, for example, it is not assumed that the adverbial adjunct positions will always be present in the winning candidate. This will be discussed in more detail in Chapter 9.

(52)
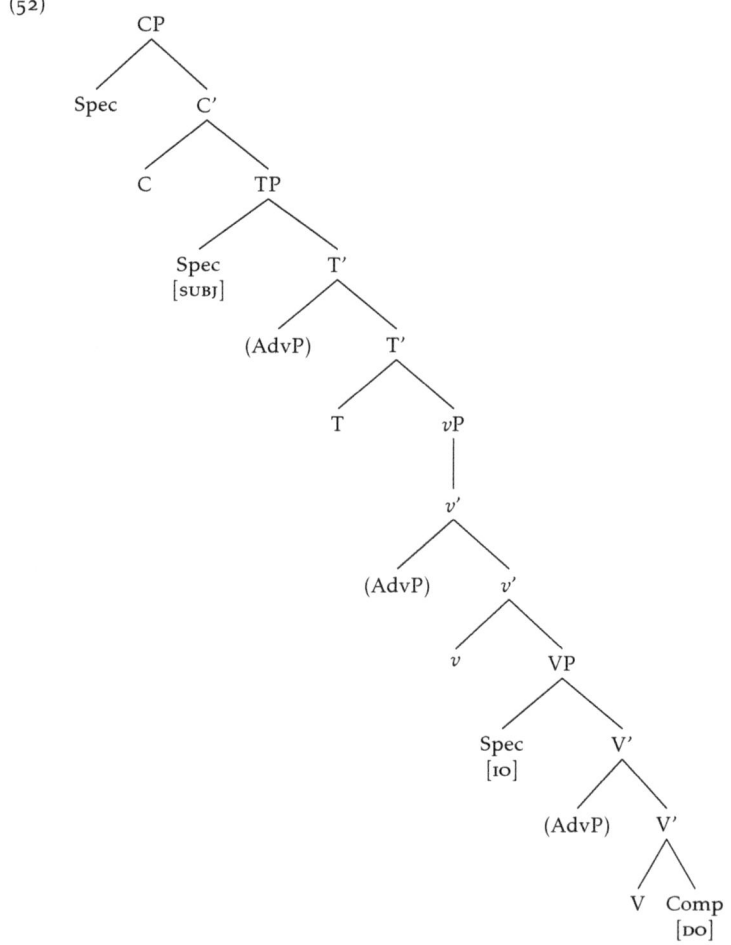

No hard evidence was found for additional low specifier positions (such as Spec,*v*P) available to subjects in the data presented by Þráinsson et al. (2012), in the blog corpus or in the survey data. Since in

OLG X-bar structures are derived from markedness constraints, we do not need to assume that they will be universally instantiated: an input–output faithfulness constraint disfavouring extra null structure can rule out empty specifiers, even when the resulting structure violates the constraint(s) responsible for enforcing X-bar; for fuller discussion, see Chapter 9.[12] Evidence that arguments which bear [+HR] morphosyntactic case can occur in V,Comp comes from unaccusative expletive constructions such as (53), which are reportedly accepted by a majority of speakers:

(53) a. Far. *Tað hava (nakrar mýs) verið (nakrar mýs) í*
EXPL have some.NOM mice.NOM been some.NOM mice.NOM in
baðikarinum
bathtub-the.DAT
'There have been some mice in the bathtub'

b. Far. *Tað eru (nakrir gestir) komnir (nakrir gestir) úr*
EXPL are some.NOM guests.NOM come some.NOM guests.NOM from
Íslandi
Iceland.DAT
'Some guests have arrived from Iceland'

It is unclear from examples like (53) alone whether the expletive and finite auxiliary occur at the left edge of TP or CP. It is reasonable to posit that the associate occurs in V,Comp in unaccusatives like (53), but in main clauses the subject position between the auxiliary and main verb could either be Spec,TP (and therefore the expletive and auxiliary must be in Spec,CP and C), or a lower specifier like Spec,vP. A quick internet search gives some hints as to where sentence-medial adverbs like *aldri* 'never' occur in such constructions, the subject phrases here indicated by square brackets:

(54) a. Far. *tí tað hava **aldri** verið [so nógvir lokalpolitikkarar] í*
because EXPL have never been so many local.politicians.NOM in
løgtinginum sum nú
parliament-the.DAT as now
'...because there have never been as many local politicians in the parliament as now'
www.oyggjatidindi.com, 'Trý lokalsjúkrahús ella Sjúkrahús Føroya?', accessed 3/6/17

---

[12] In essence, Chomsky (1995) presents a similar view when he posits Bare Phrase Structure, which argues that category labels are unnecessary since a head functions as the label of its projections, and thus specifiers are defined simply as structural relations to the head. However, the division of labour is starkly different in OLG, since inviolable constraints do not apply to GEN, which is a tree adjoining grammar, but are part of EVAL, which rules out candidates that do not conform to X-bar principles.

b. Far. *Tað hevur **altíð** verið [tónleikur] í hansara barnaheimi*
EXPL has always been music.NOM in his childhood.home.DAT
'There has always been music in his childhood home'
www.folkakirkjan.fo, 'Jóhan Kallsoy, organistur', accessed 3/6/17

c. Far. *Jenis av Rana segði, at tað hevur **aldri** verið [so nógv brúk fyri politikkinum]*
Jenis.NOM of Rana said that EXPL has never been so much.NOM need.NOM for policy-the.DAT
'Jenis av Rana said that there has never been such a need for the policy...'
www.r7.fo, 'Miðflokkurin havt landsfund', accessed 3/6/17

If we assume that in examples like (54c) the complementiser *at* is occupying C, whether or not we adopt some version of the recursive CP hypothesis (see Vikner 1995), it is at least clear that the subject phrase must be occupying a position lower than Spec,TP and lower than the sentential adverb and participle.[13] This does not clarify whether the subject can also occur between the adverb and participle in (54a–c), however. Native speaker consultants expressed doubts about the possibility of the subject occurring in this position when the adverb is present (unlike Icelandic, where this position is available, see Þráinsson 2007:316):

(55) a. Far. ?? *Tað hava altíð [góðir menn] verið í Føroyum*
EXPL have always good.NOM men.NOM been in Faroes.DAT
'There have always been good men on the Faroes'

b. Far. ?? *Tað hava aldri [innlendsk trø] verið í Føroyum*
EXPL have never native.NOM trees.NOM been in Faroes.DAT
'There have never been native trees on the Faroes'

When a modal is added, the subject occurs below both the nonfinite auxiliary and participle; the same judgement holds regarding the position between the adverb and participle, and higher subject positions are impossible (56).

(56) a. Far. *Tað má hava altíð verið [nógv fólk] í húsinum*
EXPL must have always been many.NOM folk.NOM in house-the.DAT
'There must have always been a lot of people in the house'

b. Far. ?? *Tað má hava altíð [nógv fólk] verið í húsinum*
EXPL must have always many.NOM folk.NOM been in house-the.DAT

---

[13] A reviewer notes that if (54a, c) were embedded V2 environments, it could be the case that the finite auxiliary is occupying an embedded C position and that the expletive *tað* occupies the lower Spec,CP. However, even if this is the case, it does not follow that the bracketed subject phrase must be higher than V,Comp, since it is not clear that the main verb is displaced from V.

c. Far. * Tað má hava [nógv   fólk]   altíð   verið í   húsinum
         EXPL must have many.NOM folk.NOM always been in house-the.DAT
d. Far. * Tað má   [nógv   fólk]   hava altíð   verið í   húsinum
         EXPL must many.NOM folk.NOM have always been in house-the.DAT

The adverbs *altíð* 'always', *aldri(n)* 'never' and *ongantíð* 'never' may also occur between the finite and non-finite auxiliaries, but in such sentences the subject still cannot intervene between the adverb and auxiliary, nor show up higher than the adverb:

(57) a. Far.   Tað má   altíð   hava verið [góðir   menn]   í Føroyum
              EXPL must always have been good.NOM men.NOM in Faroes.DAT
              'There must always have been good men on the Faroes'
     b. Far. ?? Tað má   altíð   hava [góðir   menn]   verið í Føroyum
              EXPL must always have good.NOM men.NOM been in Faroes.DAT
     c. Far. * Tað má   altíð   [góðir   menn]   hava verið í Føroyum
              EXPL must always good.NOM men.NOM have been in Faroes.DAT
     d. Far. * Tað má   [góðir   menn]   altíð   hava verið í Føroyum
              EXPL must good.NOM men.NOM always have been in Faroes.DAT

(58) a. Far.   Tað má   ongantíð hava verið [innlendsk trø]   í Føroyum
              EXPL must never   have been native.NOM trees.NOM in Faroes.DAT
              'There must never have been trees on the Faroes'
     b. Far. ?? Tað má   ongantíð hava [innlendsk   trø]   verið í Føroyum
              EXPL must never   have native.NOM trees.NOM been in Faroes.DAT
     c. Far. * Tað má   ongantíð [innlendsk   trø]   hava verið í Føroyum
              EXPL must never   native.NOM trees.NOM have been in Faroes.DAT
     d. Far. * Tað má   [innlendsk   trø]   ongantíð hava verið í Føroyum
              EXPL must native.NOM trees.NOM never   have been in Faroes.DAT

Thus, the higher subject position in (53) does not seem to be available when a sentence-medial adverb is present, as shown by examples (55–58). It should be noted that these judgements on the availability of subject positions in existential constructions correlate with those for Mainland Scandinavian (Vikner 1995:188, Vangsnes 2002:44), not for Icelandic (Þráinsson 2007:321–322), an indication that Faroese is moving from an Icelandic-type word order to a more Mainland Scandinavian-type one overall. Since in (53) the expletive and auxiliary could be occupying Spec,CP and C, there is no reason to hypothesise a different subject position from Spec,TP when the subject precedes the participle. Let us assume V,Comp for the post-participial subject position in this type of existential construction. Hence, there is not as yet any empirical evidence that the subject ever occurs in a specifier lower than Spec,TP and higher than V,Comp, in spite of the standard assumption that it is base-generated in Spec,vP.[14] For our purposes, the correct Faroese facts can be captured without Spec,vP existing, let alone being a subject-licensing position. It could also be the case that the adverb occupies Spec,vP rather than being adjoined, but there is no empirical reason to reject adjunction, which has been a broadly accepted analysis in the literature (Sportiche 1988; see Þráinsson 2010 for Scandinavian data).

In Table 2.1 the assumed structural positions are laid out for the Faroese sentences in (46, 50a, 51a, 54b, 56a, 58a).

Note that the notation v is used for the non-finite verb position higher than V in the cases of (50a) and (56a, 58a), but does not assume the additional functions attributed to v-heads in the Minimalist literature (e.g. introducing external arguments, see Borer 1986, Chomsky 1995, Kratzer 1996 and others); it is simply an empirically necessary non-finite verb position higher than V, for which v is a convenient notation. In OLG, licensing of arguments is the purview of feature-matching as subject to the relevant OT constraints. In Chapter 9, it is argued that these starting assumptions about the Faroese clause structure enable one to generate all of the attested Faroese predicates. Whether or not extra functional material is present (e.g. null v or Appl heads, empty specifiers) does not make any different predictions, since the OLG analysis does not rely on movement and, hence, does not appeal to restrictions on head- or specifier-movement to rule out unacceptable sentence types. Instead, the structural position of clausal elements is determined by the output of the EVAL calculation: the constraints themselves ensure that unacceptable orders are losing candidates.

A few further notes on the structures posited in Table 2.1: explicit evidence that the subject moves to Spec,CP and finite verb to C in subject-initial sentences such as (46a) is wanting, but it cannot be ruled out; for theory-internal reasons, the analysis that Spec,TP must always be occupied by an argument is preferred, a constraint that the expletive satisfies (see Section 9.6.1 for discussion). There is insufficient evidence to posit a 'split-IP' into Tense and Agreement (Pollock 1989), so this has been notated as a simple unsplit T projection. One important difference between this approach and the standard analysis of Scandinavian clause structure is that *it is not assumed that the positioning of sentential adverbs higher than the finite verb constitutes evidence of*

---

[14]Further work is needed to explore additional diagnostics for low subject positions, such as quantifier float (Sportiche 1988, McCloskey 2000, among others).

Table 2.1 Faroese clause structure

	Spec,CP	C	Spec,TP	T'	T	v'	v	Spec,VP	V'	V	V,Comp
46a			Tey		hava	aldri				lisið	bókina
46b	Tá	hava	tey		hevur	aldri				lisið	bókina
46c'		at	Jógvan	aldri	hevur	aldri				lisið	bókina
46c''		at	Jógvan	aldri	hevði					lisið	bókina
46d			hvør	altið	sigur						satt
46e		um	hon		lósu	aldri					bókina
46f			Tey			ongantið	selja	dreingjunum			teldurnar
50a	Ivaleyst	skulu	tey			ongantið		dreingjunum			teldurnar
51a	Ivaleyst	góvu	tey			altið					tónleikur
54b'	Tað		Tað		hevur	altið				verið	
54b''		hevur	tónleikur						altið	verið	
56a			Tað		má	ongantið	hava			verið	nógv fólk
58a			Tað		má		hava			verið	innlendsk trø
46g	Tann gamla bilin	vil	eg			ikki				hava	
46h			Eg		las	ikki		hana			bókina
46i			Eg		las			ongan	ikki		
46j			Eg		havi			ongan næming		sæð	
46k			Eg		havi					tosað	við ___

51

the finite verb occurring lower than T. This is not a completely novel approach: Svenonius (2002), for example, argues that adverb adjunction interacts with tense, such that adverbs like 'never' may be adjoined as high as T. Moreover, Heycock and Wallenberg (2013) restrict the set of diagnostic adverbs to negation and only a few others, such as clear manner-adverbs, even for historical Icelandic.[15] Instead, it is assumed that *v'*-adjunction is the default adverb position for 'always' and 'never' in main clauses, and we pursue the hypothesis that the tensed verb is always in T or C, thus avoiding the complication of affix-hopping should the tensed verb occur below the adverb (46c″, d–e), or of having a non-finite verb in T (56a). It is assumed that the negation word *ikki* has a similar distribution to sentential adverbs, and may be low-adjoined to V' when a shifted object precedes it (46i–k). For a detailed dialectal survey on verb and adverb placement in Faroese, see Bentzen et al. (2009); their conclusion that verb movement in embedded clauses is not readily available in Faroese (apart from in V2 contexts) is consistent with the claim that *v'*-adjunction is the default sentential adverb site in main clauses, but that in embedded clauses T'-adjunction is the norm in Faroese; sentence (46c') represents the older 'V-to-I' option. Let us posit the same VP-internal specifier site for shifted pronominal and negative-quantified objects; no explicit evidence was found that this position differs from that occupied by indirect objects in double-object constructions. Indeed, the placement of negation in ditransitives seems consistent with our hypothesis, since Faroese native speaker consultants judged either the *v'*- or V'-adjoined position for *ikki* acceptable, including when both objects are pronominal:

(59) Far. Eg   seldi (ikki) gentuni   (ikki) bókina   (*ikki)
        I.NOM sold not   girl-the.DAT not book-the.ACC not
        'I didn't sell the girl the book'

(60) Far. Eg   seldi (ikki) honum   (ikki) hana   (*ikki)
        I.NOM sold not   him.DAT not   it.ACC.F not
        'I didn't sell him it'

Therefore, it seems that *ikki* may be adjoined to any level of the *v*P or VP in ditransitives.[16] Interestingly, as (59) shows, a definite nominal

---

[15] See Þráinsson (2010) for an overview of the literature on Scandinavian adverb sites and Þráinsson (2007:79–87) for discussion of adverb sites as a diagnostic for positions of other elements in the clause.

[16] A reviewer points out that an example with a non-finite verb and *ikki* adjoined below the indirect object would be even stronger evidence for this analysis. Unfortunately,

such as *gentuni* may occur to the left of *ikki*, but true object shift of a full-DP nominal is not permitted in monotransitives, as seen in (46h) above. The reader may consult a version of Table 2.1 in Appendix A1 with every possible position elements in the clause could be occupying notated; here, only a working hypothesis is presented.

To summarise, in this section the starting assumptions regarding Faroese clause structure have been laid out. In Chapter 3 the linking theory framework is discussed, in particular regarding the relation between the above hypothesised tree structure and the optimality calculation: what constitutes the input, what are the output candidates, what relations hold between Semantic Form and levels of case, and so forth. Before detailing this framework, empirical facts are presented regarding Faroese dative experiencer arguments, and the central problem that these raise, in Sections 2.4–2.5.

2.4 Faroese Dative Experiencers

Having established a working hypothesis for the basic Faroese clause structure, we are now in a position to examine the behaviour of the pre-verbal dative experiencers that, on the surface at least, appear similar to Icelandic quirky subjects. Barnes (1986) applied the same diagnostics as Zaenen et al. (1985) to Faroese dative-subject verbs and found essentially the same results, whether for binding properties or structural position.

2.4.1 Subjecthood Tests

2.4.1.1 Reflexivisation

Barnes (1986:19–21) argues that subjects in Faroese control reflexives obligatorily rather than optionally, like objects, as shown in the contrast between (61a–b). The reader is referred to Þráinsson et al. (2012:325–329) for further evidence that this is a property of subjects in Faroese.

(61) a. Far. **Kjartan**$_i$ koyrdi nýggja bil sín$_{i/*j}$/hansara$*_{i/j}$
    Kjartan.NOM$_i$ drove new   car his.REFL$_{i/*j}$/his$*_{i/j}$
    'Kjartan drove his new car'

I could not find such examples in the corpora, and my consultants were reluctant to accept examples of ditransitives with *ikki* in which the matrix verb was not directly negated, suggesting this requires deeper investigation.

b. Far. *Jógvan_i   sá   **Kjartan**_j   á   skrivstovu síni_{i/j}/hansara*_{i/j}*
   Jógvan.NOM_i saw Kjartan.ACC_j in office   his.REFL_{i/j}/his*_{i/j}
   'Jógvan saw Kjartan in his office'

Therefore if the dative arguments are subjects, we expect the non-coindexed reading of the reflexive possessive to be unavailable when they co-occur, which does turn out to be true (62a–e):

(62) a. Far. ***Kjartani**_i   dámar væl   nýggja bil   síni_{i/*j}/hansara*_{i/j}*
         Kjartan.DAT_i likes well new   car his.REFL_{i/*j}/his*_{i/j}
         'Kjartan likes his new car a lot'

   b. Far. ***Sigmundi**_i   tørvar trygging   fyri nýggja bil   síni_{i/*j}/hansara*_{i/j}*
         Sigmundur.DAT_i needs insurance for new car his.REFL_{i/*j}/his*_{i/j}
         'Sigmund needs insurance for his new car'

   c. Far. ***Onnu**_i   manglar trygging   fyri nýggja bil   síni_{i/*j}/hennara*_{i/j}*
         Anna.DAT_i lacks insurance for new car her.REFL_{i/*j}/her*_{i/j}
         'Anna lacks insurance for her new car'

   d. Far. ***Rógva**_i   leingist altíð   eftir gamla bili sínum_{i/*j}/hansara*_{i/j}*
         Rógvi.DAT_i longs always after old car his.REFL_{i/*j}/his*_{i/j}
         'Rógvi always misses his old car'

   e. Far. ***Bettu**_i   lukkaðist til hús   síni_{i/*j}/hennara*_{i/j} áðrenn klokka 12*
         Betta.DAT_i succeeded to house her.REFL_{i/*j}/her*_{i/j} before o'clock 12
         'Betta made it to her house before 12 o'clock'

2.4.1.2 Subject–Verb Inversion

Topicalised objects cannot occur in immediate postverbal position (Barnes 1986:22).

(63) a. Far. *Hann   hitti **eg**   í gjár*
         him.ACC met I.NOM yesterday
         'I met *him* yesterday'

   b. Far. ** Í gjár   hitti hann   eg*
         yesterday met him.ACC I.NOM

   c. Far. *Í gjár   hitti **eg**   hann*
         yesterday met I.NOM him.ACC

Let us assume that this example indicates no further topicalisation is possible once an object has been preposed (Zaenen et al. 1985:450). By contrast, these dative experiencer arguments can and do occur immediately postverbally, indicating that they pattern like subjects as in (63c) rather than topicalised objects.

(64) a. Far. *Mær   dámar   sjokulátu   eftir døgurða*
         me.DAT likes.3SG chocolate.ACC after dinner
         'I like chocolate after dinner'

b. Far. *Eftir døgurða dámar* **mær** *sjokulátu*
after dinner likes.3SG me.DAT chocolate.ACC

c. Far. *Mær   tørvar   sjokulátu   ov   ofta*
me.DAT needs.3SG chocolate.ACC too often
'I need chocolate too often'

d. Far. *Ov ofta tørvar* **mær** *sjokulátu*
too often needs.3SG me.DAT chocolate.ACC

e. Far. *Mær   leingist   ofta   eftir   friði   og   náðum*
me.DAT longs.SG often after peace.DAT and quiet.DAT
'I often long for peace and quiet'

f. Far. *Ofta leingist* **mær** *eftir friði   og   náðum*
often longs.SG me.DAT after peace.DAT and quiet.DAT

2.4.1.3 Raising

The following examples include a phrase such as *í skundi mínum* 'in my haste' to demonstrate that this is not an instance of scrambling (i.e. that the subject argument is in fact in Spec,TP). Example (65) shows that raising is a property of subjects only in Faroese, since a dative-marked object may not raise; the nominative case on *Bárður* in (65b), unlike Icelandic, cannot be mistaken for object case since nominative is unavailable as a monotransitive object case in Faroese.[17] Note also that the verb *tykjast* 'seem' itself can take a dative subject (e.g. when the subject is an experiencer), though in such examples usually a clausal complement ('It seems to Jógvan that ...').

(65) a. Far. **Bárður**$_i$ *tykist í skundi sínum*$_i$ *(at) trúgva   Marjuni*
Bárður.NOM seems in haste his (to) believe.INF Marjun.DAT
'Bardur seems, in his haste, to believe Marjun'

b. Far. * *Marjuni   tykist í skundi sínum*$_i$ *(at) trúgva   Bárður*$_i$
Marjun.DAT seems in haste his (to) believe.INF Bárður.NOM

In (66) we see that the same facts hold of the dative experiencers:

(66) a. Far. **Beini**   *tykist   í   býttleika sínum (at) dáma   sjokulátu   eftir*
Beinir.DAT seems.SG in stupidity his (to) like.INF chocolate.ACC after
døgurða
dinner
'Beinir seems, in his stupidity, to like chocolate after dinner'

b. Far. **Mikkjali** *tykist   í   býttleika sínum (at) tørva   sjokulátu   ov*
Mikkjal.DAT seems.SG in stupidity his (to) need.INF chocolate.ACC too
ofta
often
'Mikkjal seems, in his stupidity, to need chocolate too often'

---

[17] Example based on Zaenen et al. (1985:448).

c. Far. **Tórhalli**   tykist   í órógv   sínum (at) leingjast ofta eftir
    Tórhallur.DAT seems.SG in unease his   (to) long.INF often after
    friði   og   náðum
    peace.DAT and quiet.DAT
    'Torhallur seems, in his unease, often to long for peace and quiet'

d. Far. **Hjalmari**   tykist   í vansketni   sínum ongantíð (at) lukkast
    Hjalmar.DAT seems.SG in carelessness his   never   (to) succeed.INF
    heim áðrenn kl. 12
    home before 12:00
    'Hjalmar seems, in his carelessness, never to make it home before 12 o'clock'

Consultants rejected raising constructions with an expletive, even when the subject occurs to the left of the prepositional phrase (ostensibly in Spec,TP), as in (67a):

(67) a. Far. * Tað tykist   **hann**   í býttleika sínum (at) drekka   øl   ov
        EXPL seems.SG him.ACC in stupidity his   (to) drink.INF beer.ACC too
        ofta
        often
        'He seems, in his stupidity, to drink beer too often'

    b. Far. * Tað tykist   í býttleika sínum **hann**   drekka   øl   ov ofta
        EXPL seems.SG in stupidity his   him.ACC drink.INF beer.ACC too often

This behaviour is the same with dative-subject verbs, which do not permit the construction:

(68) a. Far. * Tað tykist   **Beini**   í býttleika sínum (at) dáma   sjokulátu
        EXPL seems.SG Beinir.DAT in stupidity his   (to) like.INF chocolate.ACC
        eftir døgurða
        after dinner
        'Beinir seems, in his stupidity, to like chocolate after dinner'

    b. Far. * Tað tykist   í býttleika sínum **Beini**   dáma   sjokulátu   eftir
        EXPL seems.SG in stupidity his   Beinir.DAT like.INF chocolate.ACC after
        døgurða
        dinner

2.4.1.4 Control

Like nominative-subject PRO (69), a dative-subject PRO can occur in the embedded clauses of control predicates (70).

(69) a. Far. Álvur vónar, [(at) **PRO**   lesa kinesiskt]
        Álvur hopes   to PRO.NOM learn Chinese.ACC
        'Álvur hopes to learn Chinese'

(70) a. Far. Brandur vónar, [(at) **PRO**   mangla ikki kaffi]
        Brandur hopes   to PRO.DAT lack   not coffee.ACC
        'Brandur hopes not to lack coffee'

b. Far. *Bjarni vónar,* [*(at)* **PRO** *lukkast heim áðrenn klokka 12*]
   Bjarni hopes   to PRO.DAT return home before o'clock 12
   'Bjarni hopes to return home before 12 o'clock'

Dative subjects of matrix verbs can also control *nominative* PRO in the embedded clause (71a), but native speaker consultants expressed doubts as to whether a dative matrix subject could control a *dative* PRO in the embedded clause (71b–c). However, this could be due to the pragmatically odd sentences required to test the judgements, given the small number of dative-subject verbs in the language.[18]

(71) a. Far. *Ásmundi   brellist eftir,* [*at* **PRO**   *eta føroyskan   mat*]
         Ásmundur.DAT desires after to PRO.NOM eat Faroese.ACC food.ACC
         'Ásmundur yearns to eat Faroese food'
      b. Far. **Bárði · brellist eftir,* [(*at*) **PRO**   *lukkast at gera tað*]
         Bárður.DAT desires after   to PRO.DAT succeed to do it.ACC
         'Bárður yearns to succeed at doing it'

2.4.1.5 Exceptional Case-Marking

Finally, in accusative-with-infinitive/ECM constructions, the same observations apply as do for raising: nominative subjects (72) and dative arguments in quirky-case verbs (73) exhibit the same behaviour.

(72) a. Far. *Eg$_i$ helt   **Boga**   í skundi mínum$_i$ trúgva   Marjuni*
         I   thought Bogi.ACC in haste my   believe.INF Marjun.DAT
         'I thought in my haste that Bogi believed Marjun'
      b. Far. **Eg$_i$ helt   Marjuni   í skundi mínum$_i$ trúgva   Bogi*
         I   thought Marjun.DAT in haste   my   believe.INF Bogi.NOM

(73) a. Far. *Eg helt   **Súsannu**   í býttleika mínum mangla ofta sjokulátu*
         I thought Susanna.DAT in stupidity my   lack.INF often chocolate.ACC
         'I thought, in my stupidity, that Susanna often lacked chocolate'
      b. Far. *Eg helt   **Bárði**   í býttleika mínum dáma   sjokulátu   eftir*
         I thought Bárður.DAT in stupidity my   like.INF chocolate.ACC after
         døgurða
         dinner
         'I thought, in my stupidity, that Bárður liked chocolate after dinner'
      c. Far. *Eg helt   **Tórhalli**   í skundi mínum leingjast ofta eftir*
         I thought Tórhallur.DAT in haste my   long.INF often after
         friði   og náðum
         peace.DAT and quiet.DAT
         'I thought, in my haste, that Tórhallur often longed for peace and quiet'

---

[18]The verb *brellast (eftir)* 'desire, crave' does not occur in the blog corpus, but my consultants used it with a dative subject in spoken contexts.

58 Case Study: Non-Nominative Subjects

The results of all the above tests were replicated with native speaker consultants, both for when the experiencer is marked dative and when nominative case is substituted. Therefore, it appears that these Faroese dative experiencer arguments are true subjects according to the criteria typically assumed (Zaenen et al. 1985 and subsequent studies). We now have enough information to postulate the following structure for a dative-accusative case frame with V2 and a sentence-initial adverb:

(74)

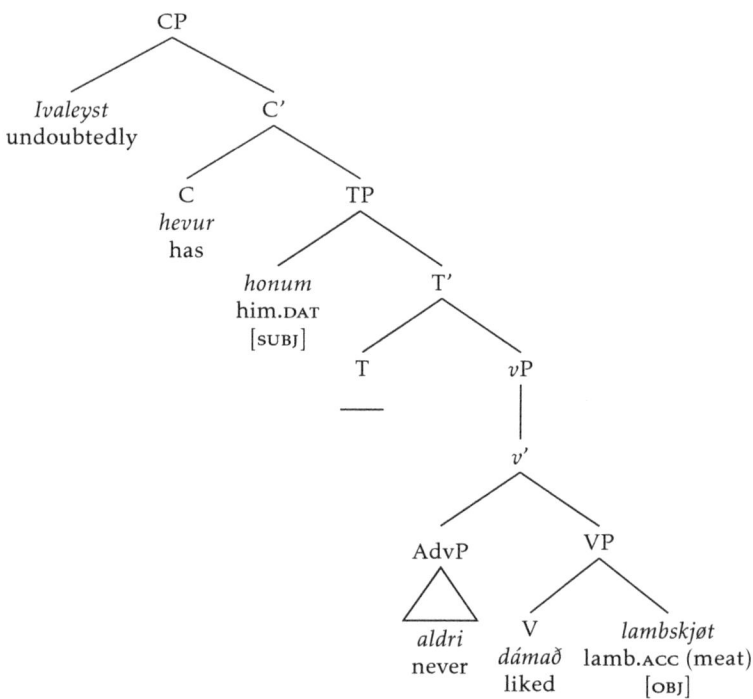

Given that this structure is very similar to (26) – an analogous Icelandic construction involving a fronted XP, V2 and a dative subject – it is surprising that the object, which is marked nominative in Icelandic, should be accusative in Faroese. If it is correct that the two arguments in such dative-subject predicates occupy the same positions in both languages, it remains to be explained why there is a difference in object case-marking.

Two obvious possibilities for the surprising accusative object case are (i) that it is *lexically* assigned, or (ii) that it is *structural* case (i.e. regular transitive object case), the position argued for here. The first option can be ruled out via diagnostics for lexical case, the main one being preservation under passivisation. If an object promoted to subject of the passive surfaces in the active with regular subject case, this constitutes one piece of evidence that the case on the object in the active is structural (Zaenen et al. 1985:445). On the other hand, if the object case is preserved when promoted to subject in the passive, we conclude that it is the result of some lexical rule applying. This contrast is illustrated in (75–76):[19]

STRUCTURAL OBJECT CASE – NON-PRESERVATION

(75) a. Far. *Málmaðurin sparkaði **bóltin** út*
goalkeeper-the.NOM kicked ball-the.ACC out
'The goalkeeper kicked the ball out'

b. Far. ***Bólturin** varð sparkaður burtur*
ball-the.NOM was kicked.NOM.SG.M away
'The ball was kicked away'

LEXICAL OBJECT CASE – PRESERVATION

(76) a. Far. *Tey trúðu **henni** kanska ongantíð*
they.NOM believed her.DAT perhaps never
'Perhaps they never believed her'

b. Far. ***Henni** bleiv kanska ongantíð trúð*
her.DAT was perhaps never believed
'She was perhaps never believed'

It should be noted, however, that not all Faroese dative-object verbs behave like (76); in fact, only a subset of verbs with quirky object case exhibit preservation in the passive. This is related to the nominative substitution property of dative subject case and is an indicator that quirky case as a system is being lost in contemporary Faroese. These issues will be discussed in further detail in Chapter 6; at this point it suffices to say that in those cases where passive is available with dative-subject verbs, the accusative never preserves but behaves like typical object case:

(77) a. Far. *Mær dámar hasar hestarnar*
me.DAT likes.3SG those.ACC horses-the.ACC
'I like those horses'

b. Far. ***Hasir hestarnir** blivu væl dámdir*
those.NOM horses-the.NOM were well liked.NOM.PL
'Those horses were well liked'

---

[19]When the tests for subjecthood are conducted on the dative arguments in passives of the same type as (76b), the result is that they behave like true subjects, not fronted objects. The same goes for passives of regular nominative-accusative monotransitives, and for those verbs with dative objects that do not preserve the dative case in the passive.

A secondary, weaker argument that these accusatives are structural rather than lexical is from lexical distribution. Simply put, accusative is the standard object case and occurs on direct objects in the vast majority of the verbal lexicon. Nominative is completely ungrammatical for these objects, and there is no discernible semantic generalisation that can be made, nor is there alternation with another object case.[20] In Chapter 4, we explore the hypothesis that the Faroese accusative object bears standard structural case by investigating object shift behaviour in survey data.

2.5 Summary of Chapter

As noted above, the main issue we intend to disentangle with respect to case-marking is why the Faroese quirky case predicates have accusative rather than nominative objects, unlike Icelandic. Previous analyses, such as the Case in Tiers model (Yip et al. 1987 and subsequent studies), suggest that in Icelandic the lexical or idiosyncratic case is in some sense a more specific rule, and (following some version of Pāṇini's Principle) applied before structural or default case.[21] Hence, in Icelandic lexical subject case is associated with the highest argument, and as a result the subject becomes unavailable as a target for the structural case-marking tier; this is the explanation for nominative object case, since accusative is hierarchically lower on the structural case tier (cf. Yip et al. 1987:223). Subsequent accounts may have adopted different notation or assumptions regarding the mapping of grammatical relations to syntax (e.g. the dependent case literature could be seen as developing the same idea), but the basic intuition is that accusative object case is blocked in Icelandic due to nominative being more prominent on a case-marking hierarchy. However, it is immediately clear that this cannot be true for Faroese, where accusative case is the norm across the board for objects when co-occurring with a

---

[20]This argument only pertains to the dative-accusative case frame; it is possible that some semantic factor could be affecting the alternation where certain verbs which take dative objects may also take accusative objects.

[21]The terms lexical, structural and default case are used here in as theory-neutral a manner as possible: by 'lexical' is meant associated with a particular verb or subset of verbs, that is, associated with arguments by lexical rule (although this is instantiated configurationally, such as by a head-complement or head-specifier relation); by 'structural' is meant the standard case assigned to a verb's arguments by means of their structural position; and by 'default' is meant the elsewhere case or last resort when all more specific cases are unavailable.

dative subject, and nominative object case is ungrammatical across the board (see Chapter 8 for discussion of purported nominative objects).

Given this research question, in the following chapters our main hypothesis is explored further, namely, that the accusative case is unavailable in Icelandic due to some requirement that a nominative-marked argument must be agreed with. In Chapter 3 the mechanisms of OLG framework are laid out. In Chapters 4–7, dative-subject predicates, passive, ditransitives and passives of ditransitives, including new data from surveys conducted on the Faroe Islands, are discussed in detail. It is demonstrated that the OLG apparatus, in addition to the clause structure assumed in Section 2.3 and constraints already proposed in the literature, is flexible enough to account for all the discussed Faroese and Icelandic sentence types while also generating a realistic factorial typology. In Chapter 8 some alternative hypotheses are investigated, concluding that while they can be altered to achieve empirical coverage, they miss generalisations that the OLG approach captures. Finally, in Chapter 9 the OLG framework is presented in much greater detail, along with an analysis of the basic Faroese sentence types in Section 2.3.

3

Overview of OLG

As mentioned in Chapter 1, OLG builds upon both generativist and connectionist models of grammar by combining formal grammatical representations with an output harmonisation defined by a ranking of violable constraints. The theory is also highly stratal, presupposing several empirically necessary levels of structure and harmonisation between levels. This chapter presents a brief overview of the fundamental components of the OLG theoretical framework, namely Linking Theory (LT) and Optimality Theory (OT). A much more in-depth presentation of the theory is given in Chapter 9; our purpose here is simply to provide the prerequisite information for the OLG analyses the in following chapters. In Section 3.1 the basic apparatus of LT is described and examples provided of how quirky case predicates in Icelandic and Faroese are represented, while in Section 3.2 key aspects of OT syntax are summarised.

3.1 Linking Theory

The LT framework was proposed by Kiparsky (1997) in order to account for phenomena relating to case, agreement, word order and thematic roles, such as loss of morphological case in the history of English (and synchronous word order changes). Kiparsky's theory in turn informed work by Wunderlich (1997) and Wunderlich and Lakämper (2001), whose Lexical Decomposition Grammar was also drawn upon by Kiparsky (2001); for further discussion of the differences between these approaches, see chapter 5 of Butt (2006). The relevant 'linking' between levels concerns a thematic representation of argument structure, which is mapped to syntax; within syntax, structural position and case inflection also undergo a mapping computation in languages that have both – though as discussed in Section 4.4.1, this is proposed to be evaluated in parallel within morphosyntax; and finally, it concerns the mapping from morphosyntax to morphology (a topic largely beyond the scope of this book). This section gives further details of the levels particularly relevant to case-marking.

3.1.1 From Conceptual Structure to Semantic Form

First, following Bierwisch (1986) and Lexical Decomposition Grammar (LDG) as proposed by Wunderlich (1997), we assume a level of Semantic Form (SF), represented as expressions in which theta-roles are lambda-abstractors over variables. This provides a hierarchy of theta-roles, where the ranking of roles is determined by depth of embedding. An example of an SF representation for the verb 'show' is given in (78):

(78)   show: $\lambda z \lambda y \lambda x$ [x CAUSE [CAN [y SEE z]]]

As Wunderlich (1997:29) argues, lexical decomposition yields an argument structural representation that captures properties of a subclass of lexemes without going beyond computation of the argument hierarchy into further granularity; in other words, SF does not represent conceptual semantics subject to contingent knowledge. Instead, SF is a restructuring of conceptual information into an argument structure that can be straightforwardly linked to syntax. Some further relevant aspects of this approach to the semantics–syntax interface are given below (Wunderlich 1997:30–33):

i. **Two-level semantics**: Conceptual Structure (CS) and SF are distinguished (Bierwisch 1983), so that SF cannot be infinitely decomposed but represents a level of sublexical semantics that feeds the input to syntax. While CS will distinguish *cat* and *dog* using contingent knowledge, SF will concern the lexical properties shared by *cat* and *dog* relevant to syntax.[1]

ii. **Semantic Form is expressed in a type-categorial language**: we assume a version of Categorial Grammar (Oehrle et al. 1988)

---

[1] For further evidence of the need for SF, see the analysis of causatives provided by Wunderlich (1997:53–65), or more recently Wunderlich (2012).

restricted to SF, with only two basic types, *individuals* and *propositions*, which combine to form more complex types; all predicates can be defined in terms of their logical type. This is represented by λ-expressions over variables.

iii. **Semantic Form is restricted**: the possible decomposition templates of a predicate are drawn from a finite, universal set, the combination of which is further constrained by principles of composition. We assume that an OT evaluation also applies to the mapping from CS to SF with domain-specific constraints, such that only well-formed SF representations are permitted to feed syntax.

iv. **Semantic Form determines argument linking**: the thematic-role hierarchy provided by SF is expressed in terms of abstract case, which is accessible to syntax, and determines syntactic argument realisation.

For further information on LDG as it relates to LT, see Kiparsky (2001) and Wunderlich (2002).[2] With these starting assumptions, we can represent dative-subject verbs as a class in both Faroese and Icelandic by the same template as two-argument verbs, but with lexical features inherited from CS that feed argument structure. The relevant lexical features are derived from the thematic role information specified by the verb lexeme, not solely the level of embedding in the argument structure; for instance, verb lexemes specifying an experiencer role are represented at SF with a feature associated with the variable that is instantiated at the level of abstract case as dative case. This is a way to capture the empirical observation that verbs with lexical case tend to form subclasses in which certain case-marking patterns reflect thematic information (see Þráinsson 2007:198–232 for a detailed overview of Icelandic and Faroese case frames with respect to theta-roles). Let us assume that the OT evaluation on the mapping from SF to abstract case instantiates thematic-role features as lexical cases, for example, a constraint conflict between ExpDat ensuring that experiencer roles receive lexical dative case, and *LexCase penalising lexical case. In this way, the universality of thematic information is retained, but the language-specific instantiation of lexical cases is a result of a particular

---

[2] See also Wunderlich (2008) for an LDG-based account of dative-nominative predicates in Icelandic.

ranking. We assume that the theta-role features are always present at SF but that constraints such as *LexCase are highly ranked in languages without inflectional case. Examples of the SF of lexical case-marking predicates are given below:[3]

(79) **Icelandic:**
líka 'like': $\lambda y_{<Th>} \lambda x_{<Exp>}$ [x LIKE y]
vanta 'lack': $\lambda y_{<Th>} \lambda x_{<Exp>}$ [x LACK y]
hjálpa 'help': $\lambda y_{<Go>} \lambda x_{<Agt>}$ [x HELP y]
stríða 'tease': $\lambda y_{<Exp>} \lambda x_{<Agt>}$ [x TEASE y]
úthluta 'assign': $\lambda z_{<Th>} \lambda y_{<Go>} \lambda x_{<Agt>}$ [x CAUSE [BE OBLIGATED [y HAVE z]]]
svipta 'deprive': $\lambda z_{<Th>} \lambda y_{<Src>} \lambda x_{<Agt>}$ [x CAUSE [y NOT HAVE z]]

(80) **Faroese:**
dáma 'like': $\lambda y_{<Th>} \lambda x_{<Exp>}$ [x LIKE y]
tørva 'need': $\lambda y_{<Th>} \lambda x_{<Exp>}$ [x NEED y]
vaska 'wash': $\lambda y_{<Exp>} \lambda x_{<Agt>}$ [x WASH y]
takka 'thank': $\lambda y_{<Exp>} \lambda x_{<Agt>}$ [x THANK y]
spyrja 'ask': $\lambda z_{<Th>} \lambda y_{<Src>} \lambda x_{<Agt>}$ [x CAUSE [CAN [y SAY z]]]

These SF representations feed abstract case, a level of argument structure that itself feeds the input to syntax. Therefore, given the divisions of labour described in this section, our model of grammar thus far can be schematised as in Figure 3.1:

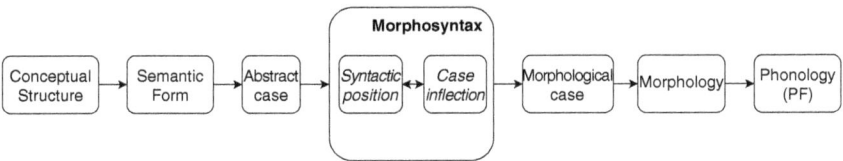

Figure 3.1 OLG grammar model

It is assumed that each arrow in the chart in Figure 3.1, excluding the relation between syntactic positions and items occupying those positions, represents an OT constraint evaluation with sets of constraints appropriate to the information accessed by the component of grammar in question. Therefore, this is a highly stratal OT model which presupposes strong inter-relatedness between levels. Although on the surface this appears to be a large number of derivational steps, 'abstract

---

[3] The crux of the OLG proposal does not rest on the specific semantic decompositions laid out in (79–80); the important information is that specific theta-roles are instantiated as specific lexical cases, for example, Experiencer → Dative, a mapping that is subject to the relevant OT evaluation.

case' and 'morphological case' are really formalisms that represent the semantics–syntax and syntax–morphology interfaces, respectively; all theories must adequately explain this flow of information, and the necessary linking computations are too often left implicit or collapsed into a single level of structure, which as argued in Chapter 1 presents problems for languages such as Finnish or Icelandic.

3.1.2 From Semantic Form to Syntax

An advantage of LT is that the information at SF relevant to case-assignment can be captured via abstract features [±H(ighest) R(ole)] and [±L(owest) R(ole)], which operate at *all* levels of grammatical structure that refer to case (i.e. argument structure, syntax and morphology). Abstract case corresponds to grammatical relations, traditionally 'subject', 'object', etc., which yield four abstract structural cases, defined featurally in (81). Here S = intransitive subject, O = object, A = transitive subject and D = dative (see Dixon 1979).

(81) **Abstract case:**
    S: [+HR+LR]
    O: [−HR+LR]
    A: [+HR−LR]
    D: [−HR−LR]

Since intransitive predicates have only a single theta-role, [+HR] alone is sufficient to define their abstract case for the constraints proposed here, although in principle the role borne by the subject is simultaneously highest and lowest in the hierarchy. Moreover, the abstract case for the object of a monotransitive can be defined simply as [−HR], which logically entails [+LR] in a two-argument predicate; likewise, [+HR] for transitive subjects entails [−LR]. (For these reasons, MAX constraints which ensure that abstract case is present in the output are satisfied by a [+HR] feature borne by the S or A argument, [−HR] borne by an O argument, and [−HR−LR] borne by a D argument.) Abstract case, then, is analogous to f-structure in Lexical–Functional Grammar frameworks (Kaplan and Bresnan 1982, Bresnan 2001), in that it represents abstract grammatical functions defined by feature values, subject to constraints on how feature values are mapped between linked levels of structure. Abstract case feeds the input to syntax, which generates phrase structures with lexical and functional items inserted, and therefore is less of a 'level' but more an interface requirement that SF information be readable to syntax. The input to syntax is therefore not strictly abstract case by itself but lexical items bearing syntactically relevant features that include abstract case features on arguments (see Section 9.4 for further discussion); information from the entire lexical branch from CS→SF→abstract case is represented in the input to the syntax evaluation. This is similar to the Numeration of items fed to syntax in some Minimalist approaches (see Chomsky 1995:225). Thus, the mapping from CS to SF and SF to abstract case can be construed as successive harmonisation cycles that take place within one pre-syntactic component of grammar.

The same binary [±HR±LR] features define morphosyntactic case, which corresponds to syntax-internal inflectional morphemes and/or structural position,[4] and morphological case, which corresponds to surface forms; both of these have the same inventory of structural cases:

(82) **Morphosyntactic case:**

NOM/ABS: [+HR]
ACC: [−HR]
ERG/GEN: [−LR]
DAT: [−HR−LR]

As Kiparsky (2001:14) mentions, the glosses of morphosyntactic features (e.g. [−HR] as 'accusative') will differ between and within languages, as the instantiation of morphology is subject to a language-specific ranking of morphological constraints. It is also noteworthy that the traditional syntactic categories of internal and external arguments are encoded by the [±HR] feature value: the VP-external position bears [+HR], VP-internal positions are [−HR] and the higher internal object position additionally [−LR].[5]

As discussed in Chapter 1, OLG follows Kiparsky (2001) in adopting an OT implementation of the mapping between abstract and morphosyntactic case, which makes straightforwardly defined predictions about the space of possible grammars generated by a given set of constraints. Here we propose three kinds of constraints on output candidates that govern this mapping: MAX, DEP and MATCH constraints.

---

[4] Moreover, in some languages without morphological case but with verbal person agreement (e.g. Swahili), agreement morphemes assign [+HR] morphosyntactic case to the subject and/or [−HR] case to the object, as mentioned in Section 1.2.1.

[5] This does not assume the classic transformational analysis of unaccusatives often associated with these terms (see Perlmutter 1978, Burzio 1986 and subsequent studies). Rather, 'internal/external' argument positions are descriptive properties of syntactic structures present in output candidates.

It is important from the outset to clarify that MAX constraints ensure that *input features/items are present in the output*, DEP constraints are violated by *features present in the output that do not have corresponding inputs*, while MATCH constraints *penalise mismatches of features within the output candidate*. Notably, this formulation of MATCH-type constraints differs from the variants of IDENT typical of other OT correspondence theories, since MATCH targets output well-formedness at the level of morphosyntax, not input–output faithfulness; they are more similar to markedness constraints in phonology, such as AGREE, which evaluate feature values at a particular level of structure.[6] All these families of constraints are defined not by featural unification, but *identity*: e.g. MAX[–HR] is violated by a [+HR] feature, an unspecified case feature or absence of a feature, and MATCHCASE is violated by a mapping such as [–HR]:[–HR–LR]. However, since OT constraints are ranked and violable, some winning output candidates will incur violations thereof.

It is also important to delineate precisely how MAX and DEP constraints are violated: by default, MAX constraints are defined throughout this work such that the relevant morphosyntactic case feature targeted is that borne by the *item*, and that the mere presence of a *position* bearing an identical feature in the output does not prevent violation. For example, an output structure with a V,Comp position bearing [–HR] still violates MAX[–HR] if the occupying item bears [+HR] case. In other words, the positional feature alone does not truly realise [–HR] independently of the corresponding item (see Section 9.4.2 for further discussion of feature realisation). The same holds of the constraint AGR[+HR], which is still violated if there is a subject position bearing [+HR] but no local argument bearing [+HR]. DEP-type constraints, on the other hand, examine the output and check whether the features there realise an input feature, effectively the inverse of the MAX type. Other than the general DEP constraint which penalises insertion of extra items, one specific sub-constraint of this type is DEP[+HR]/POS, which targets correspondence of subject *position* to an abstract case feature in the input (/POS is added for clarity and in distinction to MAX constraints; see Section 7.3 for details). It is quite plausible that other more specific DEP constraints penalising insertion of certain

---

[6] As discussed further in Section 4.4.1, I am not arguing for an additional evaluation stratum that takes syntactic positions with unassociated items as input: rather, the relevant level of mapping described by the tableaux is from abstract case to morphosyntax, and syntactic position-item feature correspondence is evaluated at this step.

types of items would be necessary, e.g. something like DEP[+HR]/ITEM, but such were not called for in the data examined here. As Kiparsky (2001) notes, his original framework assumes the abstract case as input and morphosyntactic case as output, but if data were to emerge that rendered the inverse analysis more convincing, the MAX and DEP formulations could be swapped without damaging the conclusions: each type is unidirectional in its evaluation but also symmetrical, in that the key concept is correspondence between levels.

Another distinctive feature of this framework is positional licensing of arguments; this is formalised as a feature-matching constraint (83):

(83) MATCHCASE: Assign a violation for each positional case feature matrix F[$vals_{pos}$] that is not identical to its corresponding item case feature matrix F[$vals_{item}$].

Crucially for Faroese and Icelandic, we assume that the level of morphosyntactic case is instantiated by structural position as well as case suffixes. Mismatches between positional case and case inflection may be licensed when a lexical case feature is present, which is expressed via a higher-ranked 'express lexical case in inflectional morphology' constraint, MAX[LEXCASE]. This is why it must be established where the subject and object in quirky case predicates are sitting, since positional case features partly determine which output candidate is optimally chosen. By way of illustration, (85) and (86) show hypothesised tree structures for the Icelandic sentences in (84a–b).

(84) a. Ice. Ég sá stelpan
I.NOM saw girl-the.ACC.SG
'I saw the girl'

b. Ice. Mér líkar hundurinn
me.DAT likes.3SG dog-the.NOM.SG
'I like the dog'

Icelandic:

(85)

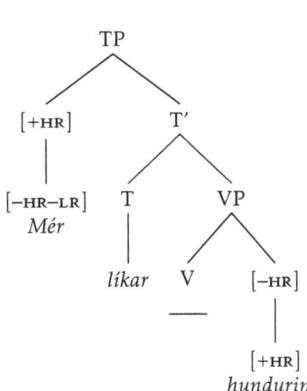

Icelandic:

(86)

In (85), neither MATCHCASE nor MAX[LEXCASE] is violated, since each positional case feature matches that of its occupying item and there is no lexical case feature in the input. In contrast, (86) shows a mismatch between the subject position case feature [+HR] in Spec,TP and the dative subject, in violation of MATCHCASE, but satisfying MAX[LEXCASE] by expressing the lexical dative case.7

Given the data discussed in Section 2.3, let us propose the basic licensing positions in Faroese to be as shown in (87). The reader is referred to Þráinsson (2007) for detailed discussion of possible argument positions in Icelandic.

Faroese:

(87)

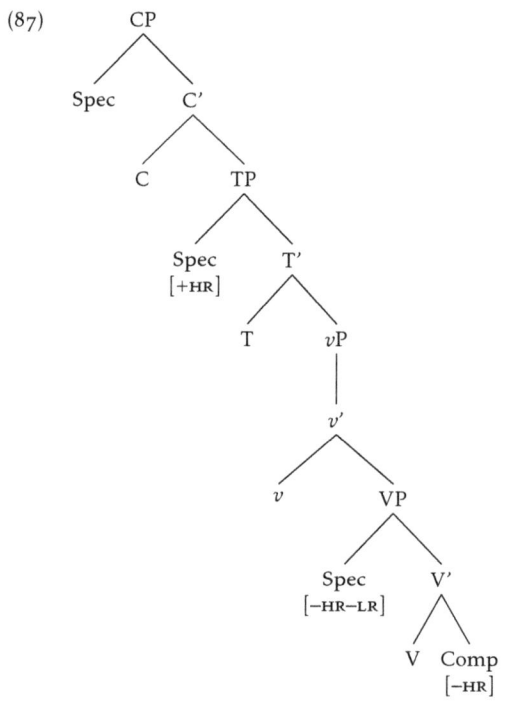

Therefore MATCHCASE is violated if the output candidate contains a position-item feature mismatch, for example, the winning candidate for a predicate with a dative subject necessarily incurs a violation

---

7 There is also a mismatch between the object position feature [−HR] and the nominative case on the object [+HR], which is argued to be a consequence of AGR[+HR] outranking MAX[−HR] in Icelandic, as discussed in Section 4.4.1.

of MATCHCASE, since the [–HR–LR] argument is occupying Spec,TP, a position bearing [+HR]. The reason non-nominative subjects are possible at all is that a constraint enforcing realisation of lexical case, MAX[LEXCASE], is ranked higher than MATCHCASE in those languages that have this phenomenon. In that sense, MATCHCASE is really about the mapping of structural position to inflectional features, that is, a purely syntactic constraint. In languages with case morphology but no evidence of positional licensing, we assume MATCHCASE to be ranked low, and thus there is a greater tolerance of mismatches between structural position and case inflection.

In summary, recognising the distinction between conceptual knowledge and the argument structure of a predicate, as well as the fact that arguments may be licensed either by structural position or by case inflection, yields a system flexible enough to account for a wide range of languages, provided the information available to each component of grammar is appropriately restricted.

3.2 Optimality-Theoretic Syntax

This section lays out starting assumptions regarding the proposed OT architecture of grammar. A far more detailed presentation of the framework is given in Chapter 9.[8] The basic OT hypotheses presented in Legendre et al. (2001:3) are also adopted as theoretical priors in OLG:

(88) a. Universal Grammar is an optimizing system of universal well-formedness constraints on linguistic forms.
 b. Well-formedness constraints are simple and general. They routinely come into conflict and are (often) violated by the surfacing form.
 c. Conflicts are resolved through hierarchical rankings of constraints. The effect of a given constraint is relative to its ranking, which is determined on a language-particular basis.
 d. Evaluation of candidates by the set of constraints is based on strict domination. For any two constraints C_1 and C_2, either C_1 outranks C_2 or C_2 outranks C_1.

---

[8]The *locus classicus* for OT is Prince and Smolensky (1993); early OT analyses of syntactic phenomena include Grimshaw (1997) and Legendre et al. (1998). For a detailed overview of OT-based approaches to syntax, see Legendre et al. (2001). Representative OT approaches to case phenomena include Kiparsky (2001), Wunderlich (2000), Optimal case in Hindi (Unpublished ms., University of Dusseldorf), Woolford (2001), de Hoop and Malchukov (2008) and others; see also references in Müller (2009) and de Hoop (2009).

e. Alternative structural realizations of an input compete for the status of being the optimal output of a particular input. The most harmonic output – the one that best satisfies, or minimally violates, the full set of ranked constraints in a given language – is the optimal one. Only the optimal structure is grammatical.
f. Every competition yields an optimal output.

These hypotheses yield an architecture of grammar minimally consisting of the following components: an INPUT; GEN, which generates a candidate set for a given input; CON, the set of universal well-formedness constraints; EVAL, the mechanism for evaluating the output candidates on the basis of the hierarchically ranked constraints of CON; and the optimal OUTPUT. This can be visualised as in Figure 3.2:[9]

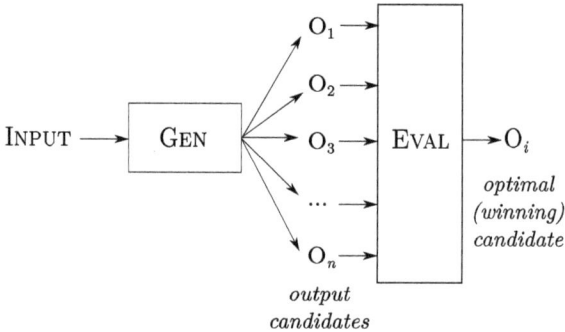

Figure 3.2 Architecture of grammar in Optimality Theory

As noted in Section 3.1, OLG assumes a modular architecture of grammar in which the passing of information between each component is subject to harmonisation; for instance, the optimal output candidate O_i of the syntactic evaluation is sent on to phonology, which has its own evaluation mechanism and domain-specific set of constraints. The main focus of this book is the syntactic component.

On this theory of syntax, both GEN and CON are universal, and grammar-particular variation is located in EVAL, which evaluates candidates against the given ranking of CON. GEN consists of a mechanism which generates output candidates consisting of tree structures with lexical and functional items already inserted; this is formally defined as a context-free grammar in Section 9.2. Hence, many malformed trees will be ruled out at EVAL, which not only contains a

---
[9]Diagram based on similar version in Müller (2009).

set of ranked violable constraints but also *undominated* (inviolable) constraints, ensuring that candidates which do not conform to X-bar principles are harmonically bounded and can never win. Thus, this approach is strikingly different from that proposed by Chomsky (1995), in which structure-building is attributed to a Merge operation. In OLG, trees are not built bottom-up but are the result of free combination of primitives in all possible ways, even though a large number of these candidates will be harmonically bounded. It may be objected that this adds complexity by stipulating losing candidates with malformed structures. However, most Minimalist approaches also stipulate inviolable constraints, such as c-selection, which do the same work as the undominated constraints at EVAL. In fact, OLG is in one sense more 'minimalist' than the Merge-based theory, in that the entirety of the component which rules out ill-formed structures is restricted to the harmonisation, rather than involving sets of inviolable constraints that operate at different stages of the derivation. For instance, c-selection (which holds of external Merge), the Extended Projection Principle (EPP) – a property of features that trigger movement during the derivation – and the Phase Impenetrability Condition (PIC) (which prevents operations on previously derived structure) are accounted for by the constraints SUBCAT, ARGSP and an interaction between DEP and MATCHDIS, respectively.[10] Furthermore, the set of output candidates at the semantics–syntax interface will not undergo further applications of Merge or other transformations: the constraints at EVAL, in principle, should account for all elements that appear in a different position than that which satisfies subcategorisation.

It is assumed that the evaluation window of the input consists of the smallest constituent necessary for all features present in the argument structure of the predicate to be discharged, typically the clause (CP or TP); therefore, the only serious contender candidates will have sufficient structure for all case and information-structural features to be realised (see Grimshaw 1997, Legendre et al. 1998, among others). Trees with additional empty structure beyond that required to express the input fully are ruled out by markedness constraints corresponding to X-bar principles; faithfulness constraints ensure that all and only the input items are represented in the output, that is, no extra material

---

[10] For further discussion of SUBCAT, see Section 9.2; for discussion of how information-structural and argument licensing constraints interact to derive both the EPP and the kinds of expletive constructions that motivate the PIC, see Section 9.6.

absent from the input, nor omission of input material (exceptions to this are filler-gap dependencies and ellipsis, see Section 9.5 for discussion). The power of OT is that even highly ranked constraints can be violated, yielding highly marked structures, such as a phrase with more than one specifier, an empty head position, or a unary branch. Crucially, this is not unconstrained but only possible with a ranking in which a faithfulness constraint dominates one of the constraints contributing to the enforcement of X-bar structure. In this way, long-established generalisations about phrase structure have a principled genesis but are not completely unviolated in every structure in every language, thus accounting for language-specific variation through a constraint ranking, yielding an optimal output which minimally violates those same principles.

Table 3.1 reiterates the precise formulations of the constraints relevant to case-marking, which are central to the analysis of the data in Chapters 4–7:

Table 3.1 Case constraints

Constraint	Formulation
Faithfulness constraints	
Max[−hr]	Assign a violation for each [−hr] abstract case feature on an input argument that is not realised by a [−hr] morphosyntactic case feature on an output argument.
Max[−lr]	Assign a violation for each [−lr] abstract case feature on an input argument that is not realised by a [−lr] morphosyntactic case feature on an output argument.
Max[LexCase] (Max[LC])	Assign a violation for each lexical case feature on an argument at the level of abstract case that does not correspond to the same lexical feature value on an argument at the level of morphosyntactic case.
Parse	Assign a violation for a null parse of the input (i.e. if the output is zero).
Markedness constraints	
MatchCase (MC)	Assign a violation for each positional case feature matrix $F[vals_{pos}]$ that is not identical to its corresponding item case feature matrix $F[vals_{item}]$.
Agr[+hr]	Assign a violation for each finite verb whose number agreement value is not identical to that of an argument bearing [+hr] morphosyntactic case in the same clause.
Subj[+hr] (S[+hr])	Assign a violation for each position bearing [+hr] (i.e. subject position) not occupied by an item bearing [+hr] case.
Dep[+hr]/Pos (Dep[+hr]/P)	Assign a violation for each [+hr] morphosyntactic positional case feature that does not realise a [+hr] abstract case feature on an input argument.

These constraints, combined with the LT and OT starting assumptions laid out in this chapter, are sufficient to account for the range of case-marking phenomena explored in this book and make predictions that are borne out empirically, as argued in the chapters which follow. Many further questions are raised by OT approaches to syntax: What material must be present at the input? How are output candidates generated? How are movement phenomena accounted for? How are syntactic features evaluated? These and other issues are discussed in detail in Chapter 9. What is essential for my analysis of the Faroese and Icelandic data is the adoption of LT and the constraints which hold of the mapping from argument structure to syntax.

3.3 Summary of Chapter

In this chapter, the basic LT and OT apparatus has been presented. The adoption of a three-level approach to case, combined with a system of ranked violable constraints, enables us to explain the Faroese and Icelandic data in a consistent way that also extends beyond Insular Scandinavian. Chapter 9 gives a thorough overview of the OLG framework, expanding upon the aspects of the theory mentioned in this section. In Chapters 4–7, new data from surveys conducted on the Faroe Islands and Iceland are discussed, as well as argumentation that OLG provides a cogent analysis thereof.

4

Faroese Dative Subjects

4.1 Introduction

In this chapter, the core Faroese and Icelandic 'quirky case' data previously mentioned in Sections 2.4–2.5 are discussed and an OLG analysis presented. It is argued that the crucial difference between Icelandic and Faroese, that which results in a DAT-NOM case frame in the former and DAT-ACC in the latter, is a different ranking of a markedness constraint enforcing agreement with a nominative argument within the clause and a faithfulness constraint ensuring realisation of structural object case. As stated in Chapter 2, it has long been established that non-nominative subjects exist in languages such as Icelandic, at least in one broadly accepted definition of subjecthood (Zaenen et al. 1985), while acknowledging the caveat that properties associated with subjects vary cross-linguistically (Keenan 1976 *i.a.*). In Icelandic, such subjects tend to co-occur with nominative-marked objects (89a), which also exhibit number, but not person, agreement with the finite verb (89b–c).

(89) a. Ice. *Mér   líkar   fiskur*
 me.DAT likes.3SG fish.NOM.SG
 'I like fish'

 b. Ice. *Mér   líka   hundar*
 me.DAT like.3PL dogs.NOM.PL
 'I like dogs'

 c. Ice. * *Honum líkum/-ið   við/þið*
 him.DAT like.1PL/2PL us/you.NOM.PL
 'He likes us/you (pl.)'

In Faroese, those verbs which mark subjects with non-nominative case, almost exclusively dative in the contemporary language, do not occur with a nominative lower argument but with an accusative, as shown in (90), which standardly does not permit object agreement at all.

(90) a. Far.   *Mær   dámar   fisk*
          me.DAT likes.3SG fish.ACC
          'I like fish'
     b. Far. * *Mær   dáma   hundar*
          me.DAT like.3PL dogs.ACC.PL
          'I like dogs'

On the surface this pattern should be surprising if previous analyses of Icelandic are to be extended to Faroese. This is partly because Icelandic was the first such language to be explored in depth in the generative literature and has long been viewed as the classic 'quirky case' language. However, there is no *a priori* reason to assume that Icelandic should be normative, nor that the Faroese phenomenon should therefore be treated as an odd variant of the Icelandic. Instead, this Faroese pattern is readily explained by the interaction between markedness and faithfulness constraints. In Section 4.2 the Faroese experiencer-subject verb data are reviewed, and in Section 4.4 an OLG analysis given. Also discussed is the observed variation in realisation of the dative subject case as well as similar variation in dative object case, which is argued to be a result of competing grammars.

4.2 Overview of Data

The central data examined here involve a small subset of psychological predicates in Faroese with a dative-marked experiencer argument ('quirky case') and an accusative-marked stimulus argument, with some optionality as to whether the experiencer is nominative or dative. It should be understood from the outset that Faroese is widely considered to be in the process of changing from an Insular to a Mainland Scandinavian morphosyntax, which manifests itself in the loss of rich morphology, including quirky case (Barnes 1986, Jónsson and Eyþórsson 2005, Þráinsson et al. 2012). Nevertheless, a 2.5 million word corpus of Faroese blog texts[1] reveals that speakers are still readily producing dative subjects with the relevant verbs, in addition to some

---
[1] Texts accessible at purl.stanford.edu/qt590wf1460 (Scannell 2011).

generalisations: (i) nominative subjects are encountered for almost all the verbs, albeit only rarely with *tørva*,² and (ii) nominative subjects are reportedly more 'informal' or 'colloquial', despite some examples also occurring in more formal registers. Examples given below are taken from the blog corpus unless otherwise noted.³

A. *dáma* 'like'

Dative subject with third person singular agreement represents the standard written and spoken form, which is available in the majority of contexts.

(91) Far. Mær   dámar   so væl myndirnar   hjá Frits Johannesen
         me.DAT likes.3SG so well pictures.DEF.ACC by Frits Johannesen
         'I like Frits Johannesen's pictures so much'

(92) Far. Eti   fiskafrikadellur. Tað dámar mær   ordiliga væl :)
         eat.1SG fish-croquettes it   likes.3SG me.DAT really well [emoji]
         'I'm eating fish croquettes. I like it (eating them) a lot. :)'

(93) Far. Magnu   dámdi   allarbest agurkina   hjá Hansinu
         Magna.DAT liked.3SG above-all cucumber.DEF.ACC of Hansina
         'Magna liked Hansina's cucumber most of all'

Nominative subjects with full verbal person agreement sometimes occur, mostly with first person singular pronouns in informal contexts; also found rarely in other contexts:

(94) Far. Mamma heldur, at   eg   dámi   skógvar   alt for væl
         Mamma thinks that I.NOM like.1SG shoes.ACC all too well
         'Mama thinks that I like my shoes far too much'

(95) Far. nakrir   støddfrøðingar   dáma   betur ikki at skoða talið
         some.NOM mathematicians.NOM like.3PL better not to look.at number-the
         0   sum eitt teljital
         zero as a   natural.number
         'Some mathematicians prefer not to look at the number zero as a natural number'⁴

---

²This is unsurprising given the results in Jónsson and Eyþórsson (2005), who find some measure of acceptability for nominative subjects with all the relevant verbs and increasing acceptability rates of nominatives among the younger generation.

³The verb *tykja* 'seem' can occur with a dative subject (see Jónsson and Eyþórsson 2005), but the patterns are very complex; for this reason this verb is left for further study.

⁴From Faroese Wikipedia article 'Teljital', accessed 3/2/18.

B. *tørva* 'need':

Dative is by far the most frequent subject case for this verb (96–97); of the 35 tokens of finite *tørva* in the corpus, only 4 occur with nominative subjects, 3 of which have plural subjects and a plural verb, e.g. (98). Nominative subjects were also rejected by a consultant for this verb, in contrast to nominatives with *dáma* and *mangla*, which were judged acceptable.

(96) Far. Okkum tørvar   at síggja aðra   list   enn føroyska
         us.DAT needs.3SG to see other.ACC art.ACC than Faroese.ACC
         'We need to see other art than (just) Faroese'

(97) Far. Eg svaraði, at mær ikki tørvaði lokabrøgd
         I answered that me.DAT not needed.SG schemings.ACC
         'I answered that I didn't need to scheme'

(98) Far. Júst hesir   báðir   samfelagsbólkar   tørva   eina
         just these.NOM.PL both.NOM.PL community.groups.NOM.PL need.PL a
         'saltvatnsinnspræning', um hesi fólkini skulu tíma   at búgva í Føroyum.
         salt.water.injection   if these folks should bother to live in Faroes
             'Indeed, both of these community groups need a 'boost' if these folks are going to trouble themselves to live in the Faroes.'

C. *mangla* 'lack, be short on' (Dan. loan)

This verb is of Danish origin and more colloquial. It is not present in Old Norse[5] and was borrowed into Danish from German *mangeln* 'lack', which itself was borrowed from Latin *mancare* 'be missing' (cognate with *mancus* 'maimed'). Dative subject is available:

(99) Far. Á nei, vit kunnu ikki, tí   vit hava onki   og okkum manglar ...
         oh no we can not because we have nothing and us.DAT lacks.3SG
         'Oh no, we cannot, because we have nothing, and we are lacking ...'[6]

However, a nominative subject is far more widespread with this verb than with *dáma*; the vast majority of tokens in the blog corpus have nominative subjects:

(100) Far. Ungdómurin undir 18 ár   manglar eisini eitt stað   at fara í
          youth.NOM under 18 years lacks.3SG also a.ACC place.ACC to go on
          vikuskiftinum
          weekend.DEF
              'Young people under 18 also lack a place to go on the weekend'

---

[5] Absent from the Old Norse poetic *Lexicon Poeticum* (1931) and prose lexicon *Ordbog over det norrøne prosasprog*, onp.ku.dk, accessed 3/21/18.

[6] Part of a paragraph where several objects are elided as indicated orthographically.

(101) Far. Mangli bæði bor   og skrúvur,   so eg mátti   út at keypa
         lack.1SG both drill.ACC and screws.ACC so I must.PST out to buy
         'I lack both a drill and screws, so I had to go out to buy (them)'7

D. *lukka(st)* 'succeed'

This verb is rare in the corpus with only three tokens, all of which have –*st* medio-passive morphology, and two of which co-occur with the expletive *tað*, though both dative and nominative occur:

(102) Far. ...lukkast   tað Sáru   at bjarga beiggjanum?
         succeeds.3SG it Sára.DAT to save brother.DEF.DAT
         'Does Sára succeed in saving her brother?'

(103) Far. Nei. Hvar fór   hon so, lukkast   tað at hitta Sáru   í í USA...
         no   where went she so succeeds.3SG it to meet Sára.DAT in in USA
         'No. So where she went, Sára managed to meet (her son) in in [sic] the USA'8

(104) Far. Og Øskufía   lukkaðist   akkurát heim áðrenn 12
         and Øskufía.NOM succeeded.SG barely home before 12
         'And Øskufía barely managed to get home before 12'

E. *leingja(st) eftir* +DAT 'long for'9

Nominative and dative subjects are attested in the corpus:

(105) Far. ...og eg   longdist   upp aftur meir eftir kavanum
         and I.NOM longed.SG up after more after snow.DEF.DAT
         'and I longed more for snow once again'

(106) Far. Mær   leingist at síggja teg
         me.DAT longs.SG to see you.ACC.SG
         'I long to see you'

Nominative subjects occur in some informal contexts, e.g. reporting what children are thinking in baby blogs:

(107) Far. Og nú leingist eg   eisini eftir teimum   :(
         and now longs.SG I.NOM also after them.DAT [emoji]
         'And now I miss them too (Grandma and Grandpa) :('

Table 4.1 summarises the occurrences of the three most frequent dative-subject verbs in the blog corpus, namely, *dáma* 'like', *tørva* 'need' and *mangla* 'lack':

---

7 I assume the tense here to be a historic present.

8 I assume this is a topicalised phrase *lukkast tað at hitta*, with a postposed dative experiencer, rather than *Sára* being the object of *hitta*, which normally takes accusative objects. The son, *sonin*, is mentioned in the next sentence fragment: *lukkast tað at finna sonin Italia*, '(she) succeeds in finding her son (in) Italy'.

9 It should be noted that dative is the expected case with this meaning of the preposition *eftir* and is therefore a typical example of a lexically specified prepositional case.

Table 4.1 Frequencies of subject case by verb token in blog corpus

Verb token	DAT subject	NOM subject	Total
dáma (3PL)	7 (38.9%)	11 (61.1%)	18
dámar	183 (93.4%)	13 (6.6%)	196
dámi (1SG)	0	9	9
dámdi	83 (96.5%)	3 (3.5%)	86
dámdu	1	2	3
dámt (SUP)	3	2	5
All dáma	277 (87.4%)	40 (12.6%)	317
mangla (3PL)	1	10	11
manglar	1	8	9
mangli (1SG)	0	5	5
manglaði	0	5	5
manglaðu	0	3	3
manglað (SUP)	0	1	1
All mangla	2 (5.9%)	32 (94.1%)	34
tørva (3PL)	0	2	2
tørvaði	2	0	2
tørvaðu	0	1	1
tørvar	29 (96.7%)	1 (3.3%)	30
tørvi (1SG)	0	0	0
tørvað (SUP)	0	0	0
All tørva	31 (88.6%)	4 (11.4%)	35

As can be seen from these statistics, each of the three verbs behaves rather differently with respect to available subject case in the blog data: *dáma* occurring a majority of the time with dative but with the option of nominative, *mangla* only rarely occurring with dative and *tørva* only rarely with nominative. Furthermore, it seems that plural subjects may bias towards nominative with an agreeing plural finite verb, particularly with *dáma* and *mangla*. These data will be discussed in greater depth in Section 5.1.

Finally, it should also be noted that there exist a small number of rare instances of accusative subjects in fossilised expressions, e.g. *Meg lystir at dansa* 'I'm raring to dance'; however, these are far from productive, and it is assumed they are not representative of the current system. Unlike Icelandic, genitive subjects are not possible in Faroese, and the genitive case has mostly fallen out of use in the contemporary language.

Very little prior work exists on these Faroese dative-subject verbs, in spite of a huge literature on similar phenomena in Icelandic. Jónsson and Eyþórsson (2005) conducted two surveys assessing the acceptability of dative versus nominative case-marking on the subject arguments of the relevant verbs, the first interviewing children and the second adults. Jónsson and Eyþórsson report that every one of the small set of Faroese verbs which still occur with dative-marked subjects in the spoken language are accepted with 'nominative substitution', where the subject is marked nominative and exhibits full person and number agreement with the verb. However, they found that acceptability of nominative subjects varied both by verb and by context. Jónsson (2009) supplements this with further survey data and presents a theoretical account of the dative–accusative pattern, discussed in Chapter 8. Þráinsson et al. (2012) also offer a fairly comprehensive descriptive overview of the quirky case facts in their grammar, including which verbs admit nominative substitution.

4.3 Surveys on Quirky Case

The author conducted two surveys on the Faroe Islands in which acceptability judgements on quirky case predicates were elicited; the results are presented in Sections 4.3.1–4.3.2.

4.3.1 Faroese Quirky Case Survey 1

4.3.1.1 Participants

The first survey was conducted at *Tilhaldið*, a community activity centre in Tórshavn. The survey was distributed on paper at a folksong meeting attended by locals aged 50+. There were 23 participants, 14 of whom answered every question, and the remaining 9 gave partial responses. No further demographic information is available for the participants.

4.3.1.2 Materials

Table 4.2 shows the 15 sentences presented for judgement. In this survey, possible object positions were tested with respect to negation *ikki* 'not', the adverb *altíð* 'always' and the participle *dámað* 'liked'. In addition, the verbs *dáma* 'like' and *tørva* 'need' were tested in sentences with plural agreement on the verb, singular or plural dative subject,

Table 4.2 Faroese quirky case verbs: Sentences in survey 1

№	μ	σ	Faroese sentence	Gloss
1	3.7	1.5	ℬ ?Mær hevur ikki altið dámað bókina	Me.DAT has.SG not always liked book-the.ACC
2	1.3	0.9	*Mær hevur bókina ikki altið dámað	Me.DAT has.SG book-the.ACC not always liked
3	4.5	0.7	Mær hevur ikki altið dámað hana	Me.DAT has.SG not always liked it.ACC
4	1.2	0.9	*Mær hevur hana ikki altið dámað	Me.DAT has.SG it not always liked
5	1.3	0.9	*Mær hevur ikki bókina altið dámað	Me.DAT has.SG not book-the.ACC always liked
6	2.6	1.6	ℬ ??Teimum man bókina ikki altið hava dámað	Them.DAT must.SG book-the.ACC not always have liked
7	1.6	1.2	*Teimum man ikki bókina hava altið dámað	Them.DAT must.SG not book-the.ACC have always liked
8	1.8	1.2	*Teimum man ikki bókina altið hava dámað	Them.DAT must.SG not book-the.ACC always have liked
9	1.8	1.2	*Teimum man ikki altið hava bókina dámað	Them.DAT must.SG not always have book-the.ACC liked
10	3.1	1.9	ℬ ?Mær dáma bátarnar	Me.DAT like.PL boats-the.ACC.PL
11	1.7	1.4	*Honum dáma bátarnir	Him.DAT like.PL boats-the.NOM.PL
12	3.6	1.7	ℬ ?Okkum dáma bátarnar	Us.DAT like.PL boats-the.ACC.PL
13	2.6	1.6	ℬ ??Tykkum dáma bátarnir	You.DAT.PL like.PL boats-the.NOM.PL
14	2.2	1.4	*Okkum torva bátarnir	Us.DAT need.PL boats-the.NOM.PL
15	3.7	1.6	ℬ ?Teimum torva bátarnar	Them.DAT need.PL boats-the.ACC.PL

Key to judgements: * = mean acceptability < 2.5, ?? = 2.5–3, ? = 3–4, no mark = mean > 4 and nominative or accusative plural object. Owing to time limitations and the means of distribution, it was not possible to include filler sentences nor to test further combinations of case and agreement in this survey. Table 4.2 shows the actual mean (μ) and standard deviation (σ) of the responses for each sentence and provides the mean judgement in the standard notation for linguistic examples. If the histogram of judgements for the sentence suggests that the distribution is bimodal, that is, where is evidence for two response groupings, one in which the sentence was rejected (mean 1–2) and one in which it was accepted (mean 4–5), such patterns are indicated by the symbol ꞛ (for bimodal) preceding the sentence.[10] The criterion used for bimodality is $2.5 \leq \mu < 4, \sigma > 1$, since a mean of ~3 without a relatively high standard deviation does not indicate bimodality but broad speaker agreement on a medial judgement. These tests were conducted for all the surveys presented in this book.

4.3.1.3 Procedure

Participants were handed a sheet of paper with the 15 sentences printed in bold font. At the top of the page the following rubric was printed:

Tú mást hava føroyskt sum móðurmál, fyri at taka lut í hesari kanning. Metið um, hvussu natúrligir hesir setningarnir eru á føroyskum. "Natúrligt" her merkir, at ein føroyingur hevði kunnað sagt tað.

'You must have Faroese as your native language to take part in this survey. Judge how natural these sentences are in Faroese. "Natural" here indicates that a Faroese could have said that.'

Directly beneath each sentence, a five-point scale was shown with empty boxes for check marks. The scale rubric was as follows: from left to right, *Als ikki natúrligt* 'Not at all natural', *Ikki sera natúrligt* 'not very natural', *Eg veit ikki* 'I don't know', *Heldur natúrligt* 'Rather natural' and *Púrasta natúrligt* 'Completely natural', with 'I don't know' in the middle of the horizontal. Participants were told to mark their judgement on the sentence by putting a cross in the appropriate box and that they should only mark one box per sentence.

---

[10] Thanks to Seth Greenstein and Rob Mina for drawing my attention to this possibility.

4.3.1.4 Results

Figure 4.1 shows mean acceptability of sentences 1–9 in Table 4.2 by word order, more specifically, the order of negative *ikki*, adverb *altíð* and the object. As can be seen in Table 4.2, the only unequivocally accepted sentence (mean acceptability > 4) is *Mær hevur ikki altíð dámað hana*, with the order Negative-Adverb-Object. As shown in Figure 4.1, this order is the only possibility with a mean acceptability approaching more than 3, that is, the object may only be located in its standard V,Comp position. The notation 'Obj.x.PolAdv' indicates whether the object precedes the polar adverb (here 'always') or not: as evident from the plot, only the order in which the object follows the adverb is possible. It should also be noted that these data are expected on the OLG analysis of object shift (Section 9.7.1), since when the finite auxiliary is in T and the main verb in V as in these examples, the

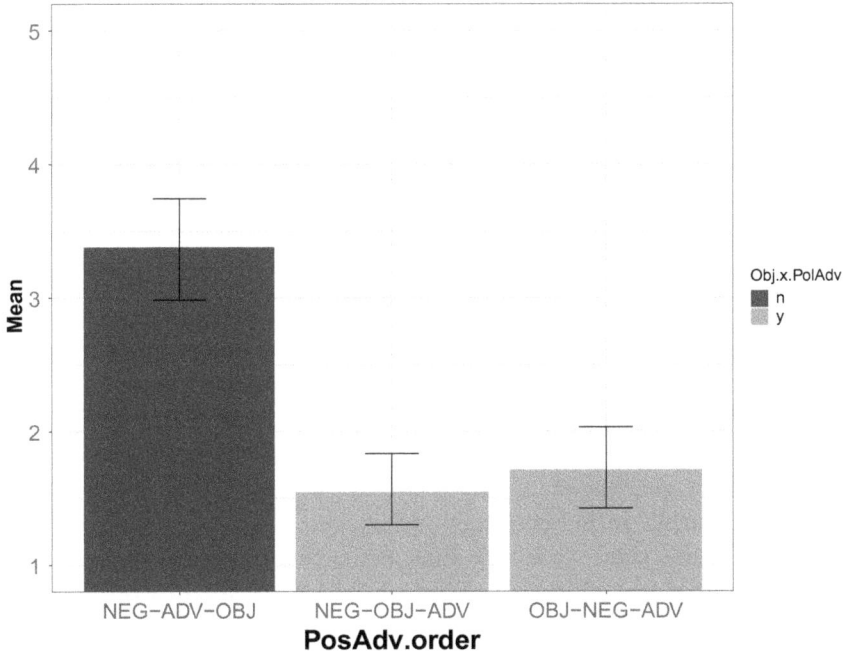

Figure 4.1 Faroese quirky case survey 1: Mean acceptability by word order

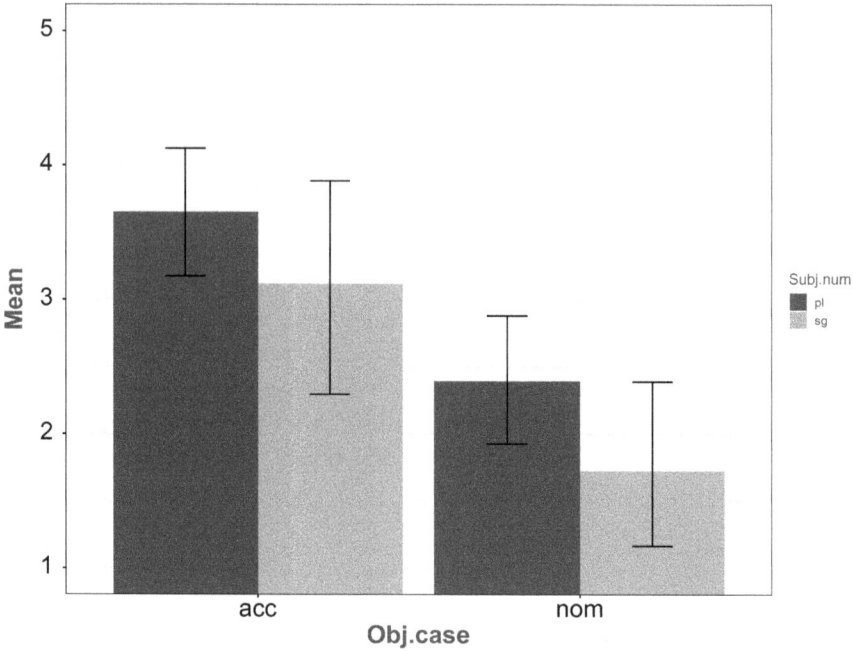

Figure 4.2 Faroese quirky case survey 1: Mean acceptability by object case and subject number

adverbs are hypothesised to be adjoined to T' or v', and so shifting the object to Spec,VP does not remove the MATCHDIS violation.

Figure 4.2 shows mean acceptability of sentences 10–15 in Table 4.2 plotted against object case and subject number. All the sentences had plural verb morphology, plural objects and dative subjects, and so agreement and non-agreement cannot be compared in this survey. However, as can be seen in Figure 4.2, the mean acceptability of singular subjects is across the board lower than that of plural. An ordered logit regression model using R (R Core Team 2012, same for all references to R hereafter) and *ordinal* (Christensen 2018) was run to test the significance of this. An ordinal regression model is appropriate for these kinds of Likert scales with ordinal responses; the proportional odds assumption, that the log of the odds of responses form an arithmetic sequence, is met for scales ranging from 'poor' to 'excellent', 'strongly disagree' to 'strongly agree', or in this case, 'not at all natural' to 'completely natural' (McCullagh 1980). Random intercepts were included for Speaker and Item. The bimodal sentences were included for this model, since the contrast is clearly between whether the sentence was completely unacceptable ($\mu \sim 1$–2.4, $\sigma < 1.5$), or there was disagreement ($\mu \sim 2.5$–4, $\sigma > 1.5$). The striking result is that nominative object case is strongly rejected compared to accusative, with a significantly worse mean than that of accusative object case ($\beta = -1.6$, $p < 0.01$). Interestingly, although the verb morphology was plural in all of sentences 10–15, some speakers wrote in a final –*r* by hand on the verb, indicating that it should have been *dámar* 'likes.3SG' or *tørvar* 'needs.3SG'. Therefore some speakers at least seem to have a preference for non-agreement with the dative subject, which is what we expect to be standard.

4.3.1.5 Discussion

While this first survey is limited in scope and grand conclusions may not be drawn from a small sample such as this, nevertheless it is clear that, as predicted, object shift is judged unacceptable with quirky case verbs when the adverbs are adjoined to T' or *v*' (i.e. when the main verb occurs in V). This suggests that when object shift is precluded, the argument in V,Comp in quirky case predicates behaves as any other object bearing structural case. If the base object position in these predicates was some other site than V,Comp, or if the accusative argument were a subject and the dative argument a topicalised object, we might expect different behaviour. In other words, as far as object shift is concerned, the theme argument with 'like' in Faroese seems to be a typical object.

The second tentative conclusion we may draw from this survey is that nominative object case is judged unacceptable across the board with the quirky case verbs *dáma* 'like' and *tørva* 'need' in Faroese. When the verb bears plural morphology, it looks like a plural subject improves the judgement over a singular subject. This suggests a preference for agreement with the subject over the object, or at least an assumption on the native speaker's part that subject rather than object agreement is intended, since otherwise the mean acceptability would be predicted to be similar for both singular and plural subjects. However, this does not say anything about the acceptability of agreement versus non-agreement.

4.3.2 Faroese Quirky Case Survey 2

The second survey on Faroese quirky case predicates was combined with the surveys on 'give' passives (see Sections 7.2.1 and 7.2.2). The discussion here is based on the combined results from both surveys. In this survey, object position was tested in quirky case predicates with respect to negation with *ikki*, negative adverbs *aldri* and *ongantíð*, both meaning 'never', and the polar quantifiers *eingin* 'no' and *nakar* 'any'. If the theme argument in such predicates exhibits typical object behaviour (i.e. occurs to the left of the main verb in shift contexts and in V,Comp in non-shift contexts), the evidence will be consistent with the analysis that the theme is a regular object.

4.3.2.1 Participants

The participants were the same as those for the surveys described in Sections 7.2.1 and 7.2.2, a total of 158, though only 46 of these fully completed their respective survey; the remaining 112 gave partial responses. See Sections 7.2.1.1 and 7.2.2.1 for further information about the participants.

4.3.2.2 Materials

Participants were presented with the following 28 sentences for judgement. These were interspersed with the 'give' passive sentences tested in the surveys described in Sections 7.2.1 and 7.2.2. The sentences were presented in the same manner as those in the Faroese 'give' passive surveys, interspersed with filler sentences and embedded in a formal or colloquial context.

4.3.2.3 Procedure

Participants were asked to provide acceptability judgements on each of the 28 Faroese sentences, presented in a different random order for each trial. A sentence would display in the Stanford Qualtrics online application[11] as in (108), excluding the English translation:

(108) Vit tosaðu stillisliga við konurnar, tá ið brádliga Hjalmar rópti, "**Mær dámdi ikki bókina.**"
'We were talking quietly to the women, when suddenly Hjalmar shouted, "I didn't like the book."'

---

[11] stanforduniversity.qualtrics.com/, accessed 4/4/18; requires Stanford University login.

Table 4.3 Faroese quirky case verbs: Sentences in survey 2

Nº	μ	σ	Faroese sentence	Gloss
1	4.9	0.2	Mær dámdi ikki bókina	Me.DAT liked not book-the.ACC
2	1.6	0.9	*Mær dámdi bókina ikki	Me.DAT liked book-the.ACC not
3	4.1	1.1	(?)Mær dámdi ikki hana	Me.DAT liked not it.ACC
4	4.9	0.3	Mær dámdi hana ikki	Me.DAT liked it.ACC not
5	4.4	0.8	Sigmundi tørvar ikki klaveriđ	Sigmund.DAT needs.SG not piano-the.ACC
6	1.5	0.9	*Sigmundi tørvar klaveriđ ikki	Sigmund.DAT needs.SG piano-the.ACC not
7	3.6	1.2	ß ?Evu tørvar ikki hann	Eva.ACC needs.SG not him.ACC
8	4.1	1.0	Evu tørvar hann ikki	Eva.ACC needs.SG him.ACC not
9	4.7	0.5	Honum leingist ikki eftir henni	Him.DAT longs not for her.DAT
10	1.3	0.7	*Honum leingist eftir henni ikki	Him.DAT longs for her.DAT not
11	4.5	0.8	Honum leingist ikki eftir sólini	Him.DAT longs not for sun-the.DAT
12	1.1	0.4	*Honum leingist eftir sólini ikki	Him.DAT longs for sun-the.DAT not
			Áđrenn eg hoyrdi Eivør...	Before I heard Eivør...
13	3.4	1.3	ß ...?hevđi mær ongan sangara dámađ	...had me.DAT no singer.ACC liked
14	1.5	0.7	...*hevđi mær dámađ ongan sangara	...had me.DAT liked no singer.ACC
			Síđani eg flutti til Lissabon...	Since I moved to Lisbon...
15	3.8	1.2	ß ...?hevur mær onga troyggju tørvađ	...had me.DAT no sweater.ACC needed
16	1.6	0.7	...*hevur mær tørvađ onga troyggju	...had me.DAT needed no sweater.ACC
			Áđrenn eg hoyrdi Eivør...	Before I heard Eivør...
17	1.6	0.8	...*hevđi mær aldri nakran sangara dámađ	...had me.DAT never any singer.ACC liked
18	4.3	0.9	...hevđi mær aldri dámađ nakran sangara	...had me.DAT never liked any singer.ACC
19	1.1	0.4	...*hevđi mær nakran sangara aldri dámađ	...had me.DAT any singer.ACC never liked
20	1.2	0.4	...*hevđi mær dámađ aldri nakran sangara	...had me.DAT liked never any singer.ACC
			Síđani tey fluttu til Lissabon, hevur teimum ivaleyst...	Since they moved to Lisbon has them.DAT doubtless...
21	2.0	1.0	...*ongantíđ nakrar troyggjur tørvađ	...never any sweaters.ACC needed
22	4.1	1.0	...(?)ongantíđ tørvađ nakrar troyggjur	...never needed any sweaters.ACC
23	1.1	0.4	...nakrar troyggjur ongantíđ tørvađ	...any sweaters.ACC never needed
24	1.1	0.4	...tørvađ ongantíđ nakrar troyggjur	...needed never any sweaters.ACC
			Hóast tey nú skulu flyta til Lissabon, man teimum...	Though they now will move to Lisbon must them.DAT...
25	1.1	0.3	...*hava aldri nakrar sólbrillur tørvađ fyrr	...have never any sunglasses.ACC needed before
26	1.5	0.9	...*hava aldri tørvađ nakrar sólbrillur fyrr	...have never needed any sunglasses.ACC before
27	3.0	1.5	ß ...??aldri hava tørvađ nakrar sólbrillur fyrr	...never needed any sunglasses.ACC before
28	1.5	0.7	...*aldri hava nakrar sólbrillur tørvađ fyrr	...never have any sunglasses.ACC needed before

Participants were told to evaluate acceptability of the embedded sentence displayed in bold font; the surrounding contextual sentence was either colloquial or formal register (see Section 7.2.1). The question *Hvussu natúrligur er hesin setningurin á føroyskum?*, 'How natural is this sentence in Faroese?' displayed above the judgement buttons for each sentence. Acceptability was rated on a five-point scale with the following descriptions:[12]

	FAROESE	ENGLISH TRANSLATION
1	*Als ikki natúrligt. Ein føroyingur kundi ongantíð sagt hetta.*	**Not at all natural.** A Faroese could never say this.
2	*Ikki sera natúrligt. Tað hevði verið løgið, um ein føroyingur segði hetta.*	**Not very natural.** It would be strange if a Faroese said this.
3	*Eg veit ikki, um ein føroyingur natúrliga hevði sagt hetta.*	**I don't know** if a Faroese could naturally say this.
4	*Heldur natúrligt. Ein føroyingur hevði kunnað sagt hetta.*	**Rather natural.** A Faroese could have said this.
5	*Púrasta natúrligt. Ein føroyingur hevði lættliga kunnað sagt hetta.*	**Perfectly natural.** A Faroese could easily have said this.

These judgement descriptions were displayed on discrete forced-choice buttons (i.e. it was only possible to select one of the above options). The buttons were displayed horizontally with *Eg veit ikki* in the centre; it could be argued that some speakers interpreted 'I don't know how natural' differently from 'a judgement between "not very natural" and "rather natural"', but it was assumed that stating uncertainty about naturalness is equivalent to a judgement between 'not very natural Faroese' and 'rather natural Faroese', and avoids having to notate point 3 on the scale as either the positive 'natural' or negative 'unnatural', or leaving the description blank, which could cause confusion. It was possible to leave an answer blank, and therefore some participants reached the end of the survey without providing responses to every question. At the end of each trial, participants were given the opportunity to provide additional comments in a text box and voluntarily to provide anonymised demographic information: age, gender and where they were from. This same format was used for all the online surveys conducted.

---

[12] The notion of acceptability was expressed as 'naturalness' on advice from native speaker linguists, as this seemed to be the best translation of the concept.

4.3.2.4 Results and Discussion

As can be seen in Table 4.3, the sentences with the highest mean acceptability are those in which the object behaviour conforms to that of typical objects. In the simple sentences 1–12, the examples with full DP objects are judged acceptable (mean > 4) when the object occurs in V,Comp, as expected. In the sentences with pronominal objects, those with shift are accepted with a higher mean in each case than the equivalent sentence without shift, apart from those with PP complements, which is expected with pronouns (see Þráinsson et al. 2012:247). Moreover, examples 13–16 show a higher mean acceptability for examples in which the negative quantified object occurs left of the verb, compared to those where it occurs in V,Comp. This is also expected since negative scrambling of this type occurs with negative quantified objects, unlike regular object shift (see Þráinsson 2007:83). Finally, the mean judgements on sentences 17–28 are greater for the examples without shift, which conforms to the observation that shift is not permitted when the finite auxiliary is in T and the main verb in V. Moreover, those examples in which the adverb is adjoined at least as high as v' have a greater mean acceptability (sentences 18, 22, 27), contrasting with examples in which it appears to be adjoined lower: on the OLG analysis of object shift, this correlates with the scope of the adverb prohibiting shift by containing the Spec,VP position.

4.3.2.5 Summary of Faroese Quirky Case Surveys

To summarise this section, we have seen two surveys which provide evidence that the theme argument in Faroese quirky case predicates behaves like a typical object with respect to object shift. This is consistent with the OLG analysis, which attributes object shift behaviour to an interaction between discourse-structure and argument-structure constraints. Objects in predicates with non-nominative–subjects essentially behave the same way as they do in those with the default nominative-accusative case frame, and so it should not be surprising if they also bear standard structural object case. Furthermore, nominative object case is rejected across the board by the native speakers sampled. It seems then that Icelandic object case, rather than Faroese, requires some additional explanation. As argued in Section 4.4.1 and following, the additional factor is a preference in Icelandic for some nominative argument to be a target of agreement, which in Icelandic outranks the constraint enforcing the realisation of structural object case.

4.3.3 Icelandic Quirky Case Survey

In order to explore the differences between the Icelandic and Faroese patterns further, another survey was conducted which tested dative-subject verbs in Icelandic. The Icelandic 'give' passives and quirky case predicates were tested within the same survey (see Section 7.4.1).

4.3.3.1 Participants

There were 28 respondents, recruited via a shared link on Facebook by native speaker consultants; no compensation was offered to participants.[13] Of these respondents, 14 fully completed the survey, while the other 14 gave partial responses. All participants were required to declare that Icelandic was their native language before taking part in the survey. Demographic information was voluntarily provided by 13 participants: of this subset, 10 were female and 3 male, with a mean age of 44.8 years ($\sigma = 15.6$ years, range 24–71); 7 were from Reykjavík or the capital region, 3 from Sauðárkrókur (north Iceland), 2 from Keflavík, one from Djúpivogur (east Iceland), and one simply said they were from the northern region (*að norðan*).

4.3.3.2 Materials

Participants were presented with 54 sentences for judgement, laid out in full in Appendix B4. These were interspersed with the 'give' passive sentences tested in the survey described in Section 7.4.1, as well as filler sentences whose judgements were known beforehand.

4.3.3.3 Procedure

Participants were asked to provide judgements on the sentences in Table 8 in Appendix B4, in the same manner as that described in Section 4.3.2.3. The Icelandic instructions and judgement descriptions were the same as those described in Section 7.4.1.3. Unlike the Faroese surveys,

---

[13]Thanks to Einar Freyr Sigurðsson and Jóhannes Gísli Jónsson for help with the survey.

the Icelandic surveys did not have the target sentences for judgement embedded in a larger context.

4.3.3.4 Results

Figure 4.3 shows mean acceptability rating plotted against plural or singular agreement on the finite verb, and whether a dative argument intervenes between the finite verb and target of agreement. As is evident, the only mean acceptability approaching 4 on the scale is plural agreement with no intervening dative. Singular agreement is generally disliked across the board, and the presence of an intervening dative reduces the overall acceptability considerably. An ordered logit regression model was run, summarised as the following:

Response ~ Agreement * Dative intervener + (1 | Speaker) + (1 | Item)

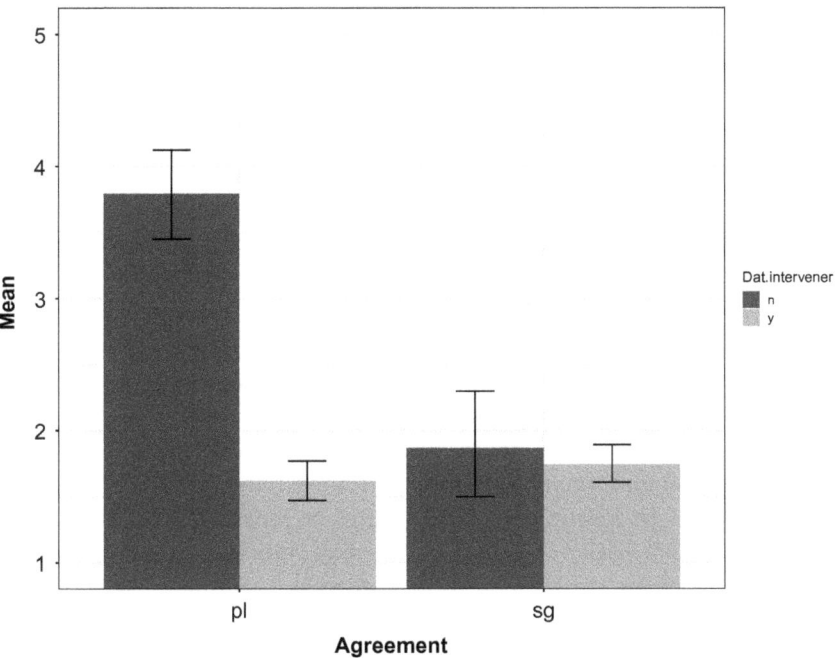

Figure 4.3 Icelandic quirky case survey: Mean acceptability by agreement and dative intervener

On this model, the fixed effect of dative intervener is very significant, with the presence of an intervener reducing acceptability ($\beta = -4.8$, $p < 0.01$). Singular agreement was also judged significantly worse on average than plural agreement ($\beta = -3.6$, $p < 0.03$). Finally, there was a significant interaction between these factors: the effect on acceptability of a dative intervener was significantly greater in plural agreement contexts than in singular agreement contexts ($\beta = 4.0$, $p < 0.02$), that is, the absence of an intervening dative improved the acceptability in the plural significantly more than it did in the singular.

The results with respect to object shift in Icelandic are as predicted: as can be seen in Table 8 in Appendix B4, the only acceptable examples (mean >4) with the finite verb in T and main verb in V are those where the object is postverbal (in V,Comp, i.e. no shift). Likewise, the examples when the main verb is in T were accepted with shift when the object was a pronoun, without shift when the object was a full DP, and accepted (albeit less consistently) with a shifted full DP object, all of which is expected given prior work.

4.3.3.5 Discussion

We may draw two conclusions from the Icelandic survey on quirky case verbs: (i) that Icelandic native speakers do show evidence of preferring number agreement with a nominative object over non-agreement (singular/default), and these speakers at least disprefer sentences where a dative argument intervenes between the finite verb and agreement target; and (ii) that the Icelandic nominative objects are true objects with respect to object shift behaviour, that is, they pattern the same way as do accusative objects in standard nominative–accusative case frames. Therefore, the question remains as framed in Chapter 2: the Icelandic nominative theme arguments in quirky case predicates trigger number agreement and undergo object shift; therefore, the question of why they are marked with nominative case cannot be answered by proposing that they are not really objects. Furthermore, our suggestion that there is a preference for agreeing with a nominative argument in Icelandic (formalised as the AGR[+HR] constraint) finds empirical support. Since only number agreement and not full person agreement is possible with nominative objects in Icelandic, this suggests that AGR[+HR] is satisfied by number agreement alone.

A reviewer notes that there is some evidence from recent studies of variation in Icelandic, such as the Icelandic part of the Scandinavian Dialect Syntax project headed by Höskuldur Þráinsson[14] and some unpublished work by Hlíf Árnadóttir (p.c.), that some speakers permit non-agreement with plural nominative objects, as indicated by the minority in my survey who largely accepted sentences with default singular agreement. This is also potentially suggestive of a competing grammars analysis, the difference being whether or not to agree with the object at all. As commented by the reviewer, from an OLG perspective, it could be that another constraint is at play that enforces agreement with subject position, or agreement only with specifier positions. The analysis would then be that this constraint is low-ranked in older Icelandic but ranked higher in a competing ranking that some younger speakers have. This all requires further investigation, but the relevant point for our discussion is that the preference for agreeing with some nominative argument in the clause is supported within the speakers' grammars who rated the sentences with object agreement higher and rejected those with singular agreement.

4.4 OLG Analysis

As is evident from the data presented thus far, an empirically adequate theory of case assignment in Faroese must minimally account for the following case frames:

MONOTRANSITIVE CASES: SUBJ-OBJ	SUBJ. CASE IN PASSIVE	DITRANSITIVE CASES: SUBJ-IO-DO	SUBJ. CASE IN PASSIVE
NOM-ACC	NOM	NOM-DAT-ACC	none
DAT-NOM (Icel.)	DAT	NOM-ACC-ACC	none
DAT$_S$-ACC	NOM		
DAT$_W$-ACC	NOM		
NOM-DAT$_S$	DAT		
NOM-DAT$_W$	NOM		
ACC-ACC (Icel.)	ACC		

In this table, subscript W indicates 'weak' dative case and subscript S 'strong' dative. These two varieties of dative case are posited due

---
[14] See websim.arkivert.uit.no/scandiasyn/scandiasyn/index.html, accessed 7/16/21.

to their behaviour with respect to nominative substitution; this phenomenon will be discussed in Section 5.1. By 'weak/strong' is meant whether the dative case borne by the subject of an active monotransitive is replaceable by nominative ('weak') or not ('strong'); the same terminology is adopted for whether the single argument of a passive bears nominative ('weak') or dative ('strong') when the counterpart active has a dative object, discussed further in Chapter 6. Passives of ditransitives will be discussed in Chapter 7. For the moment, let us leave the nominative substitution question aside and solve the simplest part of the problem, namely how to derive DAT-NOM in Icelandic versus DAT-ACC in Faroese.

4.4.1 Case and Agreement Constraints

Let us pursue the hypothesis that the key difference between Faroese and Icelandic is a different ranking of constraints that enforce two conflicting pressures: (i) that there must be a nominative argument in the clause that is flagged by agreement morphology on the finite verb, and (ii) that transitive object case must be reflected in the output when there are two input arguments. We propose the following constraints relevant to the domain of case-marking and agreement (with MATCH-CASE repeated here):

(109) MAX[–HR]: assign a violation for each [–HR] abstract case feature on an input argument that is not realised by a [–HR] morphosyntactic case feature on an output argument.

(110) AGR[+HR]: assign a violation for each finite verb whose number agreement value is not identical to that of an argument bearing [+HR] morphosyntactic case in the same clause.

(111) MATCHCASE (MC): assign a violation for each positional case feature matrix $F[vals_{pos}]$ that is not identical to its corresponding item case feature matrix $F[vals_{item}]$.

(112) MAX[LEXCASE] (MAX[LC]): assign a violation for each lexical case feature on an argument at the level of abstract case that does not correspond to the same lexical feature value on an argument at the level of morphosyntactic case.

MAX[–HR] and MAX[LEXCASE] differ from MATCHCASE in that MAX-type constraints ensure faithfulness to the input by penalising non-realisation of input features, while the MATCH-type constraint penalises output candidates with feature mismatches without directly referring to the input. In other words, MAX deals with input–output faithfulness, whereas MATCH targets a specific kind of feature-mapping within the output candidate. Nevertheless, MATCH constraints will indirectly ensure faithfulness, since the maximally faithful output candidate will also tend to have minimal feature mismatches, depending on the interactions with other constraints. MAX constraints alone do not penalise mismatches of features, but only presence/absence of a feature in the output;[15] therefore, MATCH constraints are also necessary in languages with positional licensing in order to yield the correct position-item mapping. For instance, in a predicate with two arguments and the input features [+HR] and [−HR], MAX[−HR] will not be violated even if the item bearing [−HR] occurs in a [+HR] position, such as Spec,TP, since [−HR] is still present in the output. However, MATCHCASE will be violated by the mismatch [+HR]:[−HR]. Thus the combination of positional licensing and faithfulness to abstract case rules out sentences with unacceptable argument structure.

It was noted by a reviewer that another possible analysis of position-item mismatches would involve DEP constraints penalising insertion of a role feature. For example, a dative-marked argument in object position would have [−HR]:[−HR−LR], which could violate, for example, DEP[−LR]. In some instances, this may result in different predictions from the analysis in which MATCHCASE is the relevant constraint: in case conflict situations, such as on relative pronouns in some German free relatives, not all case mismatches are equally bad, and violations higher on an obliqueness hierarchy are preferred. It is quite possible that more fine-grained DEP-type constraints are needed to account for such data, but the formulations proposed here are those which both cover the Insular Scandinavian data and seem to generate the correct factorial typologies: a DEP-type constraint would not necessarily produce the same violation profiles, and in some cases identity is really the right notion (e.g. a [+HR] item occurring in a [−HR] position). Another reviewer raised the question of levels of mapping, since my formulation of MATCHCASE refers to a different level of mapping from MAX-type constraints (position to item within syntax versus abstract case to syntax). This is an illustrative point because it also touches

---

[15]We formulate the MAX constraints relating to case such that they refer to features borne by arguments in order that an empty position bearing the correct feature does not satisfy MAX (i.e. the mere existence of an 'object position' does not satisfy MAX[−HR], only the presence of an accusative argument in the output). Positional features are hence different from features borne by arguments, since they do not fully 'realise' case unless occupied by an argument of a matching case-feature specification.

98 *Faroese Dative Subjects*

on the question of parallel versus serial evaluation. As discussed in Section 3.1, the OLG model is highly stratal in that separate evaluations are posited for mappings from abstract case to morphosyntax and morphosyntactic case to morphology. However, as argued in Section 1.2.1, these distinct but interrelated levels are empirically necessary. The question is whether it is *also* necessary to have a distinct harmonisation solely for matching the morphosyntactic case features borne by positions and their occupying items. This would need to be explored more deeply, but there is a conceptual reason for preferring a single morphosyntactic harmonisation: separating syntactic position as input from the occupying item as output effectively formalises one particular view of syntactic structure-building, since it implies a procedural, sequential step of insertion of items (whether in multiple derivations or as a single insertion). The view adopted here, where there is a single syntactic evaluation that looks at output candidates, captures the idea that candidates are fully formed structures, avoiding proliferation of derivational steps. Hence, the formulation of MATCHCASE such that it targets malformed output candidates accords with theoretical parsimony. If it is possible to capture the observed range of variation without additional levels, which does seem to be so, the onus is on the objector to demonstrate the empirical need for an extra stratum.

The following rankings are hypothesised for Faroese and Icelandic. The pair {AGR[+HR], MAX[−HR]} are differently ranked in each language, while {AGR[+HR], MATCHCASE} in Faroese and {MAX[−HR], MATCHCASE} in Icelandic are left unranked:

(113) Icelandic: MAX[LC] » AGR[+HR] » {MAX[−HR], MATCHCASE}

(114) Faroese: MAX[LC] » MAX[−HR] » {AGR[+HR], MATCHCASE}

Section 4.4.2 lays out the tableaux for the basic case frames, here ignoring nominative substitution.

4.4.2 OLG Analysis

Regarding notation, the input to the computation is at the level of abstract case, so the [+HR], [−HR] and [−HR−LR] features in the input refer to abstract nominative, accusative and dative, respectively. As for the output, the case feature matrix on the left of the colon refers to positional case, and the matrix to the right denotes the features on the item occupying that position. For instance, the notation {NOM$_{[+\text{agr}]}$

[+HR]:[+HR]} indicates that an agreed-with nominative argument is occupying Spec,TP; the positional feature is [+HR] and the item's feature is also [+HR]. Likewise, {DAT [−HR]:[DAT$_{LC}$[−HR−LR]]} indicates that a dative-marked argument occupies the position bearing [−HR] (i.e. V,Comp); the item bears lexical dative case with the feature matrix [−HR−LR]. Let us construe lexical case, notated by subscript LC, as an abstract case variable present in the input; the value of the variable is still encoded using the inventory of abstract case features (i.e. lexical dative case 'comes with' a [−HR−LR] value). The outputs on the left of the tableaux represent morphosyntactic case, the intermediate level between abstract and morphological case; we assume a separate computation of the mapping from morphosyntactic to purely morphological case, which happens at PF.

(115) **Icelandic regular monotransitive**

arg_1[+HR] arg_2[−HR]		Max[LC]	Agr[+HR]	Max[−HR]	MC
☞ a. NOM$_{[+agr]}$ [+HR]:[+HR], ACC [−HR]:[−HR]					
b. NOM$_{[+agr]}$ [+HR]:[+HR], DAT [−HR]:[−HR−LR]					*!
c. NOM$_{[+agr]}$ [+HR]:[+HR], NOM [−HR]:[+HR]				*!	*

(116) **Faroese regular monotransitive**

arg_1[+HR] arg_2[−HR]		Max[LC]	Max[−HR]	Agr[+HR]	MC
☞ a. NOM$_{[+agr]}$ [+HR]:[+HR], ACC [−HR]:[−HR]					
b. NOM$_{[+agr]}$ [+HR]:[+HR], DAT [−HR]:[−HR−LR]					*!
c. NOM$_{[+agr]}$ [+HR]:[+HR], NOM [−HR]:[+HR]			*!		*

(117) **Icelandic monotransitive with dative subject**

arg_1[DAT$_{LC}$[−HR−LR],+HR] arg_2[−HR]		Max[LC]	Agr[+HR]	Max[−HR]	MC
a. NOM$_{[+agr]}$ [+HR]:[+HR], ACC [−HR]:[−HR]		*!		*	
☞ b. DAT [+HR]:[DAT$_{LC}$[−HR−LR]], NOM$_{[+agr]}$ [−HR]:[+HR]				*	**
c. DAT [+HR]:[DAT$_{LC}$[−HR−LR]], ACC [−HR]:[−HR]		*!			*

As can be seen in tableau (117), in Icelandic object agreement satisfies Agr[+HR], which requires only that a nominative argument be marked by verbal agreement, not specifically the subject. The ranking Agr[+HR] » Max[−HR] enables us to rule out the DAT-ACC case frame for Icelandic unless the accusative object case is also lexically specified.[16] As for Icelandic predicates with two accusative arguments (e.g. *Mig vantar hníf* 'me.ACC lacks knife.ACC'), Max[LexCase] enforces the accusative on the theme as well as that on the experiencer; otherwise

---

[16]Examples of this exist in Latvian and Lithuanian, in which verbs of pain mark the experiencer argument with dative and stimulus with accusative case, the latter displaying properties of lexical rather than structural case assignment (Seržant 2013).

we would predict that nominative would surface on the theme in order to satisfy AGR[+HR].

An important question is whether it can be demonstrated that the accusative case on the theme in such examples is lexical rather than structural; an anonymous reviewer noted that some Icelandic speakers prefer the theme argument to be expressed in a PP rather than as an accusative object, and passivisation is not possible with the best illustrative verbs in question: *bresta* 'fail', *þrjóta* 'run out of, lack' (cognate with Faroese *tróta*), and *vanta* 'lack'. The Icelandic facts are complex here, since it seems that for these verbs with an accusative–accusative case frame, when dative is substituted on the subject, the object is nominative with *bresta* and *þrjóta* but remains accusative with *vanta*; this seems to be connected to the fact that when the same verbs are used intransitively, the subject which corresponds to the theme in the transitive shows up as nominative with *bresta* and *þrjóta* but accusative with *vanta* (Þráinsson 2007:188–189). However, as Þráinsson (2007:189) notes, it is not clear that preservation of accusative case on the single argument of an unaccusative is a truly analogous diagnostic to preservation under passivisation: both because there are examples of structural cases 'preserving' in the intransitive (and vice versa) and because there are often crucial semantic differences between the transitive and intransitive constructions. Disentangling this is beyond the scope of this work and would require further study of the relevant verbs with a larger pool of speakers, since there may also be inter-speaker variation. As an initial hypothesis, it is plausible that competing rankings are responsible for differing behaviour of the lower accusative, such as a Faroese-type grammar producing the dative–accusative pattern with *vanta*; this would then be expected to show reflexes in other constructions or contexts. Further discussion on dative substitution in Icelandic can be found in Section 6.4.1.

(118) **Icelandic monotransitive with accusative subject, accusative object**

$arg_1[\text{ACC}_{LC}[-\text{HR}],+\text{HR}] \ arg_2[\text{ACC}_{LC}[-\text{HR}]]$	Max[LC]	Agr[+HR]	Max[−HR]	MC
a. NOM$_{[+\text{agr}]}$ [+HR]:[+HR], ACC [−HR]:[ACC$_{LC}$[−HR]]	*!		*	
b. ACC [+HR]:[ACC$_{LC}$[−HR]], NOM$_{[+\text{agr}]}$ [−HR]:[+HR]	*!		*	**
☞ c. ACC [+HR]:[ACC$_{LC}$[−HR]], ACC [−HR]:[ACC$_{LC}$[−HR]]			*	*

By contrast, in Faroese the ranking Max[−HR] » Agr[+HR] ensures that standard accusative object case occurs on the theme argument, in spite of incurring an AGR[+HR] violation by not agreeing with a nominative argument:

(119) Faroese monotransitive with dative subject

$arg_1[\text{DAT}_{LC}[-\text{HR}-\text{LR}],+\text{HR}] \; arg_2[-\text{HR}]$	MAX[LC]	MAX[−HR]	AGR[+HR]	MC
a. NOM$_{[+agr]}$ [+HR]:[+HR], ACC [−HR]:[−HR]	*!	*		
b. DAT [+HR]:[DAT$_{LC}$[−HR−LR]], NOM$_{[+agr]}$ [−HR]:[+HR]		*!		**
☞ c. DAT [+HR]:[DAT$_{LC}$[−HR−LR]], ACC [−HR]:[−HR]			*	*

The basic pattern for dative-object verbs in Faroese is captured by the ranking MAX[LC] » MAX[−HR], which enforces the expression of lexical object case in the output. By formulating the constraints and feature matrices such that dative object case satisfies MAX[−HR], we ensure that the inverse of the DAT-ACC frame does not occur in dative-object predicates, since an additional violation of MAX[−HR] when the object is dative would result in the winner ACC-DAT:

(120) Faroese monotransitive with dative object

$arg_1[+\text{HR}] \; arg_2[\text{DAT}_{LC}[-\text{HR}-\text{LR}]]$	MAX[LC]	MAX[−HR]	AGR[+HR]	MC
a. NOM$_{[+agr]}$ [+HR]:[+HR], ACC [−HR]:[−HR]	*!			
☞ b. NOM$_{[+agr]}$ [+HR]:[+HR], DAT [−HR]:[DAT$_{LC}$[−HR−LR]]				*
c. ACC [+HR]:[−HR], DAT [−HR]:[DAT$_{LC}$[−HR−LR]]			*!	**

Finally, we generate the correct output for regular Faroese ditransitives with the constraint MATCHCASE alone, since swapping the order of the objects will incur additional violations thereof. The proposed ranking MAX[LC] » MC covers those few examples of double-object verbs with accusative indirect objects, which is assumed to be a lexically specified case.[17]

---

[17] Again, it is difficult to establish this with the passivisation diagnostic, since speakers tend to reject passives of ditransitives. My consultants also expressed uncertainty as to whether the impersonal *mann/ein*-construction (i.e. 'one asked them a question'), would take an accusative or dative higher argument with these verbs. It is plausible that the higher object receives lexical accusative since this is a very restricted type of construction in which the indirect object is more like a source: a question is asked of someone with *spyrja*, or a favour asked with *biðja* (see Section 7.1 for examples). Notably, the Icelandic constructions with the same verbs also have an accusative indirect object in a nominative–accusative–genitive case frame (Þráinsson 2007:220):

(121) a. Ice. Þeir   spurðu manninn   frétta
              they.NOM.M asked man-the.ACC news.GEN
              'They asked the man if he had any news'
       b. Ice. Ég   bað   þig   hjálpar
              I.NOM asked you.ACC.SG help.GEN
              'I asked you for help'

(122) **Faroese regular ditransitive**

arg_1[+HR] arg_2[–HR-LR] arg_3[–HR]		Max[LC]	Max[–HR]	Agr[+HR]	MC
☞ a. NOM$_{[+agr]}$ [+HR]:[+HR], DAT [–HR-LR]:[–HR-LR], ACC [–HR]:[–HR]					
b. NOM$_{[+agr]}$ [+HR]:[+HR], ACC [–HR-LR]:[–HR], DAT [–HR]:[–HR-LR]					**!
c. NOM$_{[+agr]}$ [+HR]:[+HR], ACC [–HR-LR]:[ACC$_{LC}$–HR], ACC [–HR]:[–HR]					*!

(123) **Faroese ditransitive with two accusative objects**

arg_1[+HR] arg_2[ACC$_{LC}$,–HR-LR] arg_3[–HR]		Max[LC]	Max[–HR]	Agr[+HR]	MC
a. NOM$_{[+agr]}$ [+HR]:[+HR], DAT [–HR-LR]:[–HR-LR], ACC [–HR]:[–HR]		*!			
b. NOM$_{[+agr]}$ [+HR]:[+HR], ACC [–HR-LR]:[ACC$_{LC}$–HR]], DAT [–HR]:[–HR-LR]					**!
☞ c. NOM$_{[+agr]}$ [+HR]:[+HR], ACC [–HR-LR]:[ACC$_{LC}$–HR]], ACC [–HR]:[–HR]					*

4.4.3 Factorial Typology

For the sake of clarity genitive case is excluded from the candidate set, and only the possible combinations of nominative, accusative and dative case are considered; the same constraints would also predict Icelandic predicates with genitive subjects to be possible with a ranking of Max[LC] » MatchCase. We hypothesised the ranking for Faroese in (124) and included the inputs shown in (125).

(124) **Faroese:**
Max[LC] » Max[–HR] » {Agr[+HR], MatchCase}

(125) a. NOM-ACC: /{arg_1[+HR] arg_2[–HR]}/
b. DAT-ACC: /{arg_1[DAT$_{LC}$,+HR] arg_2[–HR]}/
c. NOM-DAT: /{arg_1[+HR] arg_2[DAT$_{LC}$,–HR]}/
d. ACC-ACC: /{arg_1[ACC$_{LC}$,+HR] arg_2[ACC$_{LC}$,–HR]}/
e. NOM-DAT-ACC: /{arg_1[+HR] arg_2[–HR-LR] arg_3[–HR]}/
f. NOM-ACC-ACC: /{arg_1[+HR] arg_2[ACC$_{LC}$,–HR-LR] arg_3[–HR]}/

With four constraints, the number of logically possible grammars is 24. Five distinct output languages were generated:

(126) **Output languages**

No.	a.	b.	c.	d.	e.	f.	Example language
1	NOM-ACC	DAT-ACC	NOM-DAT	ACC-ACC	NOM-DAT-ACC	NOM-ACC-ACC	Faroese
2	NOM-ACC	DAT-ACC	NOM-DAT	ACC-ACC	NOM-DAT-ACC	NOM-DAT-ACC	(Faroese without quirky objects)
3	NOM-ACC	NOM-ACC	NOM-ACC	NOM-ACC	NOM-DAT-ACC	NOM-DAT-ACC	English, Danish
4	NOM-ACC	DAT-NOM	NOM-DAT	ACC-ACC	NOM-DAT-ACC	NOM-ACC-ACC	Icelandic
5	NOM-ACC	DAT-NOM	NOM-DAT	ACC-ACC	NOM-DAT-ACC	NOM-ACC-ACC	German

Thus we correctly predict, in addition to Faroese and Icelandic, an output type with the same case frames as Icelandic apart from ACC-ACC (i.e. German), though as argued in Section 2.2, these arguments do

---

These indirect objects form a class in which something is requested of the animate source rather than being properly a goal or recipient, an observation which also holds of the Faroese examples. Thus, the fact that a thematic generalisation can be made about such arguments is a piece of evidence that the case-marking here is more likely to be lexical rather than structural, particularly given that the canonical case for indirect objects in Faroese is dative.

not exhibit the same subjecthood properties as do those in Icelandic; we follow Wunderlich (2008) in assuming that the differing behaviour with respect to raising and control is determined by the lexical representations of the relevant verbs. The German case-marking pattern in DAT-NOM predicates is generated by the same set of constraints as Icelandic but with a different ranking: if the German ranking is AGR[+HR] » MAX[LC], accusative subjects are precluded. This captures the fact that the difference seems to be systematic, in that Icelandic licenses arguments bearing lexical subject case positionally in Spec,TP, whereas German does not appear to do so. We also generate a type without any lexical case-marking (English, Danish). Output 2 could reasonably represent a hypothetical future stage of Faroese as lexical case-marking is lost. However, as noted above, this picture is incomplete, since we must account for the substitution behaviour of the lexically marked cases in Faroese, the differences in preservation under passivisation in Faroese and Icelandic, and the issue of the passive of ditransitives. In Chapter 5, a competing grammars model is presented to explain the observed nominative substitution behaviour of Faroese dative subjects. Chapter 6 discusses results of surveys on the passive conducted on the Faroe Islands and presents an OLG analysis. Chapter 7 explores survey results on the passive of ditransitives and integrates the data into the model.

4.5 Summary of Chapter

To conclude this chapter, it has been shown that dative subjects are still in common use in Faroese, but that possibility of substituting nominative is very verb-specific and subject to other grammatical and sociolinguistic factors, discussed further in Chapter 5. We have seen that Faroese DAT-ACC predicates exhibit similar behaviour to their Icelandic DAT-NOM counterparts with respect to object shift, as revealed by survey data, suggesting that in both languages the non-dative argument is structurally an object. Moreover, the Icelandic data are consistent with the hypothesised AGR[+HR] constraint, which, given the apparent absence of nominative objects in Faroese, also favours the analysis in which the differently ranked constraints are responsible for the cross-linguistic difference in object case. This OLG analysis based on OT constraint conflict was presented, which generates the correct Faroese and Icelandic case frames for simple monotransitives and predicts attested languages within the limits of this basic model. In Chapters 6–7, more complex constructions are considered which allow us to develop the OLG model further and demonstrate the empirical validity of the approach.

5

Competing Grammars

An additional component of the OLG theory is the concept of grammar competition. Similar ideas have been articulated by Kroch (1989a,b, 1994), Pintzuk (1999), Zobl and Liceras (2005) and others as an explanation for grammatical change over time. It was noted by Kroch (1989b) that long, protracted grammatical changes, such as the rise of periphrastic *do* in the history of English, cannot be explained either as a sequence of discrete consecutive reanalyses or as dialect mixture where different systems coexist within the speech community but not the individual. Pioneering work by Ellegård (1953) showed that (a) the new form gradually increased in frequency in each syntactic environment, rather than categorically replacing the old form in a context-by-context fashion, and (b) individual authors use both old and new forms within their synchronic grammar, with variation in frequency of use. Therefore, Kroch (1989b) argued that a better approach would be to posit the availability of both forms synchronically and to attribute the increasing frequency of the new form to other factors, such as processing. An important related claim is the 'constant rate hypothesis' that use of a form increases concurrently across all environments. This was supported by the periphrastic *do* evidence, which showed that the relative strength of processing effects in each environment did *not* directly determine the rate of the rise of *do* but that the rate of increase was constant across all distributional contexts of the new form. This is an important finding, since it is consistent with the syntactic change being a categorial phenomenon that nevertheless is subject to external factors. Pintzuk (1999) built on this work, showing that the rise of Infl-medial phrase structure in Old English occurs at a constant rate in both matrix and subordinate clauses and that speakers had access to both the verb-medial and verb-final grammars, the former increasing in frequency over time. Santorini (1989, 1993) reproduced identical results for the same change in Yiddish. Subsequent proposals by Yang (2000, 2002), Wallenberg (2016) and others also presented evidence for intraspeaker competing grammars, a notion which this volume takes up with particular focus on synchronic variation.

In OLG, a grammar is a ranking of Optimality Theory (OT) constraints with a single winning output candidate corresponding to each input. Optimality Theory offers a means of capturing the concurrent nature of syntactic change across environments through constraint reranking: speakers hypothesise a different ranking for each form, which involves simultaneous privileging of a previously lower-ranked and deranking of a formerly higher-ranked constraint. Since constraints are typically postulated to be as general as possible, we expect to see changes in multiple syntactic environments, as was the case for the data examined by Kroch (1989b) and Pintzuk (1999).[1] If we pair the basic OT model with an additional premise, it is also possible to explain the varying frequency of the use of new forms: if external factors play a role in determining which ranking is accessed by speakers in a given environment, we are able to model the change statistically through weighted parameters representing these factors. Moreover, the hypothesis will be empirically testable via corpora, a task undertaken in this chapter with respect to the Faroese dative-subject verbs. Given the self-evident complexity of syntactic change processes, taking additional layers of information into account can only lead to greater understanding of the phenomena in question, provided sufficient care is taken to define the model explicitly. For this reason, the influence of sociolinguistic factors is explored in this chapter, and they are found to be statistically significant in determining selection of case. Finally, this chapter also discusses two quantitative approaches to variation, one as a means of distinguishing dialects from randomness in acceptability judgements, the other as a more sophisticated predictor of case selection, albeit with the interpretability limitations inherent to neural networks.

---

[1] See Kiparsky (2012) and Clark (2012) for more recent accounts of morphosyntactic change as constraint reranking.

5.1 Two Kinds of Dative Case

As mentioned in Section 4.4, it has been noted that Faroese verbs that typically occur with dative subjects may also occur with nominative subjects, the object remaining accusative either way (Barnes 1986, Þráinsson et al. 2012). It has not been thoroughly investigated under what circumstances this 'nominative substitution' behaviour may occur, but it has been associated with 'informal register' and 'young people's speech' (Petersen 2010); Jónsson and Eyþórsson (2005) note that nominative subjects are judged acceptable by native speakers of Faroese with all the verbs they tested, and the younger generation is more likely to accept nominative. As presented above, examples of nominative subjects are attested for all the dative-subject verbs searched for in the corpora, albeit only rarely with *tørva* 'need'. Some examples are repeated here:

(127) Far. *Mamma heldur, at **eg** dámi skógvar alt for væl*
Mamma thinks that I.NOM like.1SG shoes.ACC all too well
'Mama thinks that I like my shoes far too much'

(128) Far. *Mangli bæði bor og skrúvur, so eg mátti út at keypa*
lack.1SG both drill.ACC and screws.ACC so I must.PST out to buy
'I lack both a drill and screws, so I had to go out to buy (them)'

(129) a. Far. *Eg svaraði, at **mær** ikki tørvaði lokabrøgd*
I answered that me.DAT not needed.SG schemings.ACC
'I answered that I didn't need to scheme'
b. Far. ?* *Eg svaraði, at **eg** ikki tørvaði lokabrøgd*
I answered that I.NOM not needed.SG schemings.ACC

Jónsson (2009) proposes a 'covert nominative' analysis of this, suggesting that Faroese dative subject case, unlike that of Icelandic, is an instance of both dative and nominative case assigned to the same argument, with dative surfacing by default but with the option of nominative, though no claim is made as to when each variant may occur. Asarina (2011), building on Jónsson's account, suggests that a higher functional head is necessary to license quirky dative case in Faroese and that this head is responsible for number agreement in order to capture the purported optionality of number agreement with dative subjects in Faroese; however, again the variation is not accounted for, and unfortunately some of the Faroese data presented are inconsistent with corpora and survey results. These alternative accounts are discussed in Chapter 8; at the time of writing, these are the only attempts in the literature to account for the Faroese data reviewed in this section.

5.1.1 Accounting for 'Weak' and 'Strong' Dative Case

In order to explain the variation observed in (127–129), let us posit that multiple grammars (i.e. rankings) co-exist and are accessible to Faroese speakers. Such an account captures the observed parallel between nominative substitution on dative subject case and non-preservation in the passive of dative-object verbs, which are construed as reflexes of the same mechanism (i.e. persistent dative subject case and preserving dative object case are products of the same constraint interaction). What marks this OLG account as different from the aforementioned alternatives is that, although a ranking is categorical in the sense that only one optimal output candidate will be selected for a given input, multiple grammars co-exist for each native speaker: thus, there is no 'speaker of Icelandic A, speaker of Icelandic B', since 'Icelandic A' and 'Icelandic B' are generated by different rankings that are simultaneously accessible to one speaker. Similar conclusions have already been drawn with respect to Icelandic and Faroese data by Þráinsson (2016), who found that speaker judgements on dative substitution did not neatly fall into separate dialect groups and that the same speaker may produce two case-marking variants even within the same text. At any rate, the hypothesis that two grammars co-exist within a speaker is worth exploring further.

Figure 5.1 shows a diagram of the proposed model. The claim is that a grammar (ranking) is *probabilistically activated*, where grammar selection is determined by multiple weighted factors. These weights can be approximated through empirical investigation: corpora, judgement survey data and experimental results can be brought to bear on the question of how grammatical variants are selected. The same set of output candidates is produced by GEN, but the ranking at EVAL differs for each variant, resulting in different winning outputs. It is possible to model two competing grammars by a logistic regression, in which grammatical and contextual effects contribute to an increased or decreased probability of a grammar being selected and, therefore, a particular output candidate surfacing; for multiple competing grammars, log-linear models such as Poisson regression are appropriate. This makes for a more accurate model of grammar for three reasons: (i) it makes sense of the fact that one speaker may produce two or

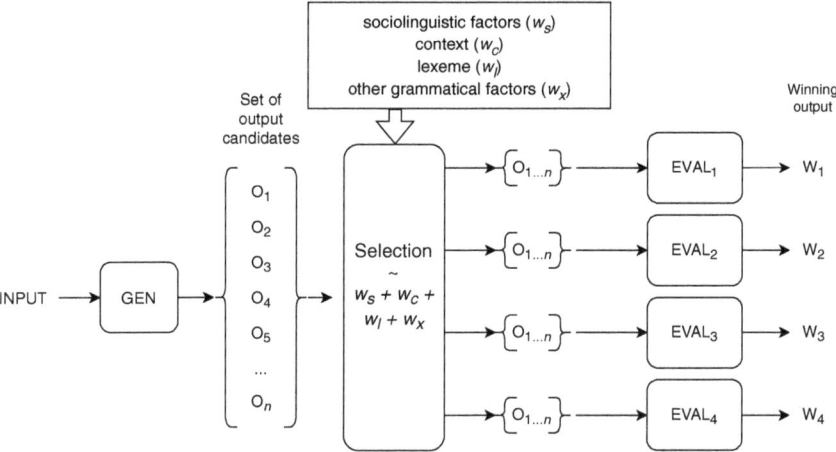

Figure 5.1 Architecture of competing grammars model

more variants, each of which requires a distinct analysis, within the same text, paragraph or even utterance; (ii) it better accounts for morphosyntactic change, since if this is viewed as constraint reranking, an account can be formulated in which several factors conspire to produce a diachronically increasing probability of one grammar being preferred over another; and (iii) it offers a cogent explanation for the loss of marked morphosyntactic features (such as 'quirky case') in acquisition, as the child's inferred grammar will decreasingly include the marked feature as the conditions change. For in-depth treatments of this idea in the acquisition literature, the reader is advised to consult Yang (2000, 2002), especially Yang (2000:31–35), which formalises a probabilistic model of learning. In this section the OLG analysis of the nominative substitution facts in Faroese dative-subject predicates is laid out, along with an explicit statistical model of the variation.

The nominative substitution behaviour of Faroese active dative-subject predicates is proposed to be a result of a different ranking of the constraints relevant to the case-marking domain. For actives, we must only add one extra constraint to those already adopted in Section 4.4.1, based on SUBJ/NOM from Kiparsky (2013):[2]

---

[2] A reviewer queried why the relevant constraint should not be a faithfulness constraint, MAX[+HR], which falls out logically from Kiparsky's framework. Some evidence that the property being targeted is strictly positional case, rather than faithful realisation of abstract nominative, comes from the 'give' passives discussed in Section 7.3. The

(130) SUBJ[+HR] (S[+HR]): Assign a violation for each position bearing [+HR] (i.e. subject position) not occupied by an item bearing [+HR] case.

With this simple constraint, the 'non-preserving/weak' grammar can be captured by the ranking S[+HR] » MAX[LC], and the 'preserving/strong' one by the ranking MAX[LC] » S[+HR]. This makes predictions about case preservation behaviour in the passive, which are shown in Chapter 6 to be borne out. For now, let us first demonstrate that the addition of this constraint captures the correct behaviour, and second present the OLG model for grammar competition.

5.2 Competing Grammars Model of Nominative Substitution

As shown in tableaux (131–132), in OT the difference can easily be accounted for by a straightforward reranking of a pair of constraints. The diachronic story is therefore that through increased probability of the ranking represented in (132) over time, the 'strong dative' grammar becomes less and less frequently activated, and consequently the lexical case-marking is lost.

(131) Faroese 'strong' dative subject

$arg_1[\text{DAT}_{LC}[-\text{HR}-\text{LR}],+\text{HR}]\ arg_2[-\text{HR}]$	MAX[LC]	MAX[−HR]	S[+HR]	AGR[+HR]	MC
a. NOM$_{[+agr]}$ [+HR]:[+HR], ACC [−HR]:[−HR]	*!				
b. DAT [+HR]:[DAT$_{LC}$[−HR−LR]], NOM$_{[+agr]}$ [−HR]:[+HR]		*!	*		**
☞ c. DAT [+HR]:[DAT$_{LC}$[−HR−LR]], ACC [−HR]:[−HR]			*	*	*

(132) Faroese 'weak' dative subject

$arg_1[\text{DAT}_{LC}[-\text{HR}-\text{LR}],+\text{HR}]\ arg_2[-\text{HR}]$	S[+HR]	MAX[LC]	MAX[−HR]	AGR[+HR]	MC
☞ a. NOM$_{[+agr]}$ [+HR]:[+HR], ACC [−HR]:[−HR]		*			
b. DAT [+HR]:[DAT$_{LC}$[−HR−LR]], NOM$_{[+agr]}$ [−HR]:[+HR]	*!		*		**
c. DAT [+HR]:[DAT$_{LC}$[−HR−LR]], ACC [−HR]:[−HR]	*!			*	*

SUBJ[+HR] constraint is intended to capture the notion that positional licensing is what counts here, since MAX[+HR] would not actually be violated by, say, an argument with abstract case [−HR] occurring in a [+HR]-bearing position: in other words, MAX[+HR] fails to rule out a morphologically accusative theme as subject, whereas SUBJ[+HR] specifically penalises oblique subjects. Another question is why this cannot be conflated with MATCHCASE, since violations of SUBJ[+HR] are always a subset of MATCHCASE violations, or a subtype such as MATCH[±HR]. The reason I chose to formulate it this way is the asymmetry between subject and object positions: the important factor is whether subject position, in OLG terms the position bearing [+HR], is occupied by a nominative argument, not whether there are other nominative arguments in the clause (e.g. occupying V,Comp).

In Chapter 6 we will see that these rankings also account for case (non-) preservation in the passive, with the addition of a constraint ruling out a null parse of the input (PARSE).

In order to construct our model, we must first decide upon which effects to include. The factors in (133) have been claimed to contribute to morphosyntactic variation in Faroese:

(133) a. **Register**: register is assumed to be a contextual feature, determined by genre and level of formality of the surrounding lexemes and constructions. In order to construct a linear model, we adopt a five-point scale for register: Least formal < Less formal < Neutral < More formal < Most formal. This is a somewhat coarse-grained operationalisation of register, since style may well be construed as more of a continuous variable, but it suffices for the demonstration of the feature's relevance. These notions build upon foundational work on style shifting by Labov (1972), who connected style to the amount of attention paid to speech;[3] work by Fasold (1972), Guy (1980) and subsequent studies on *t/d* deletion could also be seen as a phonological analogue to the competing morphosyntactic variants described here. The features considered in our register calculation include: use of vocabulary tagged as 'written language' or 'spoken language' in the most detailed Faroese dictionary *Sprotin*; genre (poetry, baby speech, political discourse, diary entries, etc.); use of 'older' morphology, such as the genitive case; use of Danish and/or English words and constructions; and use of emoji or non-standard spelling that reflects pronunciation. Of course these measures can be challenged in the specifics, but a broad categorisation of register is helpful as a way of capturing the intuition often commented on by native speakers that *talumálið* 'spoken language' and *skrivimálið* 'written language' are systematically distinct.

b. **Lexeme**: we assume the relevant feature of a lexeme in this context of variation to be its age, which depends on whether the term is considered a Danish loan or a vocabulary item directly inherited from Old Norse. To approximate this, we adopt three categories: confidence in Old Norse origin, confidence in Danish loan origin, and uncertain origin.

c. **Danish loan words and constructions**: it has been claimed that vocabulary items and constructions borrowed from Danish constitute a pressure on Faroese grammar towards a more 'Mainland Scandinavian'-type system. Since Danicisms are often reflected in the register of the text, in that a preponderance of Danicisms indicates an informal register, we exclude this factor from the model to avoid collinearity effects. It is also difficult to determine at what point Danish loanwords entered the language or whether the word happens to have a Danish cognate, given the two languages' common origin; therefore, it is difficult to devise an uncontroversial measure of how many 'Danish loans' occur in the context.

d. **Speaker age**: it has been claimed that nominative substitution is both more prevalent among young people (Jónsson 2009) and judged more acceptable

---

[3] Later studies on style shifts are also potentially relevant: work by Bell (1984), Bell and Holmes (1990), Johnstone (1995), Schilling-Estes (1998) and Eckert (2008), among others, adds to our understanding of the conscious dimension of style on the speaker's part, whereby shifts are used in some performative sense as an act of audience design, identity construction or indexation.

by the younger generation (Jónsson and Eyþórsson 2005). Since speaker age is not generally known with precision for blog authors, we also adopt a five-point scale here of estimated age group: Youngest < Younger < Middle < Older < Oldest. Tokens where nothing at all is known about the author's age are excluded. Care is needed when interpreting the role of age, since although synchronic age-graded effects are possible, age may also be an 'apparent time' proxy for the advance of a change in progress (i.e. baseline frequencies for two rankings where one is replacing the other over time). As a reviewer pointed out, these two concepts will be indistinguishable in a statistical model, which will merely show that age is a relevant factor, not how the effect should be interpreted. Although it would be preferable to have a more continuous scale for age, we are restricted by the absence of precise age data for the blog authors.

e. **Dialect:** Dialect variation is excluded since not enough is currently known about the effects of this on Faroese morphosyntax; see Þráinsson et al. (2012) for an overview. Additionally, the blog author's location or dialect background is often unknown.

In order to test this, a sample of tokens of quirky case verbs from the blog corpus was examined. The types were *dámi* 'like.1SG', *dámar* 'likes.3SG', *tørvar* 'needs.3SG', *mangli* 'lack.1SG' and *manglar* 'lacks.3SG'. All tokens of *dámi* and *mangli* occurred with nominative subjects. Since only one of 30 tokens of *tørvar* 'needs.3SG' occurred with nominative in the blog corpus, it was excluded. Both cases were included for *dámar*, and one token of *manglar* with dative was included.[4] Figures 5.2–5.4 show subject case plotted against register, lexeme and speaker age, respectively.

As can be seen in Figure 5.2, dative subjects are overwhelmingly preferred in the most formal registers, though nominative subjects are attested in all styles. Importantly, dative subjects are still possible in even the most informal register represented by baby blogs. Figure 5.3 shows that the lexeme known to be a relatively recent Danish loan, *mangla* 'lack', is almost exclusively used with a nominative subject,

---

[4] The rationale for including the dative *manglar* example but rejecting the *tørvar* with nominative is as follows: firstly, dative is the prescriptive norm with transitive uses of *manglar* and is more frequently attested in formal contexts such as news media; in contrast, nominative with *tørvar* is both non-standard and rejected by consultants, despite occurring once in the corpus. This raises the question of to what extent our model should reflect usage only or whether acceptability judgements should be factored in, effectively as a kind of bias term. Secondly, the single example of nominative with *tørvar* involves an objective relative clause, *sum kroppur okkara tørvar* 'which body.NOM.SG our needs.3SG', a more complex construction than the other transitive tokens of *tørvar* in the corpus. Further work is required to investigate the combination of internal and external factors which determine case selection, particularly since sociolinguistic constraints appear to be at play.

5.2 CG Model of Nominative Substitution   113

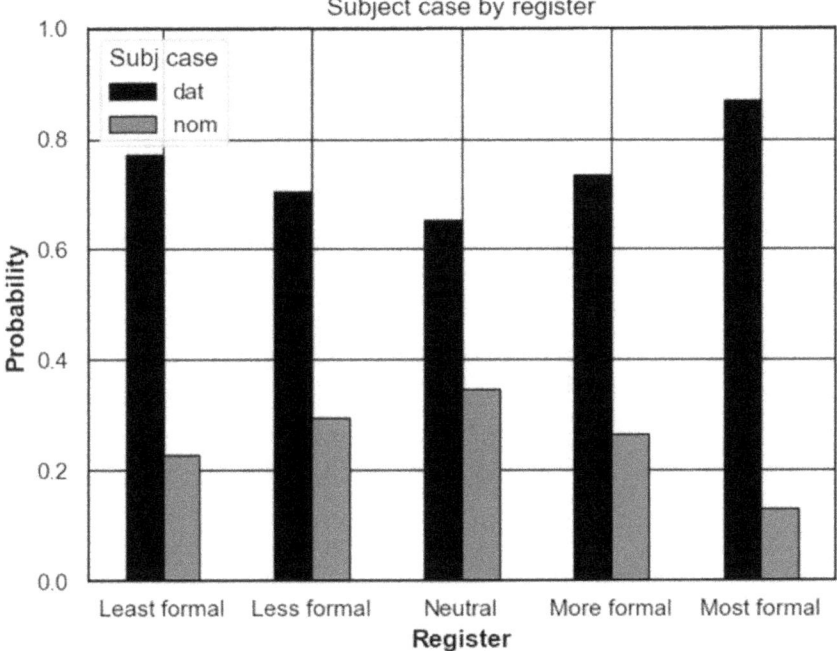

Figure 5.2 Faroese competing grammars: Subject case by register

while the Old Norse stock lexemes *dáma* 'like' and *tørva* 'need' still tend to occur with datives, even though nominatives are possible with *dáma* (and marginally with *tørva*). Finally, Figure 5.4 indicates that speakers in the younger and older age brackets are far more likely to use dative subjects with these verbs, while those in the middle bracket seem to prefer nominatives; this needs further investigation, since the expectation would be for the use of nominative relative to dative to decrease with age if nominative substitution is a change in progress. Interestingly, even the youngest age bracket still strongly prefers datives over nominatives (though it should be noted that this 'youngest' bracket is represented by words put into the mouths of children on baby blogs by their parents, and hence some influence of prescriptivism cannot be discounted).

We adopt a logistic regression model for the grammar selection, represented by subject case here. The model can be summarised thus:

$$\text{Subject case} \sim \text{Register} + \text{Lexeme} + \text{Speaker age}$$

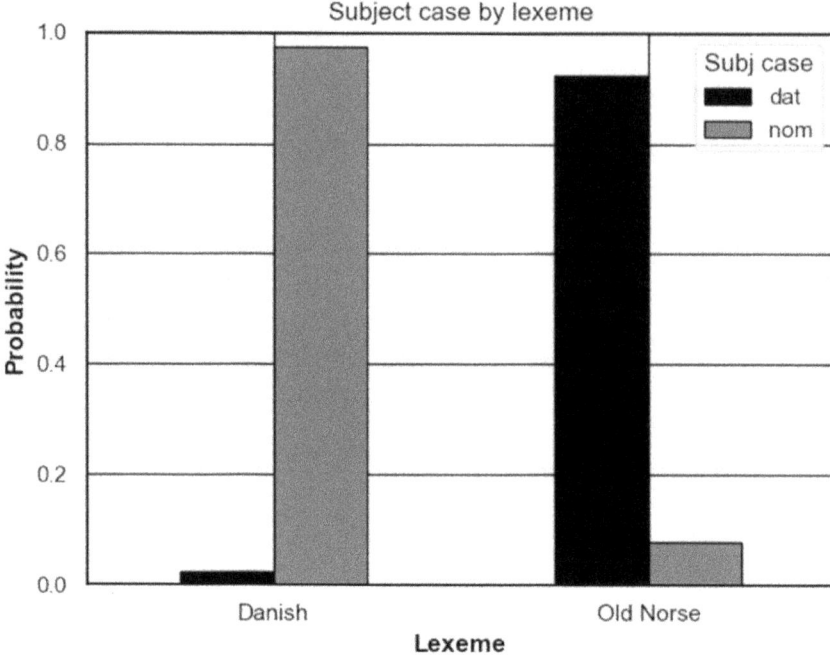

Figure 5.3 Faroese competing grammars: Subject case by lexeme

As noted above, the effect of dialect is excluded, though it may also play some role in grammar selection. Speaker and Item are excluded from the model since there will be collinearity with the other factors. The data were split (272 tokens in total) into a training and test set; the training set contained 204 tokens and the test set 68 tokens. The model was run using the Python package *scikit-learn* (Pedregosa et al. 2011). This yielded the confusion matrix shown in (134), with an accuracy rate of 0.88 on the test set, that is, 8 incorrect predictions and 60 correct predictions. In (135) additional measures of the model's predictive accuracy are given: 'precision' is the ratio of true positives over the sum of true positives and false positives, in other words the ability of the classifier not to label a sample incorrectly as nominative if it is dative. 'Recall' is the ratio of true positives over the sum of true positives and false negatives (i.e. the ability of the classifier to find the nominatives). The F-beta score can be interpreted as a weighted harmonic mean of the precision and recall, where an F-beta score reaches its best value at

5.2 CG Model of Nominative Substitution   115

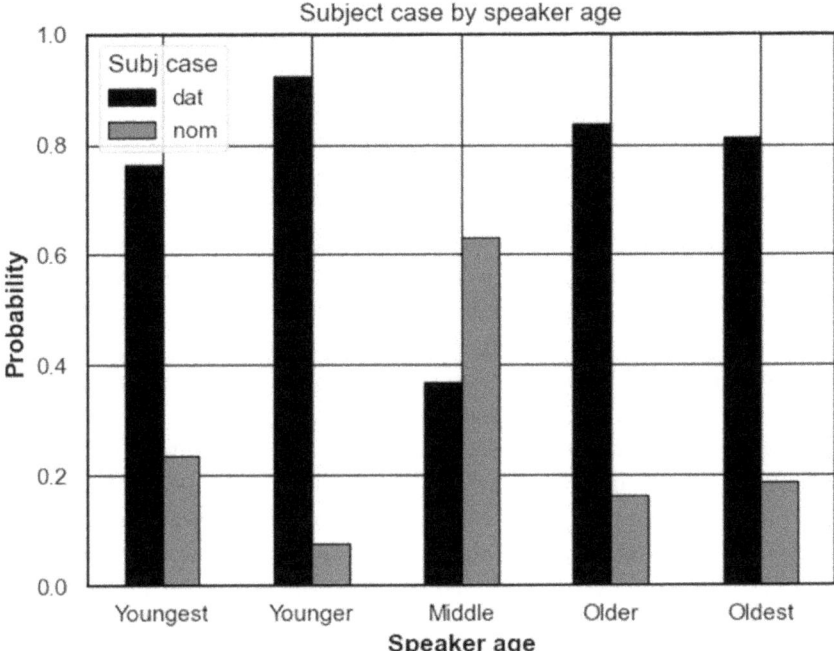

Figure 5.4 Faroese competing grammars: Subject case by speaker age

1 and worst at 0. Finally, 'support' is the number of occurrences of each class in the test set.[5] Since this is such a small dataset, we cannot draw very definite conclusions as to whether the same results would hold of a larger sample, but this is currently the largest corpus in existence of Faroese quirky case verbs in non-elicited data. With this model, we did not test the significance of the fixed effects individually, although the confusion matrix indicates that categorising the data in this way enables fairly accurate predictions.

(134) **Logistic regression model 1: Confusion matrix**

	Predicted DAT	Predicted NOM
Actual DAT	51	0
Actual NOM	8	9

---

[5]Definitions taken from http://scikit-learn.org/stable/modules/generated/sklearn.metrics.fbeta_score.html. Accessed 10/25/22.

(135) **Logistic regression model 1: Accuracy measures**

	Precision	Recall	F1 score	Support
DAT	0.86	1.00	0.93	51
NOM	1.00	0.53	0.69	17
Avg./Total	0.90	0.88	0.87	68

Similar results were reproduced with a generalised logistic regression model run in R using *glm2* (Marschner 2011). This model included the fixed effects of Speaker age, Lexeme and Register, with random effects for Speaker and Item. Owing to the small number of tokens, the effects of Speaker age and Register had to be coded as binary for the model to converge (i.e. 'Older vs Younger' and 'High vs Low'). All three of these factors emerged as significant: by far the most significant was Lexeme, where Old Norse origin (*dáma* and *tørva*) was significantly less likely to occur with nominative ($\beta = -8.6$, SE 2.0, $p < 0.01$); interestingly, the Low register was a significantly less likely context for nominative than High ($\beta = -3.8$, SE 1.7, $p = 0.03$); and the age group Younger was significantly more likely to select nominative than Older ($\beta = 3.6$, SE 1.6, $p = 0.02$). This result is somewhat weakened by the collinearity of Lexeme and Register, since it is known that Danish loanwords are more colloquial. The fact that there is a lower likelihood estimate for nominative in the Low register can be explained by relative frequency of the lexemes: the verb *dáma* 'like' occurs with far greater frequency than *mangla* 'lack' (19 tokens of *mangla* versus 75 of *dáma* in the less formal register), which is simply a consequence of 'like' being generally more frequent than 'lack' in personal blogs. Since the 'Old Norse versus Danish origin' factor is by far the most significant, it is actually expected that the higher frequency of 'like' in the informal register will bias the case selection to dative.

This second model also predicted the data with reasonable accuracy:

(136) **Logistic regression model 2: Confusion matrix**

	Predicted DAT	Predicted NOM
Actual DAT	212	2
Actual NOM	17	41

(137) **Logistic regression model 2: Accuracy measures**

	Precision	Recall	F1 score	Support
DAT	0.92	0.99	0.96	214
NOM	0.95	0.70	0.81	58
Avg./Total	0.94	0.85	0.88	272

Thus, it is possible to model case selection using a logistic regression, where the grammar that outputs nominative case is significantly less likely when the verb lexeme is of direct Old Norse stock rather than a recent Danish loan and significantly more likely when the speaker is younger. One major factor not discussed so far is how speakers exploit this case selection to convey social meaning; the following section discusses a Rational Speech Act (RSA) model of how speakers access sociolinguistic knowledge in grammar selection.

5.3 Competing Grammars and Social Meaning

It has been reported in the literature on Faroese that the nominative substitution behaviour in active quirky case verbs may indicate both language change in progress and socio-cultural associations with child speech, colloquial register and anti-purism (Jónsson and Eyþórsson 2005, Petersen 2010, Þráinsson et al. 2012). Here I argue that the best way to approach the sociolinguistic question is to assume that speakers are not making a blind, random selection of one form over another but actually have access to knowledge of style that they are able to manipulate, to some extent, in order to convey social meaning. I do not hereby claim that all sociolinguistic effects of these morphosyntactic variants are conscious or fully under the control of speakers, merely that style shifting gives evidence of sensitivity to social context, even if not entirely volitional. In brief, with respect to social meaning, grammar competition is not reducible to a statistical 'black box'. The dative–nominative variation in Faroese can be seen as an instance of a stereotype in traditional variationist terms (Labov 1972), since it is to some degree known to and commented on by speakers. Nominative substitution, like dative substitution in Icelandic, is a stigmatised variable: speakers are reported to describe it as 'bad Faroese' or 'Danish influence'. However, it is also a variable with indexical value (Silverstein 2003, Eckert 2008): a pertinent example is that of the baby bloggers, in which parents put words in the mouth of their child that convey cuteness and childlikeness. Conscious of register and the indexical field evoked by the variable, these bloggers' use of nominative with quirky case verbs is a stylistic act intended to engage the addressee, what Bell (1984) describes as audience design. The blogger engages in 'initiative shift' by triggering a switch to the non-standard variant when the child is the feigned speaker (Bell 1984:182): they construct a 'child' identity for the speaker as a kind of accommodation to the imagined listener (here, the blog reader).

This style shift can be modelled probabilistically with Bayesian reasoning in a version of the RSA model (Goodman and Frank 2016), as exemplified by Burnett (2017) in her approach to Kiesling's study on the –ING/–IN' variable in English among speakers in a fraternity (Kiesling 1998). Burnett (2017:256–257) formalises the construction of personae or identities as the combining of ideological properties that pattern together, for example {competent, incompetent, casual, delicate, masculine, feminine}; it is assumed that only some combinations of these properties can form personae (e.g. 'competent' and 'incompetent' cannot be indexed simultaneously). Burnett (2017:257) construes the indexical field as equivalent to a set of personae that it is possible to construct with a given variant (Montague 1973, Eckert 2008). The properties associated with the nominative and dative variants are given in (138). We construe 'colloquial, Danish' as elements of a persona that is young, rebellious or anti-purist, internationally minded and more influenced by Denmark and broader European culture than local Faroese culture. By contrast, dative is the unmarked or standard form, and so the indexical properties can be decomposed into elements of seriousness or maturity, a prescriptivist or puristic attitude to language, and a locally or Faroese-oriented mindset over against Danish influence. Nominative also indexes cuteness, as evinced by the use of nominative by baby bloggers; since dative is an elsewhere case with respect to this, we do not construe it as indexing 'non-cuteness' but merely as not indexing cuteness.

(138) Indexical field: Nominative versus dative case

VARIANT	INDEXICAL FIELD
DAT	{mature, purist, Faroe-centric}
NOM	{childish, cute, anti-purist, cosmopolitan}

Let us assume that the set of possible personae generated by these properties contains every possible non-contradictory combination of those indexed by the given variant, for example, a persona defined by {childish, cosmopolitan} can be indexed by use of nominative, but not {Faroe-centric, cosmopolitan} (contradictory) nor {childish, purist} (indexed by different variants). Moreover, let us assume that a persona consists of more than one indexed property, in other words, {purist} is not a persona but {purist, Faroe-centric} is.

Following Burnett (2017:258), it is assumed that the speaker makes a hypothesis about the listener's prior beliefs, which can be represented as a probability distribution over the set of available personae

5.3 Competing Grammars and Social Meaning

Pr. This information may contain assumptions about the individual speaker (e.g. 'Jógvan is young and Danish-influenced') or more general stereotypes (e.g. 'people from Suðuroy are Faroe-centric'). We assign probability weights to the personae based on these hypothesised beliefs:

(139) **Listener prior beliefs:** Jógvan, teenager

Persona	Pr(persona)
{mature}	0.025
{purist}	0.025
{Faroe-centric}	0.025
{mature, purist}	0.0194
{purist, Faroe-centric}	0.0194
{mature, Faroe-centric}	0.0194
{mature, purist, Faroe-centric}	0.0194
{childish}	0.1
{cute}	0.1
{anti-purist}	0.1
{cosmopolitan}	0.2
{childish, cute}	0.05
{childish, anti-purist}	0.05
{childish, cosmopolitan}	0.05
{cute, anti-purist}	0.025
{cute, cosmopolitan}	0.025
{anti-purist, cosmopolitan}	0.05
{childish, cute, anti-purist}	0.0194
{childish, cute, cosmopolitan}	0.0194
{childish, anti-purist, cosmopolitan}	0.0194
{cute, anti-purist, cosmopolitan}	0.0194
{childish, cute, anti-purist, cosmopolitan}	0.0194

Once the listener hears the variant used by the speaker, they adjust their beliefs according to the restricted set of personae available for that variant; for instance, if they hear the dative variant, they assign probability 0 to the persona {childish, cute}. For the speaker's part, we assume following Burnett (2017:259) that there is some utility function for them to use a variant m to construct a given persona P, formalised in (140):

(140) $U_s(P, m) = \ln(Pr(p|m))$

In other words, when the speaker wishes to construct persona P, the utility of them using variant m is the natural log of the probability of P given the indexical fields of m. For example, if we assume that teenager Jógvan wishes to construct an {anti-purist, cosmopolitan} persona, we run the model using the probability distribution in (139), which in this case predicts that he will select the nominative variant with a probability of 1.0 when constructing this persona and the dative variant, also with a probability of 1.0, when constructing the persona {mature, Faroe-centric}. A more complex example would be a blogger writing about Faro–Danish politics: in this case, there would be the conflicting pressure to use standard forms like the dative, represented by a persona {mature, purist}, but there may also be pressure to appear cosmopolitan, for example the persona {anti-purist, cosmopolitan}. One assumes that any persona with the properties {childish} or {cute} would have a very low probability in this context. An example probability distribution for this case is given in (141):

(141) **Listener prior beliefs:** Einar, political blogger

Persona	Pr(persona)
{mature}	0.1
{purist}	0.1
{Faroe-centric}	0.1
{mature, purist}	0.05
{purist, Faroe-centric}	0.05
{mature, Faroe-centric}	0.05
{mature, purist, Faroe-centric}	0.025
{childish}	0.048
{cute}	0.048
{anti-purist}	0.1
{cosmopolitan}	0.1
{childish, cute}	0.048
{childish, anti-purist}	0.01
{childish, cosmopolitan}	0.01
{cute, anti-purist}	0.01
{cute, cosmopolitan}	0.01
{anti-purist, cosmopolitan}	0.025
{childish, cute, anti-purist}	0.005
{childish, cute, cosmopolitan}	0.005
{childish, anti-purist, cosmopolitan}	0.01
{cute, anti-purist, cosmopolitan}	0.048
{childish, cute, anti-purist, cosmopolitan}	0.048

This time the calculation yields a probability of 1.0 for the dative variant when constructing the persona {mature, Faroe-centric} and 1.0 for the nominative when constructing {anti-purist, cosmopolitan}. The reason the probabilities are all 1.0 for this variable comes from an assumption behind Burnett's model that a variant is either compatible or incompatible with a persona. In other words, social meaning is treated as equivalent to descriptive meaning: use of nominative to convey childishness would then be the same as asserting 'I am childish'. However, this is not the only possibility for modelling social meaning, and there may be good reasons to see social meaning as use-conditional (Qing and Cohn-Gordon 2018). The RSA model presented here only concerns social meaning and therefore can only explain the sociolinguistic pressures on the variable, not the grammatical or lexical–semantic pressures: it may be, for example, that the persona {anti-purist, cosmopolitan} is unlikely to be conveyed via nominative case with *tørva* 'need', since this verb strongly favours the dative; in fact, this persona favours the Danish phrasal construction *hava brúk fyri* 'have need of', which is common in colloquial Faroese. Nevertheless, the RSA model provides a way of quantifying when a particular variant is more or less likely to be chosen given socio-pragmatic priors.

5.4 Bimodally Distributed Judgements: Dialects or Noisy Data?

WITH ROB MINA

An important question raised by the competing grammars model is how to distinguish between dialects (i.e. consistent variation across speakers) and uncertainty with respect to acceptability of a sentence, whether or not the latter results from intra-speaker grammar competition or simply unpredictable responses to the stimulus. This point is particularly relevant when examining judgement data that appears diverse. Returning to the first Faroese quirky case survey data repeated in Table 5.1, a number of sentences had a relatively high standard deviation from the mean (<1.5), suggesting clusters of speakers whose judgements contrast.

Histograms showing the distribution of judgements for each sentence are shown in Appendix C1. It emerges that for sentences 1, 6, 10, 12, 13 and 15, one group of respondents had a mean judgement of around 1–2, and another group of around 4–5, as in the example of sentence 10 shown in Figure 5.5. What this demonstrates is substantial *inter-speaker disagreement* over these sentences, as opposed to agreement around a judgement of 'neither particularly acceptable nor unacceptable' or 'I don't know'. This raises the question of whether it is possible to tell whether these groupings are self-consistent across sentences of the same type or whether no such consistent grouping emerges from the data. For the purposes of this discussion, sentences are considered to be of the same 'type' if they exhibit the same syntactic configuration of interest, for example, sentences 10 and 12 in Table 5.1 if we are testing groupings with respect to plain DAT-ACC monotransitives.

122 *Competing Grammars*

Table 5.1 Faroese quirky case verbs: Sentences in survey 1

№	μ	σ	Faroese sentence	Gloss
1	3.7	1.5	฿ ?Mær hevur ikki altíð dámað bókina	Me.DAT has.SG not always liked book-the.ACC
2	1.3	0.9	*Mær hevur bókina ikki altíð dámað	Me.DAT has.SG book-the.ACC not always liked
3	4.5	0.7	Mær hevur ikki altíð dámað hana	Me.DAT has.SG not always liked it.ACC
4	1.2	0.9	*Mær hevur hana ikki altíð dámað	Me.DAT has.SG it not always liked
5	1.3	0.9	*Mær hevur ikki bókina altíð dámað	Me.DAT has.SG not book-the.ACC always liked
6	2.6	1.6	฿ ??Teimum man bókina ikki altíð hava dámað	Them.DAT must.SG book-the.ACC not always have liked
7	1.6	1.2	*Teimum man ikki bókina hava altíð dámað	Them.DAT must.SG not book-the.ACC have always liked
8	1.8	1.2	*Teimum man ikki bókina altíð hava dámað	Them.DAT must.SG not book-the.ACC always have liked
9	1.8	1.2	*Teimum man ikki altíð hava bókina dámað	Them.DAT must.SG not always have book-the.ACC liked
10	3.1	1.9	฿ ?Mær dáma bátarnar	Me.DAT like.PL boats-the.ACC.PL
11	1.7	1.4	*Honum dáma bátarnir	Him.DAT like.PL boats-the.NOM.PL
12	3.6	1.7	฿ ?Okkum dáma bátarnar	Us.DAT like.PL boats-the.ACC.PL
13	2.6	1.6	฿ ??Tykkum dáma bátarnir	You.DAT.PL like.PL boats-the.NOM.PL
14	2.2	1.4	*Okkum tørva bátarnir	Us.DAT need.PL boats-the.NOM.PL
15	3.7	1.6	฿ ?Teimum tørva bátarnar	Them.DAT need.PL boats-the.ACC.PL

Key to judgements: * = mean acceptability < 2.5, ?? = 2.5–3, ? = 3–4, no mark = mean > 4

5.4.1 Bimodal Clustering: Investigating Disagreement in Judgements

co-authored with Rob Mina

If we look at a scatter plot of speaker judgements on these sentences, in which each point represents one judgement by a given speaker, and form groupings determined by the first sentence and apply that grouping to the other results, we see that an informal splitting does not prove conclusive as to whether the groups are self-consistent 'grammars' or random, but it does suggest substantial disagreement. Figure 5.6 shows the sentences with SVO word order, plural verb and plural object, and Figure 5.7 those with sentence-medial adverbs.

It is possible to investigate the question of whether apparent groupings are 'dialects' through a statistical procedure we will call bimodal clustering. This makes use of a statistic known as Krippendorff's

5.4 Bimodally Distributed Judgements 123

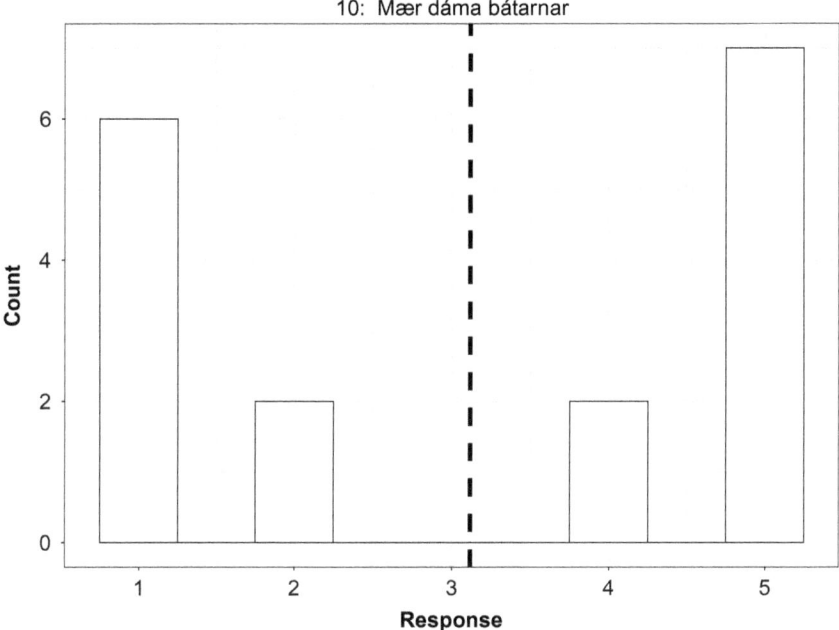

Figure 5.5 Example of a bimodal distribution of judgements

alpha, a measure of inter-rater reliability (Krippendorff 1970, 1978, Hayes and Krippendorff 2007).[6] Essentially, the goal is to test whether two self-consistent subgroups exist within a given sample of speakers. The procedure is as follows: pseudo-data is generated according to the four hypotheses given in (142). A model parameter γ is set which controls the relative size of the accepting vs. rejecting subgroups of the pseudo-data between 0 and 1, where larger values favour the accepting subgroup.

(142) 1. **Normal hypothesis**: the acceptability judgements are distributed normally according to the mean and standard deviation measured from the real data.
2. **One-grammar hypothesis**: all speakers agree on the judgement, which is consistent with the prescriptive norm; if the norm is 'acceptable', the distribution of judgements will be: {rating 5: 75%, rating 4: 25%, all other ratings: 0%}; if the norm is 'unacceptable', the distribution will be: {rating 1: 75%, rating 2: 25%, all other ratings: 0%}.

---

[6]Thanks to Rob Mina, who wrote the C++ and original Python code. The code repository is accessible at gitlab.com/robmina/krippendorff-alpha, accessed 5/8/19.

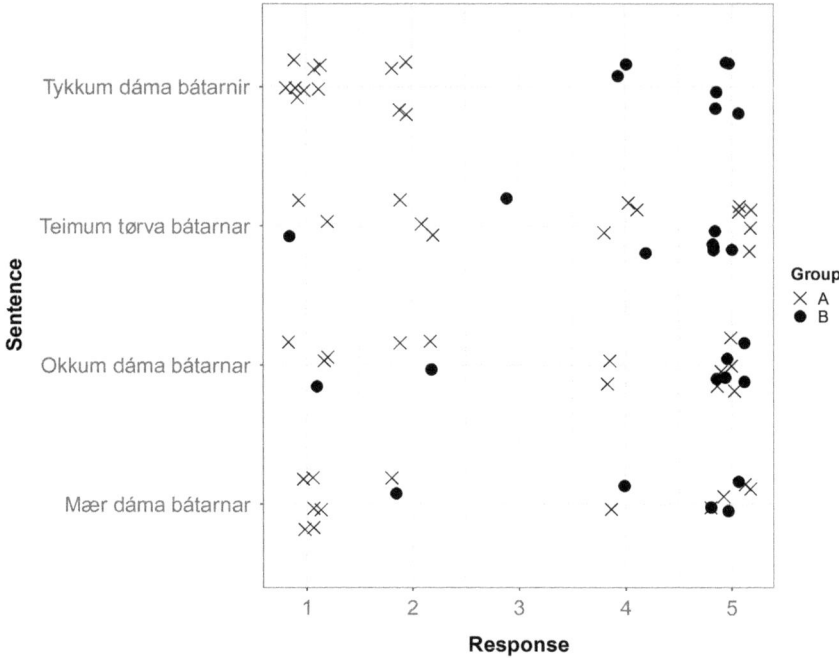

Figure 5.6 Faroese quirky case sentences with SVO word order: Scatter plot of judgements

3. **Two-grammar random hypothesis**: for bimodal sentences of the same type, speakers either accept (with probability $P = \gamma$) or reject ($P = 1 - \gamma$), but not self-consistently within the sentence type (i.e. the same speaker may accept some bimodal sentences while rejecting others).

4. **Two-grammar fixed hypothesis**: for bimodal sentences of the same type, speakers either accept (with probability $P = \gamma$) or reject ($P = 1 - \gamma$), completely self-consistently within the sentence type (i.e. the same speaker will accept or reject all bimodal sentences of that type).

Krippendorff's α is a measure of inter-speaker consistency of judgements within the sample of speakers and sentences. The α score ranges from negative values to +1, where negative values indicate systematic disagreement, 0 indicates statistically unrelated scorings, and +1 indicates perfect agreement. An advantage of using Krippendorff's alpha is that it is possible to calculate even with missing data, in this case non-attested judgements for certain speakers ('NAs'). Another score, which we will call β, measures the improvement in α achieved under

5.4 Bimodally Distributed Judgements

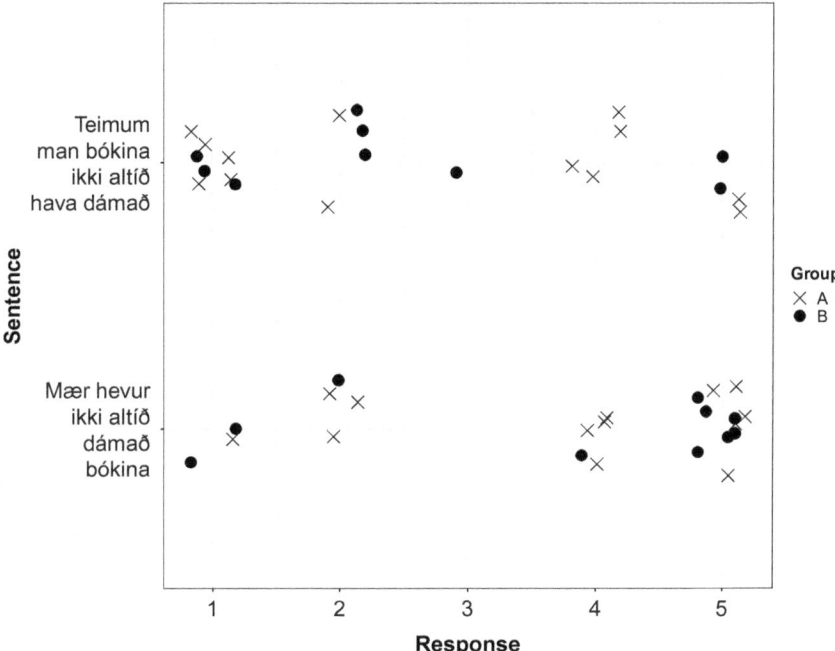

Figure 5.7 Faroese quirky case sentences with medial adverbs: Scatter plot of judgements

the optimal splitting of speakers into two sub-samples. β is calculated as follows: (α split − α unsplit) / (1 − α unsplit). This ensures that the value of β will always be between 0 and 1, even when the unsplit α is close to 1. β is expected to be larger in the case of 'two-grammar fixed', that is, greater cross-speaker agreement is found where two consistent groups actually do exist, when compared to randomness. In this way, we compare the β calculated from the actual data with that of the four hypotheses and thus arrive at an approximate metric for whether the data are more consistent with dialect groupings ('two-grammar fixed') or uncertainty ('two-grammar random').

5.4.1.1 Bimodal Clustering: Faroese Quirky Case Survey 1

This procedure was applied to the bimodal simple monotransitives from the first Faroese quirky case survey. Sentences 10–15 were considered, a total of 6, of which 4 were bimodal, with 23 speakers. Pseudo-data were generated for each of the four hypotheses in (142), and β values calculated for 40,000 trials, where a trial is a splitting of the data into two groups. Table 5.2 shows the values of γ used and the average β calculated under each hypothesis, along with the average β calculated from the real data. Owing to the large number of trials, p-values calculated from a two-tailed t-test will be very sensitive to trivial differences, and so a measure of effect size, Cohen's d is calculated instead (Cohen 1977). Cohen's d measures the difference between the mean of two variables assumed to be Gaussian; the U_3 value indicates non-overlap (i.e. the percentage of the first set of β values exceeded by the upper half of the second set). The sign of d indicates the direction of the effect. In this case, the means are calculated from a normal distribution generated from the actual mean β value ($\sigma = 0.1$), and the β values for the given hypothesis.

Table 5.2 Faroese quirky case survey 1: Bimodal clustering results

Hypothesis	γ	Avg. β	d	U_3
Normal	1.0	0.181	−0.82	0.21
One-grammar	1.0	0.165	−0.94	0.17
Two-grammar random	0.36	0.175	−0.89	0.19
Two-grammar fixed	0.36	0.258	0.18	0.57
Actual data	0.36	0.243		

As Table 5.2 shows, if the data were distributed normally, consistent with a single agreed-upon grammar, or bimodal but with random groupings, the average β generated will be around .08 lower than that of the two-grammar fixed hypothesis. The Cohen's d values are high under the normal, one-grammar and two-grammar random hypotheses, indicating that the differences in mean between these distributions and the actual β are large; for example, the U_3 value for one-grammar indicates that 83% of the set of β values on this hypothesis will be lower than the actual mean. However, the two-grammar fixed hypothesis has a small effect size in the opposite direction, indicating substantial overlap between the two-grammar fixed distribution and a Gaussian distribution generated from the actual mean β. These results can be understood as follows: β is a measure of the improvement in α for a given binary split of the data, where α measures inter-speaker agreement.

Therefore, the average β across thousands of trials of optimal splitting will reflect the likelihood of finding two self-consistent groups under that hypothesis. Hence, a higher average β is expected where greater improvement in agreement is achieved by the split (i.e. where real groupings emerge). As can be seen, while not inconsistent with other hypotheses, the actual data appear to suggest two-grammar fixed is on the right track, that is, it is probable that identifiable groupings of speakers exist. The results are perhaps easier to see in a density plot, shown in Figure 5.8; the solid black line indicates the β calculated from the actual data. The two-grammar fixed distribution peaks at a higher value of β than other hypotheses, and the actual β is closer to the modal value of β under two-grammar fixed than that of the other hypotheses.

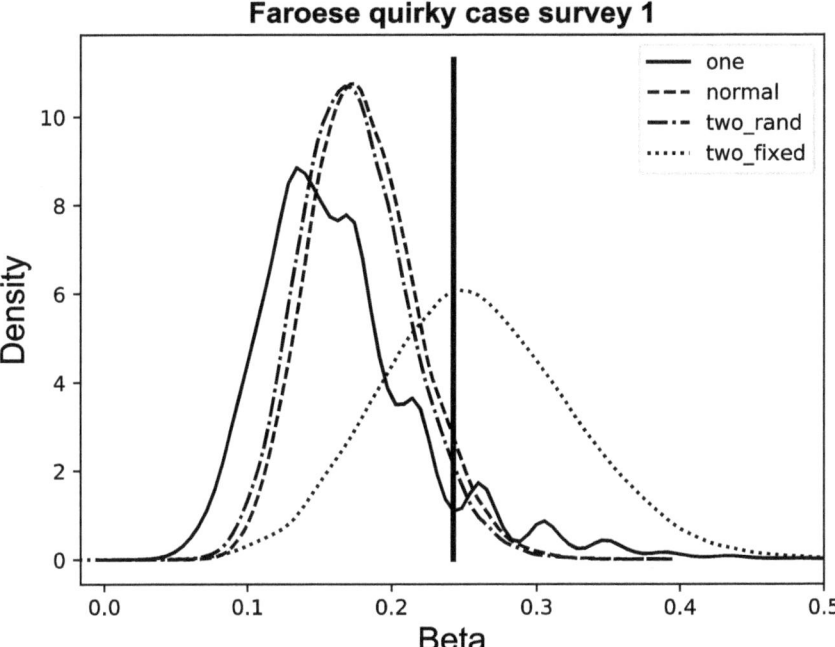

Figure 5.8 Bimodal clustering: Density plot of beta for Faroese sample

The conclusions we may draw are tentative due to the limited number of speakers and sentences, but it is intriguing that the β value calculated from the data suggests a higher probability of the two-grammar fixed hypothesis. In other words, for sentences 10–15 in Table 5.1, there seems to be a group which tends to accept and a group which tends to reject the bimodal sentences across the board (10, 12, 13 and 15) rather than an arbitrary collection of accepting and rejecting speakers per sentence. Since subject number and object case were not controlled for, it is not possible to tell whether the rejecting group judged the bimodal sentences less acceptable due to plural agreement with the subject, object agreement or, in the case of sentence 13, the nominative case on the object. Moreover, we cannot ascertain whether the accepting group considered plural agreement with the subject or object to be more acceptable. Nevertheless, this result certainly invites further investigation with a larger sample. The result does not confirm *intra*-speaker competing grammars in the sense discussed in Section 5.1, since we would have to show that the accepting and rejecting grammars are activated alternately by the same speaker; however, it does point to the existence of *inter*-speaker competing grammars in contemporary Faroese, since groups which pattern together would indicate at least two discrete rankings. By using Krippendorff's α, a measure of inter-rater agreement, we can be confident that the bimodality exists in the speaker groupings, not just the responses: the actual β (i.e. our metric of improvement in α) is most consistent with two groups of speakers whose responses show high agreement within each group, not merely two groups of responses.[7]

5.4.1.2 Bimodal Clustering: Icelandic Quirky Case Survey

The same procedure was run for the pairs of Icelandic sentences {1, 6} and {3, 8} in Table 8 (Appendix B4) in order to test whether the bimodal sentences 1 and 6 showed evidence of a dialect split. Sigurðsson and Holmberg (2008) suggest that sentences of type 1 and 6 (i.e. with singular agreement on the finite verb and a plural nominative object) are acceptable to speakers of 'Icelandic B/C' and unacceptable to speakers of 'Icelandic A'; the B and C dialects are supposed to be distinguishable by whether a plural verb in such contexts is acceptable (B) or not (C). If this held for our sample, we would expect to find subgroups of speakers patterning together in their judgements of sentences 1 and 6 when compared to sentences 3 and 8; group A

---

[7] An additional relevant question is whether speakers also select rankings probabilistically when *interpreting* sentences in a judgement task like this, or whether both are equally accessible. This requires more work, but it is interesting that some of the judgement data in Heycock et al. (2012) suggest competing grammars, a conclusion also consistent with the proposals in Yang (2000, 2002).

would reject 1 and 6 and accept 3 and 8, group B would accept 1 and 6 but reject 3 and 8, and group C would accept all four sentence types. The bimodal clustering procedure will not distinguish a three-way split, but it will give an indication of whether a group of speakers consistently accepts the types with a singular verb and rejects the plural independently of the object being pronominal or phrasal, for example. The same four hypotheses were tested under 40,000 trials, with 4 sentences (2 bimodal) and 16 speakers. Results are shown in Table 5.3:

Table 5.3 Icelandic quirky case survey: Bimodal clustering results

Hypothesis	γ	Avg. β	d	U_3
Normal	1.0	0.227	0.88	0.81
One-grammar	1.0	0.271	1.08	0.86
Two-grammar random	0.5	0.257	1.20	0.89
Two-grammar fixed	0.5	0.313	1.71	0.96
Actual data	0.5	0.153		

Table 5.3 shows quite a different story from the Faroese data. In our Icelandic sample, attempts to find an optimal split result in improved α to a considerably lesser degree than in the Faroese: the β value calculated from the actual Icelandic data is not inconsistent with any of the hypotheses but seems to indicate that two-grammar fixed is less probable due to the lower actual β. Figure 5.9 shows a density plot of the results, in which it can be seen that the actual β falls within the first quartile of the distribution under all four hypotheses (Q1 for normal = 0.182, one = 0.180, two random = 0.206, two fixed = 0.249). The Cohen's d values indicate a large effect size under all four hypotheses (i.e. the actual β differs very strongly from the mean β of the other hypotheses). For example, if one were to pick a random value of β from the two-grammar fixed hypothesis, Cohen's U_3 indicates that it would be larger than the actual β 96% of the time. This suggests that the optimal binary split of the actual data still has substantial disagreement within each subgroup of speakers, indicating there are no straightforwardly discernible dialect groupings in the data, at least with respect to this sample of judgements. Again, further investigation with a larger sample of sentences and speakers would be illuminating; however, this sample at least does not suggest a clear dialect split along

the lines of what Sigurðsson and Holmberg (2008) report. As a reviewer noted, it is also possible that a stronger prescription against using non-historical subject cases is obscuring competing grammars in Icelandic.

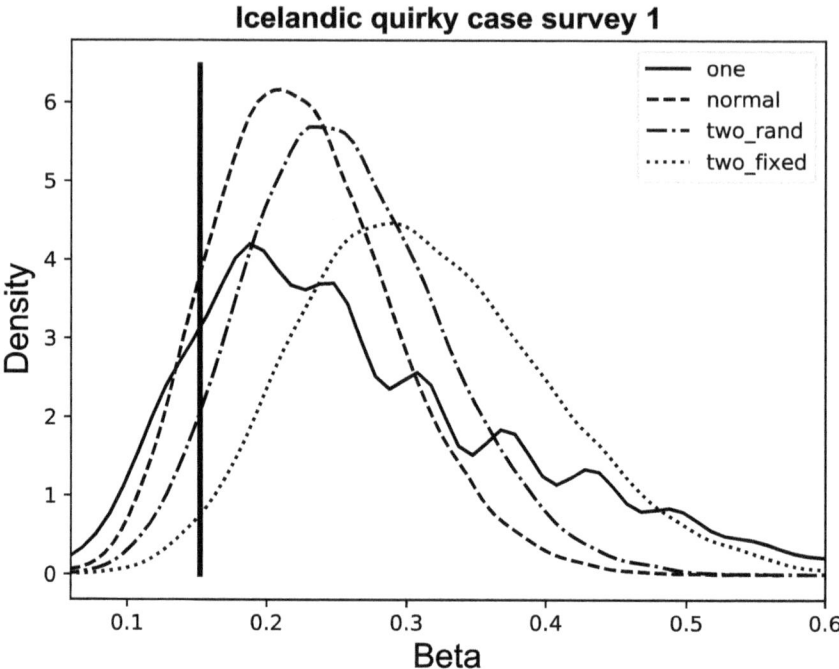

Figure 5.9 Bimodal clustering: Density plot of beta for Icelandic sample

5.4.1.3 Section Summary

To conclude our discussion of bimodal judgement data, it has been demonstrated that the bimodal clustering procedure, using the metric of average improvement in Krippendorff's α inter-rater agreement score, gives some idea of whether or not binary dialect groups exist within a judgement sample, or whether acceptance versus rejection of the bimodal sentences was effectively random. These results should be taken with the caveats that (i) these are small sample sizes, which were selected according to the limitations of the research project (means of distribution, funding, access to consultants, etc.), and (ii) the acceptability judgement task itself only provides one particular kind of window into a speaker's grammar, which inevitably will not correspond exactly to what the researcher ideally wishes to probe. Nevertheless, it is hoped that this procedure constitutes an interesting technique for distinguishing consistent speaker groupings or dialects from randomness. It would certainly be of worth to investigate both (i) the existence of dialect variation in Faroese with respect to plural agreement in dative-subject predicates, since self-consistent groupings are suggested by our data, and (ii) the dialect claims of Sigurðsson and Holmberg (2008) with a larger sample, given that these data do not seem to indicate such a split.

It is also notable that the samples investigated in this section speak only indirectly to the question of competing grammars as defined in OLG. For the Icelandic case it is, of course, plausible that each individual judgement corresponds to a different ranking being activated, but the bimodal clustering procedure does not distinguish between randomly activated competing rankings and a single 'correct' ranking that the uncertainty produced by the judgement task perhaps renders inaccessible. The concept of grammar competition proposed here is rather an attempt to account for discernible, discrete variants or forms, which are winning candidates on specific rankings, and which identifiable grammatical, contextual, processing and/or sociolinguistic factors play some role in determining. Such an account does seem to be appropriate for the Faroese data, since two groups do emerge from the bimodally distributed data. Nonetheless, substantiating evidence for competing grammars is more likely to come from corpora of usage than judgement tasks, since it is unequivocal that a certain ranking is activated when a particular variant is attested in usage, whereas an acceptability judgement neither suffices to predict usage in the positive case nor rules out the existence of a competing ranking accessible to the speaker in other contexts in the negative case.

5.5 Neural Approaches

In recent years, machine learning approaches to computational linguistic problems have exploded in popularity, particularly the use of neural networks (McCulloch and Pitts 1943, Rosenblatt 1957 and subsequent studies). Moreover, connectionist models have produced a considerable body of work in the subfields of acquisition and psycholinguistics, and to some extent in phonology (see Pearl and Goldwater 2016, Christiansen and Chater 2001, Alderete and Tupper 2018 and references in each). However, no doubt in part due to the historical beginnings of the field, these models have not been extensively explored in the theoretical syntax literature. Pater (2019) gives an overview of the development of both generative and neural network approaches to linguistic questions, especially with regards to models of language acquisition. An increasingly debated topic, the perceived usefulness of neural networks in answering theoretical linguistic questions depends to some degree on the researcher's starting assumptions; see, for example, the varying responses to Pater's article (Berent and Marcus 2019, Dunbar 2019, Linzen 2019, Potts 2019). The assumption of OLG from the outset is that fusion rather than friction of these approaches will yield better results, since adopting OT by necessity involves the premise of learned (and possibly weighted) constraint rankings along with symbolic representations. Here we will focus not on the acquisition question but on modelling the selection of competing grammars using neural networks. As already indicated by Figure 5.1 in Section 5.1, we assume that factors contributing to grammar choice are weighted and that the weights can be learned from corpora, as was demonstrated in Section 5.2 using logistic regression. Revisiting the same data, we can achieve similar results using a feed-forward neural network. See Han et al. (2012:398–408) for a straightforward explanation of the mechanics of this approach to classification, and Pater (2019:e43–e46) for a simple description of a neural network model as applied to logical AND versus XOR (exclusive 'or').

Figure 5.10 shows an example architecture of a multi-layer feed-forward neural network, which can be used to approximate a function determining case selection from the given input features. Since the only possible values for subject case with these verbs are dative or nominative, this is a binary classification problem. The network consists of an input layer, one or more hidden layers, and an output layer. The input nodes correspond to features of the training data, in our case the same variables as the logistic regression model in Section 5.2. The output layer represents the classes of interest, in this case the value of the subject case (dative or nominative, which can be represented by 0 or 1). The hidden layer nodes take as input a weighted sum of the outputs of the units from the previous layer; a logistic 'activation' function is applied to these inputs, enabling the model to capture non-linearity. With back-propagation (Werbos 1974), the error calculated at the output layer is fed backwards through the network, and the weights of each connection are adjusted to reduce the error. Since our purpose here is not to give a detailed treatment of neural networks, the reader is referred to Pater (2019) and references therein for further background.

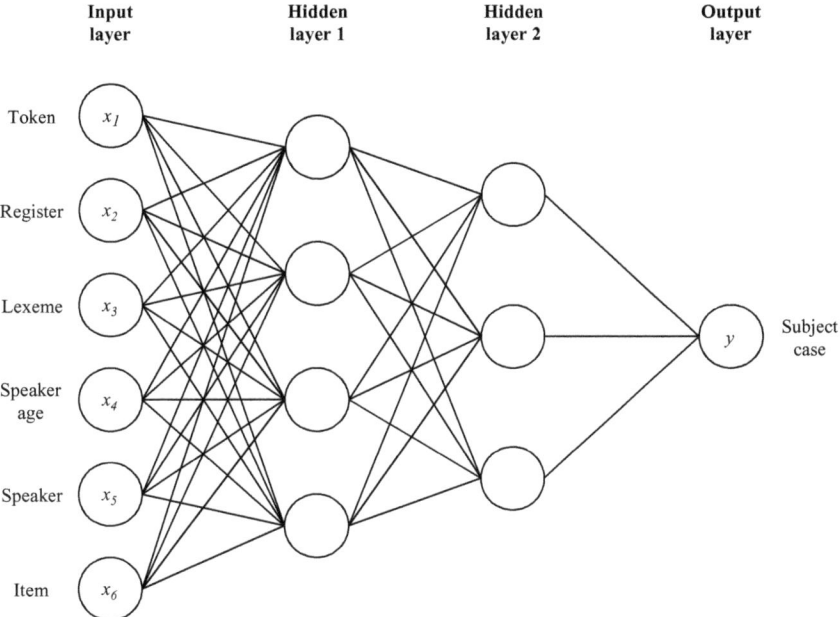

Figure 5.10 Competing grammars: Deep neural network for binary classification

Using the Python packages *keras* and *scikit-learn* (Pedregosa et al. 2011, Chollet 2015), the model was run on the same data discussed in Section 5.2, with the same input features. The features were encoded as one-hot vectors, where each category receives a value of 1 or 0 corresponding to true or false (e.g. a value of 1 for *Lexeme_Old_Norse* indicates the training example was coded as being of Old Norse origin). The input layer had a total of 48 nodes as a result of one-hot encoding. Two hidden layers were used, the first with 32 and the second with 12 nodes. The output layer consisted of two nodes, one for each output class, also one-hot encoded, with a softmax function (the same results could be achieved with a single output node, since the classification is binary). The data were randomly split into training and test sets, with a training set size of 136 tokens (75%) and test set of 68 tokens

(25%), a total of 272 tokens. Model fitting was automatically computed across 10 epochs, with 33% of the training data held aside for cross-validation, a different set for each epoch. The final validation loss was 0.33 (max 0.53, μ = 0.40, σ = 0.06), with a final validation accuracy of 0.91. The final accuracy of predicted case labels on the test set was 98.53%, an improvement over both logistic regression models (by about 8% and 4% points, respectively). The table in (143) shows the accuracy measures of the neural model:

(143) **Neural network model, 75%/25% training/test split: Accuracy measures**

	Precision	Recall	F1 score	Support
DAT	0.98	1.00	0.99	57
NOM	1.00	0.91	0.95	11
Micro avg.	0.99	0.99	0.99	68
Macro avg.	0.99	0.95	0.97	68
Weighted avg.	0.99	0.99	0.99	68

As can be seen, a neural network approach is able to achieve very high accuracy in such a classification task. It is very easy for the model to overfit with a small number of training examples. In fact, even if we train this network on only 25% of the data and leave aside 75% for testing, the results are still comparable to logistic regression, as shown in (144):

(144) **Neural network model, 25%/75% training/test split: Accuracy measures**

	Precision	Recall	F1 score	Support
DAT	0.92	1.00	0.96	165
NOM	1.00	0.62	0.76	39
Micro avg.	0.93	0.93	0.93	204
Macro avg.	0.96	0.81	0.86	204
Weighted avg.	0.93	0.93	0.92	204

Despite the absence of a larger corpus, it has at least been shown that even when the training set is a small portion of the whole, the neural approach yields high accuracy. Therefore, deep learning is a very powerful tool for approximating complex functions, such as those which produce case variation. However, the approach raises the crucial question of interpretability: while we may know that the model is learning optimised weights for the different factors determining case selection, it is not obvious how to match the highly-weighted connections between neurons to symbolic representations, for example, the precise interaction of factors that an important hidden node represents. This issue is discussed at length by Dunbar (2019), who describes it as an 'implementational mapping problem': how can representations be identified from neural network architecture?

5.5 Neural Approaches

Dunbar's challenge is articulated as follows (Dunbar 2019:e88):

> Before we can validate an abstract theory of how the system might work, we need some systematic theory of how the abstract elements and operations map to the physical implementation. Equally, if we wish to simulate learning of generative grammars with neural networks as 'hardware', particularly in the case where we do not force the networks to learn specific kinds of representations, we need some system for linking an abstract formal theory to the networks' representations. This implies making the formal theory explicit—and noting which elements of it are there to describe HOW the system does its work, rather than just characterizing WHAT it does—and then articulating HOW WE WOULD RECOGNIZE what the network is doing.

This is relevant both to the competing grammars hypothesis and to the weighted constraints of OT approaches such as MaxEnt (Goldwater and Johnson 2003). Dunbar points to various threads of literature beginning to attempt to answer this question, for example Mikolov et al. (2013), who showed that a representation of the word *king* related geometrically to that of *queen* as *man* to *woman* and argued that this implicitly encoded a semantic feature. Disentangling this problem is well beyond the scope of this book, but it is important to note that regardless of the theoretical opacity of the hidden layers, it is quite possible to restrict the input features considerably, as shown in this section. Although the precise interactions of features are not immediately apparent, some techniques have been developed to extract rules from a network (see Han et al. 2012:406–408). Network pruning, for instance, involves deleting low-impact weighted links, provided accuracy is not drastically reduced; thus important weights can be identified. Clustering algorithms can then be used to form IF-THEN statements relating input, activation and output values, such that interpretable rules can be formulated (e.g. 'IF input node 3 = 1 AND input node 7 = 0 THEN output class = 1'). While it may be the case that such methods are less useful for extracting rules from very deep networks with many hidden layers, they *can* be used when the problem is sufficiently restricted, as is the case for micro-level syntactic variation (in contrast to Dunbar 2019:94): if the researcher already has a relatively well-formed idea of which particular grammatical and/or sociolinguistic factors are relevant, these can be tested via a series of neural networks with minimally changed input features. For instance, in the Faroese nominative substitution phenomenon, other grammatical features such as tense, position of the subject or other clause-structural elements could be added or removed as input nodes. Moreover, the claim of OLG presented here is not that constraint rankings themselves are weighted but that *triggering* of a particular, discrete ranking for a given token is subject to an interaction of both internal and external factors. Hence, it may well prove fruitful to investigate the use of rule extraction to arrive at a symbolic representation of such interactions, to the extent possible – an exciting avenue for future research.

5.6 Summary of Chapter

To conclude, this chapter presented an overview of the competing grammars component of OLG. In order to account for the observed variation in Faroese subject case with the relevant verbs, it was argued that Faroese speakers have access to two competing grammars, with a different ranking of the pair {SUBJ[+HR], MAX[LC]}, that is, one constraint enforcing realisation of lexical case and another ensuring that a nominative subject occurs in Spec,TP. The same constraint, MAX[LC], conflicts with other constraints enforcing structural case, such as MAX[-HR], to derive the possibility or impossibility of lexical object case. It was proposed that the Faroese competing grammars can be modelled probabilistically: they are discrete in the sense that only one winning output candidate exists for a given input per grammar, but each grammar may be more or less likely to be activated contextually, assuming some relevant grammatical and extra-grammatical factors. A simple explicit model of this was presented, first by performing a logistic regression on data taken from the Faroese blog corpus. Moreover, the influence of sociolinguistic factors was discussed in relation to case selection, and it was shown that an RSA model can capture this dimension of meaning in an explicit way. A procedure was discussed for distinguishing dialect splits from uncertainty in acceptability judgement data; it was concluded that the Faroese data did suggest such a split, in contrast to the Icelandic data, which were not indicative of self-consistent dialect groupings (with appropriate caveats regarding the limitations of the procedure and datasets). Finally, neural network approaches were brought to bear on linguistic questions such as the morphosyntactic variation represented by Faroese nominative substitution; I showed that a deep neural network is able to achieve higher accuracy with the same data used for the simpler logistic regression models. The competing grammars hypothesis, therefore, offers an empirically sound model for exploring other morphosyntactic phenomena, especially in tandem with the impressive array of computational techniques now available.

6

Faroese Passive

6.1 Introduction

In order to test the OLG hypothesis with respect to case-marking in Icelandic and Faroese, it is necessary to investigate several sentence types beyond the simple monotransitive. The passive is particularly relevant since passivisation has been used as a diagnostic for lexical versus structural case (Zaenen et al. 1985). The notion of 'case preservation', defined by the same case on the object of the active surfacing on the subject of the passive, is important for our data since, if the accusative-marked object of the Faroese quirky case verbs bears lexical case, we expect it to 'preserve'; that is, the subject of the passive should also be accusative. Moreover, there turns out to be a relation between nominative substitution in the Faroese dative-subject verbs and case non-preservation in dative-object verbs, also connected to the Icelandic 'dative sickness' (Svavarsdóttir 1982 and subsequent studies). In this chapter, data are presented from surveys conducted on the Faroe Islands, along with an OLG analysis that accounts for the patterns observed in the Faroese data and explains both typological and intra-linguistic variation.

6.2 Survey Data

Þráinsson et al. (2012:69–70, 265–277) provide some basic information about the passive in Faroese:

- the agent is 'more frequently left out than in English' but can 'often be mentioned in a prepositional phrase with *av*, "by"';

- dative case on an object of a monotransitive is 'sometimes "preserved" in the corresponding passive subject', for example, with the verbs *takka* 'thank' and *trúgva* 'believe', but not with other verbs like *hjálpa* 'help' or *bjóða* 'invite';

- impersonal passive 'can be formed with certain intransitive verbs such as *dansa* "dance", *syngja* "sing"', as well as with 'optionally transitive' verbs whose objects can be left out, such as *eta* 'eat', *drekka* 'drink'.

At the time of writing, no other work exists on the Faroese passive; therefore, many questions remain regarding the agent phrase, case preservation and impersonal passive. To investigate further, two acceptability judgement surveys were conducted on the Faroe Islands asking participants to rate various kinds of passive sentences. In one survey, the sentences included an agent PP with *av* 'by'; in the other, this phrase was absent.

6.2.1 Faroese Passive Survey 1: No Agent Phrase

6.2.1.1 Participants

Forty-two participants were recruited using a link to a Qualtrics survey posted in the Faroese-language Facebook group *Føroysk rættstaving*;[1] no compensation was offered for participation. Twenty-two of the participants fully completed the survey; the remaining 20 gave partial responses. All participants were required to declare that Faroese is their native language before taking part in the survey, and 21 participants voluntarily provided demographic information; of this subset, 7 were male and 14 female, with a mean age of 41.6 years ($\sigma = 13.2$ years, range 25–67); 11 were from towns in *norðanfjørðs* (Northern dialect region), 7 were from Tórshavn or the area surrounding the capital and 3 were from Suðuroy.

---

[1] A discussion group on Faroese grammar and linguistic topics, which can be found at www.facebook.com/groups/185932738087033/, accessed 4/2/18. At the time of writing, the group had approximately 13,000 members.

6.2.1.2 Materials

Participants were asked to provide judgements on 25 sentences. The order of the target sentences presented for judgement was randomised and interspersed with filler sentences whose judgements were known prior to the survey. The stimuli sentences are listed in Appendix B1. Table 6.1 shows the verbs tested; both the *verða* and *blíva* auxiliaries were included, although not for every verb. A variety of argument structures were tested with respect to transitivity, for example, verbs which obligatorily take an object, such as 'hit', impersonal passives of obligatorily objectless verbs like 'dance' (excluding cognate objects) and ambitransitive verbs like 'eat'.

Table 6.1 Faroese passive sentences

No.	Verb	English	Aux.	Subject	Argument structure
1	elska	love	verða	PRON.3SG.F.NOM	SUBJ-VERB, no complement phrase
2	síggja	see	blíva	PRON.3SG.M.NOM	SUBJ-VERB, no complement phrase
3	eta	eat	verða	bread-the.NOM	SUBJ-VERB, no complement phrase
4	gloyma	forget	blíva	PRON.3SG.F.NOM	SUBJ-VERB, no complement phrase
5	mála	paint	verða	wall-the.NOM	SUBJ-VERB, no complement phrase
6	sláa	hit	blíva	PRON.3SG.M.NOM	SUBJ-VERB, no complement phrase
7	sparka	kick	verða	PRON.3SG.F.NOM	SUBJ-VERB, no complement phrase
8	eygleiða	watch	blíva	PRON.3SG.F.NOM	SUBJ-VERB, no complement phrase
9	lesa	read	verða	book-the.NOM	SUBJ-VERB, no complement phrase
10	dansa	dance	verða	impersonal	*har* expletive + temporal phrase
11	syngja	sing	blíva	impersonal	*har* expletive + locative phrase
12	drekka	drink	verða	impersonal	*har* expletive + locative phrase
13	eta	eat	blíva	impersonal	*har* expletive + locative phrase
14	mála	paint	verða	impersonal	*har* expletive + locative phrase
15	sláa	hit	blíva	impersonal	*har* expletive, no complement phrase
16	sparka	kick	verða	impersonal	*har* expletive, no complement phrase
17	lesa	read	blíva	impersonal	*har* expletive, no complement phrase

6.2.1.3 Procedure

The procedure was identical to that of the survey in which quirky case sentences were tested, laid out in Section 4.3.1.3.

6.2.1.4 Results

In Figure 6.1, mean acceptability is plotted against verb item, in addition to whether the passive was personal or impersonal (i.e. whether the expletive *har* is present).[2] As is evident, relatively high mean acceptability was elicited for the personal passives, all of which had a mean above 4 on the five-point scale. Impersonal passives were less consistently accepted, though that of 'dance' had a mean acceptability over 4. Less certainty was expressed for judgements of impersonal passives with 'eat', 'kick', 'paint', 'read' and 'sing', with 'hit' as the only verb consistently judged as completely unacceptable in the impersonal construction. In all cases, the personal passive of a given verb was judged on average more acceptable than the impersonal passive of the same verb, but in the case of 'read' and perhaps also 'kick', the difference looks to be insignificant.

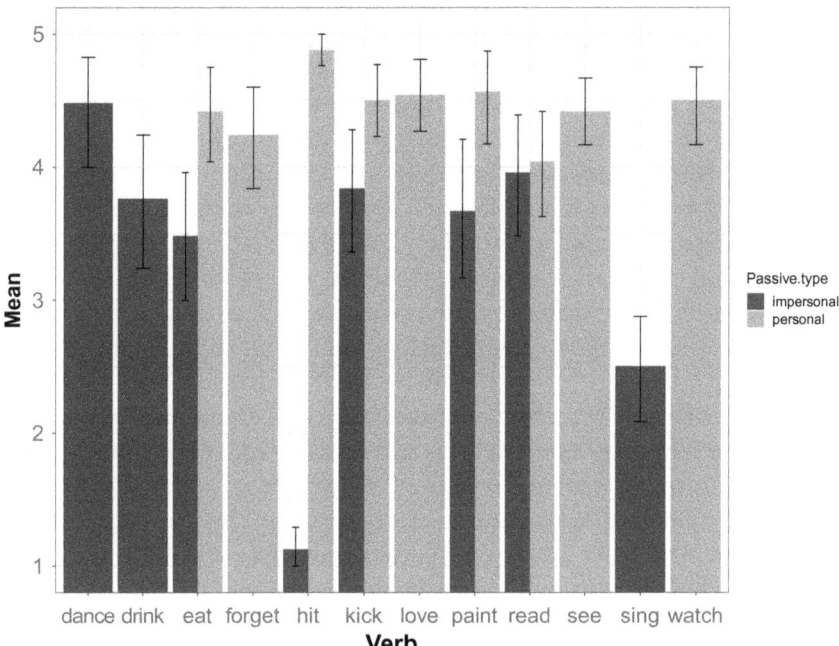

Figure 6.1 Faroese passive survey 1: Mean acceptability by verb and passive type

Ordered logit regression models were run using R and *ordinal* (Christensen 2018). Random intercepts were included for Speaker and Item. It does not make sense to test the fixed effect of verbs without

---

[2] I chose the expletive *har* 'there' instead of *tað* 'it' to avoid the confound with referential 'it'.

also considering passive type since it is quite evident that passive type interacts with verb choice, most evident in Figure 6.1 with 'hit'. Therefore, the following model was run on the subset of judgement data for verbs tested in both personal and impersonal passives ('eat', 'hit', 'kick', 'paint' and 'read'):

Response ~ Verb * Passive type + (1 | Speaker) + (1 | Item)

Taking the verb 'eat' as intercept, the verb choice of 'hit' was significant by itself ($\beta = -6.3$, $p < 0.01$). There were significant interactions with 'hit' in the personal passive ($\beta = 8.7$, $p < 0.01$) and 'read' in the personal passive ($\beta = -1.8$, $p < 0.03$): compared to the difference in mean acceptability of 'eat' in the personal versus impersonal, 'hit' was judged very significantly better in the personal than impersonal, while with 'read' the difference is significantly less. The fixed effect of passive type by itself was also significant in the subset of data with both types of passive, in that personal passive was judged significantly better than impersonal across the board ($\beta = 2.2$, $p < 0.01$). Furthermore, considering only the fixed effect of verb choice with the subset that excludes personal passive (only the verbs 'dance', 'drink' and 'sing'), it emerges that verb choice significantly affects acceptability of the impersonal passive: with 'dance' as intercept, 'sing' was judged extremely significantly worse ($\beta = -3.8$, $p < 0.01$) and 'drink' significantly worse ($\beta = -1.7$, $p = 0.01$).

In order to test the effects of auxiliary choice and animacy of the subject, the same type of model was run on different subsets of the data. Looking only at judgements for those verbs which were tested with both auxiliaries ('eat' and 'read'), the auxiliary *verða* emerged as significantly better than *blíva* ($\beta = 2.2$, $p < 0.01$), but there was also an interaction with verb choice: 'read' with *verða* improves the mean judgement over 'read' with *blíva* significantly less than is the case for 'eat' ($\beta = -2.0$, $p = 0.02$). As for animacy of the subject, the model was run only on those verbs whose subjects were present in the syntax ('eat', 'forget', 'hit', 'kick', 'love', 'paint', 'read', 'see' and 'watch'); that is, excluding impersonal passives, since although a human agent is presupposed with impersonal passives, a clearer contrast is present between the passives with overt subjects ('he was kicked', etc.). Animacy of the subject of the passive by itself did emerge as significant ($\beta = 0.4$, $p < 0.01$), though there were no data in this survey for the same verb with both animate and inanimate subjects.

6.2.1.5 Discussion

We may thus conclude from this passive survey that:

- impersonal passives were judged across the board as less acceptable in Faroese than personal passives;

- verb choice (i) interacts with passive type, such that the improvement in mean acceptability of the personal over impersonal passive differs by verb, and (ii) has a significant effect on acceptability of the impersonal when considered alone, particularly in the case of 'sing', which does not seem to permit the construction;

- the auxiliary *verða* has some effect on acceptability of the passive, though this may differ by verb;

- animacy of the subject of the passive did have a global effect on acceptability across all verbs, but interactions with verb choice or other factors were not tested.

Therefore, we ought to bear in mind the fact that although impersonal passives are acceptable in Faroese, their acceptability depends on the semantics of the verb. This suggests an analysis in which a constraint interaction allows the marked construction to occur, but its availability is determined by the lexical item – a similar phenomenon to case preservation, given that certain verbs seem to preserve case while others do not within the same language. As will be argued in Section 6.3, this may still be modelled by competing grammars, but in this scenario, the probability of the grammar permitting the construction is significantly more likely when the lexical item permitting it is present in the input. In other words, the competing grammars model for impersonal passives and case preservation may have a more significant fixed effect of lexeme than the model for nominative substitution in quirky case verbs, but the underlying constraint interaction may be the same.

6.2.2 Faroese Survey 2: Passives with Agent Phrase; Sentences with *tróta*

6.2.2.1 Participants

Thirty-seven participants were recruited using a link to a Qualtrics survey posted in the Faroese-language Facebook group *Føroysk rættstaving*;

no compensation was offered for participation. Fifteen of the participants fully completed the survey; the remaining 22 gave partial responses. All participants were required to declare that Faroese is their native language before taking part in the survey. The 15 participants who fully completed the survey voluntarily provided demographic information; of this subset, 6 were male, 8 female and 1 withheld their gender. The mean age was 43.4 years ($\sigma = 13.5$ years, range 21–60). Ten participants were from Tórshavn or the area surrounding the capital, 4 were from the northern region, and 1 from Suðuroy.

6.2.2.2 Materials

Participants were asked to provide judgements on 45 sentences. The order of the target sentences presented for judgement was randomised and interspersed with filler sentences whose judgements were known prior to the survey. The stimuli sentences are listed in Appendix B2. The verbs tested were the same as in the survey described in Section 6.2.1, with the addition of a 'by'-phrase headed by the preposition *av*, which overtly expresses an agent. Within the same survey, 16 active sentences were also tested with the verb *tróta* 'exhaust, run out of', which has been reported to occur with nominative objects (see Section 8.3 for discussion).

6.2.2.3 Procedure

The procedure was identical to that of the first Faroese passive survey, described in Section 6.2.1.3.

6.2.2.4 Results

Figure 6.2 shows mean acceptability plotted against verb and passive type. Again, ordered logit regression models were run in R using *ordinal*; as in the first survey, random intercepts were included for Speaker and Item. Results for the verb 'eat' were excluded from the model since one respondent commented: '*Har bleiv etið av øllum* does not mean that everyone ate, but that people ate all kinds of things.'[3]

Response ~ Verb * Passive type + (1 | Speaker) + (1 | Item)

---

[3] The availability of this interpretation could also be responsible for pushing the mean acceptability of the 'drink' impersonal passive above 3.

Considering the subset of verbs with data for both passive types, taking 'hit' as intercept, the fixed effect of the verb by itself was found to be significant in the case of 'paint' ($\beta = 2.1$, $p < 0.01$) and 'read' ($\beta = 2.0$, $p < 0.01$), both of which were judged better than 'hit' on average. Similarly to the first survey, personal passive was judged significantly better than impersonal across the board ($\beta = 5.0$, $p < 0.01$). However, there was also an interaction with 'paint' and the personal ($\beta = -3.4$, $p < 0.01$) as well as 'read' and the personal ($\beta = -5.0$, $p < 0.01$): the personal passive improved the mean judgement of 'hit' significantly more than it did with 'paint' or 'read'.

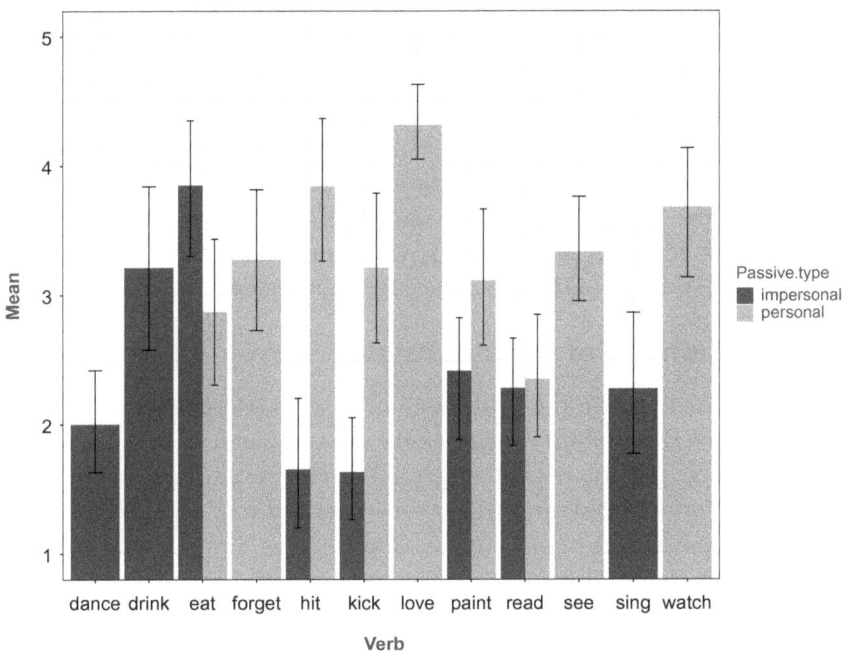

Figure 6.2 Faroese passive survey 2: Mean acceptability by verb and passive type

It was not possible to test the effect of auxiliary choice for this survey since the only usable data were for the verb 'read', and so interactions with main verb choice could not be tested. Interestingly, unlike the first survey, subject animacy did emerge as significant ($\beta = 2.6$, $p < 0.01$), with animate subjects judged better on average than inanimates. Again, however, it was not possible to test the interaction with verb choice since there were no comparable data for the same verb tested with both animate and inanimate overt subjects.

6.2.2.5 Discussion

These results show that with the addition of the agent phrase, even straightforward passives of monotransitives were never unequivocally accepted by these speakers. However, it is evident from Figure 6.2 that acceptability again depends a lot on the individual verb: 'love' is the only verb whose mean acceptability reaches above 4, while that of 'dance' does not reach above 2. Moreover, the impersonal passive was judged worse than the personal across the board but interacts with verb choice; the higher rating of 'eat' and 'drink' can be attributed to the confound with the 'all types' interpretation. Hence, this survey confirms the dependence of acceptability of the Faroese passive on verb lexeme and whether the construction is impersonal or personal, as well as the interdependence of these two factors. This survey did not shed any light on auxiliary choice, and although subject animacy had a significant effect on acceptability, we cannot draw firm conclusions since the interaction with verb choice was not tested.

6.2.3 Summary of Faroese Passive Survey Results

To summarise these findings, these small surveys on passives in Faroese revealed that acceptability judgements are significantly influenced by (i) verb choice; (ii) presence of an expletive, that is, whether the passive is personal/impersonal; and (iii) presence/absence of an agent phrase. Moreover, the factors of verb choice and personal/impersonal passive are strongly interrelated since only certain verbs admit impersonal passives, which is largely determined by the semantics of the verb lexeme. Our theory must therefore be able to handle the fact that the availability of passive is verb-specific, and even more so for the impersonal passive. In Section 6.3, an OLG analysis of the passive is presented, also dealing with the issue of case preservation.

6.3 OLG Analysis

The approach to passives adopted here is a version of that posited by Kiparsky (2013). The basic assumptions underlying linking theory are discussed in Chapter 3. Passivisation is construed as an invariant operation triggered by a passive morpheme contained in the input and operates on the basic argument structure at the level of Semantic Form. Passive is a valency-reducing operation that demotes (i.e. existentially binds) the highest non-demoted theta-role. The input for passivising a ditransitive would therefore be as in (145):

(145) gav + Passive: $\lambda z \lambda y \exists x$ [x CAUSE [BECOME [y HAVE z]]]

As discussed in Section 7.3, promoting the theme to subject in a passive will incur a violation of Max[−hr] since the abstract case [−hr] will not be realised in morphosyntax, either by the position or item which both bear [+hr]. As passivisation is demotion of the highest theta-role on this account, impersonal passive consists of valency reduction on a predicate with only one theta-role. The demoted role from the active is present in the passive argument structure with a default interpretation of [+human], unless otherwise specified in a 'by'-phrase. We can already account for the passive facts with the constraints proposed thus far, with the addition of Parse, a constraint that rules out null output; that is, the input must be realised. This ensures that marked diatheses like passive do not always lose to the corresponding active or null candidate, which otherwise would harmonically bound the passive candidate. It is assumed that null output does not violate faithfulness constraints like Max and MatchCase since there is no output to which to map. The requisite constraints are shown in (146–147):

(146) ArgSP: Assign a violation if no argument occupies subject position (Spec,TP).

(147) Subj[+hr] (S[+hr]): Assign a violation for each subject position (Spec,TP) not occupied by a nominative argument.

(148) Dep: Assign a violation for each item present in the output that is not present in the input.

(149) Parse: Assign a violation for a null parse of the input (i.e. if the output is zero).

(150) MatchCase (MC): Assign a violation for each positional case feature matrix $F[vals_{pos}]$ that is not identical to its corresponding item case feature matrix $F[vals_{item}]$.

(151) Max[LexCase] (Max[LC]): Assign a violation for each lexical case feature on an argument at the level of abstract case that does not correspond to the same lexical feature value on an argument at the level of morphosyntactic case.

Since we already have the ranking for actives in Faroese, we need only hypothesise a ranking for Parse with respect to the other constraints. The three constraints ArgSP » {Dep, Parse} are sufficient to account for the Faroese examples without lexical case; the ranking PARSE » DEP generates the impersonal passive, and DEP » PARSE rules it out. Either ranking yields the correct monotransitive passive. These different rankings are, in a similar manner to the nominative substitution facts with dative-subject verbs, two grammars that compete. However, unlike nominative substitution, the choice of grammar here depends far more on the verb semantics than on contextual or sociolinguistic factors. This can still be modelled probabilistically, but the lexical factor will be of far greater significance here. This is *not* the same as positing a lexeme-specific ranking (in contrast to Pater 2000) since the claim is that speakers still have access to the 'wrong' ranking: it is merely statistically highly improbable that they will select this ranking since the choice of verb is a highly significant fixed effect.

(152) **Intransitive passive: Impossible**

$\lambda e \exists x\, V_{PASS}$: *verða sungið* 'be sung'	ArgSP	Dep	Parse
a. V_{PASS} : *Varð sungið*	*!		
b. Expl V_{PASS} : *Tað varð sungið*		*!	
☞ c. ∅			*

(153) **Intransitive passive: Possible**

$\lambda e \exists x\, V_{PASS}$: *verða dansað* 'be danced'	ArgSP	Parse	Dep
a. V_{PASS} : *Varð dansað*	*!		
☞ b. Expl V_{PASS} : *Tað varð dansað*			*
c. ∅		*!	

(154) **Monotransitive passive**

$\lambda e \lambda y \exists x\, V_{PASS}$: *blíva sligin* 'be hit'	ArgSP	Parse	Dep
a. V_{PASS} DP_y : *Bleiv sligin hann*	*!		
☞ b. DP_y V_{PASS} : *Hann bleiv sligin*			
c. Expl V_{PASS} DP_y : *Tað bleiv sligin hann*			*!
d. ∅		*!	

Therefore, the model already adopted can straightforwardly be brought to bear on the issue of the impersonal passive. The principle is the same as that proposed to account for null expletives and nominative substitution, albeit with respect to a different pair of constraints, in this case {PARSE, DEP}. The only difference between how the nominative substitution phenomenon and the impersonal passive are modelled is the relative importance of the verb lexeme factor: it is assumed that analogous pragmatic, stylistic and sociolinguistic information is accessible to speakers in both instances. However, the grammatical factor is different in these two phenomena: nominative substitution relates to the expression of lexically marked case, while impersonal passive relates to whether or not a monadic verb can undergo argument demotion and a dummy subject be inserted. A more illustrative contrast would be that of case preservation in the passive: in both nominative substitution with dative-subject verbs and non-preservation of case with passivised dative-object verbs, realisation of lexical case conflicts with realisation of abstract case. As argued in the next section, however, case preservation has a more significant lexical-semantic factor than does nominative substitution. Thus, a similar case-substitution behaviour may be explained by the same model of grammar competition, but with different weight assigned to the relevant variables.

6.4 Case Preservation and 'Dative Sickness'

As noted by Þráinsson et al. (2012:267ff), some dative-object verbs in Faroese preserve lexical case on the subject of the passive, such as *takka* 'thank', while others do not, like *hjálpa* 'help', replacing the dative with nominative and triggering full agreement with the participle (155–156).

(155) a. Far. *Teir   takkaðu   honum.*
            they.NOM.M thanked.PL him.DAT
            'They thanked him.'
      b. Far. ***Honum*** *varð   takkað.*
            him.DAT was.SG thanked.SUP
            'He was thanked.'
      c. Far. * *Hann   varð   takkaður.*
            he.NOM was.SG thanked.NOM.M.SG

(156) a. Far. *Tær   hjálptu   okkum.*
            they.NOM.F helped.PL us.DAT
            'They helped us.'
      b. Far. ***Vit*** *blivu   hjálptir.*
            we.NOM were.PL helped.NOM.M.PL
            'We were helped.'
      c. Far. * *Okkum bleiv   hjálpt.*
            us.DAT was.SG helped.SUP

Þráinsson et al. (2012:267–268) list the following verbs as case-preserving or non-preserving:

Preserving	Non-preserving
bíða '(a)wait'	*bjarga* 'save'
dugna 'help'	*bjóða* 'invite'
takka 'thank'	*heilsa* 'greet'
trúgva 'believe'	*hindra* 'hinder'
	mjólka 'milk'
	rósa 'praise'
	steðga 'stop'

It is striking that only four verbs are listed as having dative subjects in the passive, though in the case of *takka* 'thank' and *trúgva* 'believe', they are very high-frequency verbs. By contrast, *dugna* 'help' is uncommon (not a single token of this verb occurs in the blog corpus), and *bíða* is more frequently used as a phrasal verb, *bíða eftir* 'wait for'. Therefore, it seems that as a system, Faroese has lost case preservation in the passive apart from with the two lexemes *takka* and *trúgva*, in some sense a remnant of the older Icelandic-type pattern. It is also important to note that some verbs in Faroese optionally take dative or accusative objects. Since accusative is an option for object case on such verbs, we cannot determine whether the dative is preserving or non-preserving with respect to passivisation, but the possibility of accusative seems to suggest this is an analogous case substitution to nominative substitution on dative subjects. Verbs of this type given by Þráinsson et al. (2012:260) are: *floyta* 'float, set afloat', *lyfta* 'lift', *lætta* 'lift, raise', *reiggja* 'wave, brandish', *tarna* 'delay' and *vika* 'move, budge'. The authors note that these are all verbs of movement, and in some instances there is a subtle semantic distinction between accusative and dative objects with these verbs.

How, then, to disentangle these case substitution facts? It is clear that dative-object verbs are not a homogeneous set since case may be preserved/not preserved on the passive subject and the object case is substitutable/not substitutable by accusative in the active, which may or may not convey a semantic distinction. The lexical semantics of the individual verb appear to play a large role in the case frame that surfaces, whether in the active or passive. Further work is required to establish the semantic factors relevant to case selection, a task beyond the scope of this book. However, the competing grammars model proposed thus far is versatile enough to account for both types of case substitution: that which is broadly speaking semantically 'opaque' but

6.4 Case Preservation and 'Dative Sickness' 151

may convey social meaning, such as nominative substitution, and that which conveys a semantic distinction, such as the verbs of motion. The case-preserving behaviour of the passives of 'thank' and 'believe' is less obviously either sociolinguistically or semantically motivated but seems to be a fossil of an earlier stage of the language. All three of these types, nonetheless, can be accounted for by the differing weight of the fixed effects in our model: while the choice of case is obviously categorical (option A or option B) and the grammar reflects this as a specified constraint ranking, several interacting factors may result in a speaker selecting a particular variant. In the case of the variation that communicates social or pragmatic meaning, factors other than lexical item, such as register or age, may be weighted more strongly, whereas in the case of lexical-semantic differences, the verb lexeme factor is the most significant. Finally, we currently do not know enough about case preservation in Faroese to establish which factors are most significant in choice of grammar, but the bigger point is that with a probabilistic competing grammars model – crucially, one in which the dependent variable is a discrete selection of one constraint ranking over others – the facts can be accounted for while acknowledging the sundry influences on morphosyntactic variation.

In order to capture the observed case (non-)preservation behaviour in the passive, as discussed above, this is conceptualised as two competing grammars: the 'preserving' one with the ranking MAX[LC] » PARSE » S[+HR] and the 'non-preserving' one with the ranking S[+HR] » PARSE » MAX[LC]. Diachronically, the loss of lexical case can be seen as reranking since deranking of MAX[LC] coincides with a stricter mapping from argument structure to syntactic structure, here explained by the higher ranking of S[+HR]. **Interestingly, this also makes the prediction that when the 'preserving' grammar is activated, the passive of a quirky-subject predicate will be unavailable, whereas when the 'non-preserving' grammar is activated, a quirky-subject verb will passivise with a nominative subject.** These predictions are borne out in Faroese in what at first glance appears to be the aforementioned lexical splits: quirky-subject verbs that either allow or disallow nominative substitution and quirky-object verbs that either allow or disallow preservation under passive. The verb *dáma* 'like' permits nominative substitution in the active and has a passive form with a nominative subject (157), which we know is not an adjectival use since the passive auxiliary *blíva* is used (instead of the copula *vera*).

The verb *tørva* 'need' is resistant to nominative substitution in the active (rare in the blog corpus and disliked by consultants) and does not have an attested passive (158).

(157) a. Far. Mær dámar hasar bøkurnar.
me.DAT likes.3SG those books-the.ACC
'I like those books.'

b. Far. Eg dámi hasar bøkurnar.
I.NOM like.1SG those books-the.ACC
'I like those books'

c. Far. Hon bleiv væl dámd.
she.NOM was well liked.NOM.F.SG
'She was well liked.'

(158) a. Far. Mær tørvar hasar bøkurnar.
me.DAT needs.3SG those books-the.ACC
'I need those books.'

b. Far. * Eg tørvi hasar bøkurnar.
I.NOM need.1SG those books-the.ACC

c. Far. * Hon bleiv tørvað.
she.NOM was needed.NOM.F.SG

In the same vein, a verb like *takka* whose object bears preserving dative case (i.e. the subject of the passive is dative) is accounted for by the 'preserving' grammar, while a verb like *heilsa* 'greet', with non-preserving dative on the object, is accounted for by the 'non-preserving' grammar. The following tableaux demonstrate the different rankings yielding the correct patterns:

(159) **Monotransitive with lexical subject case**

$\lambda y \lambda x_{[LC]} \lambda e$ V : *tørva* 'need'	Max[LC]	Parse	S[+HR]
☞ a. DP$_{x[LC]}$ V DP$_y$: *Mær tørvar hana*			*
b. DP$_x$ V DP$_y$: *Eg tørvi hana*	*!		
c. Ø		*!	

(160) a. **Monotransitive with 'weak' lexical subject case: Nominative substitution**

$\lambda y \lambda x_{[LC]} \lambda e$ V : *dáma* 'like'	S[+HR]	Parse	Max[LC]
a. DP$_{x[LC]}$ V DP$_y$: *Mær dámar hann*	*!		
☞ b. DP$_x$ V DP$_y$: *Eg dámi hann*			*
c. Ø		*!	

b. **Monotransitive with 'weak' lexical subject case: No nominative substitution**

$\lambda y \lambda x_{[LC]} \lambda e$ V : *dáma* 'like'	Max[LC]	Parse	S[+HR]
☞ a. DP$_{x[LC]}$ V DP$_y$: *Mær dámar hann*			*
b. DP$_x$ V DP$_y$: *Eg dámi hann*	*!		
c. Ø		*!	

6.4 *Case Preservation and 'Dative Sickness'* 153

(161) **Monotransitive passive with 'strong' lexical subject case**

$\lambda e \lambda y \exists x_{[LC]}$ V$_{PASS}$: *verða tørvað* 'be needed' || M$_{AX}$[LC]	P$_{ARSE}$	S[+HR]
a. DP$_y$ V$_{PASS}$: *Hon verður tørvað*	*!		
b. DP$_{y[LC]}$ V$_{PASS}$: *Henni verður tørvað*	*!		*
☞ c. Ø		*	

(162) **Monotransitive passive with 'weak' lexical subject case**

$\lambda e \lambda y \exists x_{[LC]}$ V$_{PASS}$: *blíva dámdur* 'be liked' || S[+HR]	P$_{ARSE}$	M$_{AX}$[LC]
☞ a. DP$_y$ V$_{PASS}$: *Hann bleiv dámdur*			*
b. DP$_{y[LC]}$ V$_{PASS}$: *Honum bleiv dámdur*	*!		*
c. Ø		*!	

(163) **Monotransitive passive with preserving lexical object case**

$\lambda e \lambda y_{[LC]} \exists x$ V$_{PASS}$: *blíva takkað* 'be thanked' || M$_{AX}$[LC]	P$_{ARSE}$	S[+HR]
☞ a. DP$_{y[LC]}$ V$_{PASS}$: *Henni bleiv takkað*			*
b. DP$_y$ V$_{PASS}$: *Hon bleiv takkað*	*!		
c. Ø		*!	

(164) **Monotransitive passive with non-preserving lexical object case**

$\lambda e \lambda y_{[LC]} \exists x$ V$_{PASS}$: *verða hjálpaðir* 'be helped' || S[+HR]	P$_{ARSE}$	M$_{AX}$[LC]
a. DP$_{y[LC]}$ V$_{PASS}$: *Teimum varð hjálpað*	*!		
☞ b. DP$_y$ V$_{PASS}$: *Teir vórðu hjálpaðir*			*
c. Ø		*!	

Hence, if we make the crucial assumption that P$_{ARSE}$ is dominated by either M$_{AX}$[LC] or S[+HR], we can capture *both* the case preservation behaviour *and* the observed correlation between unavailability of passive and non-substitutable dative subject case. The covariance of case substitution and nominative subject passives is explained by the conflict between the pressure to express lexical case and having a nominative subject. By ranking P$_{ARSE}$ such that it either dominates M$_{AX}$[LC] or S[+HR], in those instances when the preserving grammar is likely to be activated (e.g. with a lexeme like *tørva* that disprefers nominative substitution in the active), having a nominative subject does not 'save' the passive candidate since it violates M$_{AX}$[LC]; furthermore, we cannot express the lexical case on the wrong argument since this will still violate M$_{AX}$[LC], which requires the same argument in the input to be lexically case-marked in the output.

A reviewer notes that an issue with implementing competing grammars in OT is that reranking non-adjacent constraints may have knock-on effects since it predicts different interactions with other constraints in the hierarchy, which are not predicted if the competing rankings simply capture two phrase structure rules or the equivalent. This point is well taken as rerankings involving more than two adjacent constraints should only be proposed when really called for by the data. However, in this case we actually do have convincing evidence for competing grammars in which the interactions of three constraints result in ineffability of passive in (158). PARSE is needed to capture the unavailability of passive with *tørva* as the behaviour cannot be explained by the interaction of MAX[LC] and S[+HR] alone; at the same time, the availability of passive with *dáma* comes for free with this interaction. Moreover, the two proposed rankings shed light on the behaviour of lexical object case as seen in (163–164), suggesting this analysis is on the right track. In the few other places where competing rankings are proposed in this book, the rankings in question involve only a pair of adjacent constraints (see Sections 5.2 and 7.3).

6.4.1 A Word on Icelandic 'Dative Sickness'

The nominative substitution phenomenon discussed above is reminiscent of a similar, more frequently discussed phenomenon in Icelandic known as 'dative sickness': the substitution of dative subject case on verbs whose subjects standardly bear (or historically bore) accusative or genitive case (Svavarsdóttir 1982, Jónsson and Eyþórsson 2005, Þráinsson 2007:224ff). This phenomenon is somewhat different from the Faroese case substitution since Icelandic has a far larger set of commonly used verbs with non-nominative subjects, for which some thematic generalisations have been made: non-nominative subjects are always non-agentive, and dative has been associated with the experiencer role and subjects of psychological predicates in particular. Therefore, in the Icelandic phenomenon, the loss of accusative subject case to dative may reflect an analogical process in which dative-subject verbs as a class are associated with a particular thematic structure, and so accusative is the more marked form. Nevertheless, as Þráinsson (2007:224) notes, the diachronic trajectory towards regularisation in the loss of quirky case appears to be occurring in both Faroese and Icelandic, despite it being highly unlikely that they have influenced each other in this regard (by far the stronger influence on Faroese is Danish).

No explicit analysis of the Icelandic dative substitution is offered here, other than to suggest that a similar constraint interaction may be at play: MAX[LC] will enforce the realisation of accusative subject case, but perhaps a constraint preferring non-agentive, non-theme arguments to be marked dative is at play; in that sense, dative may function as a kind of 'default quirky case'. If said constraint is ranked higher than Max[LC] in the Icelandic grammar that replaces accusative with dative subject case, the 'weakening' of quirky case has both a synchronic and diachronic explanation in the competing grammars model. As the case-substituting grammar is more frequently activated over time, the input for the child acquiring Icelandic will have increasing representation of the substitution behaviour, which increases the probability of the child inferring a case-substituting grammar. This rests on the assumption that the relevant factors that promote the deranking of Max[LC] are winning out, but such factors are far from fully understood. A tentative case can be made for the role of social meaning: in a similar way to Faroese nominative substitution, in Iceland the so-called 'dative sickness' represents anti-purism since the phenomenon is frowned upon far more in Iceland than nominative substitution is in the Faroes. Further study is needed to establish the sociolinguistic and pragmatic contexts in which dative substitution is more likely to occur.

6.5 Summary of Chapter

To conclude this chapter, it has been argued that the competing grammars model proposed for nominative substitution on dative-subject verbs is also adaptable to various phenomena relating to the Faroese passive. New survey data from Faroese native speakers were presented, confirming the availability of impersonal passive in some instances but concluding that the lexical semantics of the individual verb is a particularly important factor. An analysis of the impersonal passive as a constraint conflict between Dep and Parse was laid out, which can be paraphrased by the question 'Is it worse to insert material (like an expletive) or not to have a passive form available?' Again, the ranking of {Dep, Parse} yields the (un)availability of the passive of intransitives.

It was also argued that the same constraint rankings at work in the grammars that result in nominative substitution behaviour are behind the case (non-)preservation in the passive. The ranking Max[LC] » S[+HR] results in the preservation of lexical case marking in both dative-subject verbs and passives of dative-object verbs, whereas the ranking S[+HR] » Max[LC] generates the non-preserving, substituting forms.

Moreover, an interesting correlation was observed between the typically preserving dative-subject verb *tørva* 'need' and the impossibility of passive versus the non-preserving verb *dáma* 'like' and the possibility of passive: this already falls out from the proposed model, with the addition of Parse: Max[LC] » Parse » S[+HR] predicts that it will be better to have no passive than to fail to express lexical case (even when the argument bearing said case is demoted), while S[+HR] » Parse » Max[LC] predicts that it is better to have a passive that fails to express lexical case than not to have a passive. Therefore, this model offers an explanation both for the by-verb variation in case realisation, and for the change that appears to be occurring towards a system-wide loss of quirky case.

7
Ditransitives

Faroese ditransitives are relevant to our discussion because (i) it has been reported that the dative argument, typically a recipient or goal, co-occurs with a nominative theme triggering object agreement in the passive (Þráinsson et al. 2012:272–273), a fact that would falsify the hypothesis that Faroese ranks MAX[–HR] over AGR[+HR], due to the failure to realise accusative case on the theme; and (ii) dative case in ditransitives differs from dative subject or object case in monotransitives in that it does not undergo nominative or accusative substitution. In the following sections it is argued, based on extensive survey data, that in general Faroese speakers judge ditransitive passives unacceptable across the board, regardless of whether the theme argument is nominative or accusative; the offending nominative 'object' sentences are, hence, not a problem since they are not part of the Faroese speakers' grammars. Moreover, I show that an OLG approach generates the correct Faroese ditransitive case frames while ruling out the unacceptable passive forms; it also captures the differences between the substitutable dative case in monotransitives and the dative on the recipient/goal argument in ditransitives.

7.1 Ditransitive Verbs in Faroese

The most common case-marking pattern for Faroese three-argument verbs is nominative–dative–accusative (165), which is also the default in Icelandic.

(165) a. Far. *Pápin   lænti soninum   bilin.*
father-the.NOM lent son-the.DAT car-the.ACC
'The father lent his son the car.'
b. Far. *Hon   gav gentuni   telduna.*
she.NOM gave girl-the.DAT computer-the.ACC
'She gave the girl the computer.'
c. Far. *Hann   seldi bóndanum   kúnna.*
he.NOM sold farmer-the.DAT cow-the.ACC
'He sold the farmer the cow.'

(Þráinsson et al. 2012:262)

Unlike Icelandic, other case frames have generally given way in Faroese to the default pattern, or one of the arguments shows up as a prepositional phrase (Þráinsson et al. 2012:263). Some verbs also exhibit an accusative–accusative pattern, but in most of these the second object is semantically related to the verb (166).

(166) a. Far. *Kann eg   biðja teg   eina bøn?*
can I.NOM ask you.ACC a.ACC favour.ACC
'Can I ask you a favour?'
b. Far. *Tey   spurdu meg   ein   spurning.*
they.NOM asked me.ACC a.ACC question.ACC
'They asked me a question.'

(Þráinsson et al. 2012:263)

In general, standard indirect object case in Faroese is dative. While an alternation exists with the prepositional phrase headed by *til* 'to', corresponding to English examples like 'I sent a letter to her', this is reportedly restricted to constructions where a clear directional interpretation is available (167).

(167) a. Far. *Hann   seldi kúnna   til bóndan.*
he.NOM sold cow-the.ACC to farmer-the.ACC
'He sold the cow to the farmer.'
b. Far. * *Hon   beyð   starvið   til hana.*
she.NOM offered job-the.ACC to her.ACC
'She offered the job to her.'

(Þráinsson et al. 2012:264)

The indirect–direct object order is fixed in Faroese, since ungrammaticality results when the object arguments are switched:

(168) a. Far. *Hann   seldi gentuni   telduna.*
he.NOM sold girl-the.DAT computer-the.ACC
'He sold the girl the computer.'
b. Far. * *Hann   seldi telduna   gentuni.*
he.NOM sold computer-the.ACC girl-the.DAT

c. Far. *Teir   góvu konginum   hestin.*
         they.NOM gave king-the.DAT horse-the.ACC
         'They gave the king the horse.'
d. Far. * *Teir   góvu hestin   konginum.*
         they.NOM gave horse-the.ACC king-the.DAT

(Þráinsson et al. 2012:265)

Little prior work exists on passives of ditransitives in Faroese. One example with the direct object promoted to subject is presented as grammatical in Þráinsson et al. (2012:266) without comment (169).

(169) Far. *Kúgvin   varð seld bóndanum*
           cow-the.NOM was sold farmer-the.DAT
           'The cow was sold to the farmer'

It has been claimed that the dative indirect object of a ditransitive cannot be promoted to subject, whether the case is preserved or not (unlike dative object case in monotransitives):

(170) a. Far. ?? *Bóndanum   varð seld kúgvin*
               farmer-the.DAT was sold cow-the.NOM
               'The farmer was sold the cow'
      b. Far. ? *Bóndanum   varð seld ein   kúgv*
              farmer-the.DAT was sold a.NOM cow.NOM
              'The farmer was sold a cow'
      c. Far. * *Bóndanum   varð selt eina   kúgv*
              farmer-the.DAT was sold a.ACC cow.ACC

(Þráinsson et al. 2012:270)

It is noteworthy that this contrasts sharply with Icelandic, where the dative argument is typically promoted to subject (Þráinsson et al. 2012:271–272). According to Þráinsson et al., these examples are actually judged even worse in Faroese with nominative subjects:

(171) a. Far. * *Bóndin   varð seldur kúgvin/kúnna*
                farmer-the.NOM was sold   cow-the.NOM/ACC
                'The farmer was sold the cow'
      b. Far. * *Gentan   bleiv givin teldan/telduna*
                girl-the.NOM was given computer-the.NOM/ACC
                'The girl was given the computer'

In general, Faroese consultants expressed strong doubts about passives of ditransitives. Although it has been claimed that dative-subject, nominative-object passives exist in Faroese, as in (169), in fact the author's fieldwork shows that many of the passive examples cited in Þráinsson et al. (2012:269–272) are unacceptable or highly dubious and that speakers prefer an impersonal active construction, as in (172):

(172) Far. Mann gav konunum bøkurnar
one gave women-the.DAT books-the.ACC
'One gave the women the books'

This paints a varied picture of the availability of the passive for three-argument verbs, which may well be extremely verb-specific, in the same way as the acceptability of monotransitive passives (see Chapter 6); additionally, it appears that the case and position of the arguments must be right for the ditransitive passive to be accepted at all.

7.2 Survey Data: Faroese 'Give' Passive

In order to investigate the data further, three surveys were conducted on the Faroe Islands asking native speakers for acceptability judgements on ditransitive passives, in addition to one Icelandic survey for comparison.[1] All surveys were completed online using the Stanford version of Qualtrics. The ditransitive passive stimuli varied across several dimensions: (a) word order, (b) verbal agreement morphology, (c) case of the direct object, (d) gender of the arguments. It has long been noted that there is a certain degree of diglossia in Faroese, in that the spoken language often features more Faro–Danish vocabulary and constructions, whereas there is a subset of the lexicon that tends to be used only in written or formal, literary Faroese.[2] In colloquial Faroese the passive can be avoided by the use of the impersonal *mann*-construction, which is a loan from Danish that does not exist in Icelandic (Petersen and Jónsson, p.c.). Therefore, an attempt was made to control for register by embedding the target sentences in a surrounding contextual sentence that used vocabulary from a colloquial or literary register, respectively.

---

[1] The surveys were conducted during April–June 2017. Thanks to Hjalmar P. Petersen, Jógvan í Lon Jacobsen, Bogi and Súsanna Vinther and family, Beinir Hentze Johannessen and Johann Petersen for their help. Thanks to Einar Freyr Sigurðsson and Jóhannes Gísli Jónsson for help with the Icelandic survey.

[2] See Petersen (2010) for a recent treatment of the language contact situation.

7.2.1 Faroese 'Give' Passives Survey 1: Colloquial Context

7.2.1.1 Participants

For the colloquial context survey, 23 participants were recruited from a combination of university students at Fróðskaparsetur Føroya (University of the Faroe Islands) and the Facebook group *Føroysk rættstaving*. A compensation of 10 DKK was offered for participation, though only 3 participants took up the offer. Nine of the participants fully completed the survey; the remaining 14 gave partial responses. All participants were required to declare that Faroese is their native language before taking part in the survey. The same set of 9 participants who fully completed the survey also voluntarily provided demographic information: of this subset, 5 were male and 4 female, with a mean age of 40.7 years ($\sigma = 10.7$ years, range 19–55); 3 were from Tórshavn, 2 from Sandoy, 2 from Suðuroy, 1 from Vágar and 1 from Fuglafjørður.

7.2.1.2 Materials

Participants were asked to provide acceptability judgements on 32 Faroese sentences with the verb *geva* 'give', shown in Appendix B3. These same sentences were tested in both the colloquial and formal context surveys. Passive sentences were tested in the following configurations: (i) Theme-Verb-Goal, (ii) Goal-Verb-Theme, (iii) Theme-Aux-Goal-Verb, (iv) Expl-Verb-Goal-Theme. Each order was also tested with each variant of (i) nominative or accusative case on the theme, and (ii) presence or absence of agreement; 'agreement' was defined by the inflection of the participle matching that of the theme argument, and 'no agreement' by the supine form in *–ið*.

7.2.1.3 Procedure

Participants were presented with Faroese sentences displayed as in (173), excluding the English translation:

(173) Eg fari at vitja Sigmund og Katrin í kvøld. **Eg hoyrdi frá Beini, at monnunum varð givið tveir nýggir bátar.** Tað hevði verið stuttligt at snakka um, tí Katrin kennir teir sera væl.
'I'm going to visit Sigmund and Katrin tonight. I heard from Beinir that the men were given two new boats. That would be fun to chat about, since Katrin knows them very well.'

The surrounding sentences contain the lexemes *fara* + infinitive, 'going to (immediate future)' and *snakka* 'to talk, chat', which are indicative of an informal context. Participants were told to evaluate acceptability only of the embedded sentence, which was displayed in bold font. Acceptability was rated on a five-point scale with the same descriptions as were given in the monotransitive passive surveys (see Section 6.2.1). The target sentences for judgement were randomised and interspersed with filler sentences whose judgements were known prior to the survey. Both the 'give' passives and quirky case predicates were tested within the same survey, that is, sentence types were not separated but appeared in the same block of questions, with the aim of reducing assimilation effects (Tourangeau et al. 2000).

7.2.1.4 Results

Because of the small number of responses to survey 1, our analysis of the 'give' passive is based on the combination of surveys 1 and 2. Participants in survey 1 were not identical to those in survey 2, which tested the same sentences embedded in a formal context, and there was no overlap between the sets of participants; therefore no direct comparison could be made for the same set of respondents. In spite of this, it is clear that the passives of 'give' are by and large unacceptable regardless of context: if there were an effect for context, it is reasonable to assume that the formal context would yield higher acceptability for the passive, but in both contexts no passive of 'give' had a mean acceptability of greater than 3. The results of the combination of the two surveys are presented in Section 7.2.2.4.

7.2.2 Faroese 'Give' Passives Survey 2: Formal Context

7.2.2.1 Participants

For the formal context survey, 135 participants were recruited from a combination of university students at Fróðskaparsetur Føroya and the Facebook group *Føroysk rættstaving*. Compensation of 10 DKK was offered to the university students for participation; the survey was sent out to the Facebook group without the offer of compensation. Of the participants, 37 fully completed the survey; the remaining 98 gave partial responses. All participants were required to declare that Faroese is their native language before taking part in the survey. Demographic information was voluntarily provided by 35 participants: of this subset, 15 were male, 19 female and 1 did not disclose gender. The mean age was 42.5 years ($\sigma = 12.6$ years, range 21–71). Twelve participants were from Tórshavn and surrounding area, 16 from towns *norðanfjørðs* (north of Kollafjørður), 4 from Suðuroy, 1 from Sandoy, 1 from Vágar and 1 from Mykines.

7.2.2.2 Materials

The same sentences were tested as in the first survey (see Appendix B3); the only difference between the surveys is the contextual sentence in which the sentences for judgement were embedded.

7.2.2.3 Procedure

The target sentences for judgement were embedded in a formal or literary context, given in (174).

(174) Hóast hann var heldur móður, las hann tað líta brævið, sum konan hevði lagt á borðið. Tað segði: « **Eg hoyrdi frá Beini, at monnunum varð givið tveir nýggir bátar.** » Tað hevði verið eitt áhugavert evni í samrøðuni!
'Although he was rather weary, he read the little note that his wife had left on the table. It said, "I heard from Beinir that the men were given two new boats." That would have been an interesting topic of conversation!'

The lexemes *hóast* 'although', *heldur* 'rather' and the phrase *eitt áhugavert evni í samrøðuni* 'an interesting conversation topic' indicate that this is a formal context (Jógvan í Lon Jacobsen, p.c.).

7.2.2.4 Results

The results reported in this section are based on a combined dataset from both surveys. Figure 7.1 shows mean acceptability plotted with respect to the four 'give' passive word order types, case of the theme argument and verbal agreement morphology. It should be immediately clear that regardless of word order, case of the theme and agreement, none of these sentence types are broadly accepted, and the mean acceptability for every stimulus is below 3 ('I don't know how natural'), with most being below 2 ('not very natural'). One particularly striking result is that the acceptability of one sentence type appears higher than all the others, which is the type in example (169) presented by Þráinsson et al. (2012) as grammatical: if the theme occurs in nominative case in subject position, without the goal occurring structurally higher than the verb, and with plural verb agreement, the mean acceptability approaches 3.

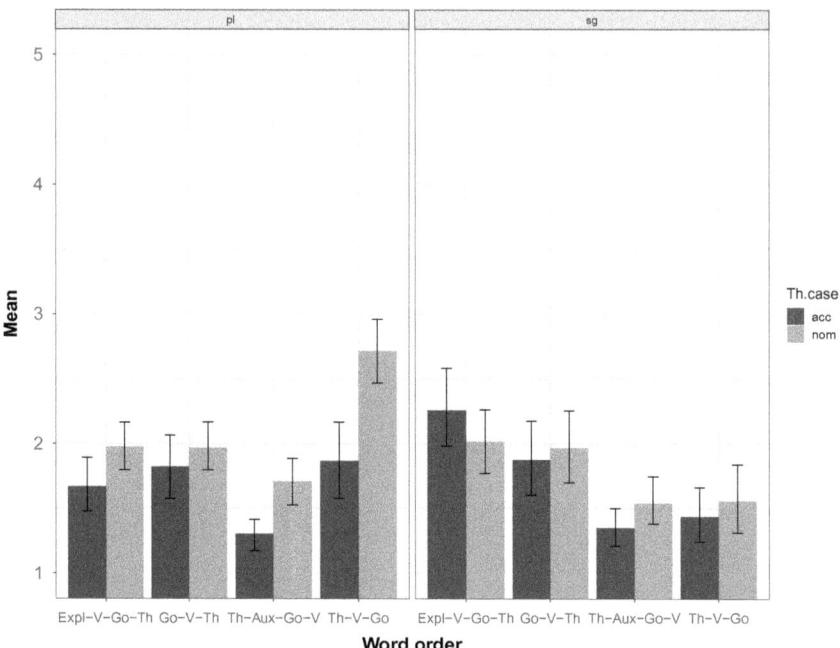

Figure 7.1 Faroese 'give' passive surveys: Mean acceptability by word order and theme case

Key to abbreviations: Expl = expletive, Go = goal argument, Th = theme argument, Aux = auxiliary, V = main verb.

In order to verify the significance of this result, the same type of ordinal regression model was run as for the monotransitive passive surveys discussed in Chapter 6. The model can be summarised thus:

Response ~ Theme case * Participle number * Word order
+ (1 | Speaker) + (1 | Item)

That is, this model tested the effect on mean acceptability of the interaction between theme case (nominative or accusative), participle number (singular or plural) and word order (Theme-V-Goal, Goal-V-Theme, Expl-V-Goal-Theme or Theme-Aux-Goal-V), with random intercepts for Speaker and Item. In this model, considering the effect of word order alone with Expl-V-Goal-Theme as intercept, the order Theme-Aux-Goal-Verb emerged as significantly worse than Expl-V-Goal-Theme

(β = −1.2, p = 0.05). The obvious significance of the Theme-V-Goal word order with plural agreement was corroborated: plural agreement improves the mean judgement in the order Expl-V-Goal-Theme to a significantly lesser degree than it does in the order Theme-V-Goal (β = -2.2, p < 0.01), in spite of the lower mean of accusative theme case across the board.

7.3 OLG Analysis

As mean acceptability of the 'give' passive is so low across the board, regardless of register, it is reasonable to rule the construction out as ungrammatical in Faroese. The fact that the only combination that has a mean acceptability approaching 3 on the scale is an agreed-with nominative theme argument in Spec,TP and that the order Theme-V-Goal is judged significantly better than Goal-V-Theme can be explained thus: ditransitive passives are ungrammatical, but if the word order and agreement morphology are the most similar to an active transitive, the sentence is judged more acceptable. Why should this be?

Passivising a verb with three arguments creates an unusual situation where abstract case, positional case and morphosyntactic case on the argument all may misalign. Since passive is construed as demotion of the highest theta-role, in a predicate with the argument structure Agent-Goal-Theme, demoting the agent will mean that the goal argument bearing [−HR−LR] at the level of abstract case will be promoted to highest role [+HR] at morphosyntactic case; the theme bears the lowest role [−HR] at both levels. Therefore, if a nominative theme occupies subject position in the passive, the case mapping will be [−HR]:[+HR]:[+HR], representing 'abstract : position : item' case, thus failing to express the abstract case in the morphosyntax and incurring a Max[−HR] violation. With these considerations, let us posit that the unacceptability of the 'give' passive is a corollary of the following constraint interaction: pressure to fill subject position with a nominative argument competes with a combined cost of either (i) promoting the recipient/goal, which violates a preference against promoting an argument bearing abstract dative case to subject, or (ii) promoting the theme, thus violating a preference that the argument promoted to subject be the highest available role. These competing pressures can be construed as a constraint interaction between S[+HR] and Parse, but with two additional constraints: one that enforces correspondence between subject *position*

166 *Ditransitives*

and the abstract case of the occupying argument (175), and (176) which ensures the realisation of structural dative case.[3]

(175) DEP[+HR]/Pos (DEP[+HR]/P): assign a violation for each [+HR] morphosyntactic positional case feature that does not realise a [+HR] abstract case feature on an input argument.

(176) MAX[−LR]: assign a violation for each [−LR] abstract case feature on an input argument that is not realised by a [−LR] morphosyntactic case feature on an output argument.

If the ranking is S[+HR] » MAX[−LR] » DEP[+HR]/P » PARSE, the null candidate will win, but the second-best contender of the passives would be nominative theme in subject position, dative goal in object position. If DEP[+HR]/P is ranked below PARSE, candidate (177a) would win as shown in (178); thus, this grammar represents the marginally attested examples of the type (169). This grammar is assumed to be statistically less probable than one in which the ranking DEP[+HR]/P » PARSE holds, hence offering a possible explanation for the doubtful acceptability judgements with respect to 'give' passives.

(177) **Faroese 'give' passive: No passive**

λzλy∃x verða givin : [x CAUSE [BECOME [y HAVE z]]]	S[+HR]	MAX[−LR]	DEP[+HR]/P	PARSE
a. Theme[−HR]:[+HR]:[+HR] V_{PASS} Goal[−HR−LR]:[−HR]:[−HR−LR]			*!	
b. Goal[−HR−LR]:[+HR]:[−HR−LR] V_{PASS} Theme[−HR]:[−HR]:[+HR]	*!			
c. Theme[−HR]:[+HR]:[−HR] V_{PASS} Goal[−HR−LR]:[−HR]:[−HR−LR]	*!			*
d. Theme[−HR]:[+HR]:[+HR] V_{PASS} Goal[−HR−LR]:[−HR]:[−HR]		*!		*
e. Goal[−HR−LR]:[+HR]:[+HR] V_{PASS} Theme[−HR]:[−HR]:[−HR]	*!			
☞ f. ∅				*

(178) **Faroese 'give' passive: Nominative theme in Spec,TP, dative goal in V,Comp**

λzλy∃x verða givin : [x CAUSE [BECOME [y HAVE z]]]	S[+HR]	MAX[−LR]	PARSE	DEP[+HR]/P
☞ a. Theme[−HR]:[+HR]:[+HR] V_{PASS} Goal[−HR−LR]:[−HR]:[−HR−LR]				*
b. Goal[−HR−LR]:[+HR]:[−HR−LR] V_{PASS} Theme[−HR]:[−HR]:[+HR]	*!			
c. Theme[−HR]:[+HR]:[−HR] V_{PASS} Goal[−HR−LR]:[−HR]:[−HR−LR]	*!			*
d. Theme[−HR]:[+HR]:[+HR] V_{PASS} Goal[−HR−LR]:[−HR]:[−HR]		*!		*
e. Goal[−HR−LR]:[+HR]:[+HR] V_{PASS} Theme[−HR]:[−HR]:[−HR]		*!		
f. ∅			*!	

It falls out nicely that, if PARSE is ranked above S[+HR], which has already been claimed for the 'preserving'-type grammar in Chapters 4–6, non-nominative arguments in subject position will be penalised less. If DEP[+HR]/P also dominates S[+HR] in Icelandic, the winner will be the candidate with a dative goal argument in subject position and a nominative theme in object position, as shown in (179).

---

[3] Very similar constraints were proposed as necessary to cover the range of Finnish data in Kiparsky (2001), including DEP-type constraints specified for nominal versus pronominal arguments.

(179) Icelandic 'give' passive: Dative goal in Spec,TP, nominative theme in V,Comp

λzλy∃x vera gefinn : [x CAUSE [BECOME [y HAVE z]]]	Max[−LR]	Parse	Dep[+HR]/P	S[+HR]
a. Theme[−HR]:[+HR]:[+HR] V_PASS Goal[−HR−LR]:[−HR]:[−HR−LR]			*!	
☞ b. Goal[−HR−LR]:[−HR−LR] V_PASS Theme[−HR]:[−HR]:[+HR]				*
c. Theme[−HR]:[+HR]:[−HR] V_PASS Goal[−HR−LR]:[−HR]:[−HR−LR]			*!	*
d. Theme[−HR]:[+HR] V_PASS Goal[−HR−LR]:[−HR]:[−HR]	*!		*	
e. Goal[−HR−LR]:[+HR]:[+HR] V_PASS Theme[−HR]:[−HR]:[−HR]	*!			
f. ∅		*!		

Candidates (d–e) in the tableaux (177–179) correspond to winners in languages that have lost morphological case-marking, such as English. The prepositional phrase recipient in the 'to' variant (i.e. 'The book was given to John') is considered here to be a distinct construction: the double-object construction and prepositional dative are not two output candidates for the same input, a position that is typically motivated by semantic differences between the constructions (see Green 1974, Oehrle 1976 and subsequent studies). Although some examples of apparent prepositional datives occur in the same configuration as double-object constructions (e.g. 'give a headache to' with heavy NP shift), as Bruening (2010, 2018) argues, it is possible to analyse the first object as rightward-projected, and therefore to see these as examples of double-object constructions with respect to their semantics (in contrast to Rappaport Hovav and Levin 2008, Ormazabal and Romero 2012 and others). Bruening (2010) provides evidence from locative inversion and scope interaction in support of this analysis; although the proposal of rightward specifiers is not adopted here, it is feasible that the structurally higher object can occur to the right of the lower object by rightward adjunction, as in (180):[4]

(180) It was a stench that would [vP give_v [VP ___v a headache [V' [PP to the most athletic constitution]]]]

The availability of the prepositional dative is assumed to be also partly determined by information structure, but detailed analysis of this variant is beyond the scope of our discussion here.[5] In English,

---

[4] Example adapted from Bresnan and Nikitina (2009:165–166).
[5] McFadden (2002) argues that the prepositional phrase recipient arose in Middle English around the same time as the loss of morphological case and the rise of positional licensing; this can be seen as a way of expressing discourse features without the flexible word order afforded by overt case-marking. In contrast, languages like German can flag argument structure via case morphology, and hence word order is more available as a means of expressing information structure. Nevertheless, it is worth noting here that modern English word order probably could not have arisen as a result of the loss of case-marking: Pintzuk (1999) showed that Infl-medial and head-initial-VP variants were innovated and rose in frequency a long time before English lost morphological case. Thus, the story is not as simple as the trade-off between available forms alone.

candidate (e) is optimal on the ranking PARSE » S[+HR] » DEP[+HR]/P » MAX[−LR]:

(181) **English 'give' passive: Goal in Spec,TP, theme in V,Comp**

$\lambda z \lambda y \exists x$ be given : $[x$ CAUSE [BECOME $[y$ HAVE $z]$]]	PARSE	S[+HR]	DEP[+HR]/P	MAX[−LR]
a. Theme[−HR]:[+HR]:[+HR] V_PASS Goal[−HR−LR]:[−HR]:[−HR−LR]			*!	
b. Goal[−HR−LR]:[+HR]:[−HR−LR] V_PASS Theme[−HR]:[−HR]:[+HR]		*!		
c. Theme[−HR]:[+HR]:[−HR] V_PASS Goal[−HR−LR]:[−HR]:[−HR−LR]		*!		*
d. Theme[−HR]:[+HR]:[+HR] V_PASS Goal[−HR−LR]:[−HR]:[−HR]			*!	*
☞ e. Goal[−HR−LR]:[+HR]:[+HR] V_PASS Theme[−HR]:[−HR]:[−HR]				*
f. ∅	*!			

With these four constraints, the number of logically possible grammars is 24. There are four possible output patterns for the 'give' passive input:

No.	OUTPUT	LANGUAGE
1	no passive	Faroese
2	Theme[NOM]-Goal[DAT]	Icelandic, German, Faroese (marginal)
3	Goal[DAT]-Theme[NOM]	Icelandic
4	Goal[NOM]-Theme[ACC]	English

In order to derive the order Theme[NOM]-Goal[ACC], which is the standard in, for example, Dutch and an option in Swedish and Norwegian, additional constraints must be at work; moreover, the details of the competition between the prepositional phrase and bare argument variants would need to be fleshed out. One can imagine an account in which the PP variant wins when input contains a [+Top] feature associated with the goal, and therefore information-structural constraints such as MATCHDIS would play a role, but the details are beyond the scope of discussion here.

7.3.1 Position of the Goal and Theme Arguments

As an addendum to the above analysis of 'give', let us briefly turn to a discussion of which positions the goal and theme arguments occupy in Faroese, facts necessary to establish given that arguments are assumed to be positionally licensed. It has been argued since at least Barss and Lasnik (1986) that the indirect object argument is structurally higher than the direct object, which has been accounted for in binary-branching frameworks via some kind of VP-shell (Larson 1988 and subsequent studies); in other words, the lower object is occupying V-,Comp and the higher object some VP-internal specifier position. In the OLG version of Linking Theory, the complement of V position is associated with a [−HR] positional case feature, and the higher specifier with a [–HR–LR] feature. Because OLG does not adopt the VP-internal subject hypothesis, there is no need to posit any additional specifiers to Spec,VP. However, it is assumed that the non-finite verb occurs in *v* and therefore precedes both object arguments.

(182)

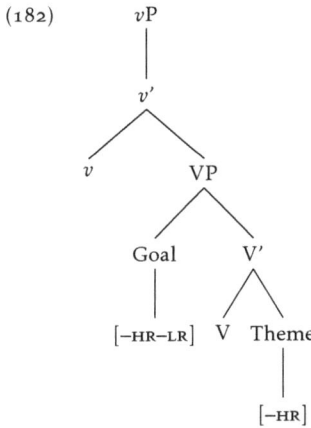

The evidence for this comes from binding asymmetries: Þráinsson (2007:128) demonstrates for Icelandic that the first object can antecede a reflexive co-indexed with the second object, but not vice versa (183); this is also shown to be not merely a linear order issue, since fronting the second object does not improve the judgement (183c).

(183) a. Ice. Þú sviptir   eiginmanninn$_i$ konu   sinni$_i$
              you deprived husband-the.ACC wife.DAT his.REFL.DAT
              'You deprived the husband of his wife.'
      b. Ice. * Þú sviptir   eiginmann   sinn$_i$ konunni$_i$
              you deprived husband.ACC her.REFL.ACC wife-the.DAT
      c. Ice. * Konunni$_i$ sviptir   þú eiginmann   sinn$_i$
              wife-the.DAT deprived you husband.ACC her.REFL.ACC

A similar test was conducted with Faroese consultants, using the double-object verb *geva* 'give', which yielded the same results:[6]

(184) a. Far. Ættleiðingarskrivstovan gav   mammuni$_i$ barn   sitt$_i$
              adoption.agency-the   gave mother-the.DAT child.ACC her.REFL.ACC
              'The adoption agency gave the mother her child.'
      b. Far. * Ættleiðingarskrivstovan gav   mammu   sínari$_i$ barnið$_i$
              adoption.agency-the   gave mother.DAT its.REFL.DAT child-the.ACC

---

[6]This comes with the caveat that further investigation of these facts with a larger speaker sample ought to be conducted, given the subtle nature of the judgements and necessity of constructing examples that are somewhat odd pragmatically.

c. Far. * Barnið_i   góvu tey mammu   sínari_i
         child-the.ACC gave they mother.DAT its.REFL.DAT
         'They gave the child to its mother'

If we assume the structure in (182) for Faroese ditransitives, this enables us to explain, via the positional licensing constraint MATCH-CASE, why we do not see nominative substitution for recipient/goal dative case, as well as why the order of the objects cannot be reversed: if the recipient/goal position is associated with [–HR–LR], an accusative argument bearing [–HR] violates MATCHCASE; likewise if a dative argument bearing [–HR–LR] is found in direct object position [–HR]. With the addition of MAX[LC], we can also account for those few ditransitive predicates with an ACC-ACC case frame, since not realising lexical accusative case on the indirect object will incur a violation thereof. The tableaux for these predicates are given in Section 4.4.2.

7.4 Survey Data: Icelandic 'Give' Passive; Other Faroese Ditransitive Passives

7.4.1 Icelandic Survey on 'Give' Passive

In order to investigate the differences between the Icelandic and Faroese case systems further, a survey was also conducted on the passive of the verb 'give' in Icelandic. The Icelandic survey also included quirky case predicates within the same block of questions as the passives.

7.4.1.1 Participants

The participants were identical to those for the Icelandic quirky case survey (see Section 4.3.3.1).

7.4.1.2 Materials

Participants were asked to provide acceptability judgements on 35 Icelandic sentences with the verb *gefa* 'give', shown in Appendix B4. Unlike the Faroese 'give' passive surveys, these were not embedded in contextual sentences. Passive sentences were tested in the following configurations: (i) Goal-Verb-Theme, (ii) Theme-Verb-Goal, (iii) Theme-Aux-Goal-Verb, (iv) Expl-Theme-Goal-Verb, (v) Expl-Goal-Theme-Verb, (vi) Expl-Verb-Goal-Theme and (vii) Expl-Theme-Verb-Goal. Each order

7.4 Icelandic 'Give' Passive, Other Faroese Passives

was also tested with each variant of (i) nominative or accusative case on the theme, and (ii) agreement/non-agreement with the theme in both case and number (where non-agreement is the supine form). Unlike the Faroese surveys, the following additional sentence types were tested: accusative participle case and intended agreement with the theme, and dative participle case and intended agreement with the goal. The additional word orders tested in Icelandic also provided data for the variable of 'dative intervention', where a dative argument intervenes between the participle and target of agreement.

7.4.1.3 Procedure

The procedure was identical to that of the Faroese surveys. Sentences for judgement were presented in a different random order for each trial, and participants were told to evaluate acceptability of the sentence which was displayed in bold font. The instruction *Segðu hversu eðlilegar þessar setningar eru á íslensku*, 'Say how natural these sentences are in Icelandic', displayed before the block of stimuli. Acceptability was rated on a five-point scale with the following descriptions:

	Icelandic	English translation
1	*Alls ekki eðlilegt. Ég gæti aldrei sagt þetta.*	**Not at all natural.** I could never say this.
2	*Ekki mjög eðlilegt. Það væri skrýtið ef ég segði þetta.*	**Not very natural.** It would be strange if I said this.
3	*Ég veit ekki hvort ég gæti sagt þetta.*	**I don't know** if I could say this.
4	*Frekar eðlilegt. Ég gæti sagt þetta.*	**Rather natural.** I could have said this.
5	*Fullkomlega eðlilegt. Ég gæti auðveldlega sagt þetta.*	**Perfectly natural.** I could easily have said this.

As in the Faroese surveys, the judgement descriptions were displayed on discrete forced-choice buttons. The buttons were displayed horizontally with *Ég veit ekki* in the centre. It was possible to leave an answer blank, and hence some participants reached the end of the survey without providing responses to every question. At the end of each trial, participants were prompted to provide voluntary additional comments and demographic information.

7.4.1.4 Results

Figure 7.2 plots mean acceptability against word order and participle case; the nominative participle in the examples is always plural (i.e.

172 *Ditransitives*

either full agreement with the nominative theme or attempted agreement with a non-nominative argument), and the notation 'nom/acc' refers to the neuter supine form of the participle, which always co-occurs with non-agreement (singular auxiliary). There are two error bars for the nominative participle judgements, since this was tested both with theme and intended goal agreement; the lower error bar is for goal agreement, which was judged at or close to 1 across the board, and the higher bar for theme agreement, whose judgements varied according to word order.

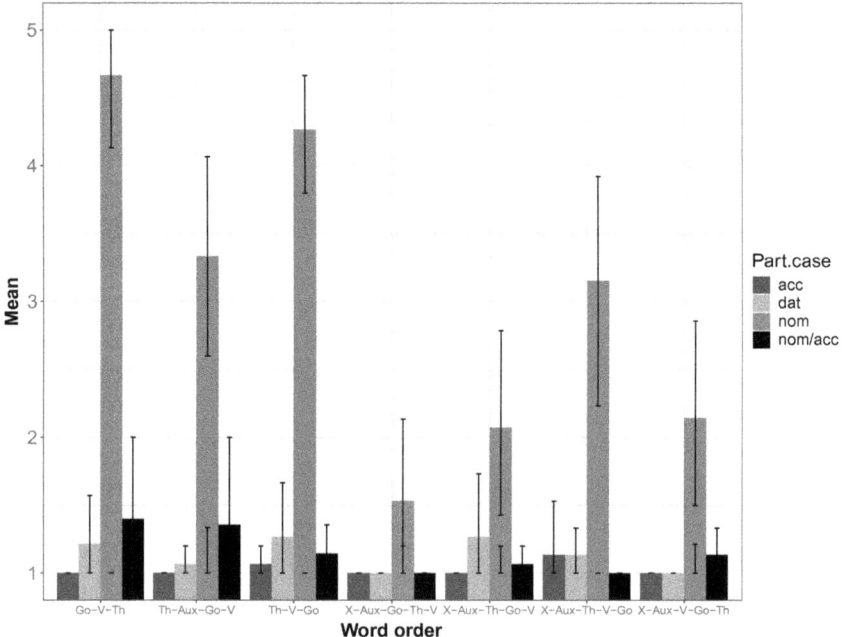

Figure 7.2 Icelandic 'give' passive survey results

As can be clearly seen in Figure 7.2, non-agreement (the supine, indicated by 'nom/acc') is completely unacceptable regardless of word order, and the same goes for sentences with the participle in the accusative or dative. Of those examples with nominative participles, the only word orders with mean acceptability greater than 4 are Goal-V-Theme and Theme-V-Goal, the former judged more acceptable than the latter. Two of the other orders, Theme-Aux-Goal-V and

Expl-Aux-Theme-V-Goal, have a mean acceptability greater than 3; it is not unexpected that these orders should be judged more natural than the other expletive constructions, since these latter also deviate from the base order Goal-V-Theme.

7.4.1.5 Discussion

These results are consistent with the analysis presented in Section 7.3, with the tableau in (179) repeated here for convenience as (185); the theme-first order, which is acceptable albeit marked, is generated by reversing the ranking of {S[+HR], DEP[+HR]/P}, shown in (186). Unlike for Faroese, it is stipulated that S[+HR] is not ranked as highly in Icelandic, given the fact that Icelandic readily allows non-nominative subjects. This is construed as competing grammars, but it could well be the case that information-structural distinctions are also behind the optionality in Icelandic, in which case MATCHDIS may be involved. The working out of the complex variation within Scandinavian is left to further research, though it seems promising to explore the role of discourse features in selection of the passive variant when more than one option exists.

(185) Icelandic 'give' passive 1: Nominative theme in Spec,TP, dative goal in V,Comp

$\lambda z \lambda y \exists x$ vera gefinn : [x CAUSE [BECOME [y HAVE z]]]	Max[−LR]	Parse	Dep[+HR]/P	S[+HR]
a. Theme[−HR]:[+HR]:[+HR] V_{PASS} Goal[−HR−LR]:[−HR]:[−HR−LR]			*!	
☞ b. Goal[−HR−LR]:[+HR]:[−HR−LR] V_{PASS} Theme[−HR]:[−HR]:[+HR]				*
c. Theme[−HR]:[+HR]:[−HR] V_{PASS} Goal[−HR−LR]:[−HR]:[−HR−LR]			*!	*
d. Theme[−HR]:[+HR]:[+HR] V_{PASS} Goal[−HR−LR]:[−HR]:[−HR]	*!		*	
e. Goal[−HR−LR]:[+HR]:[+HR] V_{PASS} Theme[−HR]:[−HR]:[−HR]	*!			
f. ∅		*!		

(186) Icelandic 'give' passive 2: Dative goal in Spec,TP, nominative theme in V,Comp

$\lambda z \lambda y \exists x$ vera gefinn : [x CAUSE [BECOME [y HAVE z]]]	Max[−LR]	Parse	S[+HR]	Dep[+HR]/P
☞ a. Theme[−HR]:[+HR]:[+HR] V_{PASS} Goal[−HR−LR]:[−HR]:[−HR−LR]				*
b. Goal[−HR−LR]:[+HR]:[−HR−LR] V_{PASS} Theme[−HR]:[−HR]:[+HR]			*!	
c. Theme[−HR]:[+HR]:[−HR] V_{PASS} Goal[−HR−LR]:[−HR]:[−HR−LR]			*!	*
d. Theme[−HR]:[+HR]:[+HR] V_{PASS} Goal[−HR−LR]:[−HR]:[−HR]	*!			
e. Goal[−HR−LR]:[+HR]:[+HR] V_{PASS} Theme[−HR]:[−HR]:[−HR]	*!			
f. ∅		*!		

7.4.2 Faroese Survey 3: Other Ditransitive Passives

To conclude this chapter on ditransitives, since it has been established that the lexical semantics of the particular verb plays a large role in case-selection, the passives of several other three-argument predicates were also tested with Faroese speakers.

174 *Ditransitives*

7.4.2.1 Participants

This survey had 18 respondents, recruited via a shared link on the Facebook group *Føroysk rættstaving*; no compensation was offered to participants. Full responses to the survey were completed by 13 respondents, while the other 5 gave partial responses. All participants were required to declare that Faroese is their native language before taking part in the survey. The 13 participants who fully completed the survey also voluntarily provided demographic information: of this subset, 7 were male and 6 female, with a mean age of 50.3 years ($\sigma = 14.1$ years, range 25–76); 8 were from Tórshavn and 5 from towns in *norðanfjørðs* (northern region).

7.4.2.2 Materials

The 31 sentences presented to participants for judgement are shown in Appendix B5. The verbs tested are shown with examples in Table 7.1; examples were tested with three word orders: (i) Theme-Verb-Goal, (ii) Goal-Verb-Theme and (iii) Theme only with a temporal phrase complement. The examples for judgement were embedded under a matrix verb of speech or cognition. In all the passive sentences the participle agreed in number and gender with the subject.

7.4.2.3 Procedure

The procedure was identical to that of the previous Faroese passive surveys (see Section 6.2.1).

7.4.2.4 Results and Discussion

In Figure 7.3, the mean acceptability of each verb is plotted against voice. As one would predict, overall the active is more acceptable than the passive, with a mean of above 4 in most cases; it appears that the passive is generally not judged acceptable, with a mean below 4 in every case. The low means of *veita* 'bestow', *bjóða* 'offer' and *flyta yvir* 'transfer' even in the active can be explained by confounds: *veita* is uncommon in the spoken language, and unfortunately incorrect inflection of the theme argument *pensión* 'pension' was tested (*–ar* GEN.SG for intended *–ir* NOM.PL); some speakers also suggested that *eftirløn* is more natural in Faroese than *pensión*. Likewise, one speaker

Table 7.1 Faroese ditransitive verbs

Verb	English	Active sentence	Passive with nom subject
læna	'lend'	She.NOM lent girl-the.DAT computer-the.ACC	Computer-the.NOM was lent
selja	'sell'	He.NOM sold man-the.DAT boat-the.ACC	Boat-the.NOM was sold
handa	'hand'	John.NOM handed me.DAT butter-the.ACC	Butter-the.NOM was handed
vísa	'show'	I.NOM showed boy-the.DAT book-the.ACC	Book-the.NOM was shown
bjóða	'offer'	We.NOM offered women-the.DAT tickets.ACC	Tickets.NOM were offered
veita	'bestow'	They.NOM bestowed men-the.DAT pensions.ACC	Pensions.NOM were bestowed
flyta yvir	'transfer'	He.NOM transferred money-the.DAT over to bank-the.ACC	Money-the.NOM was transferred
lova	'promise'	She.NOM promised me.DAT money-the.ACC	Money-the.NOM was promised

176 *Ditransitives*

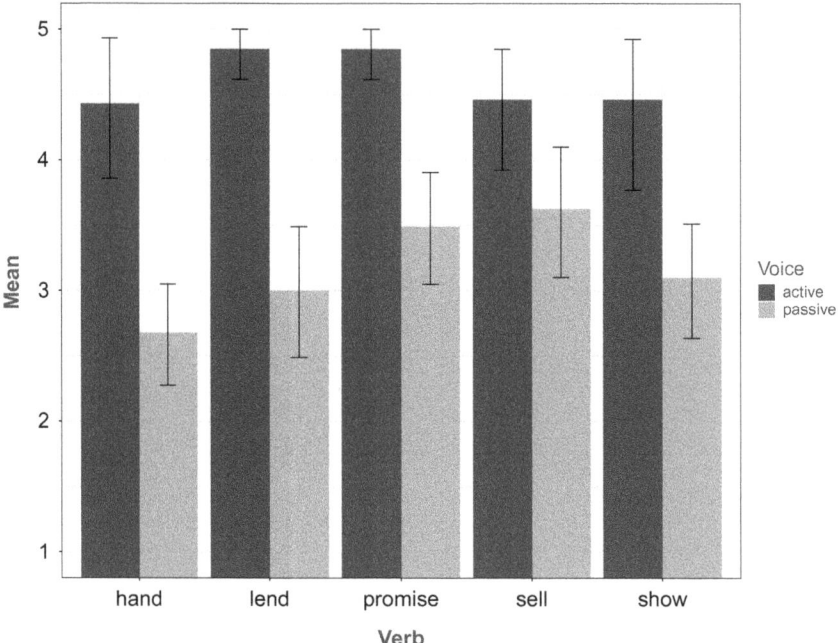

Figure 7.3 Faroese ditransitive passive survey results: Active versus passive

commented that *flyta yvir* 'transfer' is more commonly simply *flyta* without the particle *yvir*, and that *yvirføra* might be used colloquially (a Danish loan, Da. *overføre*). The verb *bjóða* 'offer' has two inflectional paradigms, a strong inflection (*buðu*), which was used in one example, and a weak inflection (*bjóðaðar*), used in the other. If some speakers reject one or other paradigm, which may exhibit dialectal variation, this could explain the lower mean acceptability of even the active with *bjóða*.

However, the acceptability of the passive is also affected by order of the arguments, consistent with the OLG analysis of the 'give' passive. Figure 7.4 shows that the order Theme-Goal is more acceptable across the board than the order Goal-Theme, apart from in the highly questioned examples with 'bestow'. With the Theme-Goal order, it is notable that the verb 'sell' has a mean acceptability between 4 and 5 on the scale, which corresponds to the example cited by Þráinsson et al. (2012:266), 'Cow-the.NOM was sold farmer-the.DAT', given as (169)

7.4 Icelandic 'Give' Passive, Other Faroese Passives

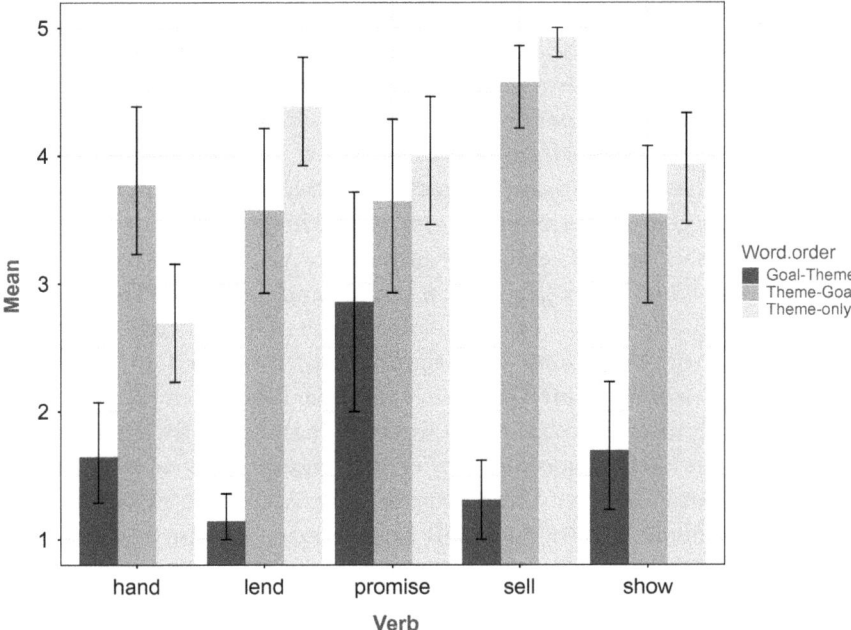

Figure 7.4 Faroese ditransitive passive survey results: Word order

above. Examples with only the theme argument were also tested, all of which had a temporal phrase following the participle (e.g. 'The boat was sold yesterday'). As can be seen again in Figure 7.4, verb lexeme has a strong effect on acceptability, which may be predictable from the semantic decomposition: 'sell' and 'lend' were most acceptable on average in comparison to 'hand', which was far more readily accepted with two arguments; this could be due to the nature of a handing event versus a selling or lending event.

The factors of voice, verb lexeme, word order, and the interaction of verb and word order were also tested for significance using an ordered logit regression model in R similar to those described in Chapters 4–7, with random effects for speaker and item. Considering the fixed effect of voice alone on the entire dataset, passive was judged significantly worse than active, as predicted ($\beta = -1.07$, $p < 0.02$). In a dataset excluding the actives and results for 'bestow' and 'offer', the effect of word order by itself was significant, in that both Theme-Goal ($\beta = 3.9$, $p < 0.01$) and Theme-only ($\beta = 2.1$,

$p < 0.01$) were judged significantly better on average than Goal-Theme. This is consistent with the analysis proposed for the 'give' passive, which rules out Goal-Theme by the relatively high ranking of S[+HR]. With the passive of 'hand' as intercept, the passive of 'promise' had a significantly greater mean acceptability ($\beta = 2.3$, $p < 0.01$). Several significant interactions between word order and verb lexeme emerged on this model: 'lend' with Theme-only order ($\beta = 5.2$, $p < 0.01$), 'sell' with Theme-only order ($\beta = 7.1$, $p < 0.01$), 'promise' with Theme-Goal order ($\beta = -2.5$, $p < 0.02$) and 'sell' with Theme-Goal order ($\beta = 3.2$, $p<0.01$). In other words, Theme-only order improved the passive of 'lend' and 'sell' significantly compared to the effect with 'hand', while Theme-Goal order improved the mean judgement of 'promise' significantly less than it did with 'hand'; finally, Theme-Goal improved the average acceptability of 'sell' significantly more so than it did with 'hand'. In all of these cases the reference level for word order was Goal-Theme. Given the small sample size, we must be cautious with our conclusions, but it seems that minimally we can ascertain that (i) ditransitive passive across the board was judged significantly worse than ditransitive active in Faroese, and (ii) Theme-Goal and Theme-only orders are judged significantly better than Goal-Theme, which was judged unacceptable overall.

7.5 Summary of Chapter

In this chapter, an overview was presented of the limited prior work on three-argument verbs in Faroese. New survey data were laid out from the Faroe Islands and Iceland on passives of 'give' and other ditransitive predicates. I posited that the same constraints adopted to account for passives of monotransitives are at work in the realisation of ditransitive passives, which in Faroese yield either null output (passive unacceptable) or the passive with Theme-Goal order: a competing grammars situation dependent on the ranking of {DEP[+HR]/P, PARSE}, but in which the ranking PARSE » DEP[+HR]/P is more likely to be selected in Faroese, hence the reduced acceptability of ditransitive passive. We proposed the pair of constraints, DEP[+HR]/P and MAX[−LR] that enforce correspondence of [+HR] abstract/positional case and realisation of dative abstract case respectively, to account for the differences between Faroese, Icelandic and English 'give' passives. I demonstrated that, at least for the overtly case-marked variants, these constraints generate the correct typology.

8

Alternative Hypotheses

It is often useful to undertake cross-theory comparison, particularly when evaluating the merits of a particular approach to a dataset which has been discussed from other theoretical perspectives. This chapter examines some alternative accounts of the core Faroese data, specifically the existence of the dative–accusative case pattern with the subset of verbs that retain lexical subject case. I argue (i) that these accounts are not explicitly articulated enough to achieve empirical coverage of the data presented in Chapters 4–7, (ii) that based on the information given, these alternatives make wrong predictions, and (iii) that OLG offers a more thoroughly worked-out system for explaining the emergence of the Faroese pattern, as well as the differences between Icelandic, Faroese and Mainland Scandinavian languages. The OLG approach, given the starting assumptions laid out in Chapters 2–3 and more fully in Chapter 9, is flexible enough to account for the full range of morphosyntactic variation, both intra- and cross-linguistically, which can be successfully modelled by competing rankings of universal, violable constraints.

8.1   Woolford (2007): An OT Account

The first theoretical account that attempts to deal with the Faroese dative–accusative pattern explicitly is a brief paragraph in Woolford (2007). As Woolford (2007) notes, the standard approach to the Icelandic dative–nominative pattern is to claim that the V-head can only license accusative case if the subject is an agent, a claim known as

'Burzio's Generalisaion' that originates in Burzio (1986). The basic assumptions are as follows: (i) that a nominative case feature is associated with Infl, (ii) that case features on heads license arguments, and in doing so assign their value to the argument (Chomsky 1995, 2001), and (iii) that experiencer subjects such as the Icelandic datives do not exhaust the nominative case feature, which (iv) takes priority over accusative assignment to the object. However, as Woolford (2007) points out, there are exceptions to Burzio's Generalisation, namely, verbs without an agent licensing accusative and verbs with an agent not licensing accusative. Moreover, the Faroese pattern represents an instance where accusative is taking priority over nominative, the opposite of assumption (iv).

Woolford (2007) accounts for this by means of a hierarchy of case markedness constraints that conflicts with a hierarchy of case faithfulness constraints, given in (187). Although these constraints derive case-marking patterns through the EVAL computation, Woolford (2007) still assumes that heads assign case, presumably via head-specifier and head-complement relations. Thus, her account differs from Kiparsky (1997, 2001) and that of OLG in that abstract and morphosyntactic case are collapsed: case is configurationally assigned, and so other means must be found to explain mismatches between thematic structure, argument positions and the case-marking on arguments.

(187) a. Markedness constraints: *ERGATIVE » *DATIVE » *ACCUSATIVE
b. Faithfulness constraints: MAX-ERGATIVE » MAX-DATIVE » MAX-ACCUSATIVE

In Icelandic dative–nominative predicates, Woolford accounts for the selection of nominative object case by the ranking MAX-DAT » *DAT » *ACC. Since the candidate with accusative object case incurs a violation of *ACC and the one with the nominative object does not, the dative–nominative pattern wins on this ranking.

(188) **Icelandic dative–nominative predicate**

NP$_{[DAT]}$ NP$_{[\ ]}$	MAX-DAT	*DAT	*ACC
☞ a. [NP$_{[DAT]}$ Infl [V NP$_{[NOM]}$]]		*	
b. [NP$_{[DAT]}$ Infl [V NP$_{[ACC]}$]]		*	*!
c. [NP$_{[NOM]}$ Infl [V NP$_{[ACC]}$]]	*!		*

However, no ranking of these constraints alone will generate the Faroese dative–accusative pattern. Woolford (2007) proposes that a higher ranked locality constraint blocks the Infl head from assigning nominative. Her motivation for the locality constraint is that nominative is not blocked VP-internally in unaccusative expletive constructions such as (189):

(189) Far. Tað eru komnir   nakrir   gestir   í gjár
           EXPL are come.NOM.PL some.NOM.PL guests.NOM.PL yesterday
           'Some guests came yesterday'

Woolford then argues that this example indicates that the presence of the 'closer' dative subject in dative–accusative predicates blocks nominative licensing, since when the dative subject is not present, nominative licensing occurs within the VP. She states that Faroese prohibits an additional NP inside the nominative case-licensing domain of Infl. This obviously rests on the assumption that there is a nominative case-checking domain, which Woolford takes to be the entire clause in both (189) and the dative–accusative predicates; the accusative case-checking domain is taken to be the VP. Woolford formulates the locality constraint as follows:

(190) PURE DOMAIN: The Case checking/licensing domain of a head must contain no NP other than the one whose Case is checked by that head.

If in Faroese the ranking PURE DOMAIN » *ACC holds, the correct outputs are generated for dative–accusative and expletive constructions:

(191) **Faroese dative–accusative predicate**

NP$_{[DAT]}$ NP$_{[\ ]}$	PURE DOMAIN	*ACC
a. [NP$_{[DAT]}$ Infl [V NP$_{[NOM]}$]]	*!	
☞ b. [NP$_{[DAT]}$ Infl [V NP$_{[ACC]}$]]		*

(192) **Faroese unaccusative**

NP$_{[\ ]}$	PURE DOMAIN	*ACC
☞ a. [∅ Infl [V NP$_{[NOM]}$]]		
b. [∅ Infl [V NP$_{[ACC]}$]]		*!

According to Woolford, since the dative subject is present within the IP in (191a), the nominative case-checking domain is 'impure'. She claims that since (191b) has no nominative argument, it has no nominative checking domain at all, and so PURE DOMAIN is not violated. It seems that the assumption is that the dative subject is not case-checked by the Infl head, and therefore would only violate PURE DOMAIN if an NP within the clause receives nominative case-marking. If the ranking for Icelandic is *ACC » PURE DOMAIN, the dative–nominative candidate will win over the dative–accusative.

The intuition behind this approach, similar to that espoused by dependent case approaches (Marantz 1991 and subsequent studies), is that arguments within some specified domain compete for case, and that realisation of accusative depends on some other language-specific factor, such as whether the case-checking domain tolerates more than one unchecked argument Woolford (2007), or whether the dative subject is a viable 'case-competitor' (Preminger 2011, 2014). While Woolford's approach attributes the contrast between Icelandic and Faroese to a markedness constraint *Acc conflicting with a locality constraint, in the OLG account we essentially adopt the inverse: a faithfulness constraint Max[–HR] (equivalent to Max-Acc) conflicts with a markedness constraint Agr[+HR]. In the simple cases, these two hypotheses cannot be distinguished empirically, but there may be good reason to avoid a locality constraint as responsible for ruling out accusative. One such issue is that the Goal-Theme order of Icelandic ditransitive passives will have a dative-marked argument within the domain of Infl that is not the one whose case is checked by Infl, thus violating Pure Domain if we assume the same definition in (190); this predicts the wrong winner.

(193) Icelandic Goal-Theme ditransitive passive (wrong winner)

Goal_[DAT] Theme_[ ]	*Acc	Pure Domain
☞ a. [Theme_[NOM] Infl [V Goal_[DAT]]]		
b. [Goal_[DAT] Infl [V Theme_[NOM]]]		*!

One question is why the regular transitive nominative–accusative pattern does not violate Pure Domain. Woolford (2007) does not make this explicit, but let us assume that the domain of Infl can only 'see into' VP when the internal argument bears nominative, since then it will be checked by Infl. In other words, VP is impenetrable to the domain of Infl with respect to Pure Domain if V assigns case to an argument, or rather, the object argument bearing accusative does not count as another argument within Infl's checking domain. Since the lower argument in (193a) bears lexical case, it is not checked by Infl and so does not incur a violation of Pure Domain: only when there is a nominative object will Pure Domain come into play. This assumption is necessary to account for dative-object predicates such as the active of verbs like 'help': if Pure Domain is violated by lexical dative object case, then we would predict accusative–dative to occur in Faroese, since either order of nominative and dative will violate Pure Domain; hence, on the ranking PURE DOMAIN » *ACC the accusative–dative pattern will win, as shown in (194). Therefore, we must change the analysis in order to account for both the Faroese nominative–dative and Icelandic dative–nominative patterns, or indeed both case-frames occurring in the same construction in the same language, as is the case for Icelandic ditransitive passives.

(194) Faroese nominative–dative predicate (wrong winner)

NP[ ] NP[DAT]	MAX-DAT	PURE DOMAIN viol. by DAT object	*ACC
a. [NP[NOM] Infl [V NP[DAT]]]		*!	
b. [NP[DAT] Infl [V NP[NOM]]]		*!	
☞ c. [NP[ACC] Infl [V NP[DAT]]]			*
d. [NP[NOM] Infl [V NP[ACC]]]	*!		*

One option is to adopt the definition of PURE DOMAIN in (190) but posit competing grammars in Icelandic, one with the ranking *ACC » PURE DOMAIN and the other with PURE DOMAIN » *ACC. The conditions under which one grammar is selected over another would depend on what selecting the Goal-Theme versus the Theme-Goal order in Icelandic communicates. If it turns out that information-structural conditions determine one output choice over another, it would perhaps call for positing two inputs and one discourse-structural faithfulness constraint, ensuring that the order of arguments reflects the information structure specified in the input.

A more fundamental question is whether PURE DOMAIN is the kind of constraint we wish to posit in the first place: what it encodes is the idea that there is a case-marking domain embedded within another (VP within IP), that the presence of a second argument must be determined by the higher head, and that the higher head can penetrate the embedded domain only if it does not case-mark the external argument. These are not necessarily problematic assumptions, but encoding them into a single constraint masks the components of the analysis: it must be assumed that (i) positional licensing and case-marking are one and the same, (ii) that case-marking is partly determined by the presence or absence of an argument within the same clause as a particular head, and (iii) that the mechanism for determining whether an argument is present is sensitive to the case-marking of that argument. A better way of encoding these claims would be to separate out licensing from identifying the presence/absence of arguments and ensuring that lexical and structural cases are expressed in the output. One could imagine the constraints as follows; let us

184 *Alternative Hypotheses*

test both claims regarding sensitivity to the presence of an argument, that is, whether the argument simply has to be present, or whether structural case is also relevant:

(195) *2VISARG (*2VA): assign a violation for each tensed clause (IP) with more than one argument visible to Infl, where a visible argument does not bear structural case (i.e. case assigned by the local head).

(196) *2ARG: assign a violation for each tensed clause (IP) containing more than one argument.

(197) MAXLEXCASE: assign a violation for each lexical case feature in the input not realised in the output.

(198) POSCASE: assign a violation for each A-position whose argument does not bear the case value specified by the local head.

With the addition of *ACC, this system is able to generate the correct facts in Faroese and Icelandic. However, tableaux (199–201) show that neither *2VA nor *2ARG are necessary: MAXLEXCASE, *ACC and POSCASE are doing all the work.

(199) Icelandic dative–nominative predicate

NP$_{[DAT]}$ NP$_{[\ ]}$	MAXLEXCASE	*ACC	POSCASE	*2VA	*2ARG
☞ a. [NP$_{[DAT]}$ Infl [V NP$_{[NOM]}$]]			**	*	*
b. [NP$_{[DAT]}$ Infl [V NP$_{[ACC]}$]]		*!	*		*
c. [NP$_{[NOM]}$ Infl [V NP$_{[ACC]}$]]	*!	*			*

(200) Faroese dative–accusative predicate

NP$_{[DAT]}$ NP$_{[\ ]}$	MAXLEXCASE	POSCASE	*ACC	*2VA	*2ARG
a. [NP$_{[DAT]}$ Infl [V NP$_{[NOM]}$]]		**!		*	*
☞ b. [NP$_{[DAT]}$ Infl [V NP$_{[ACC]}$]]		*	*		*
c. [NP$_{[NOM]}$ Infl [V NP$_{[ACC]}$]]	*!		*		*

(201) Faroese nominative–dative predicate

NP$_{[\ ]}$ NP$_{[DAT]}$	MAXLEXCASE	POSCASE	*ACC	*2VA	*2ARG
☞ a. [NP$_{[NOM]}$ Infl [V NP$_{[DAT]}$]]		*			*
b. [NP$_{[DAT]}$ Infl [V NP$_{[NOM]}$]]		**!		*	*
c. [NP$_{[NOM]}$ Infl [V NP$_{[ACC]}$]]	*!		*		*

Therefore, it seems that an OT analysis that adopts some concept of positional licensing and a constraint that penalises arguments occupying the wrong position is sufficient: the complex mechanism for determining whether another argument is present, and/or whether it is case-checked by a head, *does not seem to add anything with respect to these data*. Essentially, the easiest way to alter Woolford's analysis to account for the range of data explored in this book is to turn it into a version of our OLG analysis: MAXLEXCASE and POSCASE were deliberately notated differently from MAX[LC] and MATCHCASE to keep the hypotheses distinct, but they are the same concepts, and *ACC is merely the inverse of MAX[−HR].

8.2 Jónsson (2009): 'Covert Nominative'

Jóhannes Gísli Jónsson (2009) proposes a somewhat different account of the Faroese dative–accusative pattern. His argument is as follows: dative subjects in finite clauses have 'nominative case which is not morphologically realized' (Jónsson 2009:157). He assumes that there is a requirement for a nominative subject to appear in subject position, which he distinguishes from positional licensing, rather like our S[+HR] versus MATCHCASE. The basic idea is that both nominative and dative case are assigned, but since dative is more highly specified, if present it blocks the morphological spellout of nominative (Jónsson 2009:157). He proposes this on the basis of agreement facts: he found that many Faroese native speakers accept agreement with dative plural subjects, as shown in his examples (202–203).

(202) Far. Nógvum   kvinnum   dáma   mannfólk við   eitt sindur av búki
           many.DAT.PL women.DAT.PL like.3PL men.ACC with a   bit   of belly
      'Many women like men with a bit of belly'

(203) Far. Teimum   dáma   at vera saman   í bólki
           they.DAT.PL like.3PL to be together in band
      'They like to be together in a group'

(Jónsson 2009:157–158)

Such examples are claimed to be 'widely accepted' by Faroese native speakers (Jónsson 2009:158): fieldwork shows this to be somewhat of an oversimplification, since distributions of responses to these types were bimodal (see Sections 4.3.1 and 5.4.1.1); however, it is the case that some speakers consistently judge sentences like (202–203) acceptable, and they are occasionally produced.[1] Jónsson suggests that number agreement here is not obligatory, since this 'covert' nominative only optionally gets assigned to the subject, which already bears dative case. In other words, it is assumed that agreement must indicate the presence

---

[1] For example, there were eight tokens of teimum dáma(r), 'them.DAT like(s).3SG/PL in the blog corpus, one of which had the plural verb 'like.PL', the other seven of which had the singular.

of nominative case, even if it does not surface as such. A supplementary argument Jónsson provides is that *sjálvur* 'self', when used with a dative subject, is more acceptable when marked nominative than when marked dative; in a 2006 survey, 58.2% of participants preferred (204a), 30.6% preferred (204b), and 11.2% said both were equally acceptable.[2]

(204) a. Far. *Sjálvur dámar honum ikki at lurta eftir tónleiki*
self.NOM likes.3SG him.DAT not to listen after music
'He himself doesn't like to listen to music'
b. Far. *Sjálvum dámar honum ikki at lurta eftir tónleiki*
self.DAT likes.3SG him.DAT not to listen after music

(Jónsson 2009:159)

Jónsson (2009) argues that the covert nominative in Faroese is responsible for occurrence of accusative case on the object, and conversely that its absence in Icelandic results in the dative–nominative pattern. All relevant assumptions about case assignment are not made explicit in Jónsson (2009), but the account necessitates some sort of valuation operation where the subject receives the nominative value from T. This is standardly assumed to be the outcome of an Agree operation (Chomsky 1995), but as others have argued, this mechanism cannot be solely responsible for case assignment (Bobaljik 2008, Galbraith 2013, Preminger 2011, 2014). Indeed, it is not made clear how Icelandic fails to assign accusative case to the theme in dative–nominative predicates on this theory. Jónsson appeals to what he calls the 'Nominative First Requirement', related to the Case in Tiers idea (Yip et al. 1987 and others) that nominative is the first case available on the structural tier. However, Case in Tiers runs into a problem with double case: an argument is supposedly not permitted to receive case from both the lexical and structural tiers, but this is exactly what is required to make structural accusative case available for the object (see Yip et al. 1987). This is a tweak that was apparently never explicitly proposed for Case in Tiers theory, but it is not far from the three-level approach proposed by Kiparsky (1997, 2001) and adopted in OLG. One key difference, then, between Jónsson (2009) and the OLG approach is that both lexical and structural case are assigned by heads in the syntax for Jónsson, while in our account the winning candidate will

---

[2] One possibility is that the nominative in (204a) is an instance of default case, which in Faroese is nominative: the question *Hvør er tað?* 'Who is it?' is answered by *Eg!* 'I.NOM', not *Meg!* 'Me.ACC' (Hjalmar Petersen, Bogi and Súsanna Vinther p.c.).

8.2 Jónsson (2009): 'Covert Nominative'   187

have the optimal configuration, with the optimal morphosyntactic case-matching and the optimal mapping from abstract to morphosyntactic case *for that input*. Essentially, positions bear the features they do because of constraint interactions that rule out other candidates: constraints on the mapping from semantic roles to syntactic structure force [–HR] to be linked to V,Comp, [+HR] to Spec,TP, and so on, rather than, for example, Spec,VP bearing [–HR]. The reason that objects in monotransitives by default bear accusative case is not because the V-head assigns it into its complement within syntax but because the winning candidate for a monotransitive input (in the absence of lexical case or some other marked elements) will match positional case [–HR] to case on the argument [–HR].

While Jónsson (2009) proposes the idea of a non-realised nominative case feature within syntax, in OLG we rather take it to be a positional case which mismatches with the dative lexical case on the subject. Unlike Jónsson, we disconnect the assignment of accusative from the presence or absence of a covert nominative feature, instead positing that a constraint enforcing the realisation of abstract accusative case (Max[–HR]) conflicts with a preference that the verb agree with a nominative argument (Agr[+HR]). In other words, it is not that Icelandic lacks some feature that Faroese has, it is simply that Icelandic tolerates a case mismatch in object position provided there is a nominative argument to trigger agreement (i.e. the ranking Agr[+HR] » Max[–HR]). Proposals like Jónsson (2009) arise from the starting assumption that case-assignment happens configurationally within syntax and is driven by features on heads. Since Jónsson's account is not explicit about when a covert nominative is or is not available, it is difficult to test empirically. Because there is always the possibility of attributing variation to the presence or absence of heads or features, it could be argued that this type of approach overgenerates: one might ask whether a covert nominative ever occurs on another functional head such as *v*, or whether there are covert versions of other case features. Even if we stipulate certain case features with certain heads (e.g. nominative with T, accusative with *v* and genitive with D), covert versions would be expected to show substitution behaviour. A covert accusative on *v*, for instance, must somehow be ruled out in Icelandic when the object bears quirky case: otherwise, we would expect the object case to be replaceable by accusative in the same manner as Faroese dative subject case, which does not in fact occur. In (205) the stage of derivation prior

188 *Alternative Hypotheses*

to subject movement to Spec,TP is shown (under standard Minimalist assumptions); in (205a), covert accusative is absent and only lexical genitive case is assigned to the object by V, while in (205b), covert accusative is assigned to the argument already marked with genitive case in the same way as the proposed covert nominative in Faroese.

(205) a. [T$_{[NOM]}$ [hann v [saknar$_{V,[GEN]}$ hennar]]]
 he.[ ]   misses   her.GEN

b. *[T$_{[NOM]}$ [hann $v_{[ACC]}$ [saknar$_{V,[GEN]}$ hana]]]
 he.[ ]   misses   her.ACC

Therefore, an account like Jónsson (2009) will need to explain why (205b) is ruled out: is it the case that covert accusative is just not available in Icelandic? By contrast, data like (205) 'come with' the linking theory approach: M$_{AX}$[LC] is ranked above M$_{AX}$[–HR], and failing to express lexically marked genitive case will incur an additional violation of M$_{AX}$[LC] in (205b). Although the theory presented in Jónsson (2009) can be altered and expanded to achieve empirical coverage, the ranking M$_{AX}$[LC] » M$_{AX}$[–HR] is proposed to be responsible for a much wider range of data than a covert feature on a functional head; likewise, the Faroese ranking M$_{AX}$[–HR] » A$_{GR}$[+HR] correctly predicts the absence of nominative objects and object agreement across the language, not merely in quirky case predicates. Of course, Jónsson's covert nominative does not fail to rule out nominative objects, but it does posit a redundant element that only assigns accusative when v fails to do so, which is a highly restricted range of constructions. If we assume a set of universal constraints with grammar-specific rankings and that such constraints govern mapping relations between levels of case, we are able to capture the variation within and across languages without positing language- or construction-specific flavours of functional heads. Indeed, the OLG model of grammar is in some ways more universal than the model standardly assumed in broadly Minimalist approaches, since all languages 'have' all constraints, rather than each grammar selecting from the set of all possible functional material.

8.3 Asarina (2011)

Asarina (2011) mentions the Faroese dative–accusative pattern, adopting a version of Sigurðsson and Holmberg's (2008) proposal that Person and Number are separate probes.³ Asarina proposes that the number probe in Faroese assigns quirky dative case to the subject, whereas in Icelandic dative subject case is assigned by a lower head; she also adopts the 'covert nominative' hypothesis put forth by Jónsson (2009). However, unfortunately some of the empirical claims made in Asarina (2011) are not supported by fieldwork data. It is claimed that nominative objects exist with dative-subject verbs in Faroese (Asarina 2011:136); examples are presented from Þráinsson et al. (2004):

(206) a. Far. *Henni treyt   pening/?-ur*
               her.DAT exhausted.3SG money.ACC/?NOM.SG
               'She ran out of money'
      b. Far. *Mær   eydnaðist   *túrin/túrurin   vœl*
               me.DAT succeeded.3SG tour-the.*ACC/NOM.SG well
               'The trip turned out nicely for me'

Although this claim that Faroese has some predicates with nominative 'objects' has been repeated in the literature (Þráinsson et al. 2004, 2012), no evidence was found for this at all in the contemporary language. Of the 24 tokens of *eydnaðist* in the blog corpus, not a single one occurred with a nominative object: 1 token occurred with a nominative subject and dative object with a clausal complement,⁴ 7 tokens occurred with a nominative argument only, and the remaining 17 occurred in an expletive construction with *tað, hetta* or some non-subject XP with a dative argument in V,Comp. All consulted native speakers expressed strong doubts about the construction in (206b), preferring either *Tað eydnaðist (mær) væl* 'EXPL succeeded (me.DAT) well' or *Tururin eydnaðist (mær) væl* 'trip-the.NOM succeeded (me.DAT) well'. Furthermore, as part of the survey described in Section 6.2.2, the verb *tróta* was tested (206a) in various constructions, and I found that the verb was unacceptable regardless of case, word order or agreement. Figure 8.1a shows mean acceptability plotted against subject case and agreement, while Figure 8.1b plots mean acceptability against object case and agreement. As is evident, none of the mean judgements approach 2.5 on the five-point scale, regardless of the case frame or agreement, and so it is safe to conclude that the verb has fallen out

---

³That is, features on functional heads that receive a value by the syntactic Agree mechanism (Chomsky 1995, 2001).
⁴*Umframt katalogarbeiðið eydnaðist honum væl at gera seks frálík prent*, 'Besides, catalogue.work-the.NOM succeeded him.DAT well to make six excellent prints', 'Besides, the catalogue work gave him success in making six excellent prints', *listinblog* line 15636.

190 *Alternative Hypotheses*

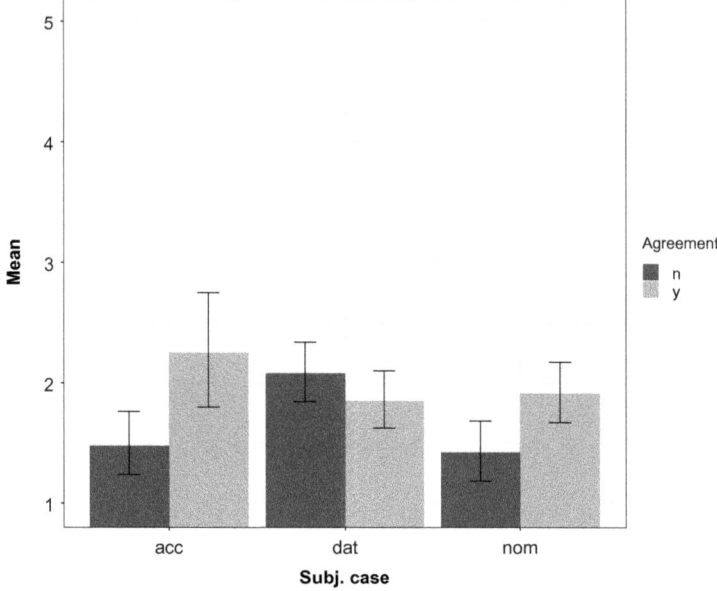

(a) Faroese survey on *tróta*: Mean acceptability by subject case and number agreement

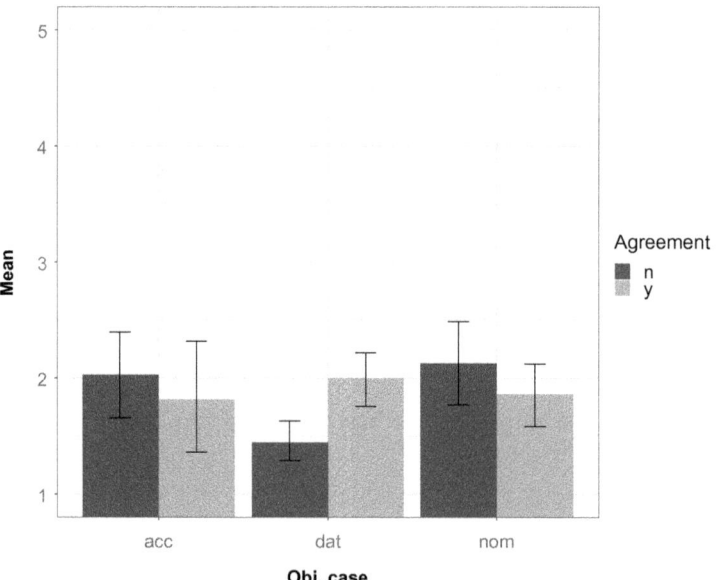

(b) Faroese survey on *tróta*: Mean acceptability by object case and number agreement

Figure 8.1 Faroese survey results on *tróta*

of use in the contemporary language. As one participant commented, 'The word *tróta* is no longer usual in Faroese'.⁵ The loss of the dative–nominative case frame can be explained as a reranking of {AGR[+HR], MAX[–HR]} from the older, Icelandic type AGR[+HR] » MAX[–HR] to the Faroese MAX[–HR] » AGR[+HR]. It could be that the examples cited by Þráinsson et al. (2004, 2012) represent an earlier stage of the language in which the ranking AGR[+HR] » MAX[–HR] was statistically more likely to be activated than in contemporary Faroese.

Asarina's account of the Faroese dative–accusative pattern is based on the timing of case assignment. If we suppose that dative subject case is assigned to the higher argument later in the derivation than in Icelandic, it could be that accusative case is assigned to the lower argument, and number agreement triggered with the higher argument, prior to the assignment of dative case (Asarina 2011:138). In other words, the dative subject in Faroese behaves like a nominative at some point before the sentence is fully derived. Asarina posits that a higher functional head than V is responsible for assigning dative case to the subject in Faroese, which she identifies as the Number head. The assumption is that this is always projected in some form, one which assigns dative case to the subject and one which does not; which form is merged depends on the verb lexeme (Asarina 2011:140). Asarina argues that if the number agreement projection can either agree with the subject and then assign case or assign case before attempting to agree with the subject, this is supposed to explain the optionality of number agreement with the dative subject in Faroese. The reason person agreement is not available with the dative is explicable if the person probe is higher in the structure than the number probe, which would mean that number agreement has already occurred before the subject ends up in Spec,TP. However, the only empirical evidence presented for splitting the person and number heads in Faroese is the fact that person agreement is not possible with a dative subject, while number agreement is attested; it is simply stipulated that the number head assigns dative. Therefore, it would need to be established (i) that the person and number heads must be separated to account for the unavailability of person agreement with the dative subject, and (ii) that the number head is able to assign dative case. By far the simpler solution is to assume positional licensing but also permit mismatches

---

⁵ *Orðið tróta er ikki longur vanligt á føroyskum.*

between subject position case and the occupying dative, and this is easiest to implement in a system of ranked, violable constraints such as OT. Moreover, we do not need to attribute the accusative object case to timing of movement operations, since accusative is the standard object case associated with V,Comp: constraint conflict, as demonstrated in Chapter 4, derives the correct case-marking patterns in Faroese and Icelandic without referencing movement at all.

8.4 Summary of Chapter

To summarise this section, various alternative possibilities to the OLG model have been presented. It was concluded that there are both conceptual and empirical reasons to favour an account which acknowledges semantic, syntactic and morphological case, that does not attribute cross-linguistic variation solely to features on functional heads but also to different rankings of markedness and faithfulness constraints, and which captures the attested intra-linguistic variation via competing grammars. New survey data showed that claims repeated in the literature that nominative objects occur in Faroese are unsubstantiated with respect to the verb *tróta*, and hence that those examples do not falsify the Max[−HR] » Agr[+HR] ranking for Faroese.

9
Syntax in OLG

9.1 Introduction

Chapter 3 provided a brief overview of Linking Theory (LT) and the basic starting assumptions behind the Optimality Theory (OT) model of grammar adopted in OLG. However, many questions remain as to the specifics of how the correct outputs are generated. This chapter broaches the major issues common to all theories of syntax. Here I propose that the OLG framework not only accounts for the data examined in Chapters 4–7, offering a deeper explanation thereof than the alternatives in Chapter 8, but also provides a model of syntax that is explicit, empirically sound and cross-linguistically tractable. Section 9.2 lays out how GEN produces output candidates, and how the word-order harmonisation derives the correct typology of headedness, including the Final Over Final Constraint. In Section 9.3, syntactic phenomena classically attributed to movement, such as filler–gap dependencies, are discussed, in addition to constraints on locality. Section 9.4 gives explicit formalisms for the syntactic features proposed in this book, and Section 9.5 provides a step-by-step derivation of an English sentence. Section 9.6 revisits the Faroese sentence types discussed in Section 2.3, providing ranking arguments for the proposed constraints; in Section 9.7, a theory of information-structural constraints is developed, and in Section 9.7.1 I show how to derive Holmberg's Generalisation from adverb adjunction and the relevant discourse constraints. Factorial typologies are provided for the proposed constraints throughout this chapter. The goal is to give a sufficiently detailed outline of the theory to be of use for future research while also providing empirical support and conceptual argumentation for the relevant components. A general familiarity with syntactic theory is assumed, in particular the notational conventions of the Government and Binding (GB)/Minimalist tradition, but the content should be accessible independently of one's theoretical perspective.

9.2 Phrase Structure

The first important question to answer in developing a theory of syntax is of course how syntactic structures themselves are generated. Most mainstream theories assume some generalised structure-building mechanism, for example Merge (Chomsky 1995). An OT model does not necessarily restrict the mechanism by which inputs are generated, although it is more consistent with OT principles to retain as much universality as possible in the generative component and membership of the set of constraints while attributing cross-linguistic differences to different constraint rankings. Therefore, following Prince and Smolensky (1993:209), Smolensky and Legendre (2006:529) and others, let us assume the 'richness of the base', that is, the set of possible inputs must be universal. In syntax, as in phonology, we construe this to mean that the set of possible inputs is a result of freely combining all primitives in all possible ways (McCarthy 2011); the set of output candidates will be the result of this combinatoric mechanism. However, it should be noted that one criticism of OT is a halting problem, since GEN would have to generate a set of candidates of arbitrary or infinite size before EVAL can begin. Instead, following Minimalist approaches, we assume that while the set of possible inputs is universal, the actual input is limited by the pre-lexical semantic primitives a speaker needs for a given sentence. In this way, we retain both the universality of the generative component and its restrictiveness, since the speaker selects a subset of available primitives from a much larger set of possibilities. The lexicon of a given language is hence a finite subset of primitives inferred by learners from the stimulus; lexical entries are formulated according

9.2 Phrase Structure

to the distribution of elements in observed grammatical structures (Smolensky 1996). The 'grammar' of GEN is minimally defined as a mechanism that generates trees with items and features occupying positions: the primitives of syntax being lexical/functional items and a hierarchical structure, analogous to phonological features occupying the positions of a hierarchical prosodic or syllable structure.

9.2.1 GEN: A Tree Adjoining Grammar

It has long been established, with argumentation dating back to as early as Chomsky (1957), that context-free grammars are insufficiently powerful to describe natural language due to phenomena such as crossing dependencies (see, e.g., Frank 2004a:675). On the other hand, fully context-sensitive grammars are overly powerful, since the set of languages generated far exceeds that of natural language; see Savitch (1987) for discussion. An alternative route has been to explore mildly context-sensitive languages, such as Tree Adjoining Grammars (Joshi et al. 1975, Joshi 1985 and subsequent studies). Since output candidates are properly trees rather than strings, we can formally define the tree-constructing mechanism as a Tree Adjoining Grammar (TAG).

Unlike context-free grammars, TAGs are tree-rewriting systems rather than string-rewriting. Instead of a start symbol, the derivation[1] begins with an initial tree and proceeds by rewriting of nodes in the tree with smaller structures called elementary trees (this and the following summary adapted from Frank 2004a:677). What constitutes the initial tree and possible elementary trees are defined as the grammar rules (i.e. part of GEN). There are two types of rewriting in this formalism: substitution and adjunction. In substitution, a non-terminal node in the existing structure is replaced by another elementary tree, with the restriction that the resulting node must have the same label as the root of the elementary tree replacing that node (Figure 9.1).

---

[1] I use this term as a loose descriptor here rather than making the stronger claim that the order of rewrite rules is somehow accessible to syntactic EVAL; my proposal is simply that the output of GEN consists of tree structures generated by tree-rewrite rules as specified here, not that derivational rules form part of EVAL *per se*.

196 *Syntax in OLG*

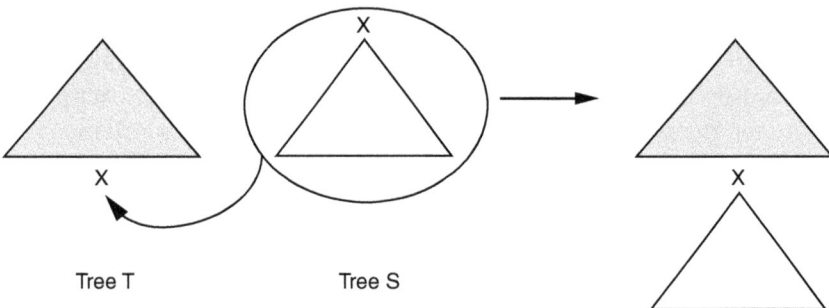

Figure 9.1 Tree Adjoining Grammar: Substitution

Adjunction, on the other hand, permits a non-terminal node anywhere in an elementary tree to be rewritten as another elementary tree called an auxiliary tree. However, adjunction is only permitted if the resulting tree has an edge node called the foot node, which dominates the structure that was dominated by the adjunction site before rewriting. This foot node must also be labelled identically to the root in order to preserve local structural relations such as parent–child or sisterhood in the original elementary tree (Figure 9.2).

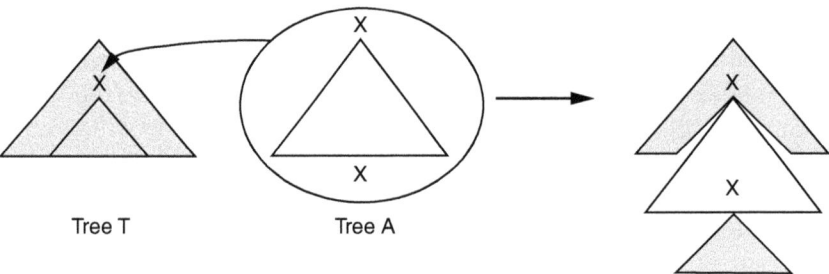

Figure 9.2 Tree Adjoining Grammar: Adjunction

Adjunction in particular permits recursive structures, since each instance of adjunction necessitates a legitimate auxiliary tree at the rewrite step and requires that the foot node have the same label as its root. The set of well-formed elementary trees is what licenses a given substitution or adjunction; the output of the TAG is therefore itself a tree produced by ordered application of the legitimate rewrite rules (Frank 2004a:678). GEN, thus, is restricted to producing output candidates that consist of trees in which each node corresponds to an elementary tree and whose child nodes are themselves elementary trees that were either substituted or adjoined.

9.2.1.1 Formal Definition

For the original mathematical definition of a TAG, see Joshi et al. (1975:138–141), with further discussion in Joshi (1985). We define the TAG here following Joshi and Schabes (1991, 1997), modified slightly for additional clarity. For a more linguistically oriented exposition of the TAG formalism, see Frank (2004b), although much of the apparatus proposed there concerns aspects of syntax handled in OLG by constraints at EVAL rather than by GEN.

(207) GEN: TREE ADJOINING GRAMMAR

> **Definition 1.1**
> A Tree Adjoining Grammar consists of a quintuple $(\Sigma, \Theta, I, A, S)$ where:
>
> i. Σ is a finite set of terminal symbols;
> ii. Θ is a finite set of non-terminal symbols: $\Sigma \cap \Theta = \emptyset$;
> iii. S is a distinguished non-terminal symbol: $S \in \Theta$;
> iv. I is a finite set of finite trees, called *initial trees*, characterised as follows:
>   - interior nodes are labelled by non-terminal symbols;
>   - the nodes on the frontier of initial trees are labelled by terminals or non-terminals; non-terminal symbols on the frontier of the trees in I are marked for substitution;
> v. A is a finite set of finite trees, called *auxiliary trees*, characterised as follows:
>   - interior nodes are labelled by non-terminal symbols;
>   - the nodes on the frontier of auxiliary trees are labelled by terminals or non-terminals; non-terminal symbols on the frontier of the trees in A are marked for substitution except for one node, called the *foot node*. In Joshi and Schabes' notation, the foot node is annotated with an asterisk (*). The label of the foot node must be identical to the label of the root node.

This version of TAG is not strictly 'lexicalised' in the sense of Joshi and Schabes (1991, 1997): although the frontier of initial or auxiliary trees usually has at least one terminal symbol, in OLG this is not enforced by GEN; rather, undominated constraints at EVAL harmonically bound candidate trees which violate subcategorisation or have superfluous empty structure. The trees in $I \cup A$ are called *elementary trees*. We call an elementary tree an XP-type elementary tree if its root is labelled by the non-terminal XP. A tree built by composition of two other trees is called a *derived tree*.

Definition 1.2 – Adjunction
Let α be a tree containing a non-substitution node n labelled by XP, and let β be an auxiliary tree whose root node is also labeled by XP. The resulting tree, obtained by adjoining β to α at node n, is built as follows:

- the subtree of n dominated by α, call it t, is excised, leaving a copy of n behind;
- the auxiliary tree β is attached at the copy of n and its root node is identified with the copy of n;
- the subtree t is attached at the foot node of β, and the root node of t (i.e. n) is identified with the foot node of β.

Adjunction is illustrated in Figure 9.3; the auxiliary tree β_1 is adjoined on the VP node in the tree α_2; the resulting tree is α_1.

Definition 1.3 – Substitution
Substitution only takes place on non-terminal nodes of the frontier of a tree, illustrated in Figure 9.4. In Joshi and Schabes' notation, the nodes on which substitution is allowed are marked by a down arrow ($\downarrow$). When substitution occurs on a node n, the node is replaced by the tree to be substituted. When a node is marked for substitution, only trees derived from initial trees can be substituted for it. In OLG, substitution is not restricted further (i.e. any non-terminal frontier node can be marked for substitution).

By definition, any adjunction on a node marked for substitution is disallowed. For example, no adjunction can be performed on any NP node in the tree α_2 in Figure 9.4. Of course, adjunction is possible on the root node of the tree substituted for the substitution node.

In the above system, an auxiliary tree can be adjoined on a node n if the label of n is identical to the label of the root node of the auxiliary tree and if n is labelled by a non-terminal symbol not annotated for substitution. This raises the question of how adjunction of auxiliary trees is restricted, for instance, nodes upon which adjunction is disallowed in a given structure or language. Unlike Joshi and Schabes (1991, 1997), however, in OLG we do not propose further constraints on adjunction to be part of GEN; instead, they are handled at EVAL. Thus, the version of TAG adopted here is essentially that of Joshi et al. (1975), in which adjunction is unconstrained beyond the description in Definition 1.2 of (207). Therefore, GEN is reduced to a tree-building mechanism with limited restrictions, allowing for greater generality and locating much of the work of enforcing syntactic well-formedness at EVAL (subcategorisation, alignment of heads and complements, filler–gap dependencies and so forth).

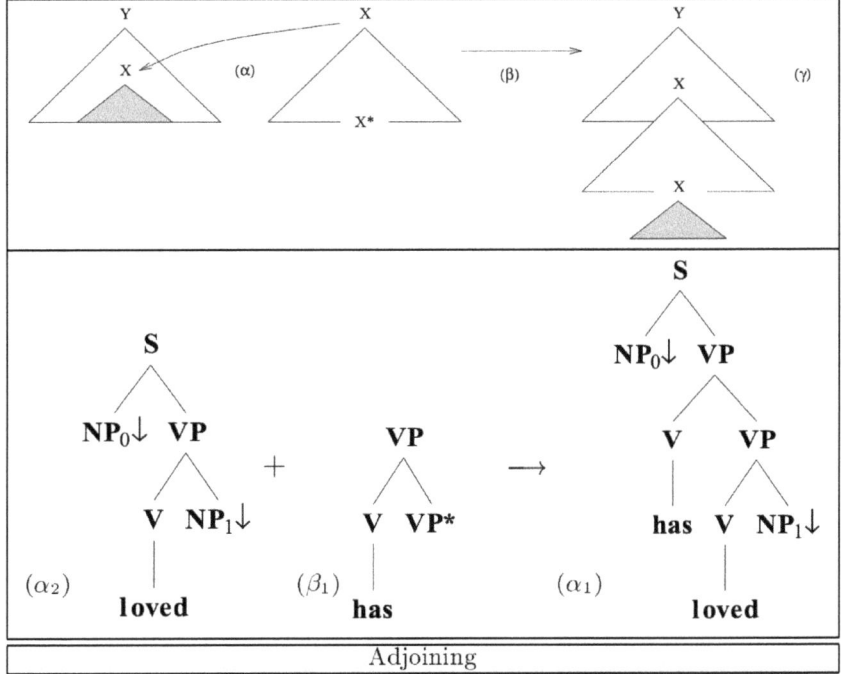

Figure 9.3 Tree Adjoining Grammar: Example of adjunction

To illustrate what the TAG might need to look like to account for the structural descriptions in this book, let us assume the following:[2]

(208) Θ = {CP, TP, VP, DP, NP, AP, PP, AdvP};
       Σ = {C, T, V, D, N, A, P, Adv};
       S ∈ Θ.

The set of non-terminals Θ and the set of terminals Σ will be straightforwardly enumerable, since the terminals are derived from universal lexical categories and the labels in the set of non-terminals are defined by the set of terminals. The set of possible elementary and derived trees for a given input will be larger than the set of well-formed tree structures for that input in that language, since the adjunction and

---

[2] vP is not included in the set of non-terminals, even though this notation is used later, because it is not assumed to be categorially distinct from VP; rather, the v-head position is an additional position occupied by items of category V.

200 *Syntax in OLG*

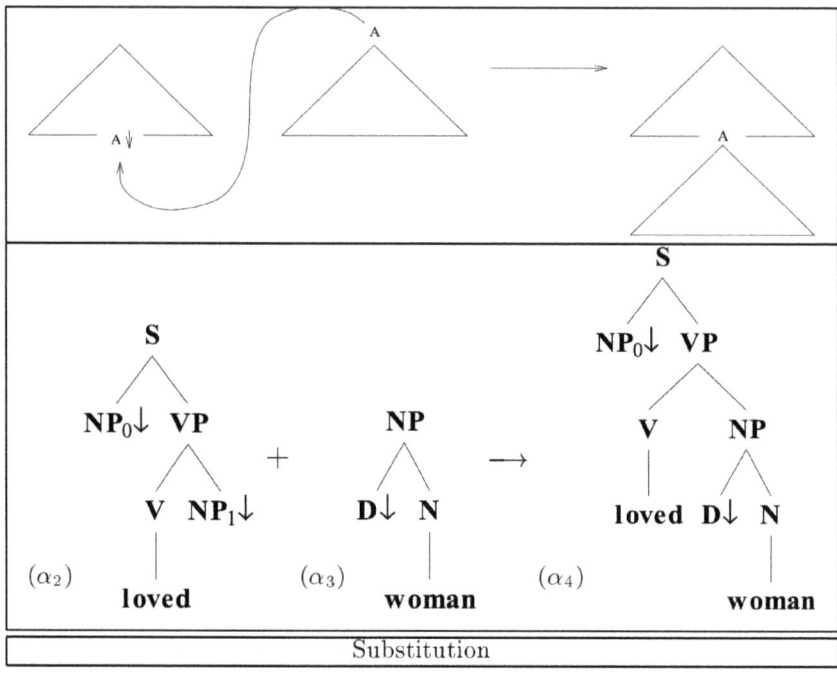

Figure 9.4 Tree Adjoining Grammar: Example of substitution

substitution definitions are category-agnostic (albeit not *label*-agnostic: a frontier XP must have its terminal node labelled X not Y). However, this is not a problem, since faithfulness constraints such as Max, Dep and Subcat will ensure that candidates produced by such rules are harmonically bounded and markedness constraints enforce X-bar theoretic structures. In this way, Gen is essentially blind to any distinction of *symbols* other than that of terminal versus non-terminal; the lexical or functional content of the symbol is relevant only to Eval. Gen also does not formally distinguish between bar levels and phrase levels: X' is merely a level of structure that is the mother of a head and sister of a specifier, concepts which are built into markedness constraints (ObHead and ObSpec) rather than Gen. The reasoning for this is that in order to permit projections without heads or specifiers, which is argued to be a more parsimonious analysis of some sentence types (see Section 2.3), the constraints enforcing them must be violable and therefore part of Eval rather than Gen. The X-bar theoretic definitions of specifier, head and complement are assumed as descriptive priors, in the same way that phonological constraints make reference to notions of 'onset' and 'coda' (Kayne 1994):

(209)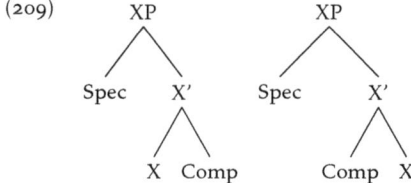

The two possible orders of heads (X) and complements (Comp) are always both generated by GEN, since there is cross-linguistic variation, and the richness of the base is assumed; alignment constraints at EVAL rule out incorrect word orders. Therefore, output candidates sent to syntactic EVAL include all logically possible orders of heads and complements present in the input. Candidates are hence *not* unordered, but both structures in (209) are always output candidates for every phrasal projection, and the candidate with the order that best satisfies the alignment constraints (for that ranking) is the winner.[3]

9.2.2 Phrase Structure Constraints

OLG attributes the bulk of the restrictions governing phrase structure to EVAL. Although endocentricity (i.e. the property that the category of a non-terminal is defined by its terminal) is handled by the label–identity requirements of GEN, compositional interpretability is governed by undominated constraints such as SUBCAT at EVAL. This captures the fact that phrase- and bar-level labels are in a sense underdetermined, since specifier and complement positions take their properties from the local head. In other words, GEN does not care about the category of an XP, merely that its head is an X not a Y; however, EVAL penalises such an X having a YP complement if X bears a subcategorisation feature that rules out YP complements.[4] **Only two undominated**

---

[3] The data examined in this book are consistent with adjuncts being evaluated at the same semantic–syntactic interface as arguments, but further work should be done to establish whether a distinct, later evaluation cycle for adjuncts is necessary. For an OT treatment of adjuncts, see Zepter (2000) Specifiers and adjuncts (Unpublished ms., Rutgers University. *Rutgers Optimality Archive* 413-0900) and the references therein.

[4] In contrast, see Narita (2014:68–76) for one recent proposal for capturing endocentricity without phrase structure rules.

constraints are necessary to account for the data under discussion here: (i) SUBCAT, which does the work equivalent to c-selection in Minimalist approaches, and (ii) *EMPTYSTRUC, which rules out unnecessary empty structure (cf. proposals in Legendre et al. 2001). They are defined as follows:

(210) SUBCAT: assign a violation for each subcategorisation feature not satisfied in the output.

(211) *EMPTYSTRUC (*EMPSTR): assign a violation for each empty position in the output that does not satisfy requirements of an input feature.

For further discussion of the features proposed here, see Section 9.4. The definition of *EMPTYSTRUC is such that subcategorised gaps and ellipsis will not be targeted by the constraint, since on this approach these phenomena are triggered by features present in the input; rather, *EMPTYSTRUC will ensure that empty specifier or complement positions beyond that required to satisfy input features will not proliferate.

As for the violable constraints responsible for phrase structure, we follow Grimshaw (2001) in positing two kinds of markedness constraints that enforce economy of projections: alignment constraints and obligatory element constraints. Alignment constraints concern the hierarchical ordering of elements in the structure. The alignment constraints are formulated as proposed by Kiparsky (2017):

(212) F<XP: assign a violation for each operator (i.e. functional head) that does not precede its operand (i.e. complement phrase) (Kiparsky 2017).

(213) HEADFINAL (HDFIN): assign a violation for each head that does not occur in the final position of its phrase (Kiparsky 2017).

(214) HARMONY (HRM): assign a violation for each phrase XP embedded in a phrase YP where XP and YP do not have the same headedness (Kiparsky 2017).

Although {F<XP, HDFIN} are sufficient to derive X-bar principles, the addition of HARMONY captures the range of attested disharmonic structures, as discussed below. The obligatory element constraints are violated when a projection does not have a head or a specifier, respectively (Grimshaw 2001:2–3):[5]

(215) OBHEAD (OBHD): assign a violation for each phrase not containing an overt head.

(216) OBSPEC (OBSP): assign a violation for each phrase not containing a specifier.

---

[5]The reason for formulating OBHEAD such that it is satisfied only by an overt head is explained in Section 9.3.

These constraints are sufficient to generate well-formed structures that obey X-bar theoretic principles. Hierarchical relations between positions, such as the notions of specifier and complement, must be referred to within syntax and, hence, are encoded in the constraints. It should be noted that these constraints are somewhat analogous to those responsible for syllable structure: for instance, OBSPEC is similar to ONSET, which requires every syllable to have an onset. Indeed, it should therefore be unsurprising if phrases without specifiers exist given that faithfulness to the input can be satisfied without them, in the same way that onsetless syllables exist without violating highly ranked faithfulness constraints. It is assumed that there is no constraint OBCOMP, since many projections consist solely of a head; similarly, it would be implausible to posit a constraint OBCODA, since there is no language in which codas are always obligatory.

9.2.3 Deriving Word-Order Typology

Head-initiality and head-finality are derived by the pair of constraints {F<XP, HDFIN}: head-initial order by the ranking F<XP » HDFIN, and head-final order by the ranking HDFIN » F<XP, as shown in the tableaux (adapted from Grimshaw 2001:5–6). The orders Head-Spec-Comp and Comp-Spec-Head are excluded, since the definition of head and complement is that they be sisters, and a specifier is by definition a left-edge position within the phrasal projection. Therefore such candidates would always incur at least one additional OBHEAD and OBSPEC violation compared to the equivalent candidates with left-edge specifiers and head-complement sisterhood, in the same way that a syllable structure such as Nucleus-Onset-Coda would violate ONSET where Onset-Nucleus-Coda would not.[6] Throughout the tableaux in this chapter, the notation $\{\alpha,\beta\}$ is used to denote an unordered set, and $[\alpha\ \beta]$ to denote a linearly ordered syntactic constituent.

(217) **Head-initial**

{Spec, H, Comp}	F<XP	HDFIN
☞ a. [Spec H Comp]		*
b. [Spec Comp H]	*!	

---

[6]It is questionable whether languages with right-edge specifiers exist: languages with ostensibly subject-final declarative word orders, such as Malagasy (VOS), do not necessarily call for a rightward-specifier analysis (Pearson 1998, 2005), nor do languages with OVS surface order, such as Hixkaryana (Mahajan 2007, Kalin 2011).

(218) **Head-final**

{Spec, H, Comp}	HdFin	F<XP
a. [Spec H Comp]	*!	
☞ b. [Spec Comp H]		*

As mentioned earlier, in order to derive disharmonic word orders while ruling out the order *[[H Comp] Op], where Op is an operator taking a complement, an additional constraint must be in operation. This restriction is known as the Final Over Final Constraint (FOFC), proposed by Biberauer et al. (2007, 2008) and subsequent studies; see Sheehan et al. (2017) for a recent overview. Kiparsky (2017) proposes the three constraints (212–214), adopted here to derive the FOFC and concomitant typological generalisations: HARMONY, ensuring that if A dominates B, A and B have the same headedness; HEADFIN, enforcing that arguments precede their predicates; and F<XP, enforcing that functional heads (operators) precede their operands. An example ranking deriving each of the possible orders is shown in (219–221):

(219)
{Op, {H, Comp}}	F<XP	HdFin	Hrm
☞ a. [Op [Comp H]]		*	*
b. [Op [H Comp]]		**!	
c. [[Comp H] Op]	*!		
d. *[[H Comp] Op]	*!	*	*

(220)
{Op, {H, Comp}}	Hrm	F<XP	HdFin
a. [Op [Comp H]]	*!		*
☞ b. [Op [H Comp]]			**
c. [[Comp H] Op]		*!	
d. *[[H Comp] Op]	*!	*	*

(221)
{Op, {H, Comp}}	HdFin	F<XP	Hrm
a. [Op [Comp H]]	*!		*
b. [Op [H Comp]]	**!		
☞ c. [[Comp H] Op]		*	
d. *[[H Comp] Op]	*!	*	*

Candidates (a), (b) and (c) are each winners on two rankings, but there is no ranking in which *[[H Comp] Op] can win, since it is always harmonically bounded. The alignment constraints are universal, as are the candidates and violations incurred by each candidate: the only difference, then, between uniformly head-initial and head-final languages is the ranking of these two constraints.[7] Therefore, in every

---

[7] One might posit a more general version of F<XP that is violated also by any head failing to precede its complement, but such a constraint derives the wrong typology of headedness (Kiparsky 2017).

grammar, under any ranking, a projection with a functional head and complement will incur a violation of {F<XP, HDFIN}, and a projection with a single element satisfies all the alignment constraints. Hence, in order to generate projections with more than a single element, the alignment constraints conflict with those requiring certain syntactic elements to be present in the structure.

The work done by the obligatory element constraints is, unsurprisingly, to ensure that projections have a head and a specifier. This also rules out completely empty structures, which despite not violating alignment constraints (since there is nothing to misalign), violate both OBHEAD and OBSPEC. Moreover, projections with a single element necessarily violate OBHEAD, OBSPEC or both. Thus, every type of projection in every grammar necessarily incurs violations of the constraints governing X-bar structure. This corollary is desirable, since it is only by constraint conflict that we derive structural economy: the combination of alignment and obligatory element constraints prohibits proliferation of empty projections (Grimshaw 2001:12–15).

Output candidates with increasing amounts of empty structure are harmonically bounded by simpler, smaller structures with fewer elements and can never win.[8] It is the job of the *faithfulness* constraints to make sure that the optimal candidate has sufficient structure for the elements in the input to be inserted and that said items are inserted in the correct positions. **In other words, the rationale behind the constraints is to achieve a more parsimonious analysis, since no empty position or structure will be present in a winning candidate unless empirically supported.** Rather than formulating GEN such that every head projects a specifier, and hence typical outputs beyond individual sentences will contain hundreds of empty specifiers or head positions that are never occupied by overt material, this approach allows us to posit only the structure that is absolutely necessary for insertion of syntactic items and the satisfying of their featural requirements. This system is thus close to that of Bare Phrase Structure (Chomsky 1994 and subsequent studies), in which the labels of non-terminals are determined by one element of the tuple created by the Merge operation (i.e. the head projects its label to the phrasal constituent). In the same way, in OLG the undominated constraints SUBCAT and *EMPTYSTRUC derive endocentricity and the minimal necessary structure for features

---

[8]Excluding the case where presence of a head is preferred over its absence; see Grimshaw (2001:11).

to be discharged. However, by positing undominated constraints as part of EVAL, not imposed on GEN as is effectively the case in Minimalism, we allow the structure-building mechanism to be as general as possible while achieving the same restrictions on tree well-formedness. As has been demonstrated in Chapters 4–7, this approach to grammar makes verifiable predictions that turn out to be consistent with the data examined, thus lending empirical support to the OLG model.

9.3 Movement, or Fillers and Gaps

9.3.1 Base Order

The linear ordering that results from the language-specific ranking of the constraints governing phrase structure is assumed to be the 'base' order, but in a different sense from that of transformational approaches. Indeed, since OLG does not posit a derivational model, base position is merely a traditional descriptor for structures in an output candidate that satisfy the word-order constraints without failing to realise input features. Therefore, *not every input will represent the base order* or *be considered to 'have' a base structure*: only that given input–output pair which fits a certain structural description.[9] In OLG it is assumed that the base position of a syntactic element is defined in (222):

(222) The base position β of a syntactic element α is that winning output candidate which:
- (i) incurs no violation of SUBCAT;
- (ii) satisfies all MATCH-type constraints targeting the syntactic features of α and β; and
- (iii) incurs no violations of higher-ranked constraints if α occurs in β.

Hence, an example of a structure that does *not* have or represent a base order would be presentational expletive constructions, in which the associate occurs in V,Comp: the winning candidate will incur a violation of MATCHCASE, since the V,Comp position bears [−HR] and the associate [+HR], as shown in (223).

---

[9]In that sense, base position is less useful terminology in a representational theory, but it can approximate a notion of markedness, in that the base order is typically less marked (e.g. polar questions versus simple declaratives in languages with subject–auxiliary inversion).

(223)
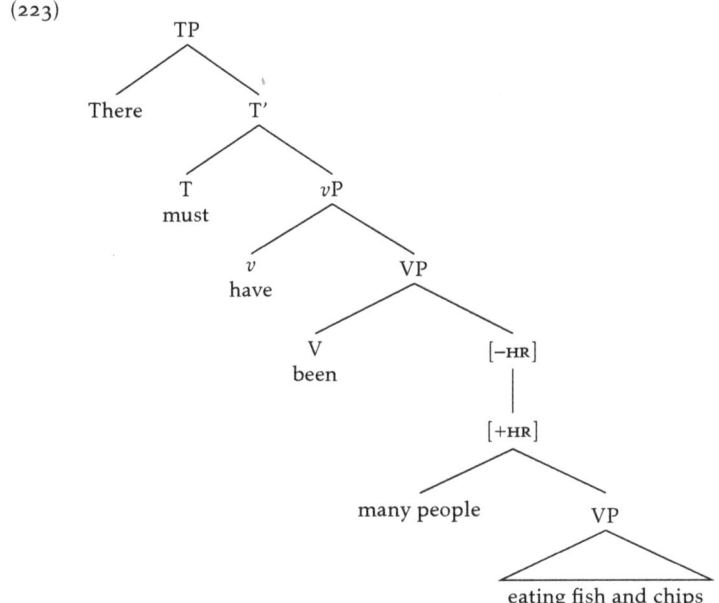

The constraints enforcing the base position will differ according to the syntactic properties of the element in question; for instance, MAX[–HR] is irrelevant to adverbs, while MATCHADV will not evaluate nominal case. The difference between MAX and MATCH must be emphasised: **where MAX constraints penalise material from the input being unexpressed in the output, MATCH constraints penalise output candidates in which the syntactic feature values are not identical on the position and occupying item**. The constraints relevant to phenomena attributed to syntactic movement are enumerated in Table 9.1; the standard OT terminology is followed in grouping faithfulness constraints as those which compare the input and output representations, and markedness constraints as those which solely evaluate the form of the output candidate (see de Lacy 2011). Both MAX and MATCHF represent classes of constraint which also have more specific subtypes; we propose only those subtypes that are empirically necessary. A full table with definitions for every constraint proposed in this book can be found in Appendix A2.

In Section 9.5 the roles played by these constraints are illustrated by an example English sentence with a wh-dependency. Regarding the constraints in Table 9.1, the base positions of several elements are

Table 9.1 Constraints governing positions of syntactic elements

Constraint	Description	Targets
\multicolumn{3}{c}{Faithfulness constraints}		
Max	Assign a violation for each feature or item present in the input that is not present in the output.	All
Dep	Assign a violation for each feature or item not present in the input that is present in the output.	All
\multicolumn{3}{c}{Markedness constraints}		
ArgSP	Assign a violation for each finite TP in which no argument occupies subject position (Spec,TP).	Spec,TP$_{[+\text{fin}]}$
MatchF	Assign a violation for each positional feature matrix F[$vals_{pos}$] that is not identical to its corresponding item feature matrix F[$vals_{item}$].	All
MatchCase	Assign a violation for each positional case feature matrix F[$vals_{pos}$] that is not identical to its corresponding item case feature matrix F[$vals_{item}$].	Argument DPs
MatchDis	Assign a violation for each positional discourse-feature matrix F[$vals_{pos}$] that is not identical to its corresponding item discourse-feature matrix F[$vals_{item}$].	All
MatchAdv	Assign a violation for each positional adverbial-adjunction feature matrix F[$vals_{pos}$] that is not identical to its corresponding item adverbial-adjunction feature matrix F[$vals_{item}$].	Adverbs
CheckTns	Assign a violation for each Tense (T) head position not occupied by an item bearing a [±fin] feature (i.e. of category V).	V-heads
VfinHi	Assign a violation for each finite verb not occurring in the highest available functional head position in the clause (CP).	V-heads

enforced as follows: for overt arguments, the base position is that which satisfies MatchCase without incurring a violation of MatchDis or other information-structural markedness constraints. For instance, an object bearing [−HR] in base position incurs no MatchCase violation; a topicalised object DP in Spec,CP does incur a MatchCase violation but satisfies the higher-ranked MatchDis by the matching of [+Top] features. As laid out in Section 9.4, both arguments and syntactic positions may also bear discourse features such as [±Foc] and [±Top]. For tensed verbs, the relevant constraint enforcing base order is CheckTns, which conflicts with the markedness constraint VfinHi that penalises finite verbs occurring in head positions lower than the highest available in the clause (CP). For adverbs, the X'-adjunction analysis is assumed, but since the position of the adverb depends both on the given adverb and on its scope, the order is determined by an adjectival-adjunction feature present on the input item. The constraint MATCHADV ensures that this adjunction feature matches that of the site (e.g. that a T'-adverb does not occur adjoined to V'). This analysis derives the correct object shift typology in Scandinavian, as discussed in Section 9.7.1. Thus, on this theory it is *not* the case that movement operations derive surface orders: instead, in cases typically assumed to be syntactic movement, the input contains features (e.g. [+Foc],[+Q]) that trigger violations of input–output faithfulness constraints if unrealised. Since SUBCAT ensures that subcategorisation violations are never present in a winning candidate, it follows that grammatical sentences with elements not present in their default position also do not violate SUBCAT.

9.3.2 Scrambling, or Word-Order Optionality

The analysis of adverb placement proposed here is also relevant to so-called cases of 'optional movement', such as optional scrambling of definites in Dutch. Diesing and Jelinek (1995) propose that referential definite objects scramble obligatorily: they must occur to the left of a sentence-medial adverb, unlike non-referential definite objects. In contrast, van der Does and de Hoop (1998) and de Hoop (2000, 2003) propose that true optionality does exist with respect to word order under certain conditions; for example, when a preceding context is provided in which there is no antecedent for 'the cat' in (224), scrambling does not force an anaphoric interpretation (de Hoop 2000:157):[10]

(224)   Context: 'Recently, Paul seems to be under stress.'
      a. Dut. *Misschien komt   dat   omdat   hij **zelden** de kat aait*
              maybe   comes that because he   seldom   the cat pets
             'That's maybe because he hardly ever pets the cat'
      b. Dut. *Misschien komt   dat   omdat   hij de kat **zelden** aait*
              maybe   comes that because he the cat seldom   pets

Both word orders in (224a–b) are claimed to be grammatical, with the non-anaphoric reading preferred for 'the cat' in both. Likewise, when a context is provided in which 'the cat' has an antecedent (e.g. 'Paul has a cat that seems to be under stress recently'), it is claimed that the anaphoric interpretation is forced for both orders in (224a–b). This suggests that word order only determines the preferred interpretation in the absence of context, an effect that can be overridden

---

[10] See Jäger (1995) and Meinunger (2000) for similar claims with respect to German scrambling of definite objects.

by an explicit antecedent. However, van Bergen and de Swart (2009, 2010) call de Hoop's analysis into question with data from two corpus studies. They found that scrambling decreases in occurrence along the definiteness hierarchy (i.e. pronouns > proper nouns > definites > indefinites); moreover, it was found that pronouns scramble almost categorically, but indefinite and definite objects, in fact, rarely scramble. Interestingly, the scrambling behaviour of definite objects was not reported to be categorical, which led the authors to propose a functional account of the data, attributing the preference to sentence planning considerations (Wasow 2002). Elements which require little planning, such as pronouns, prefer the scrambled order, whereas more complex elements, such as definite and heavy objects, require more planning and hence prefer the non-scrambled option.

How, then, does the framework adopted in this book address the empirically supported preference for the (224a) order in Dutch? In OLG, 'scrambling' is not object movement across an adverb but a different adverbial adjunction site combined with availability of the Spec,VP object position. In Section 9.7.1 an analysis of Scandinavian object shift is presented in which v'-adjoined adverbs block shift by scoping over the Spec,VP position, whereas V'-adjoined adverbs do not scope over this position and therefore permit shift as a means of satisfying a [–Foc] feature on the object. Accordingly, if we extend the hypothesis to Dutch, the difference between (224a–b) is expected to be a different adjunction site for *zelden* 'seldom': if v'-adjoined as in (224a), the object occurs in (head-final) V,Comp, while if V'-adjoined as in (224b), the object sits in Spec,VP. Since van Bergen and de Swart (2010) show that the order in (224a) is far more frequent in actual usage, the question is then why the v'-adjoined *zelden* is preferred.

The OLG approach advocated for here is in fact consistent with the sentence-processing literature. While OT syntax is not typically presented as a theory of linguistic 'performance' but rather one of 'competence' – in other words, of delimiting the inventory of all possible sentences in all languages – this does *not* entail that functional factors do not strongly influence the universal set of constraints at EVAL. Indeed, it is quite possible that late commitment on the part of the speaker (e.g. preferring non-scrambling for definites due to their lower accessibility relative to pronouns), is a functional pressure that holds of the distribution of syntactic features across the structure. In the same way that assigning [–Foc] to the Spec,VP position in Scandinavian could be a result of a pressure that discourse-heavy material should occur later, the preference for v'-adjoined adverbials in Dutch with definite objects in V,Comp could be the result of a lexical constraint ensuring that the adverb adjoins at a site prohibiting discourse-heavy material from occurring earlier. Hence, the empirical observations may be captured within a theory, such as OLG, that acknowledges functional factors as influences on the set of constraints.

9.3.3 Traces, or Co-Indexed Gaps

Another central issue regarding phenomena standardly attributed to movement is that of traces, that is, the gap position to which the filler element is in a dependency relation. In contrast to Grimshaw (2001:21–24), we do not assume that 'traces' or 'lower copies' of items that show up in higher structural positions than the base actually exist in a sense other than 'gap': the gap exists as a position in the structure, but is not manipulated as a true syntactic object.[11] Instead, we assume (following Hawkins 1999) the gap mechanism for both subcategorised and non-subcategorised gaps: a direct association or co-indexation between the wh-element and its subcategorising head (Pickering et al. 1994, Pollard and Sag 1994), here instantiated by matching features on each item, or simply an association of the filler to its gap in the latter case.

Therefore, a head position that is vacant does incur a violation of OBHEAD, even though it is the base position for an item that is pronounced elsewhere. Grimshaw (2001:21) rejects the hypothesis that OBHEAD is violated by a trace of head movement, on the basis of an analysis of subject–auxiliary inversion in English. Grimshaw argues that if only the pronounced head satisfies OBHEAD, the candidate without movement and the candidate with a trace each will violate OBHEAD once, resulting in a tie, as shown in (227). In this tableau, the constraints are formulated as follows:

(225) OBHEAD1: assign a violation for each phrase not containing a head or subcategorised head position.

(226) OBHEAD2: assign a violation for each phrase not containing an overt head.

---

[11] In OLG ellipsis is not treated as merely a 'gap' but actual deletion: constituents or sub-constituents that are unpronounced in the winning candidate are assumed to bear some input feature encoding ellipsis of the appropriate material, and a feature-realisation constraint rules out candidates in which that material is sent to PF.

(227)

{[the students]$_{[+HR]}$, have$_{[+fin][+Q]}$, read$_{[-fin]}$ [which books]$_{[-HR][+Q]}$}	OBHD1	OBHD2
a. [$_{CP}$ [$_{DP}$ Which books] have$_C$ [$_{TP}$ [$_{DP}$ the students] ___$_T$ [$_{VP}$ read ___]]]		*
b. [$_{CP}$ [$_{DP}$ Which books] [$_{TP}$ [$_{DP}$ the students] have$_T$ [$_{VP}$ read ___]]]	*	*

(227a) represents the standard analysis of subject–auxiliary inversion in English, in which the finite auxiliary is assumed to be in C. In output candidate (227a), which is supposed to win, the overt auxiliary head occurs in the higher position, with a subcategorised gap in its base position of T. In candidate (227b), which should not win, there is no C-head position at all, and therefore either formulation of OBHEAD is violated. Grimshaw states that if we adopt the OBHEAD2 formulation in which only an overt head satisfies the constraint, we are left without an explanation for inversion, and therefore we must adopt OBHEAD1. The logic is that if we only had OBHEAD2, there would be no way to rule out the loser (227b), since the empty head position would also incur a violation thereof.

However, we are only left without the explanation based on OBHEAD. If, in fact, there is a faithfulness constraint MATCHF enforcing the correct mapping of syntactic features between positions and their occupying items in the output, formulated as in Table 9.1, we have a feasible alternative hypothesis. Even though candidate (a) incurs identical violations of OBHEAD to (b), (a) does not violate MATCHF where (b) does. In languages with wh-'movement', **in wh-questions the positions C and Spec,CP, and the finite verb and wh-phrase, are each associated with a [+Q] feature**, satisfied only by matching of the positional features to those of the items occupying them; wh-in-situ languages, conversely, would locate those features in V,Comp and the finite verb 'base' (T or V). MATCHF is repeated here as (228):

(228) MATCHF: assign a violation for each positional feature matrix F[$vals_{pos}$] that is not identical to its corresponding item feature matrix F[$vals_{item}$].

This analysis would account for English subject–auxiliary inversion as shown in (229).

(229)

{[the students]$_{[+HR]}$, have$_{[+fin][+Q]}$, read$_{[-fin]}$ [which books]$_{[-HR][+Q]}$}	MATCHF	OBHD(2)
☞ a. [$_{CP}$ [$_{DP}$ Which books]$_{[+Q]:[+Q]}$ have$_{C,[+Q]:[+Q]}$ [$_{TP}$ [$_{DP}$ the students] ___$_T$ [$_{VP}$ read ___]]]		*
b. [$_{CP}$ [$_{DP}$ Which books]$_{[+Q]:[+Q]}$ [$_{TP}$ [$_{DP}$ the students] have$_{T,[-Q]:[+Q]}$ [$_{VP}$ read ___]]]	*	*

In the winner (229a), MATCHF is not violated, since the [±Q] features on Spec,CP and C have identical values to those on the occupying phrase 'which books' and 'have', respectively. In (229b), since the [−Q] feature on the T position does not match the [+Q] on 'have', a violation of MATCHF is incurred, and therefore (229b) fares worse than (229a) with respect to MATCHF.[12] Unlike some broadly Minimalist approaches, we do not posit an unpronounced $C_{[+Q]}$ head that is always present even without an overt head in C. Rather, C denotes a position that may be present/absent, occupied/not occupied or associated/not associated with [+Q], depending on the candidate. Moreover, the position is only associated with [+Q] *in the winning candidate* if [+Q] is present in the input, in the same way that V,Comp is only associated with [−HR] if the input verb takes a direct object complement. (There may, of course, be losing candidates with the features associated with the right positions but which lose due to violations of some other constraints.) Candidates with positions not associated with the input features will be harmonically bounded by violations of faithfulness constraints of the type MAX. As noted above, it is assumed that in English, [+Q] is associated with the positions C and Spec,CP, not with the finite verb base position (V or T) and V,Comp; the inverse is hypothesised for wh-in-situ languages, where the [+Q] is satisfied without the relevant items occurring elsewhere. A tree for a wh-'movement' language is shown in (230) and for a wh-in-situ language in (231).

(230)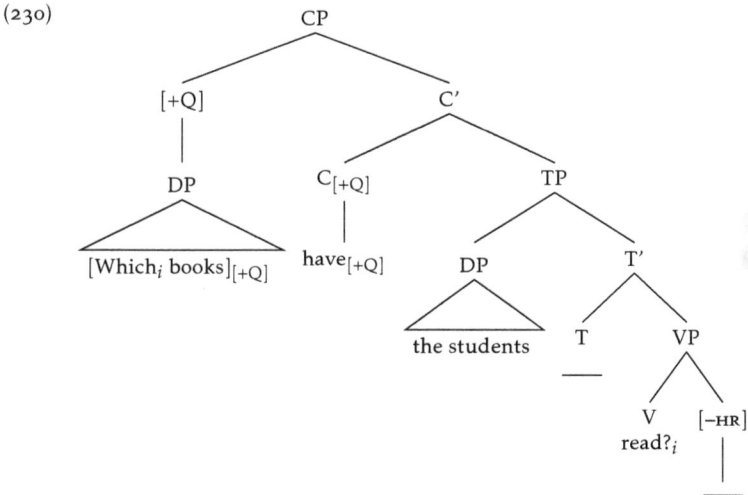

---

[12] How feature matching is evaluated is described in greater detail in Section 9.4; further discussion of English word-order constraints can be found in Section 9.5.

(231)

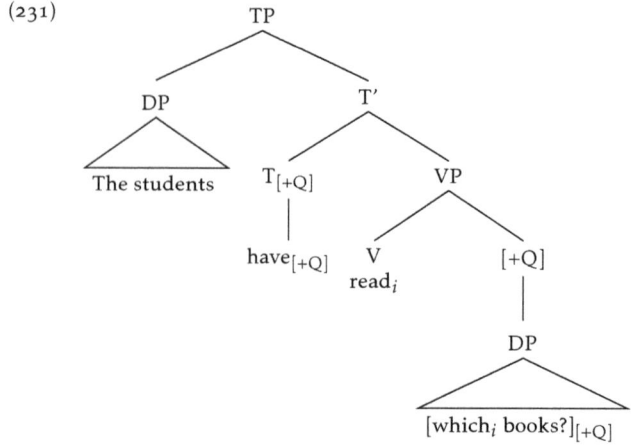

As can be seen in (230), in languages like English a subcategorised gap occurs in both T and V,Comp in the winner, incurring violations of CHECKTNS and MATCHCASE. However, MATCHF is satisfied by the matching value of the [+Q] features between Spec,CP and the wh-DP, and C and the auxiliary. In (231), MATCHF is already satisfied by the matching value of the V,Comp [+Q] and that of wh-DP in situ, as well as the [+Q] on T and the auxiliary. The [+Q] hypothesis can be extended to languages with overt morphology for polar questions, for example the Japanese sentence-final particle *ka*: unlike English do-support or Scandinavian V1, in such languages the [+Q] present in the input is morphologically instantiated rather than subject to position–item matching, and therefore candidates without the particle would incur a MAX violation.[13] Tableaux yielding the trees in (230–231) are given in (232–233), with a Mandarin example representing wh-in-situ:

(232) **English content question:**

{[the students]$_{[+HR]}$, have$_{[+fin][+Q]}$, read$_{[-fin]}$ [which books]$_{[-HR][+Q]}$}	M	OBHD
☞ a. [$_{CP}$ [$_{DP}$ Which books]$_{[+Q]:[+Q]}$ have$_{C,[+Q]:[+Q]}$ [$_{TP}$ [$_{DP}$ the students] ___$_T$ [$_{VP}$ read? ___]]]		*
b. [$_{TP}$ [$_{DP}$ The students] have$_{T,[-Q]:[+Q]}$ [$_{VP}$ read [which books?]$_{T,[-Q]:[+Q]}$]]]	**	

(233) **Mandarin content question:**

{[xuéshēng]$_{[+HR]}$, dú$_{[+fin][+Q]}$, [nǎxiē shū]$_{[-HR][+Q]}$}	M	OBHD
a. [$_{CP}$ [$_{DP}$ Nǎxiē shū]$_{[-Q]:[+Q]}$ dú$_{C,[-Q]:[+Q]}$ [$_{TP}$ [$_{DP}$ xuéshēng?] ___$_T$ [$_{VP}$ ___ v]]]	**	**
☞ b. [$_{TP}$ [$_{DP}$ Xuéshēng] dú$_{T,[+Q]:[+Q]}$ [$_{VP}$ ___ v [nǎxiē shū?]$_{T,[+Q]:[+Q]}$]]]		

---

[13] For the data examined in this book, it is sufficient to limit the scope of MAX to features that are morphologically instantiated (i.e. which have a 'host' word or morpheme), but future work may refine the formulation.

In the case of these content questions, it turns out that the same ranking MatchF » ObHead generates both languages: in English (232), wh-in-situ violates MatchF due to the [−Q]:[+Q] mismatches in T and V,Comp, while in Mandarin (233), the candidate with the sentence-initial wh-phrase incurs a violation of MatchF for the same mismatches in C and Spec,CP. The difference is between the positions to which the [+Q] features are associated. It may be objected that features rather than constraints seem to be necessary to account for movement phenomena, since when a constraint is satisfied depends on the position of the feature. However, as argued in Section 9.4, the distribution of features across structure is itself subject to harmonisation and, therefore, also under the purview of ranked universal constraints. Furthermore, other constraints are at play in both sentences (232–233), for example, MatchCase is violated by a [−hr]-bearing object occurring in Spec,CP, and an interaction between CheckTns and VfinHi derives the 'T-to-C' behaviour; these tableaux merely illustrate the role played by feature-matching in generating these two varieties of content question. Regarding such issues of word-order variation, the typology derived by the word-order constraints proposed in this book is presented in Section 9.6.2.

Therefore, we have seen that is quite possible to account for syntactic movement phenomena without explicit reference to an independent movement operation but rather to explain the observed patterns as the outcome of constraint interaction. An advantage of this approach is its flexibility to account for morphosyntactic variation with a universal set of competing pressures on well-formedness rather than a universal operation that applies 'when necessary'. The 'when' on such theories may also depend on features, but in Minimalist approaches the distribution of movement-triggering features tends to be determined by heads present at the input to syntax rather than being subject to a universal set of constraints. Conversely, by attributing universals to the set of constraints and variation to the ranking, we can be more explicit (and hence make more straightforwardly testable predictions) about the typology of possible languages with a given set of primitives.

9.3.4 A Note on Locality

The constraint-based approach to 'movement' raises questions common to representational theories, namely, how to account for locality effects.

In particular, the question of harmonic *parallelism* (a single optimisation algorithm generates the fully formed winner) versus *serialism* (multiple cyclic optimisations of smaller domains) will determine how the model captures island phenomena, for example. While the data examined in this book do not principally shed light on this issue, the way in which LT proposals would contribute to OT accounts of locality represents a fascinating avenue for future research. Here we follow Legendre et al. (1998), who posit that a general 'shortest link' constraint subhierarchy MinLink ensures that longer dependency chains are penalised (cf. Rizzi 1990): recursive application of local conjunction to the constraint Bar(rier), violated by a chain link which crosses a barrier (defined as per Chomsky 1986),[14] results in a system where chains are 'as weak as their longest link', where length of link is measured in barriers. In other words, (i) if chain C_1 is longer than chain C_2, C_1 is less harmonic than C_2; (ii) if the longest links of C_1 and C_2 are the same length but C_1 has more longest links than C_2, C_1 is less harmonic than C_2; and (iii) if C_1 and C_2 have longest links of equal length and the same number of them, harmonisation is recursively determined by examining the remaining links excluding the longest links (Legendre et al. 1998:13). This provides a principled account of a wide variety of extraction phenomena, including super-raising, wh-islands, superiority and strong island effects; it also correctly captures wh-in-situ and topicalisation in Chinese, as well as English and Bulgarian data. The reader is referred to Legendre et al. (1998) for more detailed discussion; the central point is that filler–gap dependencies are subject to optimisation that disfavours longest links, but with the advantage of the cross-linguistic flexibility provided by a violable constraint model. In this way, phenomena attributed to movement in transformational theories can be derived from the interaction of universal locality and faithfulness constraints.

9.3.5 Section Summary

A major advantage of the OLG approach is that by formulating economy constraints as part of Eval rather than economy of derivation,

---

[14]Formulating a precise definition of barrier within OLG is a task beyond our scope here, but since the notions of 'L-marking' and 'theta-governing' adopted in Chomsky (1986) require a quite distinct set of starting assumptions, this would involve reviewing in detail the empirical case for the barriers framework.

we capture the fact that gaps and insertion of expletives are tolerated only in order to satisfy some other competing pressure. Furthermore, we make more restrictive empirical predictions than accounts which posit empty specifiers and structure-altering operations: for example, presumably if a *v*-head were always present in the extended VP in all languages, it would also always project a specifier in the standard Minimalist model; this predicts that every language will have Spec,*v*P as an available syntactic position, and therefore we expect to see elements occupy this position in some sentence types. However, Spec,*v*P is not *necessary* to account for the Faroese sentence types in Table 2.1, even if it does not undergenerate. Thus, by dividing the labour such that GEN concerns only the combinatorics of lexical insertion into structures that fit a very general description, we allow for a closer matching between the data and the assigned syntactic structure. Such an approach reduces the cost of universal mechanisms like Merge by only positing structures minimally necessary for satisfying insertion and selectional restrictions.

As demonstrated in this section, on a theory without movement operations, the content of the input becomes particularly important, since it is the satisfaction of input features that determines the violation profile of an output candidate, and therefore also the winning candidate. Following standard assumptions in OT syntax, let us hypothesise that the input contains argument structure of the predicate, lexical items, information and discourse features, a hierarchy of theta-roles,[15] and functional features such as tense (Legendre et al. 2001:20). In Section 9.4 input features are discussed in greater detail, and in Section 9.5 the process of generating an English sentence is laid out.

9.4 Syntactic Features

Almost all theories of syntax have posited some form of feature-based formalism, since it is clear that a certain subset of linguistic information is syntactically 'intelligible', that is, necessary to account for the range of observed surface word orders. Feature matrices are a clear and explicit notation for such information. Indeed, some frameworks have a highly developed theory of feature inheritance and transference or

---

[15]More precisely, the hierarchical relations that derive the [±HR±LR] features rather than named roles such as Agent, Goal, Theme etc.

percolation; prominent examples being Lexical–Functional Grammar (LFG; Bresnan 1982), Generalized Phrase Structure Grammar (GPSG; Gazdar et al. 1985) and the typed feature structures of Head-Driven Phrase Structure Grammar (HPSG; Pollard and Sag 1994). In OLG, feature matrices, notated [ ], contain a possible value or values taken from the set of all possible values for that feature; feature matrices may also contain other feature matrices, such as [–HR–LR], which represents [[–HR][–LR]]. Feature-matching is notated throughout by matrices linked by a colon, in the format 'position : item'. The list of basic types below is not intended to be exhaustive but covers all necessary features to cover the data examined in this book:

(234) i. LEXICAL/FUNCTIONAL CATEGORIES:
          {N, V, A, P, Adv, D}, borne by heads and head positions
       ii. CASE FEATURES:
           morphosyntactic {[+HR],[–HR],[–HR–LR],[–LR]}, borne by arguments
           positional {[+HR],[–HR],[–HR–LR],[–LR]}, borne by argument positions
       iii. PHI-FEATURES (a subset of semantic features):
           {Pers[*val*], Num[*val*], Gend[*val*]}, borne by arguments and verbs
       iv. DISCOURSE/INFORMATION-STRUCTURE FEATURES:
           {[±Q], [±Foc], [±Top]}, borne by positions, arguments and verbs
       v. SEMANTIC FEATURES:
           {[±fin],[±aux],[adjunct:T']}, borne by positions and items of the relevant category

In the sections which follow, these features will be justified as the data present their need. It is assumed that only syntactically relevant semantic features enter the EVAL computation for syntax; hence, lexical–semantic features one might imagine, such as [+colour] or [+cognition], will only be referred to if there is empirical evidence that an attested language makes grammatical distinctions by such a feature. It is clear that the feature list in (234) contains features of several kinds: binary features, such as [±fin]; features with more than two possible values, such as Gend[m,f,n]; and categorial features that must be present on the relevant items, such as V. Therefore, formulations of feature-matching constraints must handle these distinctions. Both faithfulness and markedness constraints are necessary in the evaluation of input features, not only to enforce word orders other than the base but more generally to ensure that the broad variety of information types in (234) is correctly instantiated in the winning output. MATCH-type constraints look only at the output candidate and are therefore markedness constraints; MAX-type constraints compare input and output representations and thus fall into the category of faithfulness constraints. In order to formulate these constraints precisely, we must define notions of feature *identity* and *realisation*.

9.4.1 Feature Identity

The identity relation when evaluating values of two feature matrices is defined as in (235):

(235) **Identity**: two feature matrices $F_1[vals]$ and $F_2[vals]$ are said to be identical if, for every possible feature f, one of the following conditions holds:
  i. the value of f in F_1 is equal to the value of f in F_2;
  ii. f is not applicable in both F_1 and F_2.

In this definition 'not applicable' simply means that neither F_1 nor F_2 have the feature f. 'Every possible feature' includes all feature types listed in (234), namely, lexical category, Pers[ ], [±LR], [±Q], etc. This is not a constraint but a defined function from pairs of feature matrices to a truth value, which is a necessary prior for identity-type constraints; hence, the ability to take in any type of feature matrix is desirable. The function can be notated as in (236):

(236) $I_P : P \rightarrow \{0,1\}$, where:
P is the set of all possible $(F_i[\alpha], F_j[\beta])$ tuples;
F_i and F_j are feature matrices;
A is the set of all possible values of F_i and $\emptyset \in A$;
B is the set of all possible values of F_j and $\emptyset \in B$;
$\alpha \in A$ and $\beta \in B$;
$x \in P$.
The function I_P is defined as:
$I_P(x) := \{0 \text{ if } \alpha \neq \beta, 1 \text{ if } \alpha = \beta\}$.

Hence, the identity function only evaluates to true (i.e. two matrices are only considered identical) in the cases where *each pair of values of the same feature* is equal in both matrices (e.g. [MASC] : [MASC], [3SG] : [3SG]), or when f is not applicable in either; for example, [±fin] feature matrices are considered 'identical' with respect to a DP in an argument position, since both the position and the DP lack [±fin] (in other words, ∅ : ∅ is identical). On the other hand, a value of a feature f present in one matrix and absent from the other is *not* identical by (235) (e.g. an adverb in a [+HR] position), though such candidates will typically be harmonically bounded by SUBCAT. Moreover, a feature-bearing position without an occupying item does not satisfy either condition in (235); for instance, a V,Comp position bearing [–HR] whose corresponding argument occurs in Spec,CP, as in wh-questions, does not have a pair of identical matrices. This definition of identity allows us to formulate markedness constraints which evaluate specific subsets of features. With respect to the data in this book, we only need the following type of feature-matching constraint, different species of which enforce verbal agreement, argument licensing and discourse-feature mapping:

(237)   MATCHF(MF): assign a violation for each positional feature matrix F[$vals_{pos}$] that is not identical to its corresponding item feature matrix F[$vals_{item}$].

MATCHF will be violated once per position–item feature mismatch; for example, an item bearing the case feature [+HR] occupying a position which bears [–HR] will incur one violation, as would an item bearing the case feature [–HR–LR] occupying a position bearing [–HR]. A violation is also incurred when either the position or item feature is null (i.e. absence of a feature), for instance an empty V,Comp position bearing [–HR] whose corresponding argument occurs elsewhere in the structure, as in wh-questions. Thus, MATCHF is not a unification-type constraint but requires identical values in order to be satisfied. However, condition (ii) in the definition of identity ensures that the constraint only evaluates position–item pairs with at least one valued feature matrix: position–item pairs lacking the targeted type of feature matrices do not incur a violation (e.g. nouns do not incur an MATCHF violation by not having tense features).

9.4.2   Feature Realisation

Another important concept for defining the feature apparatus is that of 'realisation', which underlies the MAX-type faithfulness constraints. Realisation of a feature value is defined as in (238):

(238)   **Realisation**: the value of feature f is said to be realised if the output conditions of that value of f are satisfied.

The reason for the generality of the definition in (238) is that the satisfaction of the content of a feature value is highly dependent on the feature in question. The most common output condition will be presence of the morpheme or word corresponding to that feature value, but a value may also encode a specific syntactic configuration (e.g. polar question by subject–verb inversion), deletion of an element (e.g. ellipsis), or an intonational property realised at phonology (e.g. contrastive focus). The heterogeneity of output conditions is related to the broad range of morphosyntactic strategies for linking form to meaning, which cannot be flattened out into a single type. Therefore, the definition in (238) is not a necessary prior for defining MAX constraints but a description of the underlying principle. Instead, MAX constraint formulations will typically check for the presence of a particular morpheme, word, constituent, configuration, morphophonological feature (to be fed through to the next harmonisation), or the absence of any of these. Whenever the term 'realise' is used of features in this book, the definition in (238) is assumed, but the specific constraint formulation depends on the target of evaluation. To draw the analogy with phonology once again, it should not be problematic that the possible targets of MAX at syntactic EVAL differ in form and function, since the targets of phonological MAX constraints differ in several dimensions. Input–output correspondence, as defined by McCarthy and Prince (1995), holds between segments but may also target terminal and non-terminal nodes in the phonological feature hierarchy, tonal nodes or prosodic nodes (see de Lacy 2011 and the references therein).

9.4.3 Subcategorisation

The question of why one particular position is associated with one feature as opposed to another is much larger than space permits here. The answers depend on one's theory of subcategorisation, the syntax-semantics interface, and semantic compositionality. With respect to English wh-movement discussed in Section 9.3, one could imagine an account in which some set of markedness constraints prefers topics or discourse-prominent information to occur sentence-initially (see Dalrymple and Nikolaeva 2011 and others), which conflicts with constraints that require [−HR] features (i.e. direct objects) to be complements of the verb. Output candidates with features in positions unattested in real languages are likely to be harmonically bounded by the relevant constraints. Without exploring the particularities of a fully fledged theory of feature distribution across syntactic positions, a brief presentation of how 'c-selection' is accounted for in OLG is given below. The undominated SUBCAT constraint is key for ruling out candidates which violate selectional requirements (i.e. restrictions of the form 'combines with a syntactic element of type *x*'). The formulation of Subcat is repeated in (239):

(239) Subcat: assign a violation for each subcategorisation feature not satisfied in the output.

Subcategorisation features are notated by Subcat : [(*vals*),(*vals*)], where up to two places are defined, requiring an item or feature of a certain category or value in the specifier and/or complement. Subcat features may also be underspecified for place (i.e. they require an item to be present in the input but do not enforce a specific syntactic position). The definition of 'satisfied' in (239) is dependent on the feature, but the output condition is assumed to be explicitly annotated and visible to Eval. Further work may reveal the necessity for more granularity (i.e. a family of selection-related constraints), but for now let us adopt the general formulation in (239) and define the output conditions in the feature matrix itself. For examples of this, see Section 9.5.

9.4.4 Section Summary

One objection to the feature-based hypothesis presented in this section is that it adds complexity, as well as features that may not be empirically necessary. On the contrary, it is a reasonable hypothesis that a similar feature-matching evaluation lies behind several linguistic phenomena, which achieves greater cross-linguistic generality while also being more restrictive than the movement operations typically proposed in contemporary syntactic literature. Syntactic elements occur in positions that best satisfy the constraints on a given ranking, and while these constraints can and do target feature matrices, the distribution of features is itself subject to constraints. As discussed in Chapters 4–7, the Insular Scandinavian data examined can be accounted for without positing a separate movement mechanism, and the feature-based account covers the data while generating realistic typologies of possible languages.

9.5 OLG Syntax in Practice

To illustrate the proposed OLG system, in this section an analysis of one example sentence in English is laid out in detail.

(240) Which books did you say John had read?

First, (241) is the hypothesised structure of the winning candidate:

(241)
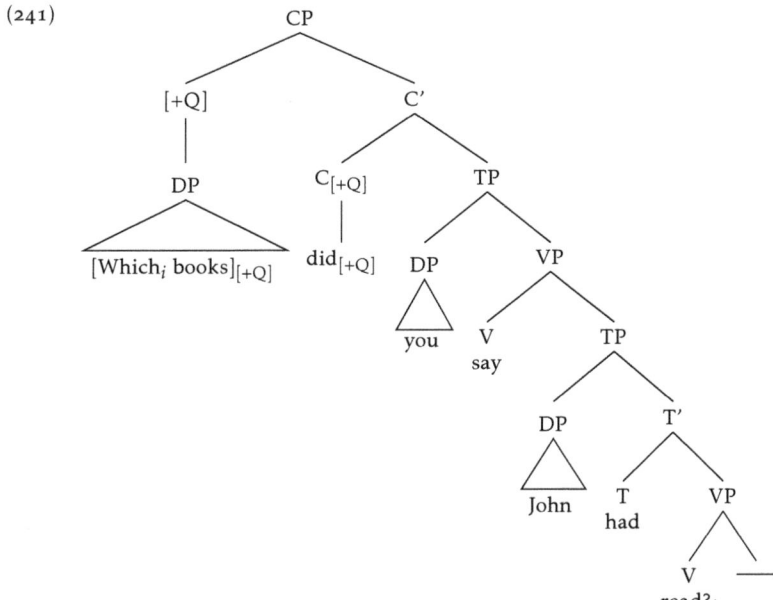

We do not assume a null C head that is realised as overt 'that' when present, but only posit C in the structure when empirically necessary; instead, the verb 'say' may subcategorise for either a TP or CP complement.[16]

9.5.1 Input to Syntax

Let us hypothesise the following input to syntactic EVAL, with the relevant feature values provided in curly brackets following the item.[17] This is not an exhaustive list of all features but a summary of those relevant to the syntactic evaluation. The input is an unordered set of non-linearised items; following standard assumptions, linearisation proper happens at PF.

---

[16] Incidentally, there is syntactic evidence for this in German: the verb *glauben* 'believe' can take a CP complement, such as *dass er gekommen ist* 'that he has come', or a TP complement, such as *er ist gekommen* 'he has come'. The clause-initial *dass* and head-final position of the auxiliary show that this is a CP complement, while the auxiliary precedes the participle in the TP complement.

[17] Key to abbreviations: Cat(egory), Pers(on), Num(ber), T(e)ns(e), Fin(iteness), Dis(course), Subcat(egorisation).

(242) you: {Cat : [N], Pers : [2], Num : [SG], Case : [+HR]}
said: {Cat : [V], Fin : [+fin], Tns : [PST], Dis : [–Q], Subcat : [(DP$_{[+HR]}$), (TP,Comp)]}
John: {Cat : [N], Pers : [3], Num : [SG], Case : [+HR]}
had: {Cat : [V$_{aux}$], Fin : [+fin], Tns : [PST], Dis : [+Q], Subcat : [(VP,Comp)]}
read: {Cat : [V], Fin : [–fin], Tns : [PST], Dis : [–Q], Subcat : [(DP$_{[+HR]}$), (DP$_{[-HR]}$)]}
which: {Cat : [D], Num : [PL], Dis : [+Q], Subcat : [(NP,Comp)]}
books: {Cat : [N], Pers : [3], Num : [PL], Case : [–HR]}

It must be stipulated that there are two [+Q] features for content questions (one on the wh-phrase and one on the finite verb), but this is not an unreasonable hypothesis, given that such questions involve both an interrogative phrase or word ('which') and the interrogative mood, which in English is realised by a sentence-initial wh-phrase and subject–auxiliary inversion.[18] GEN generates output candidates which combine the input items in all possible combinations as defined in Section 9.2. The Subcat features are made up of tuples where the first element indicates the category of constituent required and the second element the syntactic position in which to insert that constituent; however, arguments of verbs are underspecified for position, instead being selected according to abstract case features. This avoids the reduplication of information, since argument realisation varies cross-linguistically, and therefore we avoid redundancy by allowing constraints such as MATCHCASE to ensure that arguments show up in the correct position. The subcategorisation feature values are specific to *this* input (e.g. another input may have the verb 'said' selecting a DP-complement, such as 'nothing').

Hence, like most Minimalist approaches, heads do have featural requirements that will violate selection constraints if unrealised. However, EVAL may select a winner in which some syntactic element occurs elsewhere in the structure, with a subcategorised gap in the base position of that element if a MATCH or MAX constraint enforces it. One

---

[18]Further support for a general interrogative [+Q] feature comes from languages with interrogative mood morphology; one example of such a language is Central Siberian Yup'ik, which uses the interrogative conjugation even with content questions (Jacobson 1979:60):

(243) Yup. *Sameng negh-yug-sin?*
  what eat-want-INTRANS.INTERROG.2SG.S
 'What do you want to eat?'

Interrogative verbal morphology is not rare cross-linguistically: in the WALS sample of 955 (Dryer 2013), 179 have interrogative verb morphology, whereas only 13 make use of word order to express polar questions. By far the most frequent strategy is a question particle, present in 585 of the languages in the sample.

example would be a wh-phrase occurring in Spec,CP rather than object position : MatchDis is satisfied by virtue of the identity of [+Q] : [+Q], even though an additional MatchCase violation is incurred by the [−hr] : ∅ mismatch in V,Comp; in a violable constraints model, this is possible under some rankings. It is assumed that subcategorised gaps do not violate Subcat, since the gap is co-indexed with the filler, which satisfies the featural requirement.

9.5.2 Deriving an English *Wh*-Question with Do-Support

In order to capture the subject–verb inversion and do-support facts, we introduce two constraints, VfinHi and CheckTns:

(244) VfinHi: assign a violation for each finite verb not occurring in the highest available functional head position in the clause (CP).

(245) CheckTns (ChkT): assign a violation for each Tense (T) head position not occupied by an item bearing a [±fin] feature (i.e. of category V).

In (244), 'available' is defined as follows:

(246) **Availability**: a syntactic position p is said to be available if p is not occupied by an overt item.

This means that a violation of VfinHi is *not* incurred when there is a finite verb, complementiser or other overt element in C, but it *is* incurred in all other circumstances where the finite verb is in a position lower than C. As discussed in Section 9.6 these constraints are also empirically necessary to account for various word order facts in other Germanic languages (e.g. subordinate clauses in German). In languages where CheckTns is ranked below Dep, do-support does not arise, and the candidate with the finite verb in C will win. Constraint (245) may appear to be an overly general formulation if we permit any verb occupying T to satisfy it, including non-finite verbs; however, by making the combination of CheckTns and MatchF conspire to create the preference for finite verbs in T, we permit cross-linguistically rare phenomena like do-support. MatchF is the general constraint enforcing input–output faithfulness with respect to features borne by positions and items; CheckTns is effectively a more specific case of ObHead, that is, 'make sure T is occupied by a head with a [±fin] feature (i.e. a verbal head)'.

The tableau below represents the syntactic EVAL harmonisation; the input items are assumed to bear the features given in (242). For illustrative purposes, word-order harmonisation is separated into another tableau; all candidates represented in (247) conform to head-initial word orders, though it is presupposed that head-final orders are also candidates. For constraint definitions, see Table 9.1 in the preceding section. For space considerations, features are not notated in the tableau; the input features are assumed to be as in (242), while the table in (248) shows the specific causes of the violation marks for each constraint and candidate.

(247) **Which books did you say John had read?**

{you, said, John, had, read, which, books}	Max	ChkT	VFHI	Dep	M
☞ a. [CP [Which books] did_C [TP you say_T [TP John had_T [VP ready_V ?]]]]			*	**	****
b. [CP [Which books] said_C [TP you ___T [TP John had_T [VP ready_V ?]]]]		*!	*		*****
c. [CP [Which books] ___C [TP you said_T [TP John had_T [VP ready_V ?]]]]			**!		****
d. [TP You said_T [TP John had_T [VP ready_V [which books?]]]]	**!		**		**

(248)

	Max	CheckTns	VFinHi	Dep	MatchF
a.			'had' not in C	'did' bearing [+Q] inserted	V,Comp [−HR]:∅, Spec,CP ∅:[−HR], 'say' [+fin]:[−fin], 'had' [−Q]:[+Q]
b.		no item bearing [±fin] in matrix T	'had' not in C		V,Comp [−HR]:∅, Spec,CP ∅:[−HR], matrix T [+fin]:∅, 'said' [+Q]:[−Q], 'had' [−Q]:[+Q]
c.			'said' not in C, 'had' not in C		V,Comp [−HR]:∅, Spec,CP ∅:[−HR], Spec,CP ∅:[−HR], C_{[+Q]} [+Q]:∅, 'had' [−Q]:[+Q]
d.	[+Q] on 'which' and 'had' not satisfied: no [+Q] positions		'said' not in C, 'had' not in C		V,Comp [−Q]:[+Q], 'had' [−Q]:[+Q]

As noted in Section 9.3, if English were a wh-in-situ language, the [+Q] feature would already be satisfied by the DP occupying V,Comp, and so the winner would be the equivalent of (247d). Unlike the structure in (230), in (241) 'had' in the TP-complement of 'say' cannot have its [+Q] feature realised within the embedded clause, since candidates with a CP complement only win on a different input: for this input, such candidates violate SUBCAT by failing to satisfy the (TP,Comp) value of the Subcat features of 'said'.[19] Additionally, 'had' in the TP-complement in (247) does violate VFINHI, since there is no higher occupied C position within the clause. In this sentence, although DEP is violated by the winner by do-support, more costly violations are incurred in candidates (247b–d).

Here we see the difference between MAX and MATCHF: MAX compares the input and output representations, finds two instances of [+Q] and sees that its output conditions are not satisfied in either case, those conditions being that a C and Spec,CP position bearing [+Q] occur in the structure. In contrast, MATCHF solely looks at the output and sees [–Q] : [+Q] mismatches with the elements *in situ*. Hence, MAX enforces the *presence* of the conditions specified by input features (here, [+Q]-bearing positions), while MATCHF enforces the *mapping between* positions and items. All serious contenders incur two MATCHF violations due to the [–HR] feature on the wh-phrase not matching the lack of a case feature in Spec,CP, as well as the empty V,Comp not having an argument bearing [–HR]. Nevertheless, this does not incur a MAX violation since the content of the feature (namely, that the DP 'which books' is the lowest thematic role) is still present in the output by virtue of the subcategorised gap. Finally, it should be clear that it is also possible to maintain lexicalist morphology on this approach, since no lowering of tense affixes is required: CHECKTNS penalises non-realisation of tense features by ensuring that finite verbs occur in the T position.

The tableau in (249) demonstrates how word-order harmonisation occurs. It is assumed that these constraints are also part of the same syntactic evaluation as those in tableau (247).

(249) **Word-order harmonisation**

{you, said, John, had, read, which, books}	F<XP	HRM	C<XP	HDFIN
☞ a. [[Which_D books] did_C [you [say_T [John [had_T [ready _____]]]]]]				*****
b. [[Books which_D] [you [[John [[_____ ready_V] had_T]] say_T]]] did_C]	*****!		*	
c. [[Which_D books] did_C [you [[John [[_____ ready_V] had_T]] say_T]]]	***!		*	**
d. [[Which_D books] did_C [you [say_T [John [[ready _____] had_T]]]]]	*!	**		****

The ranking F<XP » HRM » C<XP » HDFIN ensures that the winner in English is consistently head-initial, with operators preceding operands. As discussed in Section 9.2, these constraints derive the FOFC while

---

[19]The reason subject–auxiliary inversion is not possible in such sentences with a CP complement either is that such candidates with the order '...that had John read' incur an additional CHECKTNS violation.

228 *Syntax in OLG*

also allowing for benign disharmony, namely, the [Op [Comp H]] order in (219). Thus, the proposed constraints derive both the correct word order for English and offer an empirically sound analysis of the phenomena of wh-movement and do-support.

Having laid out the basic starting assumptions behind OLG syntax, the next section reviews the Faroese sentence types discussed in Section 2.3 and establishes that they are generated by the OLG grammar.

9.6 Faroese Clause Structure Revisited: OLG Account

For Faroese, we propose the constraints and rankings in (250), the evidence for which will be explored in this section. A competing grammars situation is posited between {ArgSP, Dep} to account for null expletives, discussed further below.

(250) **Faroese:**
Max » {ArgSP, Dep} » {MatchF, {VFinHi » ChkT}} » {ObHd, ObSp}
{F<XP, Hrm} » {HdFin, ObSp}
C<XP unranked

In Table 9.2 (not a tableau), hypothesised winning candidates are shown for the Faroese sentences discussed in Section 2.3 with the violations they incur on the basic alignment and obligatory element constraints. In the table we do not notate the absence of a head or specifier position, which of course are responsible for some of the violations of ObHead and ObSpec. Underline indicates an empty position of the category indicated by the subscript. The violations induced DP-internally are excluded, since they will not affect the analysis here. The reader is referred to Appendix A3 for trees of all the sentences in Table 9.2.

In this section it is established that these constraints in the rankings proposed in (250) rule out serious contender (i.e. not harmonically bounded) output candidates. A valid ranking argument demonstrates conflict between constraints, a comparison between a winner and loser, and that no other constraint can do the same job (McCarthy 2011). Such an argument should hold of any of the data examined, unless additional constraints are necessary. For ranking arguments, we select sentence types where the hypothesised lower-ranked constraint is violated as many times as possible, so that loser candidates can be found

9.6 Faroese Clause Structure Revisited: OLG Account

Table 9.2 Faroese sentence types: Hypothesised winning candidates

		VFHI	CHKT	HDFIN	OBHD	OBSP
a.	[TP Tey hava_T [_vP[_v' aldri [VP lisið_V bókina]]]]	*		**	*	**
b.	[CP Tá hava_C [TP tey __T [_vP[_v' aldri [VP lisið_V bókina]]]]]		*	***	**	**
c.	[CP at_C [TP Jógvan hevur_T [_vP[_v' aldri [VP lisið_V bókina]]]]]			***	*	***
d.	[CP at_C [TP Jógvan [_T' aldri hevur_T [VP lisið_V bókina]]]]			***		**
e.	[TP hvør [_T' aldri hevði_T [VP lisið_V bókina]]]	*		**	*	*
f.	[CP um_C [TP hon [_T' altíð sigur_T [VP __v satt]]]]			***	**	**
g.	[TP Tey lósu_T [_vP[_v' aldri [VP __v bókina]]]]	*		**	**	**
h.	[CP Ivaleyst skulu_C [TP tey __T [_vP[_v' ongantíð selja_v [VP dreingjunum __v teldurnar]]]]]		*	****	**	*
i.	[CP Ivaleyst góvu_C [TP tey __T [_vP[_v' ongantíð [VP dreingjunum __v teldurnar]]]]]			***	***	*
j.	[TP Tað hevur_T [_vP[_v' altíð [VP verið_V tónleikur]]]]	*		**	*	**
k.	[TP Tað hevur_C [TP tónleikur __T [_vP[_v' altíð verið_V]]]]			***		**
l.	[TP Tað má_T [_vP hava_v [VP[_v' altíð verið [nógv fólk]]]]]	*		***		**
m.	[TP Tað má_T [_vP[_v' ongantíð hava_v [VP verið [innlendsk trø]]]]]	*		***		**
n.	[CP [Tann gamla bilin] vil_C [TP eg __T [_vP ikki [VP hava_v __V,Comp]]]]		*	***	**	**
o.	[TP Eg las_T [_vP[_v' ikki [VP __v bókina]]]]	*		**	**	**
p.	[TP Eg las_T [VP hana [_v' ikki __v __V,Comp]]]	*		**	*	**
q.	[TP Eg havi_T [VP ongan sæð_V __V,Comp]]	*		**		
r.	[TP Eg havi_T [VP [ongan næming] tosað_V [PP við_P __P,Comp]]]	*		***		*

by adding violations to the hypothesised higher-ranked constraint (Prince and Smolensky 1993:139).

9.6.1 Ranking Arguments

Given the general head-initial clause order in Scandinavian languages, let us hypothesise the ranking {F<XP, HRM} » HDFIN for Faroese. A combination tableau[20] for Table 9.2(a) is given in (251):

(251) **Ranking argument for {F<XP, HRM} » HDFIN**

{tey_[+HR], hava_[+fin], aldri, lisið_[-fin], bókina_[-HR]}	F<XP	HRM	HDFIN
☞ a. [TP Tey hava_T [_vP[_v' aldri [VP lisið_V bókina]]]]			**
b. [TP Tey hava_T [_vP[_v' aldri [VP bókina lisið_V]]]]		*W	*L
c. [TP Tey [_vP[_v' aldri [VP bókina lisið_V]]] hava_T]	*W		L

From (251) we may conclude that both F<XP and HARMONY must be ranked higher than HDFIN, since the loser candidates would only win if HDFIN were higher ranked than F<XP and HARMONY, respectively. We cannot construct a ranking argument for the pair {F<XP, HRM} from the data in Table 9.2, since no winning candidate ever violates HRM at the clause level; they must be left unranked. One potential example of a disharmonic word order in Faroese is the definite suffix, which could be analysed as a functional head D attached to the right of its N, with an additional D-head dominating the phrase containing the N if a definite adjective intervenes, as in (252).

---

[20] A tableau showing both constraint violations and whether, for a given loser, its violations of a given constraint favour the winner (W) or this loser (L).

(252) Far. [DP *tann*_D [DP [AP *stóri*_A] [NP *maður*_N] –*in*_D]]
             the   big   man   the
       'the tall man'

However, the analysis in (252) goes against the lexicalist assumption that the syntactic atomic item is the fully inflected word-form. Börjars and Donohue (2000:331) propose that the definite suffix in Faroese (as in Norwegian and Swedish, unlike Danish) only satisfies input–output faithfulness constraints if realised as a suffix to N, while the preceding definite word is a phrasal feature only satisfied by the larger DP projection. Hence, the structure for double definites would be as in (253):

(253) Far. [DP *tann*_D [NP [AP *stóri*_A] *maður-in*_N]]
             the   big   man-the
       'the tall man'

As for single definites such as *maður-in* 'man-the' without a modifier, we follow Hankamer and Mikkelsen (2002) and assume that nouns with the suffixed article enter the syntactic input as items of category D. As Hankamer and Mikkelsen (2002, 2005) show, the lexicalist approach is consistent with both the double and single definites, and so we need not stipulate a D-head position for the suffixed article. On this analysis, no violation of HARMONY is incurred within the embedded DP, and hence definite DPs do not speak to the ranking of {F<XP, HRM} one way or the other.[21]

It is difficult to construct a ranking argument for {OBHEAD, OBSPEC}, since the only way to reduce violations would be either inserting an additional head into the output to better satisfy OBHEAD, thus violating DEP, or inserting an empty specifier to do better on OBSPEC, which would be ruled out by *EMPTYSTRUC. Therefore, these are left unranked.

The ranking HRM » OBSPEC can be demonstrated by adding a specifier and removing a complement, which incurs an additional HRM violation:[22]

---

[21] We assume that candidates omitting either definite element will incur a MAX violation and that the suffix cannot occur as a prefix which would violate SUBCAT. As for the indefinite article *ein*, it is assumed to be of category D and to take an NP complement: thus, the analysis of *ein stórur maður* 'a big man' would be [DP D [NP AP N]].

[22] For ease of reading, the matrix clause is not included, but it is assumed that word-order constraints like HRM operate on full sentences, as stated in Section 9.5.

(254) **Ranking argument for** Hrm » ObSp

{... at, Jógvan[+HR], hevur[+fin], aldri, lisið[−fin], bókina[−HR]}	Hrm	ObSp
☞ a. ... [CP atC [TP Jógvan hevurT [vP[v' aldri [VP lisiðV bókina]]]]]		***
b. ... [CP atC [TP Jógvan hevurT [vP[v' aldri [VP bókinaSpec lisiðV]]]]]	*W	**L

(254b) also violates positional licensing, since Spec,VP is associated with the morphosyntactic case features [−HR−LR]. The informal generalisation could be: 'make sure an item with the correct grammatical role is occupying the correct position'. This is one of the feature-mapping phenomena that is handled by MatchF (237), repeated again in (255):

(255) MatchF: assign a violation for each positional feature matrix F[vals_{pos}] that is not identical to its corresponding item feature matrix F[vals_{item}].

If a positional feature matrix like [+HR] does not match the item's feature matrix [−HR], a violation will be incurred. MatchF will therefore rule out the mismatch of having the direct object in Spec,VP instead of V,Comp, since [−HR] does not match [−HR−LR]. Since inserting an argument into a specifier with a non-matching feature matrix incurs a violation of MatchF, the ranking MatchF » ObSpec must hold:

(256) **Ranking argument for** MatchF » ObSp

{tey[+HR], hava[+fin], aldri, lisið[−fin], bókina[−HR]}	MatchF	ObSp
☞ a. [TP Tey[+HR]:[+HR] havaT [vP[v' aldri [VP lisiðV bókina[−HR]:[−HR]]]]]		**
b. [TP Tey[+HR]:[+HR] havaT [vP[v' aldri [VP bókina[−HR−LR]:[−HR] lisiðV ____]]]]	*W	*L
c. [TP Tey[+HR]:[+HR] havaT [vP bókina∅:[−HR] [v' aldri [VP lisiðV ____]]]]	*W	*L

If the ranking ObSpec » MatchF held, one of the losers (256b–c) would win: thus, we have the partial ranking {MatchF, Hrm} » ObSp.

To test a hypothesised ranking of MatchF » ObHead, we need to look at losing candidates with fewer ObHead violations than the winner and more MatchF violations than the winner. This requires there to be either more heads (which would violate Dep), or fewer projections. The only possibility here is a candidate with *ongantið* adjoined at V', thus eliminating the vP projection,[23] combined with violations of MatchF by arguments occupying the wrong positions (257b–d).

(257) **Ranking argument for** MatchF » ObHd

{ivaleyst, gøvu[+fin], tey[+HR], ongantið, dreingjunum[−HR−LR], teldurnar[−HR]}	MatchF	ObHd
☞ a. [CP Ivaleyst gøvuC [TP tey[+HR]:[+HR] [vP[v' ongantið [VP dreingjunum[−HR−LR]:[−HR−LR] teldurnar[−HR]:[−HR]]]]]]		***
b. [CP Ivaleyst gøvuC [TP tey[+HR]:[+HR] [vP[v' ongantið teldurnar[−HR−LR]:[−HR] dreingjunum[−HR]:[−HR]]]]]	**W	**L
c. [CP Ivaleyst gøvuC [TP dreingjunum[+HR]:[−HR−LR] [vP[v' ongantið tey[−HR−LR]:[+HR] teldurnar[−HR]:[−HR]]]]]	**W	**L
d. [CP Ivaleyst gøvuC [TP teldurnar[+HR]:[−HR] [vP[v' ongantið tey[−HR−LR]:[+HR] dreingjunum[−HR]:[−HR−LR]]]]]	***W	**L

[23] Incidentally, this may suggest that in this example the adverb ought to be adjoined at V' to avoid positing unnecessary structure, but since adjunction at v' seems to be the default in other cases, we assume that some faithfulness constraint may be enforcing v'-adjunction as the elsewhere case.

If ObHead were ranked above MatchF, loser candidates like (257b–d) would win. Thus, we have the rankings MatchF » {ObHd, ObSp} and {F<XP, Hrm} » {HdFin, ObSp}. It is also impossible to test the ranking of HdFin and {ObHd, ObSp}, since there is no way of adding violations to HdFin in a consistently head-initial language like Faroese.

It is important to note that the obligatory element *markedness* constraints are doing some of the work to prohibit structures which omit heads or specifiers, which arguably could also be achieved by *faithfulness* constraints ensuring that all items in the input are present in the output (i.e. something like Max). Such a constraint is indeed necessary in order to rule out empty structures. It is also reasonable to hypothesise it being ranked higher than the obligatory element constraints, since it is more stringent: ObHead and ObSpec only ensure that already-present projections have heads and specifiers and are not violated when the projection itself is absent; Max, by contrast, is violated when any input item is not present in the output candidate.

(258) **Ranking argument for {Max, Dep} » ObHead**

{syngið}	Max	Dep	ObHd
☞ a. [$_{VP}$ *Syngið!*$_V$]			
b. [$_{VP}$ *Lesið!*$_V$]	*W	*W	L
c. ∅	*W		L
d. [$_{VP}$ *Syngið*$_V$ *væl!*]		*W	L

Here, we have evidence for the rankings Dep » ObHead and Max » ObHead.

To find a ranking of Max and Dep, we must find a winner that incurs violations of at least one of these; the most straightforward example would be expletive constructions, where *tað* or *har* is inserted despite not being present in the input (we assume, therefore, that a discourse feature in the input forces the subject to occur in V,Comp, and as a consequence, this dummy phonological material to occupy Spec,TP).

(259) **Ranking argument for Max » Dep**

{*hevur*$_{[+fin]}$, *altíð*, *verið*$_{[+fin]}$, *tónleikur*$_{[+Foc]}$}	Max	Dep
☞ a. [$_{TP}$ *Tað hevur*$_T$ [$_{vP}$[$_{v'}$ *altíð* [$_{VP}$ *verið*$_V$ *tónleikur*$_{[+Foc]:[+Foc]}$]]]]		*
b. [$_{TP}$ *Tónleikur*$_{[-Foc]:[-Foc]}$ *hevur*$_T$ [$_{vP}$[$_{v'}$ *altíð* [$_{VP}$ *verið*$_V$]]]]	*W	L

Since (259b) fails to instantiate a [+Foc] feature present in the input rather than having one in the wrong position (e.g. a non-focused subject in V,Comp), it does not violate MatchF, only Max. If we test MatchF with respect to Max » Dep, we must find a winner that does incur an

9.6 Faroese Clause Structure Revisited: OLG Account

MATCHF violation. An instance of this would be object topicalisation, as shown in (260):

(260)   Ranking argument for MAX » MATCHF

{[tann gamla bilin]$_{[-HR],[+Top]}$, vil$_{[+fin]}$, eg$_{[+HR]}$, ikki, hava$_{[-fin]}$}		MAX	MATCHF
☞ a.	[$_{CP}$ [Tann gamla bilin]$_{Ø:[-HR],[+Top]:[+Top]}$ vil$_C$ [$_{TP}$ eg [$_{vP}$[$_{v'}$ ikki [$_{VP}$ hava$_V$ ___ $_{[-HR]}$]]]]]		**
b.	[$_{TP}$ Eg vil$_T$ [$_{vP}$[$_{v'}$ ikki [$_{VP}$ hava$_V$ [tann gamla bilin]$_{[-HR]:[-HR],[-Top]:[-Top]}$]]]]	*W	L

By analogy with our treatment of focus in (259), the 'elsewhere' discourse position for objects is going to be V,Comp, which therefore is [−Top]. If MATCHF were ranked above MAX, loser (260b) would win. Therefore, we have now established the rankings MAX » {DEP, MATCHF} » {OBHD, OBSP} and {F<XP, HRM} » {HDFIN, OBSP}. The missing pieces are the rankings of {DEP, MATCHF, F<XP} and {VFINHI, CHKT, C<XP} with respect to the other constraints. These latter three constraints are motivated by the factorial typology, which must be able to generate [[H Comp] Op] word orders, such as in German, as discussed later in this section. As for {DEP, MATCHF, F<XP}, it is not possible to construct ranking arguments, so these remain unranked.

It turns out, however, that MAX » {DEP » MATCHF} is insufficient to capture some types of expletive constructions, that is, when an expletive is present (violating DEP) and all input items are expressed without violating MATCHF. One such sentence type is when adverbs occur in Spec,CP and the expletive in Spec,TP as shown in (261).

(261)	{tí, sjálvandi, vóru$_{[+fin]}$, [nøkur fólk]$_{[+HR],[+Foc]}$}		MAX	DEP	MATCHF
☞ a.	[$_{CP}$ [Tí sjálvandi] vóru$_C$ [$_{TP}$ tað [$_{VP}$ [nøkur fólk]$_{[-HR]:[+HR],[+Foc]:[+Foc]}$]]]		*		*
b.	[$_{CP}$ Sjálvandi vóru$_C$ [$_{TP}$[$_T$′ tí [$_{VP}$ [nøkur fólk]$_{[-HR]:[+HR],[+Foc]:[+Foc]}$]]]]		L		*
c.	[$_{CP}$ Sjálvandi vóru$_C$ [$_{TP}$ tí [$_{VP}$ [nøkur fólk]$_{[-HR]:[+HR],[+Foc]:[+Foc]}$]]]		L		*

Candidates like (261b–c), which violate neither MAX nor DEP, suggest that some additional constraint may be in play. Either having no Spec,TP position (261b) or putting the adverb in that position (261c) will yield a losing candidate. Let us assume that the requirement which generates expletives is that an *argument* must occupy Spec,TP, even if that argument does not bear the highest theta-role: if so, an adverb like *tí* could not satisfy that requirement. We can call this constraint ARGSP, similar to the Extended Projection Principle (EPP) (Chomsky 1981), though the standard formulation of the EPP is stronger, since it requires a *subject* argument to occupy subject position, not just any argument.

(262)   ARGSP: Assign a violation if no argument occupies subject position (Spec,TP).

234 *Syntax in OLG*

(263) **Ranking argument for** ArgSP » Dep

{tí, sjálvandi, vóru[+fin], [nøkur fólk][+HR],[+Foc]}	ArgSP	Dep	MatchF
☞ a. [CP [Tí sjálvandi] vóru_C [TP tað [VP [nøkur fólk][−HR]:[+HR],[+Foc]:[+Foc]]]]		*	*
b. [CP Sjálvandi vóru_C [TP[T' tí [VP [nøkur fólk][−HR]:[+HR],[+Foc]:[+Foc]]]]]	*W	L	*
c. [CP Sjálvandi vóru_C [TP tí [VP [nøkur fólk][−HR]:[+HR],[+Foc]:[+Foc]]]]	*W	L	*
d. [CP Sjálvandi vóru_C [TP tað [T' tí [VP [nøkur fólk][−HR]:[+HR],[+Foc]:[+Foc]]]]]		*	*
e. [CP Sjálvandi vóru_C [TP tað [VP[V' tí [nøkur fólk][−HR]:[+HR],[+Foc]:[+Foc]]]]]		*	*

The tableau in (263) raises the question of why the adverb *tí* cannot be adjoined at T' or V', since either of these apparent losing candidates satisfy the constraints we have so far the same number of times as the winner. The answer is, in fact, that candidates (263d–e) are also possible Faroese sentences: adverbs like *tí* 'therefore', *jú* 'indeed' and *bara* 'only, just', among others, have various possible attachment sites. A search of texts online in Faroese and the blog corpus yields some examples of this optionality:

(264) a. Far. [CP *Tí*   er_C [TP tað [T' millum annað   [AP sera relevant at
           therefore is   it   among other.things   very relevant to
    spyrja seg sjálvan]]]]
    ask   one- self
    'Therefore it is, among other things, very relevant to ask oneself...'
    Blog corpus, *samalsdiary* line 7578

   b. Far. [CP Ikki var_C [TP tað [T' *tí*:   [TP hugurin   at renna saman   við
           not was   it   therefore   desire-the to run together with
    bygdarfólkið bilaði honum ikki]]]]
    townsfolk-the lacked him   not
    'That was not it: he was not lacking the desire to make up with the townsfolk'
    Føroyskar bókmentir 4 vol. 3, p.116, Google Books, accessed 1/17/18

   c. Far. [TP Verið_T [VP[V' *tí*   [AP[A' altíð   [tvey vaksin saman   við
          be.IMP.PL   therefore   always two adults together with
    barninum]]]]]]
    child-the
    'Always have two adults accompanying the child'
    www.sjovarkommuna.fo, accessed 1/17/18.

(265) a. Far. [CP [Fyrsta kvøldi] var_C [TP tað [T' *bara* [nátturði og so í song]]]]
              first night   was   it   only supper and so to bed
    'The first night, it was just supper and then to bed'
    Blog corpus, *holmjohannessen* line 2320.

   b. Far. ...men so oftast   ikki, [TP[T' tí   eg gloymi_T [VP tað [V' *bara!*]]]]
           ...but so most.often not,   because I forget   it   just
    '...but most of the time not, because I just forget it!'
    Blog corpus, *roskur* line 617.

9.6 Faroese Clause Structure Revisited: OLG Account

The proposal that adverbs may adjoin to several different projections depending on the semantics is one standard way of capturing their scopal properties (Pollock 1989, Iatridou 1990, Potsdam 1998, among others), over against an alternative analysis in which adverbs occupy specifiers (Jackendoff 1981, Alexiadou 1994, Cinque 1998); see Potsdam (1998) for a review of the evidence. Here we do not attempt to solve this large problem but stipulate that, in a similar vein to presentational focus, topicalisation, and other phenomena involving syntactic expression of information structure, discourse features may be associated with the adverbs which enforce adjunction to the appropriate syntactic category. For example, a manner adverb in English, such as 'carefully', is preferably VP-adjoined, and therefore bears a V'-adjunction feature:

(266) a. They have [$_{VP}$[$_{V'}$ carefully$_{[V']:[V']}$ gathered the evidence]]
      b. They have [$_{VP}$ gathered the evidence [$_{V'}$ carefully$_{[V']:[V']}$]]
      c. ? They [$_{TP}$[$_{T'}$ carefully$_{[T']:[V']}$ have [$_{VP}$ gathered the evidence]]]

Notably, (266c) improves with contrastive stress on 'have' (i.e. 'They carefully HAVE gathered the evidence'); in that case, we hypothesise that 'carefully' bears a [T'] feature, and therefore that the lower acceptability of (266c) results from the [T'] : [V'] mismatch. Hence, if the adverb *tí* in (263) bore a feature in the input such as [Spec,CP] specifying the position needed to express the appropriate semantic information, candidates (263b–e) would incur additional MAX violations, assuming that the winner has the correct site for the adverb. This is merely a way of capturing the fact that there may be options for where to adjoin the adverb, and the input reflects this featurally in the same way as other discourse phenomena.

Since the additional constraint ARGSP has been proposed, its ranking must be established. Let us test the ranking MAX » ARGSP: the relevant losing candidates will be those that do better than the winner on ARGSP but worse than the winner on MAX. This requires a winner that incurs a violation of ARGSP (i.e. with an empty Spec,TP or a non-argument item in Spec,TP). Perhaps presentational constructions with an expletive could be brought to bear, since one possible hypothesis is that the expletive is in Spec,CP with an empty Spec,TP, and hence that the expletive always occurs in Spec,CP. However, there is a theory-internal reason to avoid this: if the descriptive generalisation is that the expletive *tað* is inserted into Spec,TP *unless* the associate subject occurs there, it makes most sense to analyse Spec,TP as the 'elsewhere' location for expletive *tað*. This analysis, however, leaves us with no way of testing the ranking of ArgSP, since there is no winner that violates it. We need to find a winning candidate with an empty Spec,TP that does not insert an expletive.

Thankfully, such constructions do exist: in Faroese, the expletive may be omitted when it follows the finite verb (Þráinsson 2007:335).

(267) a. Far. Eru ___ komnir nakrir gestir úr Íslandi?
           are   come some guests from Iceland
           'Have any guests arrived from Iceland?'
      b. Far. Í Havn regnar ___ ofta
           in Havn rains   often
           'It often rains in Tórshavn'

Example (267a) is analogous to Table 9.2(j) but without anything in Spec,TP. This example will incur a violation of ArgSP, since there is no argument in Spec,TP.[24] Let us assume the standard analysis of inversion in questions (i.e. that the finite verb occurs in C). It is necessary to account for the apparent optionality (i.e. that *tað* may either be present or omitted), and hence there are two winning candidates for the same input: we propose that this is a competing grammars situation, both of which are accessible to native speakers of Faroese given the correct conditions (Chapter 5 laid out a competing grammars proposal of syntactic variation). There is much to be said on this, but for the moment we assume two different rankings of ArgSP and Dep, with Max dominating both. Thus, the version of (267a) with the overt expletive is a losing candidate in the tableau (268) and the winner in tableau (269).

(268) **Ranking argument for Max » ArgSP » Dep**

{eru$_{[+fin],[+Q]}$, komnir$_{[-fin]}$, [nakrir gestir]$_{[+HR],[+Foc]}$, úr, Íslandi}	Max	ArgSP	Dep
a. [$_{CP}$ Eru$_{C,[+Q]:[+Q]}$ [$_{TP}$ ___T [$_{VP}$ komnir$_V$ [nakrir gestir [úr Íslandi?]]]]]		*W	L
☞ b. [$_{CP}$ Eru$_{C,[+Q]:[+Q]}$ [$_{TP}$ tað ___T [$_{VP}$ komnir$_V$ [nakrir gestir [úr Íslandi?]]]]]			*
c. [$_{TP}$ Tað eru$_{T,[-Q]:[-Q]}$ [$_{VP}$ komnir$_V$ [nakrir gestir [úr Íslandi]]]]	*W		*

---

[24]It is assumed that 'from Iceland' in this example modifies the argument 'some guests', not the entire VP.

9.6 *Faroese Clause Structure Revisited: OLG Account* 237

(269) **Ranking argument for** MAX » DEP » ARGSP

{eru[+fin],[+Q], komnir[-fin], [nakrir gestir][+HR],[+Foc], úr, Íslandi}	MAX	DEP	ARGSP
☞ a. [CP EruC,[+Q]:[+Q] [TP ___T [VP komniry [nakrir gestir [úr Íslandi?]]]]]			*
b. [CP EruC,[+Q]:[+Q] [TP tað ___T [VP komniry [nakrir gestir [úr Íslandi?]]]]]		*W	L
c. [TP Tað eruT,[-Q]:[-Q] [VP komniry [nakrir gestir [úr Íslandi]]]]	*W	*W	

A [+Q] feature violates MAX when the verb is not initial; that is, [+Q] in Faroese is expressed by the subject–verb inversion. Moreover, this difference in ranking predicts other behaviours relating to expletives elsewhere in the language: whenever it is possible to omit an expletive, the grammar in (269) will do so. It will not, however, over-zealously remove all expletives, since removing a sentence-initial expletive will incur an additional DEP violation: as we have seen, V1 expresses [+Q] (i.e. it is the default word order in questions), and so candidates with no expletive and no [+Q] in the input will violate DEP if [+Q] is in the output. In essence, [+Q] is simply a way of notating that inversion is how Faroese and other Germanic languages instantiate polar questions (rather than a verbal morpheme, for example).

Finally, although candidates (268a–b) and (269a–b) violate CHECK-TNS due to no verb occupying T, and conversely (268c) and (269c) violate VFINHI, these violations would not threaten the winner in either competing grammar if {VFINHI, CHKT} were ranked below {ARGSP, DEP}: thus, the null expletive constructions also constitute evidence for the ranking {ARGSP, DEP} » {VFINHI, CHKT}. Furthermore, the ranking VFINHI » CHKT must hold for Faroese, since the reverse would yield winners in which the finite verb always shows up in T (i.e. there would be no V2 in main clauses, as in English). The pair VFINHI » CHKT must also be ranked above {OBHD, OBSP}, since otherwise if the winner has the finite verb in C, losing candidates with the verb in T would defeat the winner, since they would remove the OBHEAD violation. Similarly to F<XP, we cannot test the ranking of C<XP in Faroese, since no winner will have a C follow its XP complement.

In brief, the following partial rankings have been demonstrated by ranking arguments:

(270) MAX » {ARGSP, DEP} » {MATCHF, {VFINHI » CHKT}} » {OBHD, OBSP}
{F<XP, HRM} » {HDFIN, OBSP}

All constraints proposed here are tested in Section 9.6.2 with respect to the languages they generate.

9.6.2 Factorial Typology: Faroese Clause Structure

What remains is to demonstrate that the proposed set of constraints generates a typology of attested and possible languages while ruling out impossible ones. A stipulated constraint ranking in (271) was run in OT Soft 2.5 (Hayes et al. 2013), first testing the inputs given in (272).

(271) **Faroese:**
Max » ArgSP » Dep » MatchF » F<XP » Hrm » C<XP » VfinHi » ChkT » HdFin » ObHd » ObSp

(272) a. /{they,have,never$_{[v']}$,read,book}/
b. /{then$_{[+Top]}$,have,they,never$_{[v']}$,read,book}/
c. /{that,John,has,never$_{[v']}$,read,book}/
d. /{that,John,never$_{[T']}$,has,read,book}/
e. /{who,never,had,read,book}/
f. /{if,she,always,says,true}/
g. /{they,read,never,book}/
h. /{doubtless$_{[+Top]}$,shall,they,never,sell,boys,books}/
i. /{doubtless$_{[+Top]}$,gave,they,never,boys,books}/

With 12 constraints, there are 479,001,600 logically possible grammars, but for the sentences in (272) without expletives, topicalisation or object shift, only 14 output language types are generated. Pernicious disharmony (i.e. the order *[[Head Comp] Op]) is never generated under any ranking. Output candidates with violations of Merge or c-Selection were not considered, nor failure to express input features such as [v'], since such candidates will be harmonically bounded.[25] No winner for these inputs incurs any violations of Max, ArgSP, Dep or MatchF; these higher-ranked constraints are necessary for expletive constructions, object shift and other diatheses.

A summary of each output pattern is given in (273). The constraints generate three types of 'T-to-C': (i) the finite verb never appears in C, (ii)

---

[25]Given our analysis of adverb adjunction, adverb placement was stipulated in the losing candidates, but we do not claim that the output languages in which that candidate wins necessarily always adjoin the adverb in that position; scope and discourse factors may enforce different adjunction sites.

9.6 Faroese Clause Structure Revisited: OLG Account

the finite verb only appears in C if there is a topicalised XP immediately preceding it, and (iii) the finite verb always appears in C. These types are listed as 'no T-to-C', 'Top(icalised XP) + T-to-C' and 'A(cross) T(he) B(oard) T-to-C' respectively. Since the difference between presence or absence of T-to-C is only detectable with a fronted XP or in embedded clauses, types (ii) and (iii) will yield the same surface orders in these sentence types: therefore, there are actually only 11 distinct output word orders for these inputs. However, the constraints do predict that in languages of type (iii) the finite verb will always appear in C, regardless of construction.

(273) **Output factorial typology**

No.	Main clause	M.c. with Aux	Embedded clause	'T-to-C'	Example language
1	VO	Aux[VO]	C[Aux[VO]]	Top + T-to-C	Faroese, Danish, Old French
2	VO	Aux[VO]	C[Aux[VO]]	no T-to-C	English
3	VO	Aux[OV]	C[Aux[OV]]	Top + T-to-C	output 4 with T-to-C
4	VO	Aux[OV]	C[Aux[OV]]	no T-to-C	Kisi, Dinka, Dongo, Nuer
5	OV	[OV]Aux	C[Aux[VO]]	Top + T-to-C	
6	OV	[OV]Aux	C[[OV]Aux]	Top + T-to-C	
7	OV	[OV]Aux	[[OV]Aux]C	Top + T-to-C	output 10 with T-to-C
8	OV	[OV]Aux / Top+Aux[VO]	C[Aux[VO]]	no T-to-C	
9	OV	[OV]Aux / Top+Aux[OV]	C[[OV]Aux]	no T-to-C	Hindi
10	OV	[OV]Aux	[[OV]Aux]C	no T-to-C	Korean, Tamil, Telugu
11	VO	Aux[VO]	C[Aux[VO]]	ATB T-to-C	Icelandic, French
12	VO	Aux[OV]	C[Aux[OV]]	ATB T-to-C	output 4 with T-to-C
13	VO	Aux[OV]	C[[OV]Aux]	ATB T-to-C	German
14	OV	[OV]Aux	[[OV]Aux]C	ATB T-to-C	output 10 with T-to-C

As the phenomena standardly analysed as 'T-to-C' and V2 are cross-linguistically rare, it should not be problematic that unattested combinations that are nevertheless logically possible (e.g. output 14) are generated. In many constructions it may not even be possible to tell whether the finite auxiliary is occupying T or C, which often yield the same surface order, particularly if fronting of a topicalised non-subject phrase is not a strategy used by the language for expressing [+Top]. Moreover, many languages whose word order profile is ostensibly the same as outputs 4 or 10 are as yet incompletely described, especially with respect to the conditions under which V2 occurs and/or whether a topicalised XP can precede the finite auxiliary, and so it is likely that more of the table cells in (273) are attested.

9.7 Information Structure

With the same set of basic clause structure constraints, the sentence types involving expletives, topicalisation or object shift were also considered (296). In dealing with these phenomena, two broad kinds of feature-matching are at play: discourse-featural positions and argument-licensing positions. Such constructions often involve a conflict between mapping of argument structure and information structure to syntax (e.g. when a positional discourse feature can only be satisfied by a mismatch in case features). In order to capture the range of data even within the Faroese sentences already seen, a more fine-grained hierarchy of constraints underneath MatchF is required:

(274) MatchCase (MC): assign a violation for each positional case feature matrix $F[vals_{pos}]$ that is not identical to its corresponding item case feature matrix $F[vals_{item}]$.

(275) MatchDis (MD): assign a violation for each positional discourse-feature matrix $F[vals_{pos}]$ that is not identical to its corresponding item discourse-feature matrix $F[vals_{item}]$.

(276) MatchAdv (MA): assign a violation for each positional adverbial-adjunction feature matrix $F[vals_{pos}]$ that is not identical to its corresponding item adverbial-adjunction feature matrix $F[vals_{item}]$.

As for the range of possible discourse features and their positions, OLG follows Choi (2001:148) in assuming that [+Foc(us)] expresses a combination of [+New] and [±Prom(inent)], the latter determined by whether focus is contrastive [+Prom] or presentational [–Prom]. [–Foc] expresses [–New] only and is underspecified for [±Prom]. [+Top(ic)] expresses [–New,+Prom], while [–Top] expresses any other combination of the features [±New,±Prom]. This captures the generalisations that focus involves drawing attention to new information regardless of discourse-prominence, while topicalisation involves making prominent some element that is not new information. A non-focused element is therefore by definition not new, while a non-topic is any element that is not *both* old *and* discourse-prominent information. In (277) the proposed positional features for Faroese are presented.

(277)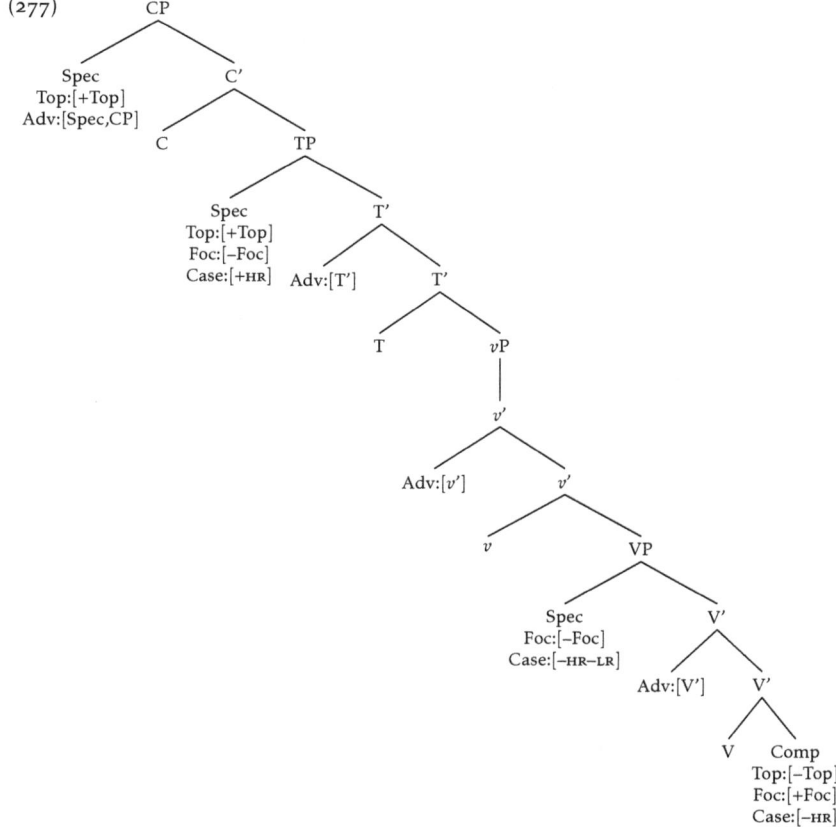

For illustrative purposes, one much-debated example is discussed in Section 9.7.1, that of object shift in Scandinavian. It is shown that variation in Scandinavian object positions can be derived straightforwardly from information-structural constraints but without any reference to movement operations, provided we assume the proposed adverbial adjunction sites.

9.7.1 Case Study: Scandinavian Object Shift

The phenomenon of object shift represents a good testing ground for the proposed information-structural constraints. The literature on this subject is vast, and only a short treatment can be given here; nevertheless, the OLG framework will provide some fresh insights into why object shift occurs. Object shift is present in all the Scandinavian languages and can be described as the occurrence of an object argument to the left of certain adverbials, notably the negative particle *ikki/ikke/ekki/inte* and negative adverbs like 'never' (see Holmberg 1986, 1997 and Þráinsson 2000, among others). Sells (2001) provides a very thorough LFG-based OT analysis of Scandinavian object shift, which more recent work by Engels and Vikner (2014) builds upon; this account is indebted to both of these works but pursues a different analysis of the constraints governing the positions of clausal constituents.[26] Swedish examples (278a–d) from Sells (2001:3) illustrate the simplest cases.

(278)   a. Swe. *Jag kysste inte Anna.*
               I   kissed not Anna
               'I did not kiss Anna'
      b. Swe. *Jag kysste henne inte.*
               I   kissed her   not
               'I did not kiss her'
      c. Swe. *Jag har inte kysst Anna.*
               I   have not kissed Anna
               'I have not kissed Anna'
      d. Swe. *Jag har inte kysst henne.*
               I   have not kissed her
               'I have not kissed her'

The pronominal object *henne* 'her' undergoes shift in (278b), but not in (278d). There is cross-linguistic variation with respect to several aspects of object shift behaviour within Scandinavian. For example, in Danish and Norwegian, the order in (278b) is the only possibility (unless the pronominal object is narrowly focused), but in Swedish, the order *Jag kysste inte henne* is also possible. In Danish, the verb occurs below sentence-medial adverbs in embedded clauses, while in Icelandic

---

[26]For another approach similar to Sells (2001), see Wallenberg (2013), who unifies object shift and some scrambling phenomena in Yiddish and other languages with head-final phrases. The proposal draws upon a similar notion of leftward alignment to that of Sells (2001) but attributes it to c-command as an LF constraint; this differs somewhat from the OLG analysis presented here, in which positional licensing does much of the work, though MATCH constraints could be seen as analogous to leftward alignment.

the verb also may occur above such adverbs in embedded clauses (279–280), which are examples from Engels and Vikner (2014:58):

(279) **Danish:**
    a. Dan. *Hvorfor læste Peter **den** aldrig?*
            why   read Peter it   never
            'Why did Peter never read it?'
    b. Dan. * *Hvorfor læste Peter aldrig **den**?*
            why   read Peter never it
    c. Dan. *Jeg spurgte hvorfor Peter aldrig **læste den***
            I asked why   Peter never read it
            'I asked why Peter never read it'
    d. Dan. * *Jeg spurgte hvorfor Peter **den** aldrig læste*
            I asked why   Peter it   never read

(280) **Icelandic:**
    a. Ice. *Af hverju las Pétur aldrei þessa bók?*
            why   read Peter never this   book
            'Why did Peter never read this book?'
    b. Ice. *Af hverju las Pétur þessa bók aldrei?*
            why   read Peter this   book never
    c. Ice. *Ég spurði af hverju Pétur læsi aldrei þessa bók*
            I asked why   Peter read never this   book
            'I asked why Peter never read this book'
    d. Ice. *Ég spurði af hverju Pétur læsi þessa bók aldrei*
            I asked why   Peter read this   book never

Only in Icelandic can full DPs also undergo object shift, whereas in Mainland Scandinavian and Faroese, only weak pronouns undergo shift (hence the Danish examples in (279) all have pronominal objects).[27] Both Sells (2001) and Engels and Vikner (2014) give detailed analyses of a broader range of data relating to this phenomenon (e.g. Swedish long object shift and variation in *let*-constructions); our intention here is not to provide such an exhaustive account but to show that the information-structural constraints adopted in OLG offer a compelling answer to the 'why' question. The analysis presented below does cover the variation under consideration, nonetheless, and shows that much can be gained from revisiting oft-discussed data from a new angle.

---

[27]See Þráinsson (2013) for a recent study of object shift in Faroese and Old Norse, which suggests that some contexts do permit full NP object shift in modern Faroese, though it is far more restricted than in Icelandic; the data in Chapter 4 are consistent with the analysis proposed in this section.

An important insight in the literature from Holmberg (1986, 1997) is that, if one assumes that V-to-T movement is blocked by certain clause-medial elements, one prerequisite for object shift to occur is that the verb must have moved out of its base position, a claim known as 'Holmberg's Generalisation'. Holmberg (1986) formulated this insight as in (281):

(281) HOLMBERG'S GENERALISATION: object shift is possible just in case the V has raised out of the VP (to a higher functional head position).

As is evident, this formulation presupposes a movement analysis in which the finite verb raises to a higher position in the structure, specifically a functional head such as T. The idea is that the object moves out of the VP in which it was base-generated, following the movement of the verb. Shift is therefore ungrammatical when the V does not leave VP, as in (282):[28]

(282) a. Swe. *Jag har henne inte kysst.
       I have her not kissed
   b. Swe. *...att jag henne inte kysste.
       that I her not kissed

However, Sells (2001:41–101) presents a compelling case that the relevant empirical generalisations about Swedish, presented in (283), hold of both shift and non-shift contexts (i.e. that movement of the verb is not truly the condition):

(283) Except for constituents in the initial topic position:
   i. An object never precedes the V of which it is an argument.
   ii. With a ditransitive verb, a direct object (DO) never precedes an indirect object (IO).

Sells' proposal is that a set of ranked alignment constraints, of the form 'X aligns left', accounts for structures with and without displaced constituents, and hence captures both generalisations (283i) and (283ii). This avoids the need to stipulate a link between verb

---

[28]Holmberg (1999) reformulates the generalisation to account for new data, so that the condition for shift is sensitive to phonologically visible intervening material. For discussion see Sells (2001:47–51).

movement and shift *à la* Holmberg, or even to adopt constraints referring to derivations, such as a restriction that objects must move in parallel (Müller 2001). Indeed, one of the advantages of Sells' account is that the syntactic alignment constraints are general and not construction-specific but still generate the correct data. In OLG, we also presuppose that constraint conflict is behind the Scandinavian object shift behaviour; however, this is achieved not through alignment constraints but by positional licensing, in particular with respect to discourse-feature positions. Such an account brings two advantages: (i) feature-matching markedness constraints are responsible for both argument licensing and discourse structure, thus avoiding the need for either transformations or construction-specific constraints, and (ii) shift is more directly attributed to discourse-functional pressures rather than only indirectly via a dependency on verb movement. In this way, the deeper functional basis of object shift is brought to the fore.

In order to account for the range of attested object shift behaviours, we follow Engels and Vikner (2014) and propose that the relevant constraint conflict involves (i) preference for a non-focused element to occur left of the extended-VP adverbial, thus avoiding focus position (V,Comp); (ii) preference for full DP objects to remain in V,Comp; and (iii) preference for any object to remain in V,Comp. Therefore, the motivation for shift is attributed to an interaction between discourse structure and the mapping from argument structure to syntax. The conflict is between objects occupying their 'canonical' position (STAY in Engels and Vikner 2014) and the syntactic instantiation of focus, such that [–Foc] elements do not occupy a [+Foc] position (their SHIFT), which is also sensitive to adverbial scope. Hence, it is quite straightforward to capture the insights from the Engels and Vikner (2014) account within the OLG framework without any dependency on syntactic movement, thanks to the feature-matching apparatus already proposed. We postulate the additional constraint (284) to account for the difference between full-DP objects and other kinds of objects (analogous to Engels and Vikner's STAYBRANCH):

(284) OBJECTDP (OBJDP): assign a violation for each V,Comp position not occupied by a full DP.

Here, a rather different approach is taken to Holmberg's Generalisation than that of Engels and Vikner (2014). Their starting assumption is that a prerequisite for object shift is movement of the finite verb to T. In the OLG account, however, the position of the adverb does not, in fact, tell us definitively where the finite verb occurs, since such adverbs may be adjoined to v', V' or T'. Instead, the finite verb *always* occurs at least as high as T once the T-head is merged and, depending on the language, may also occur in C (always in Icelandic, only under particular conditions in Danish and Faroese). Holmberg (1986, 1997:208) formulated the generalisation in terms of blocked movement: if any phonologically 'visible' category precedes the object landing site within VP, shift may not occur. This will not work under OLG assumptions, since the finite verb does not occur in V when there is no auxiliary and so is not 'visible' within VP. In a similar vein, Engels and Vikner (2014:61) adopt a constraint on order preservation: object shift is only permitted if the order of certain elements is maintained, more specifically 'an independently moved constituent A must not precede a non-adverbial constituent B if the canonical position of A (or parts of A) follows the canonical position of B'. This formulation requires more precise definitions of 'independently moved' and 'canonical', but the assumption is similar to Holmberg's in that movement across filled positions is costly.[29]

However, once we remove the assumption that the finite verb remains in V when an adverb seems to intervene, it is hard to tell what Holmberg's Generalisation, in its movement-based formulation at least, actually buys us. The data that are covered by the generalisation include (i) no shift when the object occurs left of a non-finite main verb, (ii) shift permitted with V1, (iii) no shift that results in DO-IO order in double-object constructions, (iv) variation in particle–verb constructions, and (v) variation in *let*-constructions. For reasons of space, the details of (iv–v) are not discussed here; examples of (i–iii) are shown in (285–287).[30] Following Potsdam (1998), we assume the possibility of right-adjunction of the negative particle, which is posited for (287) in Danish,

---

[29]For a far more detailed overview of issues relevant to Scandinavian object shift, negative scrambling and adverb adjunction sites, see Þráinsson (2007:65–87).

[30]Examples from Engels and Vikner (2014:13,64–81).

and more broadly in Scandinavian for ditransitives when pronominal objects appear to the left of the negative particle.

(285) **Icelandic:**
    a. Ice. [CP *Af hverju hafði*C [TP *Pétur* [*v*P[*v'* *aldrei* [VP *lesið*V *þessa bók?*]]]]]
            why   had   Peter   never   read this book
       'Why had Peter never read this book?'
    b. Ice. * [CP *Af hverju hafði*C [TP *Pétur* [VP *þessa bók* [*v'* *aldrei lesið*V?]]]]
            why   had   Peter this book   never   read

(286) **Swedish:**
    a. Swe. [CP *Kysst har*C [TP *jag* [VP *henne* [*v'* *inte*]]]]
            kissed have I   her   not
       'Kissed her, I haven't'
    b. Swe. * [CP *Kysst har*C [TP *jag* [*v*P[*v'* *inte* [VP *henne*]]]]]
            kissed have I   not   her

(287) **Danish:**
    a. Dan. [TP *Jeg gav*T [VP *hende den* [*v'* *ikke*]]]
            I gave   her it   not
       'I didn't give it to her'
    b. Dan. * [TP *Jeg gav*T [VP *den hende* [*v'* *ikke*]]]
            I gave   it her   not

What does seem consistent with Holmberg (1997) is that when V is occupied by a non-finite verb, shift does not occur, whereas it can occur when the V position is empty. However, we do not actually need a separate order-preservation or 'Holmberg's Generalisation' constraint, **or even to refer to movement/intervening material at all,** to capture these facts. The licensing constraints suffice.

'Movement across material' for object shift (i.e. the object occurring in Spec,VP), necessarily involves an additional violation of MATCH-CASE, since the target position bears [–HR–LR] features. The object remaining in V,Comp incurs a violation of MATCHDIS since [–Foc] does not match [+Foc]. These featural mismatches are shown in (288) for Danish:

(288) a. Dan. [TP *Jeg har*T [*v*P[*v'* *aldrig* [VP *set hende*[+Foc]:[–Foc]]]]]
              I have   never   seen her
       'I have never seen her'
    b. Dan. * [TP *Jeg har*T [VP *hende*[–HR–LR]:[–HR] [*v'* *aldrig set* ____[–HR]:∅]]]
             I have   her   never seen

Therefore, we attribute the costliness of shift to the licensing constraints: when the object occurs in Spec,VP, a case feature mismatch ensues, whereas the pressure to shift arises from the discourse-feature mismatch of the [−Foc] object occurring in a [+Foc] position. Why, then, can the pronominal object not occur in Spec,VP in (288b), while it obligatorily occurs there when the main verb is in T, as in (279b)? The answer relies on the position of the negative adverb. When the adverb is adjoined to v', it scopes over the entire VP, such that the Spec,VP and V,Comp positions both bear [+Foc]. In contrast, when adjoined to V', the negative adverb scopes only over V,Comp, and therefore the Spec,VP position bears [−Foc]. The contrast is shown in (289–290), where the constituents below the dotted line are within the [+Foc] scopal domain of *aldrig* 'never'. It is not assumed that Spec,VP is present in the structure of (289) in violation of *EMPTYSTRUC, only that if it were present, it would fall under the adverbial scope.

Danish: v'-adjoined adverb

(289)

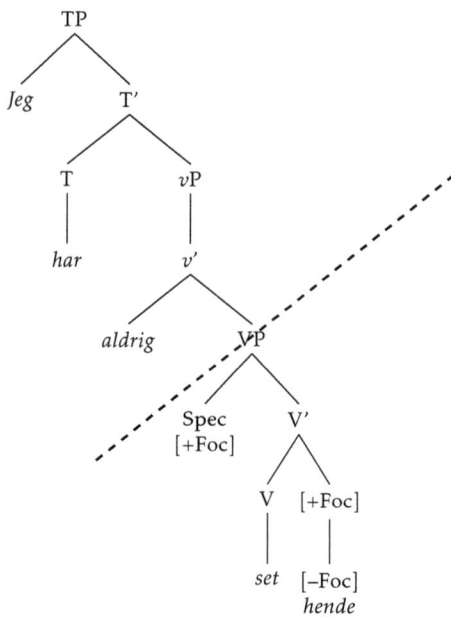

Danish: V'-adjoined adverb

(290)

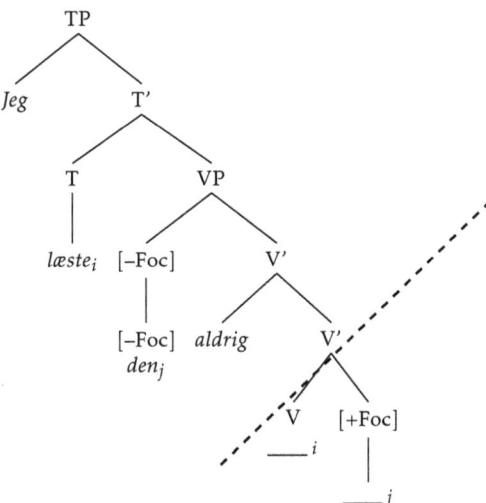

If we assume that [v'] is the only adverbial adjunction feature possible when V is occupied by a non-finite main verb, the facts fall out straightforwardly: shift will not 'save' the [+Foc] : [−Foc] mismatch in Spec,VP (i.e. remove an MATCHDIS violation) when the adverb is v'-adjoined but *does* remove the MATCHDIS violation when V'-adjoined, since then only V,Comp bears [+Foc]. The relevant feature matrices for the case of Danish pronominal shift are shown in (291):

(291) a. Dan. [TP *Jeg læste*T [VP *den*[−HR−LR]:[−HR],[−Foc]:[−Foc] [V' *aldrig* ___V
          I   read   it   never
___[−HR]:∅,[+Foc]:∅]]]

'I never read it'

b. Dan. * [TP *Jeg læste*T [vP[v' *aldrig* [VP (Spec[+Foc]) ___V
            I   read   never
den[−HR]:[−HR],[+Foc]:[−Foc]]]]]
it

As can be seen in (291b), even if *den* 'it' occurred in Spec,VP, this would not remove the MATCHDIS violation. The assumption that [v'] always occurs on negative adverbs when the main verb is finite is supported in two ways. Firstly, as an elsewhere case: [v'] is the unmarked sentential/clause-medial adverb site, but the adverb enters the input bearing [V'] when the condition of having the finite main verb in T is met. This is similar to the co-occurrence of two [+Q] features in a wh-question input: languages which convey information structure via word order may distribute the realisation of features across more than one item or constituent. Secondly, if sentential adverbs are also sensitive to tense, it is unsurprising that the adjunction sites adjacent to the tensed verb are preferred over adjunction to the non-finite verb (see Svenonius 2002 on the relation between adverb positions and tense). The conflict between MatchCase, MatchDis and MatchAdv derives the behaviour, provided the adverbs are adjoined at the right place, as shown for Icelandic examples (280a–b,285) in the following tableaux:[31]

(292) Icelandic (285): no shift with main verb in V, v'-adjunct

{af hverju,hafði$_{[+fin]}$,Pétur,aldrei$_{[v'],[+Foc]}$,lesið$_{[-fin]}$,[þessa bók]$_{[-HR],[-Foc]}$}	MA	MD	MC
☞ a. ... [TP Pétur [$_{vP}$[$_{v'}$ aldrei$_{[v']:[v']}$ [VP lesið$_V$ þessa bók$_{[+Foc]:[-Foc]}$?]]]]		*	
b. ... [TP Pétur [VP þessa bók$_{[-Foc]:[-Foc],[-HR-LR]:[-HR]}$ [V' aldrei$_{[V']:[v']}$ lesið$_V$?]]]	*!	*	*

(293) Icelandic (280a): shift with main verb in C, V'-adjunct

{af hverju,las$_{[+fin]}$,Pétur,aldrei$_{[V'],[+Foc]}$,[þessa bók]$_{[-HR],[-Foc]}$}	MA	MD	MC
a. ... las$_C$ [TP Pétur [$_{vP}$[$_{v'}$ aldrei$_{[v']:[V']}$ [VP (Spec$_{[+Foc]}$) þessa bók$_{[+Foc]:[-Foc]}$?]]]]	*!	*	
☞ b. ... las$_C$ [TP Pétur [VP þessa bók$_{[-Foc]:[-Foc],[-HR-LR]:[-HR]}$ [V' aldrei$_{[V']:[v']}$?]]]		*	*

(294) Icelandic (280b): no shift with main verb in C, v'-adjunct

{af hverju,las$_{[+fin]}$,Pétur,aldrei$_{[v'],[+Foc]}$,[þessa bók]$_{[-HR],[+Foc]}$}	MA	MD	MC
☞ a. ... las$_C$ [TP Pétur [$_{vP}$[$_{v'}$ aldrei$_{[v']:[v']}$ [VP þessa bók$_{[+Foc]:[+Foc]}$?]]]]		*	
b. ... las$_C$ [TP Pétur [VP þessa bók$_{[-Foc]:[+Foc],[-HR-LR]:[-HR]}$ [V' aldrei$_{[V']:[v']}$?]]]	*!	*	*

In summary, the restrictiveness of object shift is essentially determined by the availability of the Spec,VP position for a [–Foc] element to occur there: if the adverbial is v'-adjoined, shift cannot occur, whereas if adjoined to V', the object can occur in Spec,VP. Following Engels and Vikner (2014:47), we assume that this reflects the fact that certain adverbials mark focus, and therefore shift is a way of ensuring that a non-focused element does not occur in the adverbial's focus domain (see Engels 2012). If the focus-marking scope of the adverbial is dependent on its adjunction site, we can say that the V'-adjunction site triggers shift by marking [+Foc] in the VP-complement, whereas the v'-site has a broader scope that includes Spec,VP, and hence Spec,VP will

---

[31] The violation of MatchDis incurred for the mismatch [+Foc] : ∅ in V,Comp is also present in the winning candidates with shift.

also bear [+Foc]. This does not make different empirical predictions than the movement account, since the combination of a finite 'have'-auxiliary and a main verb in V will have either T- or v'-adjunction and therefore preclude object shift. One significant advantage of this approach over the standard analysis, namely, that the finite verb does not move from V when 'blocked' by intervening material, is that we avoid the necessity for affix-hopping. Instead, tensed verbs do always occur at least as high as T in these languages if we follow the hypothesis that adverb-placement is sensitive both to information structure and tense. Furthermore, in the OLG analysis the position of the object is not a mysterious dependency on movement but determined by independently motivated information–structure constraints. In Section 9.7.2, the factorial typology generated by the proposed constraints is presented.

9.7.2 Factorial Typology: Information Structure

With our analysis of object shift in place, we are now in a position to test the hypothesised constraints with respect to the inputs in (296). A stipulated ranking given in (295) was tested. Since it has already been demonstrated that the alignment constraints generate the correct head-initial versus head-final typology, these were not included. Expletives and topicalisation are considered apart from object shift and negative scrambling, given the specificity and cross-linguistic rarity of these latter phenomena.

(295) **Faroese:**
Max » ArgSP » Dep » MA » ObjDP » MD » MC

(296)   j.   /{music$_{[+Foc]}$,has,always,been}/
          k.   /{music$_{[-Foc]}$,has,always,been}/
          l.   /{must,have,always,been,[many folk]$_{[+Foc]}$}/
          m.   /{must,never,have,been,[native trees]$_{[+Foc]}$}/
          n.   /{I,will,not,have,[that old car]$_{[+Top]}$}/
          o.   /{I,read,not,book}/
          p.   /{I,read,not,it$_{[-Foc]}$}/
          q.   /{I,have,seen,no-one$_{[-Foc]}$}/
          r.   /{I,have,talked,with,[no student]$_{[-Foc]}$}/

With 7 constraints, there are 5,040 logically possible output languages. For expletive constructions and topicalisation of the type encountered in Germanic languages, there are four outputs generated:

(297) **Expletives and V2-topicalisation**

No.	Expletives	V2-Topicalisation	Example language
1	✓	✓	Faroese, Icelandic, German
2	✓	×	English, Malagasy
3	×	✓	Estonian
4	×	×	Irish, Turkish

Additional constraints could be included to attempt to generate the differences between languages that do have clause-initial topic XPs with and without V2, and the implications of this with respect to 'T-to-C', but this is tangential to the point that the proposed constraints generate the attested possibilities without wildly overgenerating.

As for object shift and negative scrambling, five output languages are generated by these constraints. Negative scrambling refers to the sentences with negative-quantified objects, such as (296q–r); see Þráinsson (2007:83–84) for reasons to consider this phenomenon separately from object shift.

(298) **Object shift and negative scrambling**

No.	Full DP OS	Pronoun OS	Neg. scrambling	Example language
1	×	✓	✓	Faroese, Danish
2	×	✓	×	
3	×	×	✓	German, Dutch
4	×	×	×	English
5	✓	✓	✓	Icelandic

Another advantage of adopting an OT-based approach is that it is easy to capture optionality via competing grammars (or a constraint tie). As Engels and Vikner (2014:52) note, the optionality observed with respect to object shift in some Scandinavian languages and dialects can be explained via an optional ranking of a pair of constraints. Translating their constraints into those adopted here, the following rankings generate the attested possibilities:

(299)

Language	Description	Ranking
Danish, Norwegian	no full DP OS, oblig. pronoun OS	ObjDP » MD » MC
Icelandic	optional full DP OS, oblig. pronoun OS	{ObjDP, MD} » MC
Swedish, SE Danish	no full DP OS, optional pronoun OS	ObjDP » {MD, MC}
Elfdalian, Finland Swedish	no full DP OS, no pronoun OS	ObjDP » MC » MD

Therefore, we have seen that the constraints adopted in our analysis of object shift account not only for Faroese and broader Scandinavian data but also offer a deeper explanation for information-structural phenomena without requiring additional mechanisms other than to extend LT to discourse features as well as case. Some fascinating avenues for future investigation would be to test the approach against additional sentence types relating to object shift within Scandinavian, or indeed other languages which are known to exploit a combination of morphology and word order to convey discourse functions, for example, Hungarian (see e.g. Kiss 2010), or Korean and Japanese (Kuroda 1972, Li and Thompson 1976, Huang 1984 and subsequent studies). Optimality Theory provides a straightforward means of testing hypotheses through generating factorial typologies, as well as capturing the insight that conflicting pressures yield marked phenomena, such as object shift. When combined with our extension of LT, OLG enables ostensibly disparate phenomena, such as case-marking, argument licensing and discourse structure, to be accounted for by the same basic principles.

9.8 Summary of Chapter

This chapter presented an in-depth exposition of the mechanics of the OLG approach to syntax. The proposed theoretical framework with respect to several important syntactic topics was laid out and discussed, followed by an extensive review of the Faroese clause structure facts in Section 2.3 from an OLG perspective. Ranking arguments were presented with respect to the Faroese data as far as possible, as well as reasonable typologies of real and logically possible languages, corresponding to the output permutations assuming the hypothesised inputs and constraints. I showed that the OLG approach is both flexible enough to extend beyond the data presented in earlier chapters and restrictive enough to rule out unattested sentence types, whether within a language (e.g. nominative objects in Faroese) or across all languages (e.g. the FOFC). Finally, the example of object shift in Scandinavian languages was presented as a showcase for how OLG deals with information structure: it was argued that, provided certain assumptions are adopted regarding adverbial scope, the relevant facts are derived from a simple extension of LT without construction-specific constraints or transformations. Thus, to the extent possible, the theory was shown to be both unified across subdomains of syntax and empirically sound. It is hoped that this chapter provides an explicit enough overview to function as a basis for future research while also demonstrating the strengths of this model of syntax.

10

Conclusion

10.1 Overview of Findings

In this book, a novel approach to syntax was presented, *Optimal Linking Grammar*, whose name was chosen to highlight the combination of two strands of prior literature, Optimality Theory (OT; Prince and Smolensky 1993) and Linking Theory (LT; Kiparsky 1997, 2001). In order best to motivate and test this framework, we narrowed our focus to a specific question: What is the best theory of case-marking? To arrive at any kind of compelling answer, a far broader and deeper investigation of phenomena relating to word order, case and agreement was necessary. The particular problem broached was that of an intriguing difference between dative-subject predicates in Faroese and Icelandic: why is the object marked nominative with number agreement in Icelandic but accusative with default third person singular agreement in Faroese? Our fundamental hypothesis consisted of a model of grammar that recognises three levels of case and imposes harmonisation on the mapping between levels. The key insight is that competing pressures, ranked differently between grammars, yield outputs that differ in precisely the way the Icelandic and Faroese sentence types do.

Substantial new data from the Faroe Islands and Iceland were brought to bear on the question and turned out to be consistent with the initial hypothesis: the object in both Faroese and Icelandic dative-subject predicates behaves like a regular object with respect to Scandinavian object shift, and lack of number agreement with the nominative is consistently rejected in Icelandic, thus establishing MAX[−HR] and

AGR[+HR] as the right constraints. The rankings MAX[−HR] » AGR[+HR] for Faroese and AGR[+HR] » MAX[−HR] for Icelandic were shown to capture the crucial difference between the two languages with respect to case-marking in dative-subject predicates; in this way, the difference was shown not to be idiosyncratic or language-specific but systematic and predictable. Moreover, the behaviour of case-preservation and availability of the passive with quirky case verbs in Faroese is correctly predicted by the proposed model: two grammars are synchronically accessible to Faroese speakers, one which results in case-preservation and non-availability of passive, the other which yields non-preservation and the passive with nominative subject. The inter-relatedness of these patterns is lost on a theory with only construction-specific constraints or filters but readily explicable by a grammar-specific ranking that accounts for several related morphosyntactic phenomena. The competing grammars model was also tested via statistical and computational methods and shown to provide insight into sociolinguistic factors in case selection.

Finally, the OLG model was argued to be not only conceptually self-consistent and empirically sound but also shown to generate realistic typologies of cross-linguistic variation. It was demonstrated that all the constraints proposed for Faroese and Icelandic do in fact generate attested languages and rule out unattested types. I argued that such a model of grammar both achieves descriptive adequacy and offers deeper explanations for a wide range of linguistic phenomena. It was shown that by extending the LT assumptions to discourse features, information-structural phenomena such as Scandinavian object shift also find a ready explanation that sheds new light on an old problem. Moreover, in Chapter 9 an explicit and detailed description of all important components of the theory was given in tandem with data-driven argumentation. It is hoped that this will provide a basis for future research on syntax and how it interfaces with other components of grammar. In the following section, some unanswered questions are presented which may serve as intriguing routes for further investigation.

10.2 Avenues for Future Research

10.2.1 Dative-Accusative Case Frames

A fascinating avenue for investigation is that of languages with similar case-marking patterns but from disparate families: for instance, the dative–accusative case frames attested in languages as diverse as Nepali, Lithuanian, Basque and Wangkumara. In each case, several questions will need to be answered in order to reach an appropriate analysis, including (i) whether the dative argument is a true subject according to the criteria described in Chapter 2, (ii) what the agreement patterns are, if applicable, (iii) what syntactic positions are available for each argument, (iv) whether semantic generalisations can be made about the choice of case, and (v) whether the accusative-marked argument behaves like lexical or structural case according to language-appropriate diagnostics, to name but a few. Once these facts are in place, however, the OLG framework presented in this book can be straightforwardly brought to bear on new data, even if the constraint conflicts responsible for the observed patterns turn out to be quite different from those behind Icelandic and Faroese. For instance, dative–accusative case frames are encountered in Lithuanian with verbs of pain (Seržant 2013:189–190):

(300) a. Lit. *Man skauda galvą*
me.DAT aches.3SG head.ACC.SG
'I have a headache'
b. Lit. *Man sopa galvą*
me.DAT aches.3SG head.ACC.SG
'I have a headache'

Alongside the pattern in (300), a nominative-marked body part argument is possible, albeit less common (301); additionally, a construction is available in which the body part is expressed as a locative phrase (302):

(301) Lit. *Man skauda galva*
me.DAT aches.3SG head.NOM.SG
'I have a headache'

(302) a. Lit. *Man skauda po krūtine*
me.DAT aches.3SG under chest.INS.SG
'I have pains under my chest'
b. Lit. *Man skauda šone*
me.DAT aches.3SG side.LOC.SG
'I have pains in my side'

The three alignments DAT-ACC, DAT-NOM and DAT-LOC exhibit only minor semantic differences; DAT-ACC is the most common, with DAT-LOC being more marked and subject to restrictions such as size of the body part (e.g. it cannot be used with *dantis* 'tooth'). There seems to be a distinction between DAT-LOC and DAT-ACC/NOM, in which the locative construction emphasises an affected area of pain versus a holistic focus on the type of pain (not the body part). Interestingly, however, DAT-ACC and DAT-NOM appear to be semantically interchangeable and probably variants of the same construction. Seržant (2013:192), in fact, draws an explicit parallel to Icelandic and Faroese: evidence from Old Lithuanian and modern Latvian indicates that the dative–nominative case frame is the older of the two, and that dative–accusative represents a change towards canonical object case-marking. Seržant suggests that this is a similar diachronic trajectory to that of Old Norse/Icelandic dative–nominative via the Faroese dative–accusative pattern to modern Norwegian nominative–accusative. More in-depth investigation is required to substantiate this, but it would certainly be a fascinating point of comparison if it turns out that similar constraint conflicts, such as a reranking of {AGR[+HR], MAX[–HR]}, plausibly led to these patterns in the Baltic languages.

Another interesting parallel with Faroese is found in Finnish possessive constructions, where pre-posed *itse* 'self' can be either nominative or adessive; this mirrors the nominative substitution behaviour of *sjálvur* 'self' in examples like (204) in Section 8.2 (Kiparsky, p.c.):

(303) a. Fin. *Itse   minulla   on samantyyppinen kurjenpolvi*
self.NOM me.ADESS is same-type-of   geranium.NOM
'I have the same type of geranium myself'

b. Fin. *Itselläni   minulla   on kolme lasta*
self.ADESS me.ADESS is three child.PART
'As for myself, I have three children'

An even closer parallel with Faroese could hold, since the possessum bears abstract accusative according to one analysis (Kiparsky 2001:322):

(304) Fin. *Meillä   on heidät*
us.ADESS is them.ACC
'We have them'

Moreover, in such possessive constructions, the standard pattern is non-nominative possessor with third person singular verb morphology, but examples are also found with plural agreement, which is considered non-standard (Kiparsky, p.c.):

(305) Fin. *Heillä   ovat   omat   vahvuutensa   ja   heikkoutensa*
them.ADESS are.PL OWN.NOM.PL strengths.GEN.SG and weaknesses.GEN.SG
'They have their own strengths and weaknesses'

Again, several questions regarding these data would need to be answered, but if it turns out that nominative substitution is also a consistent pattern in Finnish, this would present a good opportunity to test the competing grammars hypothesis further. For example, if nominative agreement with a non-nominative possessor conveys social meaning or is predictable from other contextual factors, this would be a candidate for a competing grammars analysis. Moreover, our expectation would be that constraint interaction such as a ranking of AGR[+HR] » MAX[LC] (*mutatis mutandis*) would hold of the 'substituting' grammar, and that a conflict such as MAX[−HR] » *[−HR], as proposed by Kiparsky (2001:363–364), would be responsible for examples like (304). Hence, OLG provides the technical apparatus for exploring hypotheses relating to case and agreement beyond Insular Scandinavian and makes testable predictions about the kinds of variation we expect to see.

10.2.2 Diachronic Changes in Case Systems

Approaches based on similar starting assumptions to OLG have already been shown to account for the evolution of case and agreement systems in the Indo-Aryan languages (Deo and Sharma 2006, Kiparsky 2017). For instance, Hindi exhibits a system in which two case-frames are possible with ergative-subject verbs, namely, ERG-NOM and ERG-ACC; when an ergative subject is present, subject-verb agreement does not occur. If the object is nominative-marked, number and gender object–verb agreement occurs (306); if the object is accusative, default third person singular agreement morphology shows up on the verb (307):

(306) Hin. *Rām-ne   chiḍiyā   dekh-ī*
Ram.M-ERG bird.F.NOM see-PERF.F.SG
'Ram saw a sparrow'

(307) Hin. *Sita-ne   Radha-ko   dekh-ā*
Sita.F-ERG Radha.F-ACC see-PERF.M.SG
'Sita saw Radha'

Deo and Sharma (2006) attribute the lack of agreement in (307) to the case-marking present on both arguments, which might suggest an analysis where case-marking happens first and then blocks agreement from occurring. However, as Deo and Sharma also note, this is not the case for Nepali, where subjecthood appears to be the relevant property of an agreed-with argument – in other words, non-nominative case-marking does not block agreement (308):

(308) Nep. *mai-le mero luga   dho-en*
      I-ERG my   clothes.NOM wash-PERF.1SG
      'I washed my clothes'

Yet another possibility is illustrated by Gujarati, where object agreement occurs in the presence of an ergative subject regardless of the case-marking on the object (309–311):

(309) Guj. *Sita-e   kāgal   vāc-yo*
      Sita.F-ERG letter.M.NOM read-PERF.M.SG
      'Sita read the letter'

(310) Guj. *Sita-e   Raj-ne   pajav-yo*
      Sita.F-ERG Raj.M-ACC harass-PERF.M.SG
      'Sita harassed Raj'

(311) Guj. *Raj-e   Sita-ne   pajav-i*
      Raj.M-ERG Sita.F-ACC harass-PERF.F.SG
      'Raj harassed Sita'

Thus, non-nominative subjects across Indo-Aryan occur with at least three agreement patterns, depending on the language: (i) the subject is agreed with regardless of case, (ii) the object is agreed with regardless of case, (iii) the object is agreed with if and only if marked nominative, otherwise agreement 'fails'. There are also instances of dative subjects in these languages, but unlike Faroese, it appears that in Hindi, Nepali and Gujarati, they do not co-occur with accusative objects (Deo and Sharma 2006:384). Moreover, subject agreement never occurs on the verb if the subject is marked dative, genitive or locative. Therefore, the precise set of constraint interactions will differ from those proposed in our analysis of Icelandic and Faroese.

Nevertheless, Kiparsky (2017) shows that with the addition of constraints penalising agreement with cases other than nominative, we arrive at a compelling account of case-marking in the Indo-Aryan languages, including historical changes thereof. For instance, if a reranking of {S[+HR], MAX[–HR]} above {MAX[LC], MAX[–LR]} over time is assumed, the correct diachronic trajectory is predicted: first, subject agreement spreads from the most prominent nominative (Apabhraṃśa or Early Modern Indo-Aryan) to the subject argument regardless of case (Modern Nepali); second, agreement with the object (Gujurati) is lost, resulting in subject agreement only (Bengali); third, ergative subjects (Nepali) are replaced with nominative (Bengali); and finally, accusative object case replaces older nominative (Old to Modern Nepali). Kiparsky's analysis is consistent with the facts reported in Deo and Sharma (2006) and parallels the constraint reranking proposed in this book to account for the observed trajectory from Icelandic/Old Norse via Faroese to a Norwegian-type system. In this way, OLG offers a framework which builds on preceding OT- and LT-based accounts of the diachrony of case, providing additional support for the role of constraint reranking in morphosyntactic change.

Therefore, a fascinating area for further study would be change in case systems beyond Indo-European languages. An example would be the relatively well-documented origins of the directional case suffixes in the Uralic languages, not merely in order to account for the grammaticalisation of postpositions (about which much has been written), but ideally to arrive at a set of constraints that generate the full range of attested case systems within that family, potentially bringing fresh insight to an old question (see Oinas 1961, Sinor 1988, Abondolo 1998, Honti 2006, Kittilä and Ylikoski 2011, Aikio and Ylikoski 2016 and others). An additional topic within Uralic would be to explore the typology of possessive constructions like the Finnish examples (303–305) above; for example, Hungarian also exhibits dative possessor case in such constructions but with a nominative possessum (Demszky, p.c.). Moreover, Finnic languages use the possessive construction to express experiential meanings such as bodily sensations, pain and other feelings, such as compassion. In Estonian and Karelian 'pity' constructions, the experiencer–possessor is adessive and the feeling–possessum nominative; in the equivalent Veps construction, the experiencer is allative. If there is an overt object of pity, it is partitive in Karelian and Veps but elative in Estonian (Lees 2015:373–375). Such variation in argument realisation would serve as a suitable case study for testing the OLG framework further, particularly if it turns out that the Finnish patterns in (303–305) find parallels in the broader Uralic family that differ minimally in agreement and case-marking. A targeted survey of historical changes in Uralic possessive constructions would certainly be illuminating with respect to the theory proposed in this book.

10.2.3 Adverbial Adjunction and Information Structure

One important claim made in this book regarding the clause structure of English and Faroese is that so-called 'V-to-T' movement, or in OLG terms the finite verb occurring in T, cannot be ruled out merely by the position of the sentential adverb (see Section 2.3). In other words, it is plausible that even when a sentence-medial adverb occurs higher than the finite verb, it is, in fact, adjoined to T', and the finite verb is in T. This hypothesis comes with several advantages that turn out to make sense of a wide range of data and allow us to generate a realistic typology of possible word orders with respect to both 'T-to-C' (Section 9.6.2) and Scandinavian object shift (Section 9.7.1). These advantages include (i) an avoidance of affix-hopping, which would introduce an additional mechanism where none is needed; (ii) having T as a consistent base position for finite verbs, in the sense described in Section 9.3.1; and (iii) acknowledging the inter-relatedness of adverbal scope, information structure and positions of clausal elements, which is less easily captured on accounts that stipulate blocked movement.

However, much further investigation is needed to understand the implications of this proposal, especially in terms of those phenomena where the standard analysis assumes successive head movement, affix-hopping or some combination thereof. A more comprehensive study of the Scandinavian object shift-related data discussed in Sells (2001) and Engels and Vikner (2014), such as *let*-constructions or so-called long object shift, would yield more insights into plausible constraint rankings and formulations but also offer more opportunities to falsify the adverbial-scope hypothesis advanced in Section 9.7.1. Likewise, a plethora of Icelandic (and other Scandinavian) facts relating to adverb positions are discussed in both Þráinsson (2007) and Þráinsson (2010) and could not be broached here. Beyond North Germanic, we need not look much further than the other major European languages to find a wide treasury of sentence types against which the claims of OLG can be tested, for which many questions about adverbial adjunction remain inadequately answered (see Haider 2000, Ernst 2001, Cinque 2004, Haumann 2007 and others). In particular, the relation of sentence-medial adverbs to finite verb positions has only received brief treatment here; it would be instructive to bring further evidence to bear on the question of how adverbial scope interacts with tense or finiteness. Indeed, non-finite clauses represent another data source for testing the OLG hypotheses, for example, a cross-linguistic investigation of positions available to medial adverbs, negation and overt subjects in a non-finite clause such as exceptional case-marking constructions (briefly mentioned in Section 2.4).

A second claim of OLG is that the same feature-matching apparatus can be extended from case to discourse features, adopting the inventory proposed by Choi (2001). Both Korean and Japanese offer opportunities to test this proposal, in particular the interaction between overt morphology such as topic and case markers, word order and so-called radical *pro*-drop (see Otani and Whitman 1991, Hoji 1998, Kim 1999 and subsequent studies on null objects; Miyagawa 1989, Sadakane and Koizumi 1995, Takahashi 2010, among others, and Hong 1991, Chung 1998, Yoo 2003 and others for work on case-marking in Japanese and Korean, respectively). The literature on these topics is vast, but still there is a relative lack of in-depth OT-based treatments of the relevant syntactic phenomena. If the positional licensing hypothesis turns out to be consistent with facts such as scopal differences between nominative and accusative objects in Japanese (Tada 1992) or the various types of case-stacking in Korean (Yoon 2004, Wunderlich 2014), this would provide further compelling cross-linguistic evidence that OLG is on the right track. Japanese and Korean are of particular interest due to the fusion of case-marking and discourse functions in the system of particles; we expect that the same inventory of MAX- and MATCH-type constraints proposed to account for the Insular Scandinavian facts will play some role in deriving the patterns in these languages if the universality of the constraint set of EVAL is the correct model.

10.2.4 Other Topics

As this book has touched on a wide variety of issues in syntactic theory, as well as methodological concerns, there are multiple further possibilities that follow on from the proposed OLG framework; here we will briefly mention a few of these.

The procedure for distinguishing dialect groupings in judgement data laid out in Section 5.4 is, to our knowledge, the only attempt of its kind to apply the Krippendorff alpha statistic in this manner. An exciting possibility would be to use the same bimodal clustering procedure on other sets of acceptability judgements, whether from further surveys in Icelandic and Faroese or testing against completely different data. In addition, the procedure itself could be developed further in order to identify more potential subgroups, for example if three or more dialects were hypothesised.

The OT model adopted here is 'classic' in the sense that constraints are ranked in strict domination hierarchies, and the winning candidate is selected deterministically; in OLG, the competing grammars model assumes a probabilistic grammar *selection*, but the selected ranking is fixed and discrete. In contrast, several variants of OT have been developed in which constraint evaluation is stochastic (i.e. the output is a probability distribution over GEN rather than a single winner). For example, Stochastic OT (Boersma 1998), Noisy Harmonic Grammar (Boersma and Pater 2016) and Maximum Entropy approaches (Smolensky 1986, Goldwater and Johnson 2003 and subsequent studies) all represent possible alternative models of the OT EVAL component, which yield different predictions (see Hayes 2017 for a recent summary). Rethinking the OLG architecture with a stochastic EVAL would be a hypothesis worthy of exploration, particularly regarding the possibility of capturing the competing grammars behaviour within a single EVAL rather than a probabilistic selection among discrete rankings. Moreover, it has been mathematically proven that MaxEnt models have convergent learning algorithms (Smolensky 1986); similar work on the mathematical foundations of the neural network approach to competing grammars described in Section 5.10 would also be fruitful.

Owing to the languages and data of focus in this book, some aspects of the OLG model of grammar received less attention; for instance, in order to formulate locality constraints that account for phenomena such as wh-islands, detailed analysis of the relevant empirical evidence would be required (see Section 9.3.4 for a brief summary). A considerable amount of OT syntax literature already exists on these topics (Ackema and Neeleman 1998, Legendre et al. 1998, Fanselow and Ćavar 2001, Heck and Müller 2003 and others), but the positional licensing assumptions of LT remain under-explored in this regard, and much of the preceding work starts from a derivational perspective, such as adopting a phase- or phrase-level harmonisation window (Müller 2002, Fischer 2006). Additional research is needed to establish whether the sentence-level optimisation domain, when combined with LT positional licensing, is consistent with data beyond those examined in this book.

Furthermore, the treatment of some topics outside the main empirical foci in the book is far from exhaustive and invites additional investigation. For example, there are various aspects of object shift phenomena not discussed in Section 9.7.1, including within the Scandinavian languages: 'long' object shift across a subject, for instance, occurs in Swedish and seems analogous to scrambling phenomena found in languages such as German, Yiddish, Japanese and Korean. While there is insufficient space in this volume to explore all dimensions of such phenomena, as more data emerge and are discussed, it is hoped that the sketches given here can serve as starting points for new pathways of analysis.

Finally, the central goal of this book has been to develop a theory of the syntactic component of grammar and its interfaces with argument structure and lexical semantics, and to a lesser extent with morphology. An area of future integration would be to define in greater detail the syntactic representations fed to morpho-phonology, as well as constraints on the distribution of licensing features across the syntactic structure (more properly a concern of semantic compositionality). These interface phenomena received some preliminary treatment here but would benefit from much deeper investigation and hypothesis testing.

10.3 Final Summary

In conclusion, this book has presented an approach to syntax that combines positional licensing, an Optimality Theoretic model of output harmonisation, and a probabilistic selection of competing grammars. This hypothesised architecture of grammar was tested against a substantial amount of data from the Insular Scandinavian languages, Icelandic and Faroese. In particular, the phenomenon of non-nominative subjects or 'quirky case' was examined in depth, focusing on the puzzle of the dative–accusative case frame in Faroese in comparison to the Icelandic dative–nominative. The proposed OLG framework was shown to account for a wide range of sentence types in these languages, including passives, ditransitives and object shift. New survey data from fieldwork conducted on the Faroe Islands and Iceland were brought to bear on the key questions, and OLG analyses were laid out which offer cogent explanations for the observed patterns; moreover, the proposed accounts were bolstered by rigorous statistical models and factorial typologies, where appropriate. A competing grammars model was demonstrated to account for morphosyntactic variation in Faroese with respect to both grammatical and sociolinguistic factors, predicting the correct empirical patterns regarding nominative substitution and availability of the passive. Alternative approaches to the Faroese dative–accusative predicates were discussed, with the conclusion that while some insights can be gained from these, the OLG model requires fewer *ad hoc* stipulations and enables us to account for a wide range of data both within the language and cross-linguistically. A detailed description of the OLG model of syntax was laid out, with the aim of providing sufficient background for further research within this framework. Finally, several topics were suggested for additional investigation, including dative–accusative predicates beyond Faroese, diachrony of case systems, adverbial adjunction and other understudied areas with respect to the theoretical strands woven together in OLG. It is hoped that this book will serve not only as a resource for those interested in the Insular Scandinavian data but also as a guide for syntacticians who wish to integrate the advantages of OT, LT and probabilistic modelling of variation into a more holistic approach to grammar.

References

Abondolo, Daniel (ed.). 1998. *The Uralic Languages*. London and New York: Routledge.

Ackema, Peter, and Ad Neeleman. 1998. Optimal questions. *Natural Language and Linguistic Theory* 16.443–490.

Aikio, Ante, and Jussi Ylikoski. 2016. The origin of the Finnic l-cases. *Fenno-Ugrica Suecana Nova Series* 15.59–158. Stockholm: Stockholms Universitet.

Alderete, John, and Paul Tupper. 2018. Connectionist approaches to generative phonology. In S. J. Hannahs and Anna R. K. Bosch (eds.), *The Routledge Handbook of Phonological Theory*, 360–390. London: Routledge.

Alexiadou, Artemis. 1994. *Issues in the Syntax of Adverbs*. Unpublished PhD dissertation, University of Potsdam.

Allen, Cynthia. 1995. *Case Marking and Reanalysis: Grammatical Relations from Old to Early Modern English*. Oxford: Clarendon Press.

Andrews, Avery. 1976. The VP complement analysis in Modern Icelandic. *NELS* 6.1–21.

Angantýsson, Ásgrímur. 2007. Verb-third in embedded clauses in Icelandic. *Studia Linguistica* 61.3.237–260.

Asarina, Alevtina (Alya). 2011. *Case in Uyghur and Beyond*. Unpublished PhD dissertation, Massachusetts Institute of Technology.

Baker, Mark C. 2008. *The Syntax of Agreement and Concord*. Cambridge: Cambridge University Press.

Barðdal, Jóhanna. 2001. The perplexity of DAT-NOM verbs in Icelandic. *Nordic Journal of Linguistics* 24.1.47–70.

Barðdal, Jóhanna. 2002. 'Oblique subjects' in Icelandic and German. *Working Papers in Scandinavian Syntax* 70.61–99.

Barðdal, Jóhanna, and Þórhallur Eyþórsson. 2003. The change that never happened: The story of oblique subjects. *Journal of Linguistics* 39.439–472.

Barnes, Michael. 1986. Subject, nominative and oblique case in Faroese. *Scripta Islandica* 37. 13–46.

Barnes, Michael. 1992. Faroese syntax – Achievements, goals and problems. In Jonna Louis-Jensen and Jóhan H. W. Poulsen (eds.), *The Nordic Languages and Modern Linguistics* 7, 17–37. Tórshavn: Føroya Fróðskaparfelag.

Barss, Andrew, and Howard Lasnik. 1986. A note on anaphora and double objects. *Linguistic Inquiry* 17.347–354.

Bell, Allan. 1984. Language style as audience design. *Language in Society* 13.2.145–204.

Bell, Allan, and Janet Holmes. 1990. *New Zealand Ways of Speaking English*. Clevedon & Philadelphia: Multilingual Matters.

Bentzen, Kristine, Piotr Garbacz, Caroline Heycock and Gunnar Hrafn Hrafnbjargarson. 2009. On variation in Faroese verb placement. *Nordlyd: NORMS Papers on Faroese* 36.2.78–102.

Berent, Iris, and Gary Marcus. 2019. No integration without structured representations: Response to Pater. *Language* 95.1.e75–e86.

van Bergen, Geertje, and Peter de Swart. 2009. Definiteness and scrambling in Dutch: Where theory meets practice. *NELS* 38.113–124.

van Bergen, Geertje, and Peter de Swart. 2010. Scrambling in spoken Dutch: Definiteness versus weight as determinants of word order variation. *Corpus Linguistics and Linguistic Theory* 6.2.267–295.

Biberauer, Theresa, Anders Holmberg and Ian Roberts. 2007. Disharmonic word-order systems and the Final-Over-Final-Constraint (FOFC). In A. Bisetto and Francesco Barbieri (eds.), *Proceedings of XXXIII Incontro di Grammatica Generativa*, 86–105.

Biberauer, Theresa, Anders Holmberg and Ian Roberts. 2008. Structure and linearization in disharmonic word orders. In C. B. Chang and H. J. Haynie (eds.), *Proceedings of the 26th WCCFL*, 96–104.

Bierwisch, Manfred. 1983. Semantische und konzeptuelle Represantation lexikalischer Einheiten. In Růžička and Wolfgang Motsch (eds.), *Untersuchungen zur Semantik*, 61–99. Berlin: Akademie Verlag.

Bierwisch, Manfred. 1986. On the nature of semantic form in natural language. In Friedhart Klix and Herbert Hagendorf (eds.), *Human Memory and Cognitive Capabilities*, Part B, 765–783. Amsterdam: Elsevier.

Bobaljik, Jonathan. 2008. Where's phi? Agreement as a post-syntactic operation. In Daniel Harbour, David Adger and Susana Béjar (eds.), *Phi Theory: Phi Features across Interfaces and Modules*, 295–328. Oxford: Oxford University Press.

Boersma, Paul. 1998. *Functional phonology: Formalizing the Interactions between Articulatory and Perceptual Drives*. Unpublished PhD dissertation, University of Amsterdam.

Boersma, Paul, and Bruce Hayes. 2001. Empirical tests of the Gradual Learning Algorithm. *Linguistic Inquiry* 32.45–86.

Boersma, Paul, and Joe Pater. 2016. Convergence properties of a gradual learning algorithm for Harmonic Grammar. In John J. McCarthy and Joe Pater (eds.), *Harmonic Grammar and Harmonic Serialism*, 389–434. Sheffield: Equinox.

Borer, Hagit (ed.). 1986. *The Syntax of Pronominal Clitics*. San Francisco: Academic Press.

Börjars, Kersti, and Mark Donohue. 2000. Much ado about nothing: Features and zeros in Germanic noun phrases. *Studia Linguistica* 54.3.309–353.

Bresnan, Joan (ed.). 1982. *The Mental Representation of Grammatical Relations*. Cambridge, MA: MIT Press.

Bresnan, Joan. 2001. *Lexical–Functional Syntax*. Oxford: Blackwell.

Bresnan, Joan, and Tatiana Nikitina. 2009. The gradience of the dative alternation. In Linda Ann Uyechi and Lian-Hee Wee (eds.), *Reality Exploration and Discovery: Pattern Interaction in Language and Life*, 161–184. Stanford: CSLI Publications.

Bruening, Benjamin. 2010. Double object constructions disguised as prepositional datives. *Linguistic Inquiry* 41.287–305.

Bruening, Benjamin. 2018. Double object constructions and prepositional dative constructions are distinct: A reply to Ormazabal and Romero 2012. *Linguistic Inquiry* 49.1.123–150.

Burnett, Heather. 2017. Sociolinguistic interaction and identity construction: The view from game-theoretic pragmatics. *Journal of Sociolinguistics* 21.2.238–271.

Burzio, Luigi. 1986. *Italian Syntax*. Dordrecht: Reidel.

Butt, Miriam. 2006. *Theories of Case*. Cambridge: Cambridge University Press.

Choi, Hye-Won. 2001. Binding and discourse prominence: Reconstruction in 'focus' scrambling. In Géraldine Legendre, Jane Grimshaw and Sten Vikner (eds.), *Optimality–Theoretic Syntax*, 143–169. Cambridge, MA: MIT Press.

Chollet, François. 2015. *Keras*. Available at keras.io, accessed on 5/6/19.

Chomsky, Noam. 1957. *Syntactic Structures*. Berlin: Mouton de Gruyter.

Chomsky, Noam. 1965. *Aspects of the Theory of Syntax*. Cambridge, MA: MIT Press.

Chomsky, Noam. 1970. Remarks on nominalization. In Roderick A. Jacobs and Peter S. Rosenbaum (eds.), *Readings in English Transformational Grammar*, 184–221. Waltham, MA: Ginn.

Chomsky, Noam. 1975. *The Logical Structure of Linguistic Theory*. New York: Springer.

Chomsky, Noam. 1981. *Lectures on Government and Binding*. Dordrecht: Foris.

Chomsky, Noam. 1986. *Barriers*. Cambridge, MA: MIT Press.

Chomsky, Noam. 1994. Bare Phrase Structure. *MIT Occasional Papers in Linguistics*, vol. 5. Cambridge, MA: MIT Press.

Chomsky, Noam. 1995. *The Minimalist Program*. Cambridge, MA: MIT Press.

Chomsky, Noam. 2001. Derivation by phase. In Michael Kenstowicz (ed.), *Ken Hale: A Life in Language*, 1–52. Cambridge, MA: MIT Press.

Christiansen, Morten H., and Nick Chater (eds.). 2001. *Connectionist Psycholinguistics*. Westport, CT: Ablex.

Christensen, Rune H. B. 2018. *Ordinal: Regression Models for Ordinal Data*. R package version 2018.4-19. Available at www.cran.r-project.org/package=ordinal/, accessed on 8/5/18.

Chung, C. 1998. Argument composition and long-distance scrambling in Korean: An extension of the complex predicate analysis. In Erhard Hinrichs, Andreas Kathol and Tsuneko Nakazawa (eds.), *Syntax and Semantics 30*, 159–220. New York: Academic Press.

Cinque, Guglielmo. 1998. *Adverbs and Functional Heads: A Cross-Linguistic Perspective*. Oxford: Oxford University Press.

Cinque, Guglielmo. 2004. Issues in adverbial syntax. *Lingua* 114. 683–710.

Clark, Brady. 2012. Subjects in early English: Syntactic change as gradual constraint reranking. In Dianne Jonas, John Whitman and Andrew Garrett (eds.), *Grammatical Change: Origins, Nature, Outcomes*, 256–274. Oxford: Oxford University Press.

Creissels, Denis. 2006. A typology of subject and object markers in African languages. In F. K. Erhard Voeltz (ed.), *Studies in African Linguistic Typology*, 43–70. Amsterdam: Benjamins.

Cohen, Jacob. 1977. *Statistical Power Analysis for the Behavioral Sciences*, 2nd ed. Cambridge, MA: Academic Press.

Cole, Peter, Wayne Harbert, Gabriella Hermon and Shikaripur N. Sridhar. 1978. On the acquisition of subjecthood. *Studies in the Linguistic Sciences* 8.42–71.

Dalrymple, Mary, and Irina Nikolaeva. 2011. *Objects and Information Structure*. Cambridge: Cambridge University Press.

Deo, Ashwini, and Devyani Sharma. 2006. Typological variation in the ergative morphology of Indo-Aryan languages. *Linguistic Typology* 10.369–418.

Derbyshire, Desmond D. 1977. Word order universals and the existence of OVS languages. *Linguistic Inquiry* 8.3.590–599.

Diesing, Molly, and Eloise Jelinek. 1995. Distributing arguments. *Natural Language Semantics* 3.2.123–176.

Dixon, Robert M. W. 1979. Ergativity. *Language* 55.59–138.

van der Does, Jaap, and Helen de Hoop. 1998. Type-shifting and scrambled definites. *Journal of Semantics* 15.393–416.

Donohue, Cathryn. 2004. *Morphology Matters: Case Licensing in Basque*. Unpublished PhD dissertation, Stanford University.

Dryer, Matthew S. 2013. Polar questions. In Matthew S. Dryer and Martin Haspelmath (eds.), *The World Atlas of Language Structures Online*. Leipzig: Max Planck Institute for Evolutionary Anthropology. Available at wals.info/chapter/116, accessed on 8/3/18.

Dunbar, Ewan. 2019. Generative grammar, neural networks, and the implementational mapping problem: Response to Pater. *Language* 95.1.e87–e98.

Eckert, Penelope. 2008. Variation and the indexical field. *Journal of Sociolinguistics* 12.453–476.

Ellegård, Alvar. 1953. The auxiliary *do*: The establishment and regulation of its use in English. In Frank Behre (ed.), *Gothenburg Studies in English*. Stockholm: Almqvist and Wiksell.

Engels, Eva. 2012. *Optimizing Adverb Positions*. Amsterdam: John Benjamins.

Engels, Eva, and Sten Vikner. 2014. *Scandinavian Object Shift and Optimality Theory*. New York: Springer.

Ernst, Thomas. 2001. *The Syntax of Adjuncts*. Cambridge: Cambridge University Press.

Fanselow, Gisbert, and Damir Ćavar. 2001. Remarks on the economy of pronunciation. In Gereon Müller and Wolfgang Sternefeld (eds.), *Competition in Syntax*, 107–150. Berlin: Mouton de Gruyter.

Fasold, Ralph. 1972. *Tense Marking in Black English*. Arlington: Center for Applied Linguistics.

Fischer, Silke. 2006. Matrix unloaded: Binding in a local derivational approach. *Linguistics* 44.913–935.

Frank, Robert. 2004a. Restricting grammatical complexity. *Cognitive Science* 28.669–697.

Frank, Robert. 2004b. *Phrase Structure Composition and Syntactic Dependencies*. Cambridge, MA: MIT Press.

Fritzenschaft, Agnes, Ira Gawlitzek-Maiwald, Rosmarie Tracy, and Susanne Winkler. 1990. Wege zur komplexen syntax. *Zeitschrift für Sprachwissenschaft* 9.52–134.

van der Gaaf, W. 1904. *The transition from the impersonal to the personal construction in Middle English*. Heidelberg: Carl Winter. (Reprinted 1967, Amsterdam: Swets & Zeitlinger.)

Galbraith, Daniel. 2013. *Positional and Morphological Case in Faroese*. Unpublished MPhil dissertation, University of Cambridge.

Galbraith, Daniel. 2017. *Faroese and Icelandic syntactic survey data: Quirky case predicates, mono- and ditransitive passives, object shift and position of negative adverbs*. Stanford Digital Repository. Available at purl.stanford.edu/nd533ns7207, accessed on 10/25/22.

Gazdar, Gerald, Ewan Klein, Geoffrey K. Pullum and Ivan A. Sag. 1985. *Generalized Phrase Structure Grammar*. Cambridge, MA: Harvard University Press.

Goldwater, Sharon and Mark Johnson. 2003. Learning OT constraint rankings using a Maximum Entropy model. In Jennifer Spenader, Anders Eriksson and Östen Dahl (eds.), *Proceedings of the Stockholm Workshop on Variation within Optimality Theory*, 111–120. Stockholm: Stockholm University.

Goodman, Noah D., and Michael C. Frank. 2016. Pragmatic language interpretation as probabilistic inference. *Trends in Cognitive Sciences* 20.11.818–829.

Green, Georgia M. 1974. *Semantics and Syntactic Regularity*. Bloomington, IN: Indiana University Press.

Grimshaw, Jane. 1997. Projection, heads and optimality. *Linguistic Inquiry* 28.373–422.

Grimshaw, Jane. 2001. Economy of structure in OT. Unpublished ms., Rutgers University. *Rutgers Optimality Archive* 434–0601.

Guy, Gregory R. 1980. Variation in the group and the individual: The case of final stop deletion. In William Labov (ed.), *Locating Language in Time and Space*, 1–36. New York: Academic Press.

Haider, Hubert. 2000. Adverb placement – Convergence of structure and licensing. *Theoretical Linguistics* 26.95–134.

Haider, Hubert. 2010. *The Syntax of German*. Cambridge: Cambridge University Press.

Halle, Morris. 1973. Prolegomena to a theory of word formation. *Linguistic Inquiry* 4.3–16.

Halle, Morris, and Alec Marantz. 1993. Distributed Morphology and the pieces of inflection. In Kenneth Hale and S. Jay Keyser (eds.), *The View from Building 20*, 111–176. Cambridge, MA: MIT Press.

Halle, Morris, and Alec Marantz. 1994. Some key features of Distributed Morphology. In Andrew Carnie and Heidi Harley (eds.), *MITWPL 21: Papers on Phonology and Morphology*, 275–288. Cambridge, MA: MITWPL.

Han, Jiawei, Micheline Kamber and Jian Pei. 2012. *Data Mining: Concepts and Techniques*. Amsterdam: Elsevier.

Hankamer, Jorge, and Line Mikkelsen. 2002. A morphological analysis of definite nouns in Danish. *Journal of Germanic Linguistics* 14.2.137–175.

Hankamer, Jorge, and Line Mikkelsen. 2005. When movement must be blocked: A reply to Embick and Noyer. *Linguistic Inquiry* 36.85–125.

Haumann, Dagmar. 2007. *Adverb Licensing and Clause Structure in English*. Amsterdam: Benjamins.

Hawkins, John A. 1999. Processing complexity and filler-gap dependencies across grammars. *Language* 75.2.244–285.

Hayes, Andrew F., and Klaus Krippendorff. 2007. Answering the call for a standard reliability measure for coding data. *Communication Methods and Measures* 1.77–89.

Hayes, Bruce. 2017. Varieties of noisy harmonic grammar. In Jesney Karen, Charlie O'Hara, Caitlin Smith and Rachel Walker (eds.), *Proceedings of the 2016 Annual Meeting on Phonology*. Washington, DC: Linguistic Society of America.

Hayes, Bruce, Bruce Tesar and Kie Zuraw. 2013. OTSoft 2.5. Software package, accessible at www.linguistics.ucla.edu/people/hayes/otsoft/.

Heck, Fabian, and Gereon Müller. 2003. Derivational optimization of wh-movement. *Linguistic Analysis* 33.97–148.

Henderson, Brent. 2011. Agreement, locality, and OVS in Bantu. *Lingua* 121.5.742–753.

Heycock, Caroline, Antonella Sorace, and Zakaris Svabo Hansen. 2010. V-to-I and V2 in subordinate clauses: An investigation of Faroese in relation to Icelandic and Danish. *Journal of Comparative Germanic Linguistics* 13.61–97.

Heycock, Caroline, Antonella Sorace, Zakaris Svabo Hansen, Sten Vikner and Frances Wilson. 2012. Detecting the late stages of syntactic change: The loss of V-to-T in Faroese. *Language* 88.3.558–600.

Heycock, Caroline, and Joel C. Wallenberg. 2013. How variational acquisition drives syntactic change: The loss of verb movement in Scandinavian. *The Journal of Comparative Germanic Linguistics* 16.127–157.

Hoji, Hajime. 1998. Null object and sloppy identity in Japanese. *Linguistic Inquiry* 29.127–152.

Holmberg, Anders. 1986. *Word Order and Syntactic Features in the Scandinavian Languages and English*. Unpublished PhD dissertation, University of Stockholm.

Holmberg, Anders. 1997. The true nature of Holmberg's Generalization. *NELS* 27.203–218.

Holmberg, Anders. 1999. Remarks on Holmberg's generalization. *Studia Linguistica* 53.1–39.

Holmberg, Anders, and Þorbjörg Hróarsdóttir. 2003. Agreement and movement in Icelandic raising constructions. *Lingua* 113.997–1019.

Hong, K.-S. 1991. *Argument Selection and Case Marking in Korean*. Unpublished PhD dissertation, Stanford University.

Honti, L. 2006. Eräästä ugrilaisten kielten postpositioperäisestä kaasussuffiksien perheestä. *Journal de la Société Finno-Ougrienne* 91.81–91.

de Hoop, Helen. 2000. Optional scrambling and interpretation. In Hans Bennis, Martin Everaert and Eric Reuland (eds.), *Interface Strategies*, 153–168. Amsterdam: Royal Netherlands Academy of Arts and Sciences.

de Hoop, Helen. 2003. Scrambling in Dutch: optionality and optimality. In Simin Karimi (ed.), *Word Order and Scrambling*, 201–216. Oxford: Blackwell.

de Hoop, Helen. 2009. Case in optimality theory. In Andrej Malchukov and Andrew Spencer (eds.), *The Oxford Handbook of Case*, 88–101. Oxford: Oxford University Press.

de Hoop, Helen, and Andrej Malchukov. 2008. Case-marking strategies. *Linguistic Inquiry* 39.565–587.

Hrafnbjargarson, Gunnar Hrafn. 2001. An Optimality Theory analysis of agreement in Icelandic DAT-NOM constructions. *Working Papers in Scandinavian Syntax* 68.15–47.

Huang, James. 1984. On the distribution and reference of empty pronouns. *Linguistic Inquiry* 15.531–574.

Huang, C.-T. James, and Ian Roberts. 2016. Principles and parameters of Universal Grammar. In Ian Roberts (ed.), *The Oxford Handbook of Universal Grammar*, 307–354. Oxford: Oxford University Press.

Iatridou, Sabine. 1990. About Agr(P). *Linguistic Inquiry* 21.4.551–577.

Iggesen, Oliver A. 2013. Number of cases. In Matthew S. Dryer and Martin Haspelmath (eds.), *The World Atlas of Language Structures Online*. Leipzig: Max Planck Institute for Evolutionary Anthropology. Available at wals.info/chapter/49, accessed on 6/19/18.

Jackendoff, Ray. 1981. *X̄ Syntax: A Study of Phrase Structure*. Cambridge, MA: MIT Press.

Jacobson, Steven A. 1979. *A Grammatical Sketch of Siberian Yupik Eskimo*. Fairbanks, AK: University of Alaska.

Jäger, Gerhard. 1995. Topic, scrambling, and Aktionsart. In Inga Kohlhof, Susanne Winkler and Hans Bernhard Drubig (eds.), *Proceedings of the Göttingen Focus Workshop*, 19–34. Tübingen: Arbeitspapiere des SFB 340 'Sprachtheoretische Grundlagen für die Computerlinguistik'.

Jäger, Gerhard. 2007. Maximum Entropy models and Stochastic Optimality Theory. In Annie Zaenen, Jane Simpson, Tracy Holloway King, Jane Grimshaw, Joan Maling and Chris Manning (eds.), *Architectures, Rules, and Preferences: Variations on Themes by Joan W. Bresnan*, 467–479. Stanford: CSLI Publications.

Jespersen, Otto. 1927. *A Modern English Grammar on Historical Principles*, vol. 3. London: Allen & Unwin.

Johnstone, Barbara. 1995. Sociolinguistic resources, individual identities, and public speech styles of Texas women. *Journal of Linguistic Anthropology* 5.183–202.

Jónsson, Jóhannes Gísli. 1997–1998. Sagnir með aukafallsfrumlagi. *Íslenskt mál og almenn málfræði* 19–20:11–43.

Jónsson, Jóhannes Gísli. 2009. Covert nominative and dative subjects in Faroese. *Nordlyd: NORMS Papers on Faroese* 36.2.142–164.

Jónsson, Jóhannes Gísli, and Þórhallur Eyþórsson. 2005. Variation in subject case marking in Insular Scandinavian. *Nordic Journal of Linguistics* 28.223–245.

Joshi, Aravind K. 1985. How much context-sensitivity is required to provide reasonable structural descriptions: Tree adjoining grammars. In David Dowty, Lauri Karttunen and Arnold Zwicky (eds.), *Natural*

Language Parsing: Psychological, Computational and Theoretical Perspectives, 206–250. Cambridge: Cambridge University Press.

Joshi, Aravind K., Leon S. Levy and Masako Takahashi. 1975. Tree adjunct grammars. *Journal of Computer and System Sciences* 10.1.136–163.

Joshi, Aravind K., and Yves Schabes. 1991. Tree-adjoining grammars and lexicalized grammars. University of Pennsylvania Department of Computer and Information Science: Technical Report No. MSCIS-91-22.

Joshi, Aravind K., and Yves Schabes. 1997. Tree-adjoining grammars. In Grzegorz Rozenberg and Arto Salomaa (eds.), *Handbook of Formal Languages, Vol. 3: Beyond Words*, 69–123. Berlin and Heidelberg: Springer.

Kalin, Laura. 2011. *Hixkaryana: The Derivation of Object Verb Subject Word Order*. Master's thesis, UCLA.

Kaplan, Ronald M., and Joan Bresnan. 1982. Lexical-Functional Grammar: A formal system for grammatical representation. In Joan Bresnan (ed.), *The Mental Representation of Grammatical Relations*, 173–281. Cambridge, MA: MIT Press.

Kayne, Richard S. 1994. *The Antisymmetry of Syntax*. Cambridge, MA: MIT Press.

Keenan, Edward. 1976. Towards a universal definition of subject. In Charles Li (ed.), *Subject and Topic*, 303–333. Cambridge, MA: Academic Press.

Kiesling, Scott Fabius. 1998. Men's identities and sociolinguistic variation: The case of fraternity men. *Journal of Sociolinguistics* 2.69–99.

Kim, Soowon. 1999. Sloppy/strict identity, empty objects, and NP ellipsis. *Journal of East Asian Linguistics* 8.255–284.

Kiparsky, Paul. 1997. The rise of positional licensing. In Ans van Kemenade and Nigel Vincent (eds.), *Parameters of Morphosyntactic Change*. Oxford: Oxford University Press.

Kiparsky, Paul. 2001. Structural case in Finnish. *Lingua* 111.315–376.

Kiparsky, Paul. 2012. Grammaticalization as optimization. In Dianne Jonas, John Whitman and Andrew Garrett (eds.), *Grammatical Change: Origins, Nature, Outcomes*, 15–51. Oxford: Oxford University Press.

Kiparsky, Paul. 2013. Towards a null theory of the passive. *Lingua* 125.7–33.

Kiparsky, Paul. 2017. Typologies as fitness landscapes: Modeling word order change. Presentation at University of Oslo, *Workshop on Variation and Change in the Scandinavian Verb Phrase*, May 16, 2017.

Kiss, Katalin É. 2010. *The Syntax of Hungarian*. Cambridge: Cambridge University Press.

Kittilä, Seppo, and Jussi Ylikoski. 2011. Remarks on the coding of Goal, Recipient and Vicinal Goal in European Uralic. In Seppo Kittilä, Katja Västi and Jussi Ylikoski (eds.), *Case, Animacy and Semantic Roles*, 29–64. Amsterdam: Benjamins.

Koenig, Jean-Pierre, and Karin Michelson. 2015. Invariance in argument realization: The case of Iroquoian. *Language* 91.1–47.

Kratzer, Angelika. 1996. Severing the external argument from its verb. In Johan Rooryck and Laurie Zaring (eds.), *Phrase Structure and the Lexicon*, 109–137. Dordrecht: Kluwer.

Krippendorff, Klaus. 1970. Estimating the reliability, systematic error, and random error of interval data. *Educational and Psychological Measurement*, 30.1.61–70.

Krippendorff, Klaus. 1978. Reliability of binary attribute data. *Biometrics* 34.1.142–144.

Kroch, Anthony. 1989a. Reflexes of grammar in patterns of language change. *Language Variation and Change* 1.199–244.

Kroch, Anthony. 1989b. Function and grammar in the history of English: Periphrastic *do*. In Ralph Fasold and Deborah Schiffrin (eds.), *Language Change and Variation*, 133–172. Amsterdam: John Benjamins.

Kroch, Anthony. 1994. Morphosyntactic variation. In Katharine Beals, Jeanette Denton, Robert Knippen et al. (eds.), *Papers from the 30th*

Regional Meeting of the Chicago Linguistics Society: Parasession on Variation and Linguistic Theory. Chicago: Chicago Linguistic Society.

Kuroda, Sige-Yuki 1972. The categorical and thetic judgment: Evidence from Japanese syntax. *Foundations of Language* 9.153–185.

Labov, William. 1966. *The Social Stratification of English in New York*. Washington, DC: Center for Applied Linguistics.

Labov, William. 1972. The isolation of contextual styles. In William Labov, *Sociolinguistic Patterns*, 70–109. Philadelphia, PA: University of Pennsylvania Press.

Labov, William. 2001. *Principles of Linguistic Change, Vol. 2: Social Factors*. Oxford: Blackwell.

Labov, William. 2007. Transmission and diffusion. *Language* 83.2.344–387.

de Lacy, Paul. 2011. Markedness and faithfulness constraints. In Marc Oostendorp, Colin J. Ewen, Elizabeth Hume and Keren Rice (eds.), *The Blackwell Companion to Phonology*, vol. III, ch. 63. New York: John Wiley.

Larson, Richard K. 1988. On the double object construction. *Linguistic Inquiry* 19.335–391.

Launey, Michel. 1981. *Introduction à la langue et à la littérature aztèques 1*. Paris: L'Harmattan.

Lees, Aet. 2015. *Case Alternations in Five Finnic Languages: Estonian, Finnish, Karelian, Livonian and Veps*. Leiden: Koninklijke Brill.

Legendre, Géraldine, Jane Grimshaw and Sten Vikner (eds.). 2001. *Optimality-Theoretic Syntax*. Cambridge, MA: MIT Press.

Legendre, Géraldine, Paul Smolensky and Colin Wilson. 1998. When is less more? Faithfulness and minimal links in wh-chains. In Pilar Barbosa, Daniel Fox, Paul Hagstrom, Martha McGinnis and David Pesetsky (eds.), *Is the Best Good Enough? Optimality and Competition in Syntax*, 249–289. Cambridge, MA: MIT Press.

Levin, Lori, and Jane Simpson. 1981. Quirky case and lexical representation of Icelandic verbs. *Chicago Linguistic Society* 17.185–196.

Li, Charles, and Sandra Thompson. 1976. Subject and Topic: A new typology of language. In Charles Li (ed.), *Subject and Topic*, 459–489. New York: Academic Press.

Linzen, Tal. 2019. What can linguistics and deep learning contribute to each other? Response to Pater. *Language* 95.1.e99–e108.

Lockwood, William B. 1977. *An Introduction to Modern Faroese*. Tórshavn: Føroya Skúlabókagrunnur.

Mahajan, Anoop. 2007. Reverse engineering two word order generalizations. Presentation at *GLOW in Asia VI: Parametric Syntax and Language Acquisition*, The Chinese University of Hong Kong, December 27–29, 2007.

Marantz, Alec. 1991. Case and licensing. In Germán F. Westphal (ed.), *Proceedings of ESCOL '91*, 234–253. Baltimore: University of Maryland.

Marschner, Ian C. 2011. glm2: Fitting generalized linear models with convergence problems. *The R Journal* 3.2.12–15.

Marten, Lutz, and Jenneke van der Wal. 2014. A typology of Bantu subject inversion. *Linguistic Variation* 14.2.318–368.

Meinunger, André. 2000. *Syntactic Aspects of Topic and Comment*. Amsterdam: John Benjamins.

McCarthy, John J. 2011. *Doing Optimality Theory: Applying Theory to Data*. New York: John Wiley.

McCarthy, John, and Alan Prince. 1995. Faithfulness and reduplicative identity. In Jill Beckman, Laura W. Dickey and Suzanne Urbanczyk (eds.), *University of Massachusetts Occasional Papers in Linguistics* 18.249–384. Amherst, MA: GLSA Publications.

McCloskey, Jim. 2000. Quantifier float and wh-movement in an Irish English. *Linguistic Inquiry* 31.57–84.

McCullagh, Peter. 1980. Regression models for ordinal data. *Journal of the Royal Statistical Society* 42.2.109–142.

McCulloch, Warren S., and Walter Pitts. 1943. A logical calculus of the ideas immanent in nervous activity. *The Bulletin of Mathematical Biophysics* 5.4.115–133.

McFadden, Thomas. 2002. The rise of the *to*-dative in Middle English. In David W. Lightfoot (ed.), *Syntactic Effects of Morphological Change*, 107–123. Oxford: Oxford University Press.

Mikolov, Tomas, Kai Chen, Greg Corrado and Jeffrey Dean. 2013. Efficient estimation of word representations in vector space. Available at arxiv.org/abs/1301.3781, accessed on 5/6/19.

Miyagawa, Shigeru. 1989. *Structure and Case Marking in Japanese: Syntax and Semantics 22*. New York: Academic Press.

Montague, Richard. 1973. The proper treatment of quantification in ordinary English. In Jaakko Hintikka, Julius M. E. Moravcsik and Patrick Suppes (eds.), *Approaches to Natural Language: Proceedings of the 1970 Stanford Workshop on Grammar and Semantics*, 221–242. Dordrecht: Reidel.

Müller, Gereon. 2001. Order preservation, parallel movement, and the emergence of the unmarked. In Geraldine Legendre, Jane Grimshaw and Sten Vikner (eds.), *Optimality-Theoretic Syntax*, 279–313. Cambridge, MA: MIT Press.

Müller, Gereon. 2002. Harmonic alignment and the hierarchy of pronouns in German. In Horst Simon and Heike Wiese (eds.), *Pronouns: Grammar and Representation*, 205–232. Amsterdam: Benjamins.

Müller, Gereon. 2009. Optimality-Theoretic Syntax. '*Comparing Frameworks*' lectures, Utrecht Institute of Linguistics (OTS), September 24–26, 2009. Text available at home.uni-leipzig.de/muellerg/mu235.pdf, accessed on 8/5/18.

Narita, Hiroki. 2014. *Endocentric Structuring of Projection-Free Syntax*. Amsterdam: John Benjamins.

Oehrle, Richard. 1976. *The Grammatical Status of the English Dative Alternation*. Unpublished PhD dissertation, MIT.

Oehrle, Richard T., Emmon Bach and Deirdre Wheeler (eds.). 1988. *Categorial Grammars and Natural Language Structures*. Dordrecht: Reidel.

Oinas, Felix J. 1961. The development of some postpositional cases in Balto-Finnic languages. *Mémoires de la Société Finno-Ougrienne* 123. Helsinki: Suomalais-Ugrilainen Seura.

Ormazabal, Javier, and Juan Romero. 2012. PPs without disguises: Reply to Bruening. *Linguistic Inquiry* 43.455–474.

Otani, Kazuyo, and John Whitman. 1991. V-raising and VP-ellipsis. *Linguistic Inquiry* 22.345–358.

Pater, Joe. 2000. Nonuniformity in English stress: The role of ranked and lexically specific constraints. *Phonology* 17.2.237–274.

Pater, Joe. 2009. Weighted constraints in generative linguistics. *Cognitive Science* 33.999–1035.

Pater, Joe. 2019. Generative linguistics and neural networks at 60: Foundation, friction and fusion. *Language* 95.1.e41–e74.

Pearl, Lisa, and Sharon Goldwater. 2016. Statistical learning, inductive bias, and Bayesian inference in language acquisition. In Jeffrey Lidz, William Snyder and Joe Pater (eds.), *The Oxford Handbook of Developmental Linguistics*, 664–695. Oxford: Oxford University Press.

Pearson, Matthew. 1998. Predicate raising and 'VOS' order in Malagasy. In Ileana Paul (ed.), *The Structure of Malagasy*, vol. 2. UCLA Occasional Papers in Linguistics, No. 20.

Pearson, Matthew. 2005. The Malagasy subject/topic as an A'-element. *Natural Language and Linguistic Theory* 23.2.381–457.

Pedregosa, Fabian, Gaël Varoquaux, Alexandre Gramfort et al. 2011. Scikit-learn: Machine Learning in Python. *Journal of Machine Learning Research* 12.2825–2830.

Perlmutter, David M. 1978. Impersonal passives and the unaccusative hypothesis. *Proceedings of the Annual Meeting of the Berkeley Linguistics Society* 38.157–189. Berkeley: Berkeley Linguistics Society.

Petersen, Hjalmar P. 2010. *The Dynamics of Faroese–Danish Language Contact*. Heidelberg: Universitätsverlag Winter.

Pickering, Martin J., Stephen Barton and Richard Shillcock. 1994. Unbounded dependencies, island constraints and processing complexity. In Charles Clifton Jr, Lyn Frazier and Keith Rayner (eds.), *Perspectives on Sentence Processing*, 199–224. Mahwah: Lawrence Erlbaum Associates.

Pintzuk, Susan, 1999. *Phrase Structures in Competition: Variation and Change in Old English.* New York: Garland.

Pollard, Carl, and Ivan Sag. 1987. *Information-Based Syntax and Semantics, Vol. 1: Fundamentals.* Stanford: CSLI Publications.

Pollard, Carl, and Ivan Sag. 1994. *Head-Driven Phrase Structure Grammar.* Chicago: University of Chicago Press.

Pollock, Jean-Yves. 1989. Verb movement, Universal Grammar, and the structure of IP. *Linguistic Inquiry* 20.3.365–424.

Potsdam, Eric. 1998. A syntax for adverbs. *WECOL* 27. Fresno: California State University.

Potts, Christopher. 2019. A case for deep learning in semantics: Response to Pater. *Language* 95.1.e115–e124.

Preminger, Omer. 2011. *Agreement as a Fallible Operation.* Unpublished PhD dissertation, MIT.

Preminger, Omer. 2014. *Agreement and Its Failures.* Linguistic Inquiry Monograph 68. Cambridge, MA: MIT Press.

Prince, Alan, and Paul Smolensky. 1993. *Optimality Theory: Constraint Interaction in Generative Grammar.* Citations from Rutgers Optimality Archive version [Aug. 2002], accessible at roa.rutgers.edu/files/537-0802/537-0802-PRINCE-0-0.PDF.

Qing, Ciyang, and Reuben Cohn-Gordon. 2018. Non-descriptive/use-conditional meaning in Rational Speech Act models. Presentation at *Sinn und Bedeutung* 23, September 5–7, 2018. Centre de Lingüística Teòrica, Universitat Autònoma de Barcelona.

R Core Team. 2012. *R: A language and environment for statistical computing.* R Foundation for Statistical Computing. Austria: Vienna. www.R-project.org/.

Rappaport Hovav, Malka, and Beth Levin. 2008. The English dative alternation: The case for verb sensitivity. *Journal of Linguistics* 44.129–167.

Rizzi, Luigi. 1990. *Relativized Minimality.* Cambridge, MA: MIT Press.

Rögnvaldsson, Eiríkur. 1995. Old Icelandic: A non-configurational language? *NOWELE* 26.3–29.

Rohrbacher, Bernhard. 1994. *The Germanic Languages and the Full Paradigm: A Theory of V to I Raising*. Unpublished PhD dissertation, University of Massachusetts, Amherst.

Rosenblatt, Frank. 1957. The perceptron: A perceiving and recognizing automaton. *Project PARA*, Report 85-460-1. Ithaca: Cornell Aeronautical Laboratory.

Sadakane, Kumi, and Masatoshi Koizumi. 1995. On the nature of the 'dative' particle *ni* in Japanese. *Linguistics* 33.5–33.

Santorini, Beatrice. 1989. *The Generalization of the Verb-Second Constraint in the History of Yiddish*. Unpublished PhD dissertation, University of Pennsylvania.

Santorini, Beatrice. 1992. Variation and change in Yiddish subordinate clause word order. *Natural Language and Linguistic Theory* 10.4.595–640.

Santorini, Beatrice. 1993. The rate of phrase structure change in the history of Yiddish. *Language Variation and Change* 5.257–283.

Savitch, Walter J. 1987. Context-sensitive grammar and natural language syntax. In Walter J. Savitch, Emmon Bach, William Marsh and Gila Safran-Naveh (eds.), *The Formal Complexity of Natural Language*, 358–368. Dordrecht: Springer.

Scannell, Kevin. 2011. *Corpus of Faroese-Language Blogs*. Stanford Digital Repository. Available at purl.stanford.edu/qt59owf146o.

Schilling-Estes, Natalie. 1998. Investigating 'self-conscious' speech: The performance register in Ocracoke English. *Language in Society* 27.53–83.

Sells, Peter. 2001. *Structure, Alignment and Optimality in Swedish*. Stanford: CSLI Publications.

Seržant, Ilja A. 2013. Rise of canonical objecthood with the Lithuanian verbs of pain. *Baltic Linguistics* 4:187–211.

Sheehan, Michelle, Theresa Biberauer, Ian Roberts and Anders Holmberg. 2017. *The Final-Over-Final Condition: A Syntactic Universal*. Linguistic Inquiry Monograph 76. Cambridge, MA: MIT Press.

Siegel, Dorothy. 1974. *Topics in English Morphology*. New York: Garland.

Siewierska, Anna. 2013. Verbal person marking. In Matthew S. Dryer and Martin Haspelmath (eds.), *The World Atlas of Language Structures Online*. Leipzig: Max Planck Institute for Evolutionary Anthropology. Available at wals.info/chapter/102, accessed on 6/19/18.

Sigurðsson, Halldór Ármann. 1989. *Verbal Syntax and Case in Icelandic*. Unpublished PhD dissertation, Lund University.

Sigurðsson, Halldór Ármann. 1991. Icelandic case-marked PRO and the licensing of lexical arguments. *Natural Language and Linguistic Theory* 9.327–363.

Sigurðsson, Halldór Ármann. 1996. Icelandic finite verb agreement. *Working Papers in Scandinavian Syntax* 57.1–46.

Sigurðsson, Halldór Ármann. 1997. Öðruvísi frumlög. In Anna Agnarsdóttir and Torfi Tulinius (eds.), *Milli himins og jarðar. Maður, guð og menning í hnotskurn hugvísinda*, 299–306. Reykjavík: Háskólaútgáfan.

Sigurðsson, Halldór Ármann. 2004. Agree and agreement: Evidence from Germanic. In Werner Abraham (ed.), *Focus on Germanic Typology*, Studia Typologica 6, 61–103. Berlin: Akademie Verlag.

Sigurðsson, Halldór Ármann, and Anders Holmberg. 2008. Icelandic dative intervention. In Roberta D'Alessandro, Susann Fischer and Gunnar H. Hrafnbjargarson (eds.), *Agreement Restrictions*, 251–279. Berlin: Mouton de Gruyter.

Silverstein, Michael. 2003. Indexical order and the dialectics of sociolinguistic life. *Language and Communication* 23.193–229.

Sinor, D. (ed.). 1988. *The Uralic Languages: Description, History and Foreign Influences*. Handbuch der Orientalistik 8: Handbook of Uralic Studies 1. Leiden: E. J. Brill.

Smolensky, Paul. 1986. Information processing in dynamical systems: foundations of Harmony Theory. In David E. Rumelhart and James L. McClelland (eds.), *Parallel Distributed Processing: Explorations in the Microstructure of Cognition*, vol. 1, 194–281. Cambridge, MA: MIT Press.

Smolensky, Paul. 1996. On the comprehension/production dilemma in child language. *Linguistic Inquiry*, 27.4.720–731.

Smolensky, Paul, and Geraldine Legendre. 2006. *The Harmonic Mind: From Neural Computation to Optimality-Theoretic Grammar (Cognitive Architecture)*, vol. 1. Cambridge, MA: MIT Press.

Sportiche, Dominique. 1988. A theory of floating quantifiers and its corollaries for constituent structure. *Linguistic Inquiry* 19.3.425–449.

Svavarsdóttir, Ásta. 1982. Þágufallssýki: Breytingar á fallnotkun í frumlagssæti ópersónulegra setninga. *Íslenskt mál* 4.19–62.

Svenonius, Peter. 2002. Subject positions and the placement of adverbials. In Peter Svenonius (ed.), *Subjects, Expletives, and the Extended Projection Principle*, 199–240. Oxford: Oxford University Press.

Tada, Hiroaki. 1992. Nominative objects in Japanese. *Journal of Japanese Linguistics* 14.91–108.

Takahashi, Masahiko. 2010. Case, phases, and nominative/accusative conversion in Japanese. *Journal of East Asian Linguistics* 19.319–355.

Taraldsen, Knut Tarald. 1995. On agreement and nominative objects in Icelandic. In Hubert Haider, Susan Olsen and Sten Vikner (eds.), *Studies in Comparative Germanic Syntax*, 307–327. Kluwer: Dordrecht.

Terrill, Angela. 2003. *A Grammar of Lavukaleve*. Berlin: Mouton de Gruyter.

Þráinsson, Höskuldur. 2000. Object shift and scrambling. In Mark Baltin and Chris Collins (eds.), *Handbook of Contemporary Syntactic Theory*, 148–202. Oxford: Blackwell.

Þráinsson, Höskuldur. 2007. *The Syntax of Icelandic*. Cambridge: Cambridge University Press.

Þráinsson, Höskuldur. 2010. Predictable and unpredictable sources of variable verb and adverb placement in Scandinavian. *Lingua* 120.1062–1088.

Þráinsson, Höskuldur. 2013. Full NP object shift: The Old Norse puzzle and the Faroese puzzle revisited. *Nordic Journal of Linguistics* 36.2.153–186.

Þráinsson, Höskuldur. 2016. There is no 'Icelandic A and B' nor 'Faroese 1 and 2'. Presentation delivered at *GLAC* 22, Reykjavík, 5/21/16.

Þráinsson, Höskuldur, Hjalmar P. Petersen, Jógvan í Lon Jacobsen and Zakaris Svabo Hansen. 2004. *Faroese: An Overview and Reference Grammar*, 1st ed. Reykjavík and Tórshavn: University of Iceland and University of the Faroe Islands.

Þráinsson, Höskuldur, Hjalmar P. Petersen, Jógvan í Lon Jacobsen and Zakaris Svabo Hansen. 2012. *Faroese: An Overview and Reference Grammar*, 2nd ed. Reykjavík and Tórshavn: University of Iceland and University of the Faroe Islands.

Tourangeau, Roger, Lance J. Rips and Kenneth Rasinski. 2000. *The Psychology of Survey Response*. Cambridge: Cambridge University Press.

Vangsnes, Øystein Alexander. 2002. Icelandic expletive constructions and the distribution of subject types. In Peter Svenonius (ed.), *Subjects, Expletives, and the Extended Projection Principle*, 43–70. Oxford: Oxford University Press.

Vergnaud, Jean-Roger. 2008 [1977]. Letter to Noam Chomsky and Howard Lasnik on 'Filters and Control', April 17, 1977. In Robert Freidin, Carlos P. Otero and Maria Luisa Zubizarreta (eds.), *Foundational Issues in Linguistic Theory: Essays in Honor of Jean-Roger Vergnaud*, 3–15. Cambridge, MA: MIT Press.

Vikner, Sten. 1991. Relative *der* and other C^0 elements in Danish. *Lingua* 84.109–136.

Vikner, Sten. 1995. *Verb Movement and Expletive Subjects in the Germanic Languages*. Oxford: Oxford University Press.

Wallenberg, Joel C. 2013. Scrambling, LF, and phrase structure change in Yiddish. *Lingua* 133.289–318.

Wallenberg, Joel C. 2016. Extraposition is disappearing. *Language* 92.e237–e256.

Wasow, Thomas. 2002. *Postverbal Behavior*. Stanford: CSLI Publications.

Werbos, Paul J. 1974. *Beyond Regression: New Tools for Prediction and Analysis in the Behavioral Sciences*. Unpublished PhD dissertation, Harvard University. Cambridge, MA.

Woolford, Ellen. 2001. Case patterns. In Geraldine Legendre, Jane Grimshaw and Sten Vikner (eds.), *Optimality-Theoretic Syntax*, 509–543. Cambridge, MA: MIT Press.

Woolford, Ellen. 2007. Case locality: Pure domains and object shift. *Lingua* 117.1591–1616.

Wunderlich, Dieter. 1997. Cause and the structure of verbs. *Linguistic Inquiry* 28.27–68.

Wunderlich, Dieter. 2002. Argument linking types approached from the perspective of LDG. In Hidekazu Suzuki (ed.), *Report of the Special Research Project for the Typological Investigation of Languages and Cultures of the East and West 2001, Part II*, 777–799. University of Tsukuba.

Wunderlich, Dieter. 2008. The force of lexical case: German and Icelandic compared. In Kristin Hanson and Sharon Inkelas (eds.), *The Nature of the Word: Studies in Honor of Paul Kiparsky*, 587–620. Cambridge, MA: MIT Press.

Wunderlich, Dieter. 2012. Lexical decomposition in grammar. In Markus Werning, Wolfram Hinzen and Edouard Machery (eds.), *The Oxford Handbook of Compositionality*, 307–327. Oxford: Oxford University Press.

Wunderlich, Dieter. 2014. Variations of double nominative in Korean and Japanese. In Doris Gerland, Christian Horn, Anja Latrouite and Albert Ortmann (eds.), *Meaning and Grammar of Nouns and Verbs*, 339–372. Düsseldorf: Düsseldorf University Press.

Wunderlich, Dieter, and Renate Lakämper. 2001. On the interaction of structural and semantic case. *Lingua* 111.277–418.

Yang, Charles. 2000. Internal and external forces in language change. *Language Variation and Change* 12.231–250.

Yang, Charles. 2002. *Knowledge and Learning in Natural Language*. Oxford: Oxford University Press.

Yip, Moira, Joan Maling and Ray Jackendoff. 1987. Case in tiers. *Language* 63.217–250.

Yoo, Eun-Jung. 2003. Case marking in Korean auxiliary verb constructions. In Jong-Bok Kim and Stephen Wechsler (eds.), *The Proceedings of the 9th International Conference on HPSG*, 413–438. Stanford: CSLI Press.

Yoon, J.-H. 2004. Non-nominative (major) subjects and case stacking in Korean. In Peri Bhaskararao and Karumuri V. Subbarao (eds.), *Non-Nominative Subjects*, vol. 2, 265–314. Amsterdam: Benjamins.

Zaenen, Annie, Joan Maling and Höskuldur Þráinsson. 1985. Case and grammatical functions: The Icelandic passive. *Natural Language and Linguistic Theory* 3.441–483.

Zobl, Helmut, and Juana M. Liceras. 2005. Competing grammars and parametric shifts in second language acquisition and the history of English and Spanish. In David Bamman, Tatiana Magnitskaia and Colleen Zaller (eds.), *Proceedings of the 30th Annual Boston University Conference on Language Development*. Somerville, MA: Cascadilla Press.

Index

abstract case, 3, 7, 9–13, 18, 20, 21, 64–68, 97, 98, 110, 147, 149, 165, 166, 178, 224
acquisition, 2, 24, 25, 108, 109, 131
adverbial adjunction, 210, 241
   in Faroese, 50, 52, 235
   and information structure, 50, 52, 235, 261, 265
   interaction with Scandinavian object shift, 247, 249, 251
agreement, *see also* object agreement, 4, 6, 8–10, 13–17, 19, 20, 23, 29, 30, 38, 62, 76–78, 82, 86, 87, 92–96, 99, 107, 128, 149, 157, 160, 161, 163, 165, 171, 172, 185, 187–189, 191, 220, 255, 257–261
argument structure, 3, 9, 33, 41, 42, 62–66, 71, 73, 75, 97, 140, 147, 151, 165, 167, 217, 240, 245, 265

Basque, 256
bimodal clustering, 121, 122, 124, 126, 128, 130, 263
Burzio's Generalisation, 179

c-selection, 73, 202, 221, 238
case
   constraints governing, 19, 67, 69, 70, 73, 75, 95, 96, 98, 100, 102, 179, 180, 182, 184, 185, 187, 191, 255, 258, 260, 261
   levels of, 2, 8, 10, 11, 17, 21, 62, 64, 65, 67, 69, 70, 96
case preservation, 8, 26, 31, 58, 100, 110, 138, 139, 143, 146, 148, 149, 151, 153, 255
   behaviour of DAT in Faroese passive, 150
   non-preservation of ACC in Faroese passive, 59
competing grammars, 2, 4, 5, 8, 9, 22–26, 31, 77, 95, 103, 106, 108, 121, 128, 130–132, 135–137, 143, 150, 151, 153, 155, 173, 178, 183, 192, 228, 236, 252, 255, 256, 259, 264–266
   architecture of model, 108
   as model of case substitution, 150, 152, 153
   as model of Faroese passive, 146, 148, 150, 152, 153

grammatical factors, 24, 112
probabilistic activation, 25, 26, 108, 136, 148, 264, 265
social factors, 24, 112, 114, 117, 119, 120, 135, 136, 150, 265
Conceptual Structure (CS), 62–65, 67
connectionism, 1, 62, 131, 133, 135
constraints
    change as re-ranking, 105, 106, 109, 110, 151, 153, 191, 258, 260, 261
    faithfulness, 20, 22, 47, 68, 73, 74, 76, 77, 96, 97, 109, 147, 180, 182, 183, 192, 200, 203, 205, 207, 209, 212, 213, 216, 218, 220, 225, 230–232
    inviolable/undominated, 47, 73, 197, 201, 206, 221
    markedness, 22, 27, 47, 68, 73, 74, 76, 180, 182, 200, 202, 207, 208, 218, 220, 221, 245
    ranking arguments, 228, 230, 231, 233, 235, 236
control predicates, 35, 38–42, 103
    in Faroese, 56
covert nominative hypothesis, 107, 184, 185, 187, 188

Danish
    influence on Faroese, 24, 117–120, 154, 160
    object shift, 242, 243, 246, 247, 249, 253

dative–accusative case frame, 58, 60, 82, 100, 179–181, 185, 188, 191
    cross-linguistically, 256
dative experiencers, 31, 39, 53–55, 58
    verbs in Faroese, 77, 79, 80
dative intervention
    in Icelandic, 16, 92, 94, 95
dative sickness in Icelandic, 138, 148, 154
dative subjects, 6, 12, 24, 31, 34, 38, 55, 57–59, 61, 70, 76–80, 82, 86, 87, 103, 107, 108, 112, 150, 153–155, 157, 181, 182, 185–187, 189, 191, 256, 260
    in Faroese, 22, 52, 53, 55, 56, 58, 61, 107, 114, 179, 180, 182, 184, 185, 187, 188
    in Icelandic, *see* non-nominative subjects
diachronic change, 24, 25, 105, 108, 110, 150, 151, 154, 256, 258–261, 265
dialects, 29, 52, 95, 105, 106, 108, 112, 114, 139, 176, 252, 263
    bimodal clustering as test for, 121, 122, 124, 126, 128, 130, 136
Distributed Morphology (DM), 10
ditransitives, 11, 12, 29–31, 45, 52, 61, 96, 101–103, 147, 157, 159, 160, 167, 170, 173, 174, 177, 178, 182, 183, 244, 247, 265

constraints governing
  passive, 166
in Faroese, 30, 44, 45, 102,
  157
give-passive in Icelandic, 166
order of objects in Faroese,
  158, 159, 161, 163, 165,
  168, 176, 178
order of objects in Icelandic,
  168
passive in Faroese, 30,
  157–159, 161, 163, 165
passive in Icelandic, 30
possible word orders in the
  passive, 167
do-support, 214, 225, 227, 228
double object construction, *see*
  ditransitives
Dutch
  scrambling in, 209, 210, 252

ellipsis, 202, 221
Exceptional Case Marking (ECM)
  in Faroese, 56, 58
expletive constructions, 16, 37,
  155, 173, 206, 217, 233,
  235, 238, 240, 251, 252
  in Faroese, 47–50, 56, 80,
    140, 146, 181, 189, 232,
    233, 236, 237

factorial typology, 18, 23, 32, 61,
  97, 193, 233, 265
of constraints governing case,
  102
information-structural
  constraints, 251, 253
of sentence types discussed
  under Faroese clause
  structure, 238, 239

faithfulness, *see* constraints,
  faithfulness
Faroese
  clause structure overview,
    43–45, 47, 48, 50, 52
  clause structure: OLG
    analysis, 228, 230, 231,
    233, 235, 236
  dative subjects survey data,
    82, 85–88, 90
  ditransitive (non-GIVE)
    passive survey data, 173,
    174, 178
  GIVE-passive survey data,
    161, 163, 165
  passive survey data, 139, 140,
    142, 144, 146
  weak and strong dative case,
    107, 110, 152, 153
features
  discourse features, 240, 241,
    246, 247, 249, 251, 253,
    261, 263
  feature mapping, 2, 11, 17,
    21, 67, 69, 70, 73, 96,
    210, 212, 214–216, 218
  identity definition, 219, 220
  realisation definition, 220
  syntactic features overview,
    216, 218, 220
fieldwork, 2, 7, 8, 23, 26–28, 30,
  31, 80, 159, 185, 189,
  265
filler-gap dependencies, 74, 193,
  198, 210, 212, 214–216,
  223, 225, 227
Final-Over-Final Constraint
  (FOFC), 193, 204,
  227

294 *Index*

Finnish
  evidence for levels of case, 10
  possessive construction with ADESS, 258

generative grammar, 1, 62, 135
German
  dative experiencers in, 39–41
  negative scrambling in, 252
  subordinate clause word orders, 233

Head-Driven Phrase Structure Grammar (HPSG), 1, 10, 218
Holmberg's Generalisation, 31, 193, 244, 246, 247

Icelandic
  dative subjects survey data, 92, 94
  GIVE-passive survey data, 170, 171, 173
  overview of oblique subjects, 34–39
impersonal passive, 34
  in Faroese, 29, 138, 140–143, 146, 148, 155
Indo-Aryan languages
  changes in case systems, 259, 260
inflection, *see also* morphological case, 4, 9, 12–14, 18, 20, 21, 27, 63, 65, 67, 69, 71, 161, 174, 176
information structure, 242, 244, 261
  constraints governing, 240, 241, 244, 246, 247, 249, 251, 253

input to syntax
  OLG definition of, 223
island phenomena, 215, 263

Krippendorff's alpha, 122, 124, 126, 128, 130, 263

language acquisition, *see* acquisition
lexical case, 6, 8, 13, 18–21, 24, 26, 31, 58, 59, 64, 65, 69–71, 98–100, 103, 110, 136, 138, 147–149, 151–153, 155, 182, 184, 187, 256, 258
Lexical Decomposition Grammar (LDG), 62, 64, 65
Lexical-Functional Grammar (LFG), 1, 10, 66, 218, 242
lexicalism, 10, 13
Linking Theory (LT), 2, 5, 8, 10, 22, 23, 31, 53, 62, 64, 65, 67, 75, 146, 168, 188, 193, 216, 253–256, 261, 264, 266
  extension to information structure, 240–253
  overview of, 9–18
Lithuanian
  verbs of pain, 256
locality, 215, 263

machine learning, 5, 131, 133, 135
markedness
  constraints, *see* constraints, markedness
  hierarchies of, 4, 18, 206
maximum entropy (MaxEnt), 27, 135, 263
Merge, 73, 191, 193, 194, 205, 206, 216, 217, 238, 246

Minimalism, 2, 31, 33, 34, 50, 67, 73, 188, 193, 194, 202, 206, 213, 215–217, 223, 224
morphological case, 3, 9–13, 15, 16, 34, 42, 62, 67, 99, 167, 192
morphosyntactic case, 9, 12, 13, 20, 21, 23, 47, 67–69, 96, 98, 99, 147, 165, 166, 180, 187, 231
morphosyntactic variation, 2, 4, 23, 27, 111, 117, 135, 136, 151, 179, 215, 236, 266
    intra-speaker, 26
    synchronic, 105
movement, 1, 23, 45, 50, 52, 73, 75, 188, 192, 193, 209, 211, 213, 215–217, 222, 241, 244–247, 251, 262
    in OLG approach, 207, 210, 212, 214–216

neural networks, 131, 133, 135
nominative objects, 6, 11, 14, 19, 20, 23, 24, 29–31, 39, 60, 61, 87, 91, 94, 95, 103, 128, 144, 180, 182, 188, 189, 192, 253
    in Icelandic, 19
    impossible in Faroese, 22, 30, 157, 188, 191
nominative substitution, 24, 59, 82, 96, 98, 102, 103, 107–109, 111, 113, 117, 135, 138, 143, 148–151, 153, 155, 170, 258, 259, 266

competing grammars as model of, 110, 112, 114
    in Faroese, 24, 26, 77, 79, 80, 138, 146, 150, 152–154, 157, 255
non-nominative subjects, 2, 4–6, 19, 21, 31, 34, 39, 42, 71, 76, 91, 154, 173, 260, 265
    cross-linguistically, 258, 260
    in Faroese, *see* dative subjects
    in Icelandic, 18, 19, 21, 33, 36, 61, 76, 100, 179, 180, 182, 184, 255
null expletives
    in Faroese, 7, 148, 228, 236, 237
object agreement, 87, 95, 128, 157, 260
    in Icelandic, 6, 7, 13, 99
    not permitted in Faroese, 77, 188
object case
    accusative, 6–8, 11, 21, 29, 58, 60, 87, 94, 99, 100, 150, 180, 192, 260, 261, 263
    comparison of Icelandic and Faroese dative-subject predicates, 6
    dative, 42, 77, 96, 101, 108, 150, 159, 182, 189
    in Faroese dative-subject predicates, 22, 28, 58, 76, 100
    in Icelandic dative-subject predicates, 19
    nominative, *see* nominative objects

on indirect objects in Faroese, 158
object position, 12, 29, 30, 45, 67, 70, 82, 87, 97, 110, 166, 170, 187, 210, 225, 241
  comparison of Icelandic and Faroese dative-subject predicates, 6
object shift, 8, 22, 23, 28, 44, 53, 60, 85, 87, 91, 94, 103, 209, 210, 238, 240–247, 250–253, 256, 262, 265
  cross-linguistically, 263
  in Faroese, 28, 87, 90
  in Icelandic, 28, 94
  in Scandinavian languages, 241, 242, 244, 246, 247, 249, 251, 253, 255
Optimal Linking Grammar (OLG), 7, 8, 10, 12, 17, 22, 23, 27, 29–32, 35, 45, 47, 50, 61, 62, 67, 71–73, 75–77, 85, 91, 95, 98, 103, 104, 106, 108–110, 131, 132, 136, 138, 146, 157, 168, 176, 179, 180, 182, 184, 186–188, 192, 193, 197, 205, 210, 211, 216, 218, 221, 222, 228, 240, 242, 243, 245, 246, 251, 253, 256, 257, 259, 261–266
  approach to syntactic movement, *see* movement
  definition of GEN, 195, 197, 198, 201
  introduction to, 5, 8–27

syntactic features in, *see* features
Optimality Theory (OT), 2, 4, 5, 8, 10, 13, 14, 16–18, 20, 22, 23, 27, 31, 32, 45, 50, 62, 64, 65, 67, 68, 70, 71, 103, 106, 110, 132, 135, 153, 179, 184, 192–194, 207, 210, 216, 217, 238, 242, 252, 253, 255, 261, 263–265
  overview of, 18, 72, 73, 75

passive, 11, 12, 22, 24, 26, 28–31, 34, 35, 38, 40, 59, 61, 88, 92, 96, 100, 101, 103, 108–111, 138–140, 142–148, 150–157, 159–166, 168, 170, 173, 174, 176–178, 182, 183, 256, 265
  acceptability of agent phrase in Faroese, 144, 146
  as diagnostic for lexical case, 8, 21, 59
  constraints governing, 146, 148, 152, 153
  impersonal, *see* impersonal passive
  Linking Theory approach, 147
phrase structure, 4, 66, 74, 106, 153, 201, 202, 206
  comparison of OLG and Bare Phrase Structure, 205
  constraints governing, 193, 201, 203, 204, 206, 207, 225, 227

positional licensing/case, 2, 4, 11–14, 16, 17, 20, 37, 40–42, 67, 69–71, 96–98, 109, 147, 165, 167, 168, 170, 178, 183, 184, 187, 191, 208, 231, 240, 242, 245, 263–265
purism
   in Faroese, 117, 119, 120

quirky case, *see also*
      non-nominative subjects, 3, 19, 20, 22, 24, 28, 31, 32, 53, 57, 59, 60, 62, 69, 76, 77, 82, 86–88, 91–94, 102, 107, 109, 112, 115, 117, 121, 122, 125, 128, 138, 140, 143, 151, 154–156, 162, 170, 187, 188, 256, 265

raising, 38, 41, 57, 103, 216
   in Faroese, 55
Rational Speech Act (RSA) model, 26, 31, 117–120, 136
reflexives, 35, 38, 42, 169
   in Faroese, 53

scrambling, *see also* Dutch, scrambling in, 28, 55, 91, 209, 210, 242, 251, 252, 265
Semantic Form (SF), 3, 8, 9, 11–13, 31, 53, 62–67, 147
serialism, 96
social meaning, 23, 24, 26, 31, 117, 119, 120, 151, 155, 259

statistical models, 5, 24, 28, 109, 112, 265
   logistic regression, 5, 31, 108, 113, 114, 116, 132, 134, 136
   ordered logit regression, 86, 93, 140, 141, 144, 163, 176
Stochastic OT, 27, 263, 264
structural case, 3, 7, 10, 11, 22, 60, 66, 67, 87, 99, 100, 136, 138, 183, 184, 186, 257
subcategorisation, 197, 198, 200, 201, 205, 207, 209, 211, 212, 214, 219–227
subject case, 20, 24, 59, 60, 79, 81, 103, 112, 113, 130, 132, 136, 179, 189
   accusative, 6, 19, 24, 81, 103, 154
   dative, *see* dative subjects
   genitive in Icelandic, *see* non-nominative subjects
   nominative, 4, 11, 24, 25, 27, 34, 57, 78–80, 82, 107, 112, 136, 151, 153, 159, 185, 189, 256
subject position(s), 10, 12, 13, 20, 30, 39, 42, 49, 50, 68, 70, 95, 110, 147, 163, 165, 166, 185, 192, 208, 233
   in Faroese, 45, 47, 48, 50, 52, 70
   in Icelandic, 37
subject–verb agreement, *see* agreement
subject–verb inversion, 35, 39, 220, 225, 237
   in Faroese, 53, 55

subjecthood, 6, 7, 31, 34, 35, 38, 39, 53, 76, 103, 260
  diagnostics for, 35, 39, 40, 53, 55, 56, 58
  of Icelandic oblique subjects, 35, 36
syntactic features, *see* features
syntactic movement, *see* movement

thematic/theta-roles, 3, 9, 13, 21, 33, 35, 41, 62–64, 66, 102, 147, 154, 165, 180, 217, 227, 233
traces, 210, 211
transformational approaches, 1, 10, 67, 73, 206, 216, 245, 254
Tree Adjoining Grammar (TAG), 195, 197, 198

Universal Grammar (UG), 2, 18, 71, 72

V-to-T/I, 44, 52, 244, 261
  in Faroese embedded clauses, 44

wh-movement, *see also* filler-gap dependencies, 221, 228
word order
  base order, 206, 207
  constraints governing, 203, 204, 207, 210, 225, 227
  in Faroese, *see* Faroese, clause structure overview

X-bar theory, 47, 73, 198, 200–205

Zaenen et al. (1985)
  on Icelandic non-nominative subjects, 33, 35, 37, 52, 53, 55, 58, 138

For EU product safety concerns, contact us at Calle de José Abascal, 56-1°, 28003 Madrid, Spain or eugpsr@cambridge.org.

www.ingramcontent.com/pod-product-compliance
Ingram Content Group UK Ltd.
Pitfield, Milton Keynes, MK11 3LW, UK
UKHW040051310825
462435UK00018B/324